MW00764766

A GUIDE TO
Operating Systems: Troubleshooting and Problem Solving

Tom Badgett

Michael J. Palmer

Niels Jonker

COURSE
TECHNOLOGY

Thomson Learning™

ONE MAIN STREET, CAMBRIDGE, MA 02142

Australia • Canada • Denmark • Japan • Mexico • New Zealand • Philippines
Puerto Rico • Singapore • South Africa • Spain • United Kingdom • United States

A Guide to Operating Systems: Troubleshooting and Problem Solving is published by Course Technology.

Associate Publisher:	Kristen Duerr	*Quality Assurance Manager:*	John Bosco
Senior Acquisitions Editor:	Stephen Solomon	*Marketing Manager:*	Susan Ogar
Product Manager:	David J. George	*Composition House:*	GEX, Inc
Production Editor:	Debbie Masi	*Text Designer:*	GEX, Inc.
Development Editor:	Deb Kaufmann	*Cover Designer:*	Efrat Reis
Associate Product Manager:	Laura Hildebrand		

© 1999 by Course Technology, a division of Thomson Learning

For more information contact:

Course Technology
1 Main Street
Cambridge, MA 02142

Or find us on the World Wide Web at: http://www.course.com.

Asia (excluding Japan)
Thomson Learning
60 Albert Street, #15-01
Albert Complex
Singapore 189969

Latin America
Thomson Learning
Seneca, 53
Colonia Polanco
11560 Mexico D.F. Mexico

Japan
Thomson Learning
Palaceside Building 5F
1-1-1 Hitotsubashi, Chiyoda-ku
Tokyo 100 0003 Japan

South Africa
Thomson Learning
Zonnebloem Building,
Constantia Square
526 Sixteenth Road
P.O. Box 2459
Halfway House, 1685
South Africa

Australia/New Zealand
Nelson/Thomson Learning
102 Dodds Street
South Melbourne, Victoria 3205

Canada
Nelson/Thomson Learning
1120 Birchmount Road
Scarborough, Ontario
Canada M1K 5G4

UK/Europe/Middle East
Thomson Learning
Berkshire House
168-173 High Holborn
London
WCIV 7AA United Kingdom

Business Press/Thomson Learning
Berkshire House
168-173 High Holborn
London WCIV 7AA United Kingdom

Thomson Nelson & Sons LTD
Nelson House
Mayfield Road
Walton-on-Thames
KT12 5PL United Kingdom

Spain
Paraninfo/Thomson Learning
Calle Magallanes, 25
28015-MADRID
ESPANA

Distrubution Services
Thomson Learning
Ceriton House
North Way
Andover, Hampshire SP10 5BE

International Headquarters
Thomson Learning
International Division
290 Harbor Drive, 2nd Floor
Stamford, CT 06902-7477

All rights reserved. This publication is protected by federal copyright law. No part of this publication may be reproduced, stored in a retrieval system, or transmitted in any form or by any means, electronic, mechanical, photocopying, recording, or otherwise, or be used to make a derivative work (such as translation or adaptation), without prior permission in writing from Course Technology.

Trademarks
Course Technology and the Open Book logo are registered trademarks and CourseKits is a trademark of Course Technology. Custom Edition is a registered trademark of Thomson Learning.

The Thomson Learning Logo is a registered trademark used herein under license.

Some of the product names and company names used in this book have been used for identification purposes only and may be trademarks or registered trademarks of their respective manufacturers and sellers.

Disclaimer
Course Technology reserves the right to revise this publication and make changes from time to time in its content without notice.

ISBN 0-7600-1142-7

Printed in Canada

4 5 6 7 8 9 10 WC 03 02 01 00

BRIEF TABLE OF CONTENTS

TABLE OF CONTENTS

INTRODUCTION

This book is very basic. It also covers complex material. A paradox? In a way, yes. Any broad-based discussion of operating systems must, perforce, be somewhat complex, but the operating system also is the most basic component of any computer system. So, basic and complex does, indeed, describe the contents of this book.

But you needn't be concerned. This basic-complex discussion begins at the beginning with a description of general operating system concepts, including how system-level software works with your computer hardware. From there, you'll read detailed descriptions of individual operating systems—DOS, Windows and its various configurations, MAC OS, and UNIX. You'll learn how each of these systems works with specific hardware components such as printers and modems, and you'll review basic procedures such as OS initial installations, OS upgrades, hardware driver installation, and more. Chapters eight and nine deal with networking and connectivity issues, and so the discussion of operating systems extends to Novell NetWare and Windows NT Server, the two most widely used network operating systems.

In addition, you can review your progress in learning these topics with extensive Hands-on projects, key terms, and review questions at the end of each chapter.

FEATURES

To aid you in fully understanding Operating Systems concepts, there are many features in this book designed to improve its pedagogical value.

- **Chapter Objectives.** Each chapter in this book begins with a detailed list of the concepts to be mastered within that chapter. This list provides you with a quick reference to the contents of that chapter, as well as a useful study aid.

- **Illustrations and Tables.** Numerous illustrations of operating system screens and components aid you in the visualization of common setup steps, theories, and concepts. In addition, many tables provide details and comparisons of both practical and theoretical information.

- **Hands-on Projects.** The goal of this book is to provide you with the practical knowledge and skills to troubleshoot desktop operating systems in use in business today. To this end, along with theoretical explanations, each chapter provides numerous Hands-on projects aimed at providing you with real-world implementation experience.

- **Chapter Summaries.** Each chapter's text is followed by a summary of the concepts it has introduced. These summaries provide a helpful way to recap and revisit the ideas covered in each chapter.

- **Review Questions.** End-of-chapter assessment begins with a set of review questions that reinforce the ideas introduced in each chapter.

- **Case Projects.** Located at the end of each chapter are several case projects. These extensive case examples allow you to implement the skills and knowledge gained in the chapter through real-world operating system support and administration scenarios.

HARDWARE AND SOFTWARE REQUIREMENTS

You can study the operating system concepts in this book without any hardware. Screen shots and other illustrations help support the discussions presented here. However, to get the most of this material you should step through the Hands-on projects. For this, you'll need access to at least one computer and operating system. To pursue a complete, broad-based study of operating systems as presented in this book, you will need several computers and operating systems.

Here are suggestions for each of the operating systems covered here:

DOS

DOS is the most basic of the operating systems covered in this book. To conduct the exercises for DOS presented here you will need only a basic computer: 80386 processor, 2 Mbytes of RAM, and a floppy disk drive. For some applications you can actually get by with even less hardware, but even more hardware is a good thing. For example, an 80486 computer, 8 Mbytes of RAM, floppy drive, and hard disk.

Windows 3.x

Windows 3.x uses a basic graphical user interface and requires slightly more hardware support for adequate operation. Recommended is an 80486-based computer with 4 Mbytes of RAM, floppy drive, and 500 MByte hard drive. This will let you conduct the exercises suggested in this book. However, if you really are going to use a Windows 3.x machine for real work, a step up to 8 Mbytes of RAM, 1 GB hard drive, and CD-ROM drive is recommended.

Windows 95

Windows 95 represents a major upgrade from Windows 3.x. The user interface is improved and the system is improved operationally as well. Although you can run Windows 95 on essentially the same hardware configurations as recommended for Windows 3.x, you'll find the machine slow and sometimes frustrating. A truly functional Windows 95 installation includes a Pentium 100 CPU, 16 Mbytes of RAM (at least!), 2 GB hard drive, floppy disk, and CD-ROM drive. You'll be amazed at how much improved Windows 95 operation will be with at least 32 Mbytes of RAM.

Windows 98

Windows 98 is a significant step up from Windows 95, and it needs a similar increase in hardware capability for successful operation. You can use the same configuration for Windows 98 as was suggested for Windows 95, but if you use all of Windows 98's capabilities—active desktop, direct World Wide Web interface, Internet communications, and so on—then you'll crave more hardware. A Pentium II running at 233 MHz, 64 Mbytes of RAM, 4 GB hard drive, floppy disk, and CD ROM will run Windows 98 nicely.

 ## Mac OS

As with Windows, Mac OS has many versions. Earlier versions can get by with basic hardware, but the latest Mac OS needs a machine comparable to one for Windows 98. You can get along with a basic IMAC (G3 processor) and 32 Mbytes of RAM for Mac OS 8.x. However, as with Windows 98, more RAM—64 or 128 Mbytes—will give you a more pleasant Mac OS experience.

 ## UNIX

Virtually any medium to high-end Intel box can make a reasonable UNIX platform, say 200 MHz Pentium or faster and 64 Mbytes of RAM. This is particularly true if you're experimenting with versions of Linux. However, if you are putting UNIX through commercial paces, doing real work with it, you should consider a RISC-based workstation, say a Sun or HP machine with as much RAM as you can afford. A machine with 250 to 500 Mbytes of RAM in a commercial environment isn't all that uncommon.

TEXT AND GRAPHIC CONVENTIONS

Wherever appropriate, additional information and exercises have been added to this book to help you better understand what is being discussed in the chapter. Icons throughout the text alert you to additional materials. The icons used in this textbook are described below.

 The Note icon is used to present additional helpful material related to the subject being described.

 Each hands-on activity in this book is preceded by the Hands-on icon and a description of the exercise that follows.

 Tips are included from the author's experience that provide extra information about how to attack a problem or what to do to in certain real-world situations.

 The Cautions are included to help you anticipate potential mistakes or problems so you can prevent them from happening.

 Case Project icons mark each case project. These are more involved, scenario-based assignments. In these extensive case examples, you are asked to implement independently what you have learned.

INSTRUCTOR'S MATERIALS

The following supplemental materials are available when this book is used in a classroom setting. All of the supplements available with this book are provided to the instructor on a single CD-ROM.

Electronic Instructor's Manual. The Instructor's Manual that accompanies this textbook includes:

- Additional instructional material to assist in class preparation, including suggestions for lecture topics, sample syllabi, lesson plans, suggested lab activities, tips on setting up a lab for the hands-on assignments, and alternative lab setup ideas in situations where lab resources are limited.

- "Quick Quizzes" corresponding to the material in each chapter to rapidly assess whether concepts have been retained.

- Solutions to all end-of-chapter materials, including the Project and Case assignments.

Course Test Manager 1.3. Accompanying this book is a powerful assessment tool known as the Course Test Manager. Designed by Course Technology, this cutting-edge Windows-based testing software helps instructors design and administer tests and pre-tests. In addition to being able to generate tests that can be printed and administered, this full-featured program also has an online testing component that allows students to take tests at the computer and have their exams automatically graded.

PowerPoint presentations. This book comes with Microsoft PowerPoint slides for each chapter. These are included as a teaching aid for classroom presentation, to make available to students on the network for chapter review, or to be printed for classroom distribution. Instructors, please feel at liberty to add your own slides for additional topics you introduce to the class.

ACKNOWLEDGMENTS

No book is the work of just the people whose names appear on the front cover. The complexity of this project, especially, required the help of many skilled and capable people. Special thanks go to Product Manager Dave George who kept the other production people—including the authors—focused and on schedule, even under hardships and setbacks. Thanks, too, to Deb Kaufmann, whose capable manuscript editing—and in some cases significant reorganization and rewriting—helped make the final product readable and logical. She, too, proved a flexible, capable team member who rolled with the punches more than she should have had to.

Much of the Macintosh technical help came from Les Jones and Jonathan Cooper, both employees of U.S. Internet, dedicated Mac users and good writers.

Then there are dozens of Course Technology folk who saw to the layout and design of this project, who worked on concept and marketing and without whom this book could never have been published. Thanks to them all for their hard work and dedication. And thanks to you, the reader, for purchasing this book, whether as part of a required course or by your own choice. You are the reason we did this in the first place.

OPERATING SYSTEM THEORY

This book is a study guide and reference for the operating systems used on most modern computers. In the following chapters, we will take an in-depth look at MS-DOS/PC DOS, Windows 3.1 and its variants, Windows 95/98, Windows NT, UNIX (focusing on the Linux variation), and Macintosh OS. This chapter deals with some of the theoretical concepts common to all operating systems. It is one of the few chapters in the book that is primarily theoretical, and was placed at the beginning of the book to give you an understanding of some general operating system theory. With this theory under your belt, you will have a frame of reference to understand operating system specifics as they are discussed later.

AFTER READING THIS CHAPTER AND COMPLETING THE EXERCISES YOU WILL BE ABLE TO:

- Understand what an operating system does
- Describe the types of operating systems
- Understand the history of operating system development
- Discuss single-tasking versus multitasking
- Differentiate between single-user and multi-user operating systems
- List and briefly describe current operating systems

UNDERSTANDING OPERATING SYSTEMS

An **operating system** (or **OS**) is a set of basic programming instructions to the lowest levels of computer hardware, forming a basic layer of programming **code** on which most other functions of the computer are built. In its lowest form, the operating system takes care of what are known as basic **input/output (I/O)** functions, which let other programs easily talk to the computer hardware. It is essentially the task of the I/O functions to take requests from the software a user runs (the application software) and translate them into low-level requests that the hardware can understand and carry out. In general, an operating system serves as an interface between application software and hardware, as shown in Figure 1-1. Operating systems perform the following tasks:

- Handle input from the keyboard
- Handle output to the screen and printer
- Handle communications using a modem
- Control input/output with all bus devices, such as a network interface card
- Control information storage and retrieval using various types of disk drives

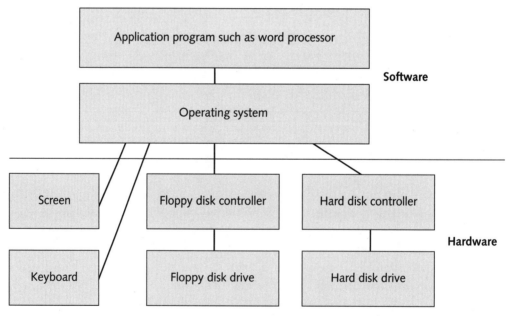

Figure 1-1   General configuration for all operating systems

The operating system communicates directly with all these devices. Some operating system programs exchange information with specific hardware (chips) inside the computer at specific times to get things done. This code is typically referred to as a **device driver**. A separate device driver is usually present for each individual device inside the computer, as shown in Figure 1-2. In general, operating systems have a standardized way to communicate with a certain type of device driver. The device driver then contains the actual code (instructions) to communicate with the chips it needs to address. This way, if another piece of hardware is introduced into the computer, the operating system code does not have to change as long as the functionality of the new hardware is reasonably similar to that of existing drivers. All that needs to be done to make the computer capable of communicating with the new device is to load a new driver into the operating system.

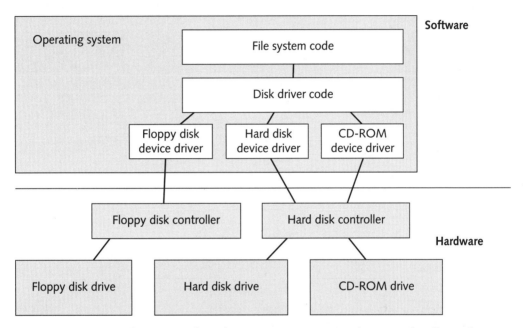

Figure 1-2   Device drivers interface the operating system with various hardware devices

A good example is a **CD-ROM** drive. CD-ROM drives for computers were introduced a long time after many operating systems were written. However, since they are similar to other types of disk drives, most operating systems can be expanded to use CD-ROM drives by loading a few simple drivers for the operating system. You may encounter device drivers that interface with your operating system for other devices, including:

- Scanners
- Printers
- Specialty devices such as digital cameras
- Other video input devices
- Audio transfer hardware

In addition to communicating with computer hardware, the operating system communicates with the application software running on the machine (Figure 1-3 on the next page). Application software is a fairly vague term; it could mean a word processor, spreadsheet, database, computer game or many types of other applications. Basically it means any program a user may choose to run on the machine. If an application program accesses a piece of hardware—say, the keyboard to see if the user has pressed a key, the screen to show the user a message, or the disk drive to read or write a file—it sends a request to the operating system to get the job done. For the application programmer (the person who actually created the application) this is a great deal! She does not have to know exactly how to manipulate the chips in the computer to communicate with keyboard, screen or printer. She only has to know how to communicate with the operating system.

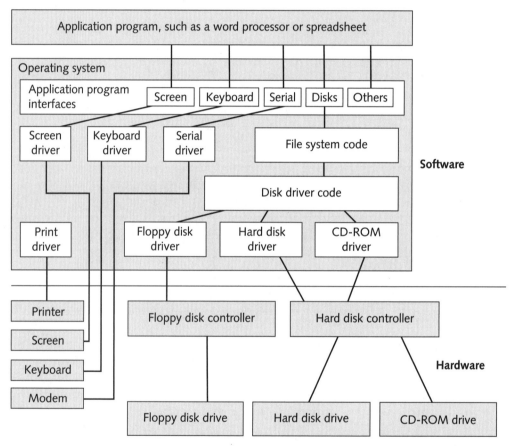

Figure 1-3   Application programs communicate with hardware through the operating system

You can therefore say that in its most basic form, an operating system provides a level of indirection among the application programs, the user, and the computer. This level of indirection allows application programmers to concentrate on applications that will run on any hardware, as long as the operating system can control it. In other words, an application program can submit to the operating system a general request, such as "write this information to a disk," and the operating system handles the details. The application programmer doesn't have to worry about how to queue the data, how to update the disk directory, or how to physically copy the data from memory to the disk drive.

Of course there are some applications—particularly those that are designed for DOS or UNIX—that access hardware devices directly. Many programmers designed code to do this to improve overall application performance, but this frequently occurred at the expense of software compatibility. Although software performance may be improved by writing directly to I/O ports or other hardware devices, it isn't necessarily good programming practice.

The general operating system we've been describing provides only the most basic input and output functions, so it is called a **Basic Input/Output System**, or **BIOS**. Every PC has a BIOS, which is stored in **Read Only Memory**, or **ROM**. ROM is a special kind of memory that does not lose its contents when the power is removed from the computer. Whenever you turn on your PC, the machine wakes up and jumps to a startup program inside the BIOS. This program initializes the screen and keyboard, tests some essential computer hardware such as the **Central Processing Unit (CPU)** and memory, initializes the floppy drive and other disk drives, and then loads other parts of the operating system that can provide more advanced functionality for application programs. Figure 1-4 shows a general conceptual drawing of various operating system components.

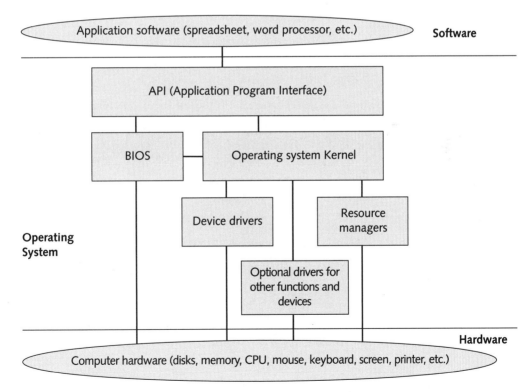

Figure 1-4 General operating system design

The elements in Figure 1-4 include the following, from the application down:

- *Application software*, such as a spreadsheet or word processor
- *API (Application Program Interface)*, software designed to communicate with the application software and with the user. The API translates requests from the application into code that the operating system Kernel can understand and pass on to the hardware device drivers, and translates data from the Kernel and device drivers so the application can use it. This is the part of the operating system most visible to users.
- *BIOS*, which provides the basic input/output functions to communicate with system devices such as disks, monitor, and keyboard. BIOS resides in ROM, so it is always present in the computer. It usually loads other operating system parts on startup.
- *Operating system Kernel*, the core of the operating system that coordinates operating system functions, such as control of memory and storage. The Kernel communicates with the BIOS, device drivers, and the API to perform these functions.
- *Device drivers*, programs that take requests from the API via the Kernel and translate them into commands to manipulate specific hardware devices, such as disks, tapes, keyboards, modems, printers, etc.
- *Resource managers*, programs that manage computer memory and central processor use
- *Optional drivers,* for other functions and devices
- *Computer hardware*, disks, storage, CPU, mouse, keyboard, monitor, printer, and so on.

Although all operating systems incorporate the basic I/O functions, the operating systems you are accustomed to, such as MS-DOS, Microsoft Windows, or UNIX include many additional functions. Examples include the logic to handle files, time and date functions, memory management, and other more advanced features to deal with the various devices connected to the system. Some features that most modern operating systems have in common are:

- Provide an interface between the computer hardware and application programs
- Act as an intermediary between the user and applications
- Provide a user interface into computer hardware and application programs
- Manage memory and central processor use
- Manage peripheral devices such as printers, monitors, keyboards, and modems

TYPES OF OPERATING SYSTEMS

There are many types of computer systems intended for very different purposes, and that therefore work in very different ways. The functions a computer requires to a large extent dictate what the operating system will do and how it will do it. As an example, the computer in a microwave oven needs device drivers for the **LED (Light Emitting Diode)** display, numeric keypad, and door close switches, whereas the computer in a television needs drivers to listen to the remote control and to tell the tuner to change the channel. The same goes for various types of small and large computers; a computer designed to handle a high volume of numerical operations for a large number of users probably needs some different functions than the PC used to run a word processor.

In general, operating systems are organized by the size, type, and purpose of the computer on which they run. In this book, we deal with personal computer (PC) operating systems. PC-class computers are designed for individual users to perform tasks such as word processing, database management, and to network with other computers. Over the years, PCs have gotten faster, more complex and more powerful, offering the user more features. As a result, many PCs now can handle complex operations that go beyond simply running a user's application software. This has resulted in advanced, elaborate operating systems that are designed to deal with more hardware and to provide advanced functions. The lines of division by size, type, and purpose are therefore getting a little more vague every day. Hardware is getting more compact every day and the operating systems are getting more complex. As operating systems get more complex, functionality is also enhanced. (Interestingly enough, prices on these smaller, more powerful machines are declining at the same time.)

For example, 20 years ago corporate computing was confined to mainframe- and minicomputer-class devices. These were refrigerator-sized or larger computers that required a full staff to manage them. The operating systems for these machines were quite complex and often included such intrinsic functions as text editing (not quite "word processing," by today's standards), database management, networking, and communications. There were few PC-class devices at the time. Those that were available were capable of minimal functionality and used what could only be described as rudimentary operating systems. Many of those early devices didn't support any storage hardware (disk drives), or if they did it was frequently serial, low-density tape. In this comparison it should be easy to see that operating systems for large machines were very different from the operating systems used for small ones.

At the same time, applications for these machines were written with efficient code so they could maximize all of the resources on the computer. As a result, the appearance, programming, and management were very terse and basic in appearance.

To a lesser extent, this is still true today. There are still "big" machines and "small" machines, except that none of today's computer equipment is physically large. The days of room-sized, or even refrigerator-sized computers are about gone. A "big" machine today simply has more processing power, more memory, more storage (disk drive capacity), stronger communications, and so on. To operate these more powerful computers, more powerful and more capable operating systems are employed. For example, a company that sells computer time to thousands of other users—an Internet service provider, for example—requires computers capable of performing multiple tasks for many users at the same time.

Although the computers used for such installations don't look much different from the PC or Macintosh designed for a single user, they are quite different inside. They use a network operating system (such as a version of UNIX or Windows NT) or another multitasking, multi-user operating system; they may include multiple CPUs or have stronger than usual I/O capabilities. The differences are significant, but also subtle. For example, Linux is a popular desktop operating system (used by a single person) based on UNIX, and it is also applied in the Internet business as a network operating system to power Web servers, mail servers, and for other multi-user applications. Again, the hardware used for an individual Linux box is likely much different from the design of these Internet service computers, even though the operating system is the same. On the other hand, even with the enhanced hardware, an Internet service provider wouldn't likely replace Linux or any other multi-user operating system on these machines with Windows 95, and certainly not with MS-DOS.

So called "high-end" workstations are used by engineers for graphical design, or by editors for film design and animation. Again, these machines may look much like a school or home PC, but inside they include extremely fast hard disk controllers, high speed networking interfaces, 3D graphics interfaces, lots of memory, and often support for multiple CPUs. The needs of these workstations are very different from the multitasking, multi-user needs of an Internet server, but they, too, have specialty requirements that can't be met by some operating systems. Although some graphics applications use Linux or UNIX, Windows NT or Mac OS are more popular foundations for these applications. Yet Windows NT and Mac OS are also popular for business and much simpler graphics applications than engineering and movie editing.

So there must be other factors that differentiate high-end from low-end computers. The main factor is the application software used with the machines. Remember we said the differentiation among computers is getting more vague. We've shown some of these factors, but the confusing concept is that even high-end applications often can run on what would be considered low-end machines, and they might even share an operating system in common. When this is the case, the main differentiating factor is the hardware: speed of the disk controller, size and speed of the hard disk, amount of memory, or type of display adapter.

One way to look at computer and operating system differences is to consider that there are really two main groups of machines: older, large machines with traditional operating systems and newer, small hardware with similar but specialized operating systems. In general, mainframe-class computers are used to conduct massive calculations or to manipulate huge amounts of data. These machines are common at scientific institutions, banks, and insurance companies. They are built to quickly perform tasks such as keeping track of thousands of checking account balances. Most of their work is done in batches—clearing two million checks and updating their associated bank accounts—instead of single, sequential repetitive tasks. When the batch job is finished—all checks have been posted, for example—the statements can be printed. These large operating systems are designed to perform these batch processes. In addition, there often are large numbers of clerks and ATM machines that use this computer to do daily transactions. They all share the resources, or processor time, of the large machine. These systems are referred to as **time-sharing systems**.

Notice that these time-sharing systems, and other large computers, frequently conduct what are termed **batch processes**. Today's smaller, interactive systems are more prone to use **sequential processing**, where each process request is completed and the data returned before the next process is started.

Medium-sized computers, which are replacing these large systems at an incredible rate, can perform many of the same tasks with less hardware because new hardware is faster and more efficient. Many of these machines run a real-time operating system instead of the batch-oriented systems used on mainframes. **Real-time systems** are what most of us are familiar with today. PC-based operating systems such as Windows 95 or Windows NT interact directly with the user—even multiple users—and respond in real time with the required information. In this environment multiple users can do many different things on the machine at the same time. Still, all users are using one machine or a group of a few machines to do all their work. This is known as a **multi-user environment**.

The newest type of large computing and operating system environments are known as **client/server systems**. Again, hardware is physically smaller, faster and more efficient than the older machines. And where the actual work is done also is very different. In the two systems above, all work is being done on the big machine. In the client/server model, only a small part of the work is being done on the central computer or computers. It may hold all the data and files, it may even perform some of the database functions or calculations required, but much of the work is performed at the client side, the computer at the user's desk. If you have used PC-class computers in a networked environment, chances are you have used the client/server model at least to some degree. A Macintosh computer running Mac OS, or a minimally-configured Windows 95 machine connected to a network that includes a Windows NT server, for example, is well suited for client/server operations, with the correct server and client applications software. Notice, again, the importance of the combination of operating system and application. Operating system differences are beginning to narrow, but the applications that run on them help differentiate how the computer is used. Client/server computing was not possible until the PC was introduced. After all, it requires a computer at the user's desk, a facility that was not available until the introduction of the PC.

A SHORT HISTORY OF OPERATING SYSTEMS

The history of operating systems is a very elaborate subject. As a matter of fact, there are many books on just this subject. This short history is not meant to be comprehensive; it merely presents enough background information to show how some of the features in modern PCs and PC operating systems work.

Initially, computers were used as large automated calculators to solve all sorts of mathematical and statistical problems. Computers were extremely large, often taking up entire rooms. Although you can legitimately trace the history of today's digital computers back one hundred years or more, there were no practical designs used by significant numbers of people until the late 1950s and early 1960s. Scientists programmed these computers to perform precise tasks, the exact tasks for which they were built. The operating systems were rudimentary, often not able to do more than read punched cards or tape, and write output to Teletype machines: a tape or deck of cards was loaded, a button was pushed on the machine to indicate the input was ready, the machine started to read the tape and perform the operations requested. If all went well, the work was done and the output was generated. This output would be sent to the Teletype, and that was that.

Yes, there was computer history before this point, but it did not involve any sort of operating system. Any program that the computer ran had to include all logic to control the computer. Since this logic was rather complex, and not all scientists were computer scientists, the operating system was the tool that allowed non-computer scientists to use computers for their purposes. That reduced programming work and increased efficiency. Obviously, there was not all that much to "operate" on, mainly the punch card and punch tape readers for input, and the Teletype printer for output. There also was not that much to operate with; memory capacity was very limited and the processing speed of the computer was slow. The art in operating systems design, therefore, largely was to keep them very small and efficient.

It did not take long (in terms of world history, at least) before computer applications evolved that could actually do something useful for a broader audience. Although computers of the late 1960s and early 1970s were crude by today's standards, they were quite capable and handled extremely complex tasks. These computers contributed to the development of space travel, submarine-based ballistic missiles, and a growing global financial community. This period also saw the beginning of a global, computer-based communications system called the Internet. Applications became logically more complex, requiring larger programs and larger amounts of data. With more useful applications being developed, the wait to "run" programs became longer.

As always, necessity was the mother of invention. Input and output devices were created; computer memory capacity and speed were increased. With more devices to manage, operating systems became more complex and extensive, but the rule of thumb (small and fast) was still extremely important. This round of evolution, which really began to take off in the mid-1970s, included the display terminal, a Teletype machine with a keyboard that did not print on paper, but projected letters on a screen. The initial "glass Teletype" was later followed by a terminal that could also show simple graphics. The magnetic tape drive, used to store and retrieve data and programs on tape, could store more and was less operator intensive than paper tape. It was quickly followed by numerous incarnations of magnetic disks.

The next evolution was the ability to share computer resources among various programs. After all, if a computer were very fast and it could quickly switch among various programs, you could do several tasks seemingly all at once and serve many people simultaneously. Some of the operating systems that evolved in this era are long-lost to all but those who worked directly with them. But there are some notable players that were responsible for setting the stage for the full-featured functionality we take for granted today. Digital Equipment Corporation's PDP-series computers, for example, ran the DEC operating system, simply known as OS, in one version or another. A popular version was OS/8, which came in various versions, such as Release 3Q, which was released in 1968. The PDP series could also run Multics, which was the basis for the development of the first version of UNIX, a multi-user, multitasking operating system. The original UNIX was developed at AT&T Labs in 1969 by Kenneth Thompson and Dennis Ritchie, as an improvement on Multics, an operating system available for the PDP machines that is widely considered to be the first multi-user, multitasking operating system. Later Digital VAXs used VMS, a powerful, multitasking, multi-user system that was strong on networking. IBM mainframes made a series of operating systems popular, including GM-NAA I/O in the early 1960s, an operating system which effectively enabled the machine to perform batch processing jobs. The letters "GM" indicate the company for which this OS was originally developed. Many others would follow, including CICS, which is still in use today. However, this company's minicomputers used OS/VM and TS, systems aimed at batch processing and time-sharing applications.

Programming computers at this time was still a very complicated process best left to scientists. In the mid 1960s, right after the first interactive computer game was invented at MIT, a simple programming language was developed, aimed at the non-programmer. It was dubbed **BASIC, Beginner's All-Purpose Symbolic Instruction Code**. A few years later, in 1975, Bill Gates discovered BASIC and became interested enough to write a compiler for it, which he sold to a company called MITS (Micro Instrumentation Telemetry Systems), the first company to produce a desktop computer that was fairly widely accepted and that could actually conduct useful work at the hands of a knowledgeable programmer. That same year he dropped out of Harvard to dedicate his time to writing software. Other programming languages introduced at about this time included other versions of BASIC supplied by various computer manufacturers, Pascal, and C. In addition, Microsoft and others, only a couple of years later, released FORTRAN, COBOL and other mini- and mainframe computer languages for desktop machines. There were in those times also highly proprietary languages that gained some popularity—languages that were primarily designed for database programming, for example—but they neither lasted nor are they significant to our discussion in this book.

The introduction of the microcomputer in the mid-1970s was probably the most exciting thing ever to happen to operating systems. These machines typically had many of the old restrictions, including little speed and little memory. Many a microcomputer came with a small operating system in ROM that did no more than provide elementary screen, keyboard, printer, and disk input and output. Bill Gates saw an opportunity, and wrote his Disk Operating System, or **DOS**. This was the first product of his brand new company, Microsoft. And it was the first widely distributed operating system for microcomputers that had to be loaded from disk or tape. There were earlier systems, including CP/M (Control Program/Microcomputer) that used some of the features and concepts of the existing UNIX operating system designs, but when IBM adopted MS-DOS for their new machine, the die was cast.

When IBM introduced the first PC in 1981, it caused a revolution—not necessarily because the machine itself was revolutionary (many would argue that it was not), but because it was designed around an "open standard." Anyone who wanted to was welcome to make PCs that worked like IBM's PC, or hardware that would work with it. And when IBM needed an operating system for their PC, they bought a license for Microsoft DOS (MS-DOS *with a* hyphen). IBM dubbed their new operating system PC DOS (*without* a hyphen), and Bill Gates once again showed his entrepreneurial spirit. He approached all the people now making PC hardware, and sold them licenses to MS-DOS. The vendors needed MS-DOS to be truly compatible with the IBM PC, and Microsoft was the only game in town. It is reported that Microsoft had more than 100 companies licensing the DOS system in less than two years.

What did this MS-DOS do? It provided the basic operating system functions described earlier in this chapter, and it was amazingly similar to what had been used before on larger computers. It supported very basic functions such as keyboard, disk and printer I/O, and communications with the outside world. As time went on, more and more support functions were added, including such things as hard disks. Then graphical interfaces became the thing of the day; initially Microsoft sat by and didn't do much. They enhanced the operating system with graphical support, after Apple Computer introduced their own PC, the Macintosh.

The Macintosh was introduced in 1984, and it seemed to be light years ahead of the IBM PC. Its operating system actually had a standard graphical interface, at a time when MS-DOS was still text-based. Also, the Macintosh OS managed the computer memory closely for the software, something DOS did not do. And because Mac OS managed all computer memory for the application programs, you could start several programs sequentially and switch among them. It was also years ahead in such things as printer management. In DOS, a program was on its own when it came to controlling the printer; all DOS did was provide the most rudimentary interface. On Mac OS, many I/O functions were part of the operating system.

Microsoft, however, did not fall far behind. In 1990 Microsoft introduced an extension to their DOS operating system that provided a graphical interface and many of the same functions as the Mac OS, called Microsoft Windows. The first Windows was in essence an operating environment running on top of an operating system, made to look like a single operating system. Windows today is more unified than the early versions.

The incarnations of operating systems since those days have been numerous; maybe five versions of Windows and eight of Mac OS. Today, they are both very similar in what they can do and how they can do it; they have a wealth of features and drivers that makes the original DOS look elementary. But their principal functions are unchanged: to provide an interface between the application programs and the hardware, and provide a user interface for basic functions such as file and disk management. In DOS, many of these functions were actually performed by the application software that interfaced with the operating system.

Let's review the important pieces of operating system development history. Although pre-1980s computing history is interesting, it doesn't hold much relevance to what we do with computers today. Table 1-1 shows the major milestones in operating system development. Note that we mention 16- and 32-bit operating systems in the table. In general, a 32-bit operating system is more powerful and faster than a 16-bit system. We'll give you more information on this difference in Chapter 2.

Table 1-1   Operating System Releases

Operating System	Approximate Date	Bits	Comments
UNIX (Bell/AT&T)	1968	8	First widely used multi-user, multitasking operating system for use on minicomputers.
CP/M	1975	8	First operating system that allowed serious business work on small personal computers. VisiCalc, released in 1978, was the first business calculation program for CP/M, and to a large extent made CP/M a success.
MS-DOS	1980	16	First operating system for the very successful IBM PC family of computers. Lotus 1-2-3 was to DOS in 1981 what VisiCalc was to CP/M. Also in 1981, Microsoft introduced the first version of Word for the PC.
PC DOS	1981	16	IBM version of Microsoft MS-DOS.
Mac OS	1984	16	The first widely distributed operating system that was totally graphical in its user interface.
Windows 3.0	1990	16	First usable version of a graphical operating system for the PC. Earlier releases, such as Windows 286, were not significant to this discussion.
Windows for Workgroups	1993	16	First version of Microsoft Windows with peer-to-peer networking support for the PC.
Windows NT	1993	32	Microsoft's first attempt at bringing a true 32-bit, preemptive multitasking operating system to the world of personal computing, with integrated networking functionality.
Windows 95	1995	16/32	A much improved user interface, with increased support for hardware and mostly 32-bit code. Native support to run 32-bit applications, and many networking features.
Windows 98	1998	32	Many bug fixes to Windows 95, more extended hardware support and now fully 32 bit.
Windows 2000	1999?	32	The next generation in the Windows operating system. With the introduction of Windows 2000 Professional version, hardware and software have caught up to the point where the most powerful Windows operating system will run on all machines. This OS will come in several versions including Professional, Server, Advanced Server, and Datacenter.

And what have all of these PCs done to the dynasty of the big machines? They have changed their role. Many big machines are now obsolete; others are used for calculation and data storage, as back-end functions for the PC. Even in this arena they are being threatened today, as PC operating systems and hardware are extended further and further.

Many older operating systems are no longer around because of hardware changes. In the next chapter, we will look more closely at hardware architecture and what it means for the operating system. A good example of hardware that is no longer a feasible option to run an OS on is the Z80 CPU produced by Zilog. When the cheaper and more flexible Intel 8088 and 8086 microprocessors were introduced in the IBM PC, the MS-DOS platform was a more attractive choice for most users. The Z80 and CP/M slowly died out. The same happened to some operating systems that used the IBM PC hardware for other reasons. A prime example is IBM's own OS/2 operating system. The system required extensive hardware, and it could not run older MS-DOS applications. Many people wished to continue to run DOS applications, so OS/2 was not a big hit. Because new software for OS/2 was slow to come, and offered no substantial new features, users were hesitant to use OS/2. Today, you will find OS/2 mainly in environments where it is used to interface to large IBM mainframes with custom-developed applications. For an operating system to be successful, many things have to work together: availability of hardware and application programs, the right mix of features, and a little luck.

SINGLE-TASKING VERSUS MULTITASKING

There are a few aspects of operating systems that deserve a closer look. As we've pointed out, today's PC operating systems go way beyond basic I/O. In practice, almost every resource in the computer, such as the memory and the **microprocessor** (central processing unit or CPU), are now being managed by the operating system. This is both good and bad; it results in a lot more consistency and a lot of added functionality. However, application programs can no longer directly access hardware in creative ways as they could under DOS. A good example of this is the chip used to make sound. This chip includes an electronic timer that can be accessed by external programs. Many older DOS programs use this chip as a timer to halt program execution for a specified period of time. This is done by manipulating the internal workings of the chip directly from the application program without the intervention of MS-DOS. A Windows program could not do this, since Windows is firmly in control of the chip in question at all times.

One of the major reasons for giving the operating system so much control over resources is to facilitate **multitasking**, a technique that allows a computer to run two or more programs at the same time. Since most personal computers have only one CPU chip, which can in general only do one thing at a time, multitasking is generally achieved by splitting processor time between applications, switching so rapidly that the user is not aware of any discontinuity.

There are two general types of multitasking. The first method is known as **cooperative multitasking**. In this method, the operating system hands over control to a program, sits back, and waits for the program to hand control back to the operating system. The assumption here is that the program will do some work, and then give control back to the operating system. If for some reason the program does not hand control back to the operating system, however, it means that this one program will hog the CPU until its operations are complete, while all other programs on the computer are on hold. If the one program does not release control, for example because it has gotten stuck in an endless loop, the operating system may never get control back. As a result, no other programs can run until the computer is reset—an undesirable scenario. This could also be a problem if some of the programs on the computer are time sensitive. If a program that needs to collect some data every second or that must update a clock every so often is running, a cooperative multitasking environment may cause some trouble. You will find this behavior in such operating systems as Windows 3.1; if you format a floppy disk and try to play Solitaire at the same time, you will find that you cannot play a card until the floppy disk is completely formatted. Figure 1-5 shows the basic concept of cooperative multitasking.

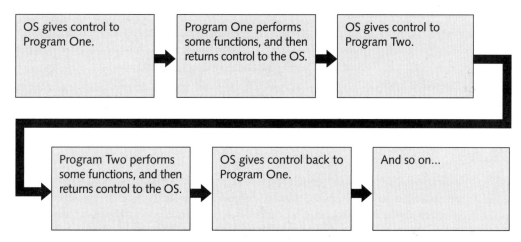

Figure 1-5   Cooperative multitasking basics

A better method would be the second alternative, **preemptive multitasking**, illustrated in Figure 1-6 on the next page. In this scenario, the operating system is in control of the computer at all times. It will let programs execute a little bit of code at a time, but immediately after the code has executed, it will force the program to relinquish control of the CPU back to the operating system. It then picks the next program, and repeats the same process. Because the operating system is in charge, it has a large amount of control over how much of the computer's resources are allocated to each program. As a result the computer will have to use more of its processor power and memory to support the operating system, but the behavior of programs and the computer as a whole will be a little more predictable. Playing Solitaire while formatting a floppy disk in Windows NT is not a problem; preemptive multitasking will result in both processes getting some CPU time to do their job. Windows 95 and Windows 98 are both preemptive multitasking systems, but you can still format a floppy disk and play Solitaire at the same time. The reason is that the program code used to format the floppy disk has been rewritten to be more cooperative. If you were to compare the speed and response of Solitaire on a Windows 98 machine against the speed and response of Solitaire on a Windows NT machine while both are formatting a floppy disk, you will see a slight difference in favor of Windows NT.

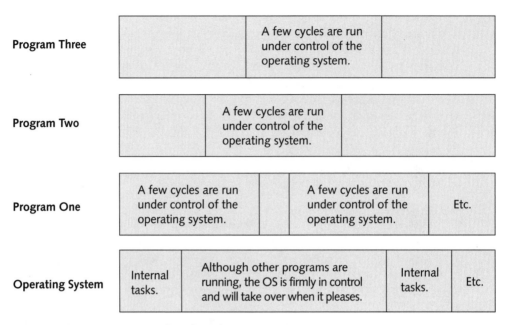

Figure 1-6   Preemptive multitasking basics

There are still some single-tasking operating systems being used on PCs. A **single-tasking** operating system executes one program at a time (see Figure 1-7). To do something else, one program has to be stopped, and a new program has to be loaded and executed. Since there is normally never a situation in which there are multiple programs trying to use the same resources, single-tasking operating systems are a lot simpler. This is however considered older technology, and as new operating systems are released, they are seldom single-tasking. An example of a single-tasking operating system would be MS-DOS. New single-tasking operating systems are only found in computers with very limited processor capacity, such as Personal Digital Assistants (PDAs). An exception is Windows CE, which is designed for PDAs but also can be multitasking. In addition, the Apple Newton, now an older product, is still available and can handle basic multitasking.

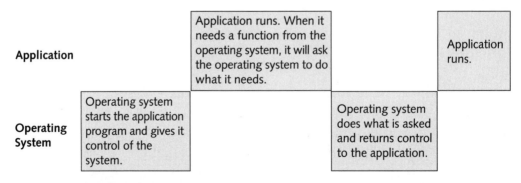

Figure 1-7   Single-tasking operating system

A special note needs to be made of a hybrid called a **task-switching** operating system. This system has many of the device management functions of the multitasking operating system, and it can load multiple application programs at once. It will however only actively execute one of these applications. If the user wants to use another application, they can ask the operating system to switch to that task. When the switch is made, the operating system gives control to the newly selected task. Obviously, many of the problems associated with switching among various applications and their use of various devices do not have to be dealt with, making this a less complicated type of operating system. This is also considered an older technology that isn't used in any of the new PC operating systems. Many versions of the Mac OS are task-switching, as are some of the operating systems found on older PCs made by companies such as Atari (the ST series) and Commodore (the Amiga series—though some now use UNIX), which focused more on the home computer market. You can see the concept of task switching in Figure 1-8.

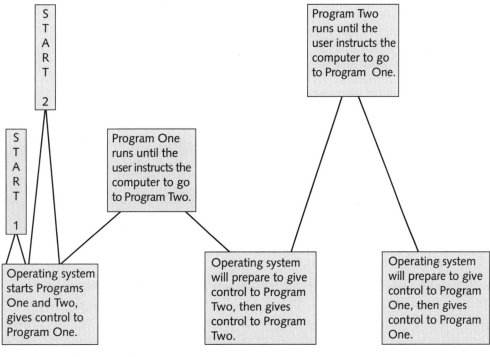

Figure 1-8   Task-switching

SINGLE-USER VERSUS MULTI-USER OPERATING SYSTEMS

Some operating systems, in addition to being able to run multiple programs at the same time with multitasking technology, can also allow multiple *users* to use an application at the same time. These are known as **multi-user** operating systems. A system that is a multi-user system is almost by definition also a multitasking system. Most multi-user systems use preemptive multitasking technology. All of the operating systems covered in this book initially were designed as single-user systems, with the exception of UNIX, which is a multi-user operating system by design. UNIX has been included here since its role in business seems to be increasing over recent years, even though UNIX is over 25 years old.

You might think that the operating systems used to run client/server networks would be considered multi-user operating systems; however, this is not always the case. An OS can be multitasking without being multi-user. For example, although one computer on the network may act as a network server, making files or printers available to many other computers and thereby to many other users, the operating system that performs those tasks is not always a multi-user operating system. In general, to qualify as multi-user, the operating system needs to allow multiple users to run individual applications simultaneously. For this reason many client/server operating systems are not strictly multi-user. Some experts predict that client/server computing will eventually make multi-user systems obsolete. A good example of an operating system that is multitasking but not multi-user is Windows 95.

CURRENT OPERATING SYSTEMS

The operating systems surveyed in this book are the most common in today's computing environment: MS-DOS or PC DOS, Windows 3.1, Windows 3.11, Windows 95/98, Windows NT, UNIX, and Apple Macintosh Mac OS. In Chapter 2 you will be introduced to each of these in more detail. This section gives a brief summary.

The most popular OS in corporate America as this book is written is probably Windows 3.1, Windows 3.11, or Windows for Workgroups 3.11. Although there are newer Windows versions, including Windows 95, Windows 98, and Windows NT, the earlier releases are still widespread. They are stable, will run on many computers, are familiar to many people, and are able to meet computing needs for a wide population. It is also possible to use Windows 3.1 with older and more resource-limited machines, machines that would not be able to run Windows 95/98 or Windows NT. The exact requirements for the various hardware platforms will be discussed in Chapter 2.

Some of the more elaborate computers will run newer versions of Microsoft Windows. Windows 95 (as in 1995, not the 95th release) is a very popular operating system, although much of corporate America has not yet upgraded from older Windows versions. Windows 95 brings new functions, as does its newer sibling, Windows 98. Microsoft says that Windows 98 is the last version in the Windows 9x line. Many people have not upgraded to Windows 95 or 98 because they are happy with what they have, or because the computer resources required are not available. There are also programs that, despite Microsoft's claims, will not work on Windows 95/98.

Windows NT (for New Technology) is also found in various versions, including 3.51 and 4.0, in many corporate environments. If you need a big, fast PC to run Windows 3.x, 95 or 98, say an Intel 80486 with 16 MB of RAM, you need a *very* big, *very* fast machine for Windows NT, in particular for version 4.0, say an Intel Pentium with 32 MB of RAM. This operating system is expensive, much more complicated than Windows 3.1 or 95/98, but it has some distinct advantages for users in a networked environment. These advantages will be discussed in the next chapter.

We will also look at a very dynamic multi-user operating system called UNIX. There are many flavors of UNIX. We will look at a group of UNIX operating systems called the POSIX Compliant, System V, Release 4 systems (pronounced "System 5, Release 4" or "S5R4" for short). POSIX is an interface standard supported by both schools of UNIX and non-UNIX operating systems like Windows NT. It was designed so applications could be source-compatible across multiple operating systems.

Still hanging on, especially in education and the graphics industry, is the Mac OS operating system for Apple Macintosh computers. In certain sectors, this OS is strongly represented, but typically you will not find it much in corporate America. You *will* find the Mac OS in education—colleges and some secondary schools—and in the graphics industry, particularly in video editing.

In Chapter 2, we will take a closer look at the individual operating systems mentioned here. You will read more about hardware required to run an operating system, which versions you will see in what environment and for what reason, and we will discuss in greater detail where you will typically find what operating system and why.

CHAPTER SUMMARY

You should now have a good idea of how an operating system works in general terms. You should have an understanding of the input and output functions provided by the BIOS and the other parts of the operating system. We introduced the concept of device drivers and the functions the operating system provides to application programs. We briefly discussed the types of operating systems in use, and the differentiation that can be made based on the computer environment in which the operating system is used.

We provided a short operating system history, which touched on some of the highlights in computer development from an operating system point of view. We introduced you to single-tasking operating systems, which run only one application at a time, and multitasking operating systems, which can run multiple applications at once. The single-user operating system can only service one user at a time, while the multi-user operating system will service multiple users at once.

Finally, we briefly described some modern PC operating systems you will find in use today. This should provide good background for the following chapter, which will provide a comparison of the basic features of some of today's popular operating systems.

KEY TERMS

- **BASIC** — Beginner's All-purpose Symbolic Instruction Code. An English-like computer programming language originally designed as a teaching tool, but which evolved into a useful and relatively powerful development language.

- **batch processing** — A computing style frequently employed by large systems. A request for a series of processes is submitted to the computer; information is displayed or printed when the batch is complete. Batches might include processing all of the checks submitted to a bank for a day, or all of the purchases in a wholesale inventory system, for example.

- **BIOS** — Basic Input/Output System. Low-level computer program code that conducts basic hardware and software communications inside the computer. A computer BIOS basically resides between computer hardware and the higher level operating system, such as DOS or Windows.

- **CD-ROM** — Compact Disk Read Only Memory. A hardware device used to play and in some cases to record computer data, music, and other multimedia information in a write once, read many format.

- **client/server systems** — A computer hardware and software design wherein different portions of an application execute on different computers or on different components of a single computer. Typically client software supports user I/O and the server software conducts database searches, manages printer output, and the like.

- **code** — Instructions written in a computer programming language.

- **cooperative multitasking** — A computer hardware and software design wherein the operating system hands off control to an application temporarily and waits for the application to return control to the operating system.

- **CPU** — Central processing unit. In today's computer, typically a single chip (the microprocessor) with support devices that conducts the majority of the computer's calculations.

- **device driver** — Computer software designed to provide the operating system and applications software access to specific computer hardware.

- **DOS** — Disk Operating System. The generic computer code used to control many low-level computer hardware and software functions. Also, the specific name for the operating system popular with IBM-compatible PC computers.

- **I/O** — Input/output.

- **LED** — Light Emitting Diode. An electronic device frequently used to display information in electronic devices such as watches, clocks, and stereos.

- **microprocessor** — A solid state electronic device that controls the major computer functions and operations. See also CPU.

- **multi-user** — A computer hardware and software system that is designed to service multiple users who access the computer's hardware and software applications simultaneously.

- **multi-user environment** — A computer environment that supports multi-user access to a computer's hardware and software facilities.

- **operating system (OS)** — Computer software code that interfaces with user application software and the computer's BIOS to allow the applications to interact with the computer hardware.

- **preemptive multitasking** — A computer hardware and software design for multitasking of applications in which the operating system retains control of the computer at all times. See cooperative multitasking for comparison.

- **real-time systems** — An operating system that interacts directly with the user and responds in real time with required information.

- **ROM** — Read Only Memory. Special memory that contains information that is not erased when the power is removed from the memory hardware. ROM is used to store computer instructions that must be available at all times, such as the BIOS code.

- **sequential processing** — A computer processing style in which each operation is submitted, acted upon, and the results displayed before the next process is started. Compare to batch processing.

- **single-tasking** — A computer hardware and software design that can manage only a single task at a time.

- **task-switching** — A single-tasking computer hardware and software design that permits the user or application software to switch among multiple single-tasking operations.

- **time-sharing systems** — A central computer system, such as a mainframe, that is used by multiple users and applications simultaneously.

REVIEW QUESTIONS

1. One company created a revolution of sorts when it introduced an open standard in desktop computer hardware. Which company was this?

2. Which of the following statements is true of a computer's BIOS?

    a. It conducts high-level software and hardware operations.

    b. It communicates with the computer hardware at the lowest, most basic levels.

    c. It is required in some form of all computer systems.

    d. It serves as an intermediary between the operating system and computer hardware.

3. The _____ operating system was the first system used by IBM for its PC computer.

4. Microsoft's Bill Gates wrote what computer operating system?

5. What is the main difference between a cooperative multitasking system and a preemptive multitasking system?

6. Apple Computer Corporation's operating system is called _____.

7. The most prevalent operating system on current desktop computers is not necessarily the newest one. What is this operating system?

8. _____ is a technique that allows a user or a computer application to switch among multiple applications, running one program at a time.

9. The hardware device that conducts the majority of a computer's calculations is a solid state processor called a _____. With support chips, this chip is called the Central _____ _____ or _____.

10. One of the earliest widely used programming languages was called BASIC, which stands for _____.

11. Linux is a low-end operating system rarely used for serious computer applications. True or False?

12. Very large early business computers were called _____.

13. The medium-sized computers that preceded PCs and that were used for serious business and engineering applications were called _____.

14. Microsoft Windows was the first graphics-oriented user interface for small desktop computers. True or False?

15. The more powerful the computer, the larger it has to be. True or False?

HANDS-ON PROJECTS

PROJECT 1-1

Today's Internet is a rich resource for finding current and historical computer information.

To view a World Wide Web page that shows additional history about the information covered in this chapter:

1. Point your browser to this online address:

   http://www.tcm.org/html/history/timeline/index.html

2. Answer the following questions based on your investigation of this Web page:

   a. The IBM PC, introduced in 1981, used what type of central processing unit (CPU)?

   b. This first desktop CPU ran at what clock speed?

   c. Who was Bill Gates' original partner in founding the Microsoft Corporation and in what year did they found the company?

d. What promotion technique did Apple use to introduce the first Macintosh in 1984? What short-lived IBM computer was introduced that same year?

e. Microsoft introduced the first successful version of Windows in 1990. What version was it and what was the official introduction date?

3. Point your browser to this online address:

http://www.digitalcentury.com/encyclo/update/mits.html

4. Answer the following questions based on your investigation of this Web page:

a. Who were the co-developers of the MITS Altair computer, mentioned earlier in this chapter? (Point of interest: one of the authors of this book, Tom Badgett, worked with the second developer, who was also the namesake for another popular early computer called the Sol, as joint technical editors for Computers and Electronics magazine in New York. For a picture of the Sol computer, point your browser here: **http://204.117.207.9/hcs/museum/sol.jpg**)

b. What two Boston-based programmers responded to the first Altair ads with excitement because they had a computer program that might run on it?

5. Point your browser to this online address:

http://www.realtime–info.be

6. Answer the following questions based on your investigation of this Web page:

a. How many copies of Windows 3.0 did Microsoft sell, according to this source?

b. In what year was Microsoft Windows 3.0 introduced?

c. What important new feature was introduced with this version of Windows?

PROJECT 1-2

Regardless of the operating system you have access to, you can study its facilities.

To enter commands and discover some information about your DOS or Windows operating system:

1. If you are running a version of DOS or Microsoft Windows, display the C:/ prompt (ask your instructor how to do this if necessary), type the command **ver** and press **Enter**. You will see a display that shows what version of the DOS operating system you are using. Note that even Windows, a graphical user interface, contains some DOS elements.

2. At the DOS prompt, type the command **chkdsk** and press **Enter**. You should see a detailed display that describes some of your system components, hard disk size, amount of memory, and other information about the system.

3. At the DOS prompt, type **mem /c** and press **Enter**. This command shows how your computer's memory is being used.

4. Type **Exit** and press **Enter** to exit DOS.

To discover some information about your Windows 95/98 or NT operating system:

1. In Windows 95, 98, or Windows NT, double-click **My Computer** on your desktop, click **Help** and choose **About Windows** from the pull-down menu. This dialog box tells you what version of Windows you are using, whether it has been updated with service packs, copyright dates, and other information. You will need this information if you have to contact technical support for your operating system.

2. Press and hold **Ctrl** and click the **Exit** icon (the X at the upper-right corner of the topmost dialog box) to close all of the open windows.

To discover some information about your Mac OS operating system:

1. In Mac OS, click on **Help** at the right side of the main menu bar and choose **Help** from this menu to display the Apple Guide. Click on **Look for** and type **read text aloud**. You should get a detailed description of the process. Look for other topics of interest to see how Mac OS handles online Help.

2. Click the **Close icon** at the upper-right corner of the display to close any open window.

To enter commands and discover some information about your UNIX operating system:

1. At a UNIX system prompt, type the command **ls –la** and press **Enter**. You will see a list of files and directories as well as attributes of these objects.

2. At a UNIX prompt, type **man ls** and press **Enter**. Now you will see a Help file (manual) that describes how the list command works and shows you additional switches.

3. Type **Exit** and press **Enter** to exit a UNIX session (check with your instructor if you need to use a different exit command).

PROJECT 1-3

Microsoft Windows 95 and later, and Windows NT are good examples of widely distributed multitasking operating systems.

To start several applications and view some information about their operation:

1. Click **Start** on the taskbar.

2. Point to **Programs**.

3. Choose **Windows Explorer**. The Windows Explorer utility opens. Now you will open several other applications.

4. Click **Start**, **Programs**, **MS-DOS Prompt** to open a DOS prompt.

5. Click **Start**, **Programs**, **Accessories**, **Notepad** to open the Notepad word processor.

6. Click **Start**, **Programs**, **Accessories**, **Calculator**. Now Windows Explorer, a DOS Prompt, Notepad, and Calculator are all running.

7. Press **Ctrl+Alt+Del** to display the Task List Dialog box (or the Close Program dialog box in Windows 98). You can press this keyboard combination at any time to display active programs. Close this dialog box.

8. Click **Start**, **Programs**, **Accessories**, **System Tools**, **Resource Meter**. If you do not see the Resource Meter option, it has not been installed on your machine. In this case, close all open windows and skip steps 9–12. Otherwise, click **OK** to place the Resource Meter on your taskbar tray.

9. Double-click the **Resource Meter** icon on the taskbar tray. This utility shows how much of your system resources are being used.

10. Close one or more of the open programs and notice the effect on the Resource Monitor.

11. Close all of the open programs.

12. Right-click the **Resource Monitor** icon and choose **Exit**.

CASE PROJECT

In this project you have been asked to help expand the basic computer installation of your employer. Presently the company has two relatively old computers, one a Macintosh running Mac OS and the other a PC-compatible running Windows 3.11. The plan is to purchase two more computers now and to expect future expansion within the next six months.

1. Given that your company is involved in fairly traditional business computer activities including accounting, word processing and some spreadsheet work, what operating system do you think should be recommended based on the discussion of operating system capabilities in this chapter?

2. Future requirements require a fairly substantial expansion, including several computers connected to a central server. What operating system would be a logical choice for this central network server? (Make a stab at this one. You'll get more information on this topic a little later in this book).

3. You have been told that one employee uses the Macintosh for newsletter and other internal graphics work. Requirements in this area aren't likely to grow soon. Should you make any changes to the Macintosh computer?

4. Long range plans call for the establishment of a multi-user environment where perhaps dozens of users will access a single central computer over a local network, possibly from remote locations. Based on the information in this chapter, what two current operating systems would you choose for this application? Which one do you think is the strongest candidate for this multi-user application, all other considerations aside?

CURRENT PC OPERATING SYSTEMS

This chapter provides a look at the most popular operating systems used in business today, and provides some additional detail on the way computer hardware interacts with the operating system. You will become acquainted with the general characteristics of each of the operating systems, their strengths and weaknesses, and the hardware requirements to run them. This overview will help you place the operating systems in the work environment, so that you can decide which operating system to apply when new machines are installed or when existing machines are upgraded. You will also be able to identify situations in which the wrong operating system is used.

AFTER READING THIS CHAPTER AND COMPLETING THE EXERCISES YOU WILL BE ABLE TO:

- Understand the characteristics of the hardware platform, such as design type, speed, cache, address bus, and data bus
- Describe the basic features and system architecture of popular PC processors
- Identify the basic features and characteristics of popular PC operating systems

Understanding Computer Hardware

As you learned in the previous chapter, one of the main functions of the operating system is to provide the interface between the various application programs running on a machine and the hardware inside the machine. The hardware includes the Central Processing Unit (CPU; also called the processor or microprocessor); a more general hardware classification is the system architecture (SA) used in the machine.

The CPU is the chip that actually does the computational and logic work. Most modern PCs have one such chip, and are referred to as **single-processor machines**. Note, however, that for complete functionality the CPU requires several support chips. There are also machines that have multiple CPUs; many have two, some have as many as 64 or more. These machines are generally referred to as **multiprocessor machines**. You will take a closer look at single-processor and multiprocessor machines later in this chapter. CPUs can be classified by several factors, the most important of which are:

- Design type
- Speed
- Cache
- Address bus
- Data bus

Each of these factors is considered in the following sections.

Design Type

Two general CPU designs are used in today's computers: **CISC (Complex Instruction Set Computer)** and **RISC (Reduced Instruction Set Computer)**. The main difference between the two is the number of different instructions the chip can process. When a program executes on a computer, the CPU reads instruction after instruction from the program to perform the tasks the program wants completed. When the CPU has read such an instruction, it carries out the operations associated with it. In the current generation of PCs, the CPU can process as many as 20 million complex operations per second on the low end, and as many as half a billion on the high end. Clock speed and CPU design are the factors that determine how fast operations are executed. Future CPUs for PCs will be able to perform several billion operations per second. Obviously, it is convenient for the programmer to have available many instructions to do many different operations.

Let's say for example that the programmer wants to multiply two numbers. It would be convenient to give the CPU the two numbers, then tell it to multiply them, and display the result. Since different kinds of numbers (such as integers and real numbers) need to be treated differently, it would be nice if there were functions to perform this multiplication on all number types. You can see that as we require the CPU to perform more and more functions, the number of instructions could get quite large. At the same time the **instruction set**, or the list of commands the CPU can understand and carry out, can get quite complex. As programs perform more functions, the instruction set gets more complicated. A processor that works according to this model is therefore called a Complex Instruction Set Computer (CISC) CPU. When a CISC CPU gets a command, it typically invokes some parts of the CPU itself to carry out the command. When a command is finished and the CPU gets the next command, it will typically use the same parts of the chip it used before to carry out this command.

The CISC CPU has its advantages and disadvantages. A big advantage is that you need only general-purpose hardware to carry out commands. If you later want to add new commands to a new revision of your chip, that likely can be done with the same general-purpose hardware. Another big advantage is that the chip is mainly driven by software, which is in general cheaper to produce than hardware. Major disadvantages to the CISC design are the complexity of hardware that can perform many functions and the on-chip software needed to make the hardware do the right thing. An even bigger disadvantage is, ironically, the need to continually reprogram the on-chip hardware. If you use the same part of the chip to add a number as you use to multiply a number—two functions that are obviously related but slightly different—you will need to reconfigure the hardware in between the multiplication and the addition operations. This reconfiguration takes a little time, which is one reason a CISC chip can be a little slower than other designs.

Also, when you use general-purpose hardware to perform specific functions, the functions won't always be executed in the most efficient way, which tends to slow down the CPU's execution of program code. One solution to this problem would be to customize hardware for specific functions. You can add a module that is optimized to do all computational functions (a math coprocessor), for example. Such a trick will increase CPU performance, but it will increase the price as well. Fast hardware is expensive.

Considering these disadvantages of the design of the CISC CPU, it will be easy to understand the idea behind the other major CPU design, the Reduced Instruction Set Computer (RISC) CPU. The complex operations it has to carry out slow down a CISC CPU, because all sorts of hardware on the chip have to be set up to perform specific functions. The RISC CPU design, on the other hand, requires very little setup for specific tasks; it has hardware on the chip that is specially designed and optimized to perform particular functions. As mentioned before, the disadvantage of this approach is that you need a lot of hardware to carry out instructions, which will make the chip more expensive because it is more complex. This is the main reason a RISC CPU has so few instructions; most of the instructions it performs are conducted by hardware on the chip that is dedicated to perform just that function. Since most of the hardware on the RISC CPU is not shared among many instructions, RISC CPUs typically use a technique called **pipelining**, which allows the processor to operate on one instruction at the same time it is fetching one or more subsequent instructions from the operating system or application. The difference between the RISC approach and the CISC approach is best explained by the example in Figure 2-1 on the next page, which shows how each design carries out five multiplications.

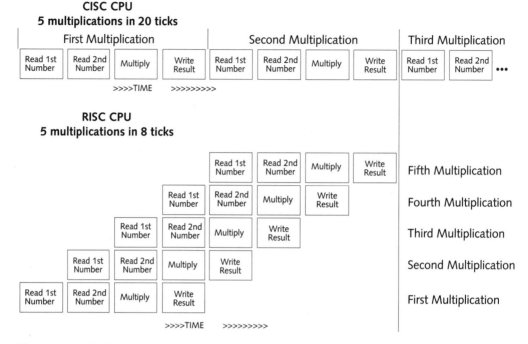

Figure 2-1   CISC versus RISC processing

The general steps required to perform the multiplications are as follows:

1. Read the first number out of memory.

2. Read the second number out of memory.

3. Multiply the two numbers.

4. Write the result back to memory.

5. Repeat steps 1–4 for each of the four remaining multiplications.

On a simple CISC CPU, the CPU will first be configured to get (read) the numbers. It will then read the numbers. Now the CPU will be configured to multiply the numbers. Then the numbers will be multiplied. Now the CPU will be configured to write the result to memory. Then the numbers will be written to memory. If you wish to multiply five sets of numbers in this way, the whole process has to be repeated five times.

On a simple RISC CPU, the process looks slightly different. A piece of hardware on the CPU will be dedicated to reading the first number. When this operation is complete, another piece of hardware will read the second number. When that operation is complete, yet another piece of hardware will perform the multiplication, and when that is complete yet another piece of hardware will write the result to memory. So far, no difference between how the RISC model and the CISC model complete the operation. But if this operation has to happen five times in a row, the piece of RISC hardware dedicated to obtaining the first number from memory will obtain the first number for the second operation while the second number for the first operation is obtained. And while the first two numbers are being multiplied, the second number for the second operation will be retrieved from memory, while the first number for the third operation will be obtained. As the first result is written back to memory, the second multiplication will be performed, while the second number for the third operation will be read from memory, while the first number for the fourth operation will be read from memory, and so on. As you can see, when a large number of operations must be performed, the RISC CPU's pipelining design does it a lot more efficiently than a CISC CPU.

SPEED

The speed of a CPU defines how fast it can perform all the operations expected of it. There are many ways to indicate speed, but the most obvious indicator is the **internal clock speed** of the CPU. As you may know, a CPU runs on a very rigid schedule along with the rest of the computer. The clock provides this schedule to make sure that all the chips know what to expect at what time. The internal clock speed tells you how many clock pulses, or *ticks* are available per second. Typically, the CPU will perform some action on every tick. The more ticks per second, the faster the CPU will execute commands, and the harder the electronics on the CPU have to work. The clock speed for a CPU can be as low as 1 million ticks per second (1 megahertz or MHz) or even lower, and as high as 500 million ticks per second (500 MHz). The faster the clock, the faster the CPU, the more expensive the hardware. Also, as more components are needed to make a CPU, the chip uses more energy to do its work. Part of this energy is converted to heat, causing faster CPUs to run warmer.

This leads to another advantage of the RISC CPU design: RISC CPU hardware is less complicated than CISC CPU hardware, so a RISC CPU can operate at higher clock speeds. RISC CPUs operating at clock speeds of 500 MHz have been around for years. Some designs are now available that run at speeds of up to 800 MHz. CISC chips running at 400 MHz have only recently become available, and there are not yet any production CISC chips that run faster than 450 MHz.

In addition to performing fast operations inside the CPU, the chips also must be able to communicate with the other chips in the machine. This is where the **external clock speed** of the CPU comes in. While a CPU may internally run at a speed of 200 or 400 MHz, it will typically use a lower clock speed to communicate with the rest of the machine. The reason for this is again, to a large extent, cost. It would be extremely expensive to make every component in the computer run as fast as the CPU. It is therefore common practice to run the other components in the computer at a reduced clock rate. Usually, the external clock speed is one-half, one-third, or one-fourth the speed of the internal CPU clock. This is the speed at which the processor can communicate with the memory and the other devices in the computer.

CACHE

If a CPU wants to get a few numbers out of memory, and its internal clock speed is twice as fast as its external clock speed, it will obviously have to wait on the external clock, which could be very inefficient. To get around this problem, most modern CPUs have **cache**

memory built into the chip. This memory is extremely fast, and therefore expensive. It typically runs at the same speed as the processor. If a number the processor needs is stored in the cache memory on the CPU, it probably won't have to wait to obtain that number. This memory is referred to as **Level 1 (L1) cache**. Some CPUs have one more level of cache memory, which is typically on a separate chip. This is called **Level 2 (L2) cache**, and it typically runs at the same speed as the external CPU clock. It is, in general, still accessible faster than the other memory in the computer, but it isn't as fast as the Level 1 cache. The amount of L1 and L2 cache will, especially for larger CPUs, determine the speed of the CPU. In many cases, up to 90% of the data a CPU needs to transfer to and from memory is present in either the L1 or L2 cache when the CPU needs it. This is because there is a specialized piece of hardware called the **cache controller** that predicts what data will be needed and makes that data available in cache before it is needed. Most modern CPUs also can use the cache to write data to memory, to ensure that the CPU will not have to wait when it wishes to write results to memory. You can see that intelligent, fast cache controllers and large amounts of L1 and L2 cache are important components for increasing the speed of a CPU.

ADDRESS BUS

The **address bus** is an internal communications pathway that specifies the source and target addresses for memory reads and writes. It is instrumental in the transfer of data to and from computer memory. The address bus typically runs at the external clock speed of the CPU. The address, like all data in the computer, is in digital form and conveyed in the form of a series of bits. The width of the address bus is the number of bits that can be used to address memory. A wider bus means the computer can address more memory, and therefore store more data or larger, more complex programs. For example, a 16-bit wide address bus can address 64 kilobytes (KB) (64,000 bytes) of memory. This bus size is no longer found in PCs sold today. However, it will appear in the discussion of system architecture later in this chapter. Most PCs today use a 32-bit address bus, which allows them to address roughly 4 billion (4,000,000,000) memory addresses, or 4 gigabytes (GB). However, you will see later that many systems, although they have a 32-bit address bus, cannot actually address that much memory. New processors being developed today have even wider address buses, some as wide as 64 bits, allowing them to address over 1.8 *quintillion* bytes of memory!

For Intel family machines this addressing is set in a specific way:

- 8088/8086 – 20-bit - 1 MB
- 286/386SX – 24-bit – 16 MB
- 386DX/486/Pentium – 32-bit – 4 GB
- Pentium Pro – 36-bit – 64 GB

DATA BUS

The **data bus** allows computer components such as the CPU, display adapter, and main memory to share information. The number of bits in the data bus indicates how many bits of data can be transferred from memory to the CPU or vice versa in one clock tick. A CPU with an external clock speed of 25 MHz will have 25 million ticks per second to the external bus. If this CPU has a 16-bit data bus, it could theoretically transfer 50 MB (50,000,000 bytes) of data to and from memory every second. (One byte consists of 8 bits, so 25 million times 16 bits divided by 8 bits per second equals 50 MB per second). A CPU with an external clock speed of 25 MHz and a 32-bit data bus could transfer as much as 100 MB per second (25 million times 32 bits divided by 8 bits per byte). That is twice as much data in the same time period, so in theory the CPU will work twice as fast.

There are a couple of catches here. First, the software must be able to instruct the CPU to use all of the data bus, and the rest of the computer must be fast enough to keep up with the CPU. Most CPUs work internally with the same number of bits as it does on the data bus. In other words, a CPU with a 32-bit data bus typically will be able to perform operations on 32 bits of data at a time. Almost all CPUs can also be instructed to work with chunks of data narrower than the data bus width, but in this case the CPU will not be as efficient, since the same number of clock cycles will be required to perform an operation whether or not all bits are used.

POPULAR PC PROCESSORS

The following sections give an overview of the CPUs most often found in current or recent use on PCs.

INTEL

The most popular CPUs in use in PCs today are designed by Intel. The first player in this line of processors was the **8088**, the CPU found in the original IBM PC. It originally had an internal and external CPU clock speed of roughly 4.7 MHz, and there was no L1 or L2 cache. Cache memory wasn't needed because the memory ran at the same speed as the external and internal CPU clock. The address bus on the CPU was 20 bits wide, a number chosen to enable the computer to address 1,048,576 bytes of memory, or 1 MB. This was 16 times the customary 65,536 bytes (commonly referred to as 64K) of memory common on CPUs in those days, something many engineers thought would be more than a personal computer would ever need. The address bus of this CPU was 8 bits wide, but internal operations could be performed either with 8 or 16-bit logic. The 8-bit data bus made it cheap and easy to build computers around the chip.

The 8088 was followed by the **8086**, which was the first Intel CPU to have a 16-bit data path. Apart from that, it was identical to the 8088. Later on, clock speeds on these CPUs increased to as much as 20 MHz. Intel has built on this CPU ever since, following it up with other processors that became popular in PC computers. The 80286 was the beginning of the **80x86** line, with more advanced chip functionality to provide more commands to the end user, and higher clock speeds of 8, 16 or later even 20 MHz. This chip also ran at identical internal and external clock speeds and had no L1 and L2 cache.

The 80386 introduced a 32-bit address and data bus, even higher clock speeds of 16, 20 and later even 40 MHz. This chip was the first in the Intel 80x86 chip family that could perform operations using 32 bits of data at a time. Because the chips were so fast, running at speeds over 16 MHz, these were the first Intel chips in this line to support external, or L2, cache. The internal and external clocks on the chip were still the same, but more new instructions were introduced. Like the 8088 and 8086 combination, this chip also came in two data port variations. The 80386 was officially called the 80386DX and had a 32-bit data path. For reasons of economy, there was also an 80386SX, which had a 16-bit external data path and 24-bit address bus width.

The next chips released were the 80486 family, the first line of chips in which Intel used different internal and external clocks. This chip is the first one to have L1 cache on the chip, which runs at the internal CPU speed, as well as features for external L2 cache, which runs at the speed of the external clock. Unique in the 80486 was the inclusion of hardware dedicated to performing mathematical operations. Some 486 models, the initial ones known as DX chips, ran at the same internal and external clock speed. Newer models, identified as DX2 or DX4 chips, run internally at twice or four times the external clock. This is the last series of chips Intel made that had a "little brother" with a reduced data path, referred to as the 80486SX.

After the 80486 chip family, Intel left the 80x86 numbering scheme and started naming chips. The first model with a name was the **Pentium**. *Penta* is the Greek word for five, so this is really the 80586 if Intel had followed their previous conventions. More instructions were added and L1 cache was made more efficient. Otherwise not much differed from the 80486. Next came the **Pentium Pro**, which is optimized for running 32-bit instructions faster than a Pentium chip. Then Intel released something called the **Multimedia Extension** or **MMX**. These chips are nearly identical to a regular Pentium, but they have a few new instructions to deal with multimedia—for example graphics and video—and the chip design is optimized for handling large amounts of data. The data bus is 32 bits wide with a 36-bit address bus; the chip will run at external clock speeds of up to 66 MHz, and at internal clock speeds as fast as 233 MHz.

The newest Intel CPUs at the time this book is written are the chips in the **Pentium II** family. Added features on these chips include an internal clock that has been raised to as high as 450 MHz, with future releases planned at 500 MHz. External clock speed for these chips is 66 or 100 MHz. Unique in the Pentium II design is the inclusion of L1 cache, running at internal clock speed, as well as L2 cache, running at external or twice external clock speed, built right onto the CPU module. Table 2-1 summarizes the development of Intel CPUs.

Table 2-1 Intel CPUs

CPU	Introduced	Data Bus/ Address Bus Bits	Int Clock MHz	Ext Clock MHz	Cache
8088	1978	8/20	4–8	4–8	No
8086	1978	16/20	4–16	4–16	No
80286	1982	16/24	8–40	8–40	No
80386SX	1985	16/24	16–40	16–40	No
80386DX	1985	32/24	16–40	16–40	No
80486SX	1989	16/24	16–80	16–40	Yes
80486DX	1989	32/24	16–120	16–40	Yes
Pentium	1993	32/28	16–266	16–66	Yes
Pentium Pro	1995	64/28	33–200	33–50	Yes
Pentium II	1997	64/36	66–450	66–100	Yes

A very important feature of the whole line of Intel CPUs discussed here is backward compatibility, which means that a significant number of features from an older chip will function on a newer chip. Code written to run on an 8088 processor will run on any newer CPU without change. Since the 8088 code is only 16-bit code, it will not use many of the advanced features of the newer CPUs, therefore it will run slower than code written especially for the CPU. But the code will run without being rewritten, which is one of the major reasons for the success of the Intel line of CPUs.

MOTOROLA

Motorola is the next most popular CPU maker. Its line of CISC CPUs is used in many older Macintosh computers, as well as in many UNIX machines. The popular models include the 68000, 68020, 68030 and 68040. The development of the features in the chips is roughly similar to the development in the Intel line; with the 68020 showing many similarities to the 80286, the 68030 similar to the 80386, and the 86040 similar to the 80486. Although there are major differences between the Intel and Motorola chip lines, and they are in no way interchangeable, their development was similar.

The 680x0 processors instruction sets are divided into supervisory instructions, which are intended for use by an operating system, and user instructions, which are intended for use by a program. This, and the memory layout of these CPUs, made them very popular for task switching, multitasking, and multi-user operating systems. The latest entry in this line of CPUs is the 68060, but this chip is aimed at the market for embedded devices; Motorola will not market this chip to computer vendors so as not to compete with their new high-end chip, the PowerPC chip.

PowerPC

Although Motorola continues to develop chips in the 68xxx line, modern Macintosh computers do not use this line of chips. A new non-compatible line of chips—chips that use different instruction sets and a different general architecture than the 68xxx line—was developed jointly by IBM, Motorola, and Apple Computer. These are RISC chips known as the **PowerPC** line. The initial PowerPC chips, known as model 601, 602, 603 and 603e, were all similar in design and functionality. As the model number increased, so did the internal clock speeds, L1 cache size, and the efficiency of the chip designs. The newest chip in this line is the **G3** (for 3rd generation), with an external clock speed of up to 100 MHz, an internal clock speed of up to 300 MHz, and 32-bit address and data buses.

Other Processors

It is useful to mention a few other RISC processors briefly, one of which is the SPARC processor designed by Sun Microsystems. SPARC CPUs have gone through many incarnations and are the most popular RISC processor on the market today. The address bus on the most modern SPARC CPU, the UltraSPARC II, is 32 bits wide and the data bus is 64 bits wide. The internal clock on this chip is available at speeds up to 450 MHz, and 100 MHz for the external clock. L1 cache is as much as 256 KB, while external, on-CPU-module L2 cache can be as much as 2 MB. You'll primarily see various implementations of the UNIX operating system running on these CPUs, performing high-end engineering and networking duties. The most popular operating system using the chip is Sun Microsystem's SunOS UNIX, also known as Solaris. There are now also versions of Linux and BSD UNIX available for SPARC architectures.

Another CPU of interest is the Alpha CPU designed by Digital Equipment Corporation (DEC). This CPU also has a 64-bit data bus and a 32-bit address bus. Internal clock speed can be as high as 750 MHz, with external clock speeds up to 100 MHz at the time this book was written. Like the SPARC CPUs mentioned above, Alpha chips are strong in the UNIX environment as well as with Windows NT. And, like the SPARC, Alpha chips will be found in machines conducting heavy networking, engineering, and graphics duties. There are now many proprietary devices such as file servers, firewall products and routers that run custom operating systems on an Alpha architecture.

There are of course many other CPUs, and there are many details about these chips that are beyond the focus of this book. The CPUs discussed here are those that are most popular in PCs today.

System Architecture

In addition to the CPU, many other parts are needed to make a functional computer. The design of the CPU and its surrounding parts is referred to as the **system architecture**. The main architectures are centered on a particular CPU type. What is known as the IBM PC architecture is centered on one of the Intel 80x86 CPUs. Intel architecture is generally divided into three classes: one consisting of the 8088, 8086 and 80286, one consisting of the 80386 and 80486, and one consisting of the Pentium and its variations.

The memory architecture that was implemented in the PC had some problems. Since the CPU had only a 16-bit data bus, it could only handle a 16-bit wide address internally. That would have meant that it could only address 64 KB of memory, which was obviously not enough. To get around this problem, memory was divided into 16 segments of 64 KB each. In addition to just pointing to an address, the CPU would refer to one of these "segments." When the original PC architecture was designed, ten of these segments were assigned for user memory, making the PC able to address 640 KB of memory as one continuous block. At the time it seemed like more than enough. The highest segment, number 16, was reserved for the BIOS part of the operating system, and numbers 11 through 15 were used for expansion cards, such as video, disk, and communications controllers. When the architecture was expanded to a 32-bit address and data bus, the lower end of the memory architecture was left unchanged, and additional memory was placed beyond the 1 MB memory limit of the old 16-bit architecture. This resulted in main memory with a "hole" between 640 KB and 1 MB.

The original Intel architecture design haunted software and hardware designers for several years as they tried to use more than 1 MB of memory. Program code would run in the first 640 KB of RAM, then you had to jump above 1 MB (on later machines that had more than 1 MB of memory) to store anything else. The memory between 640 KB and 1 MB was reserved for system use. Any IBM PC or clone on the market today has this notorious "hole" in memory. It is required to make sure that newer hardware architectures are compatible with older ones.

Although this design allowed these machines to use 1 MB of memory, they could use it only 64 KB at a time. This resulted in some interesting, and sometimes difficult, programming solutions as application software became more complicated.

The Macintosh architecture has a Motorola chip or one of the PowerPC chips at its center. This architecture is generally divided into four classes: Macs with a 68000 or 68020, Macs with a 68030 or 68040, Macs with a 60X PowerPC chip, and Macs with a G3 chip. Most PowerPC-based Macintoshes have 64-bit paths to memory, ROM, and video.

The DEC Alpha architecture has the Alpha chip as its center, and needs no further distinction, as is the case with many other architectures including the above-mentioned SPARC architecture. As you become acquainted with the operating systems in the next sections, you can refer to the various architectures mentioned here to confirm which architecture can be used, and which architecture is recommended to run the operating system in question.

Keep in mind that new processors, new operating systems, and updated system architectures are released all the time. You will find that new operating systems are typically enabled by newer system architectures. You will therefore also find that machines of an older architecture will run older operating system software. The operating systems covered in this book were chosen for two reasons. Either they are older, but still in use in today's business world, or they are current and you will see them installed on the new computers of today and the near future.

POPULAR PC OPERATING SYSTEMS

The operating systems in today's computers offer a wide range of features and benefits, yet each has its limitations. You can use the following sections to assess each according to your needs.

MS-DOS AND PC DOS

Microsoft wrote the original operating system for the IBM PC hardware platform, called **MS-DOS** or more simply, DOS. DOS will run on any of the Intel 80x86 or Pentium-class CPUs implemented in a PC hardware platform. You may also see references to **PC DOS**, a slightly different operating system based on the Microsoft version, customized and marketed by IBM.

The letters **DOS** stand for **Disk Operating System**, and that is the focus of this operating system. It is written entirely as 16-bit code, which is what makes it compatible with the 8088 and 8086 processors, and the oldest class of PC hardware architecture. The primary function of DOS is to provide common interfaces to disk functions by implementing a relatively simple file system. Depending on the version of DOS you study, it will support a series of devices, such as floppy disks and hard disks. Most specialty devices, such as CD-ROM drives and tape drives, require special drivers not included in the operating system.

DOS is a single-tasking, single-user operating system. You will find that most programs operating under DOS use a simple text-based command-line user interface. You can see a typical DOS screen in Figure 2-2.

```
C>dir

 Volume in drive C is 123
 Volume Serial Number is 2C1D-19D4
 Directory of C:\

CONFIG   SYS           713   08-06-98   6:27p
COMMAND  COM        93,812   08-24-96  11:11a
AUTOEXEC BAT         4,320   08-06-98   6:27p
WRPLOG   TXT           489   08-06-98   6:11p
BORLAND          <DIR>       08-06-98   6:11p
PROGRAMS         <DIR>       08-06-98   6:11p
DOCUMENT         <DIR>       08-06-98   6:26p
CICOMNDD LOG           450   09-12-98  11:08p
        5 file(s)        99,774 bytes
        3 dir(s)     41,831,680 bytes free

C>mkdir test

C>cd test

C>cd
C:\TEST\

C>
```

Figure 2-2   Typical DOS screen

2

In DOS, there is no built-in support for a graphical user interface. Since DOS does not offer any security features, or any way to limit the access users have to the functions of the computer, it is generally thought of as a high-maintenance operating system. You will find that MS-DOS is still widely used, especially with older machines where the system architecture will not support much more than DOS.

As you learned in the section on system architecture, the original 16-bit architecture for the IBM PC was able to address only 640 KB of memory, a limitation that is still very visible in DOS. Any DOS program can run in this 640 KB of what is known as **base memory**. Some of this memory is taken up by DOS and the drivers it uses, leaving less memory for applications to use.

With the memory and disk requirements of software growing and growing, PCs running DOS today can run a very limited range of software. There are special drivers in newer DOS versions that enable you to use memory beyond the 1 MB memory limit, but these drivers require specially written software to make use of them. Another drawback of DOS is that it does not support networks by default. A lot of optional software, such as support for CD-ROMs, memory above 1 MB, and tape drives, is included in the newer DOS versions. However, these options are not required to run DOS in its most basic form.

A nice thing about DOS is that the basic operating system files are small enough to fit on one floppy disk. You will find that in many cases DOS is used on PCs as the stepping stone to install other operating systems. You won't see DOS as the only operating system on any modern machine, but it is still around on older hardware either by default or because the applications it is supporting need DOS. Refer to Table 2-2 for a brief list of advantages and disadvantages of DOS.

Table 2-2 DOS Advantages and Disadvantages

Advantage	Disadvantage
Runs on minimal hardware	Doesn't support some newer hardware features
Small size. Early versions could fit on a single floppy disk	Includes minimal utilities and user support features
Requires minimal memory. Some applications run faster under DOS	Early versions can't support large memory of new machines
Command line interface gives operator direct control	Command line interface requires considerable knowledge and training

When you start a machine running DOS, it presents you with a way to communicate with it, known as a **shell**. Since DOS has no graphical user interface, you must type in commands to make DOS work, and some of these commands are less than intuitive. Some commands are built into the shell, these are known as the built-in, **internal**, or **intrinsic commands**. Other commands are stored in separate programs, known as **external commands**.

A few important internal commands are used to navigate the DOS system of disks and directories, which you will learn in more detail later. The following are some of the most frequently used internal commands, which you can type directly at the command prompt:

- VER (check the version of DOS running)
- DIR (gives a directory listing)
- CD (changes directories)
- MKDIR or MD (make a new directory)
- RMDIR or RD (remove a directory)
- COPY (copy files from one directory to another)
- DEL (delete files)

When you type VER, DOS will respond to you with the name and version of the operating system. This can be very helpful, as it will let you know what version you're working with.

DIR provides you with a directory listing, or a list of all files in the current **directory** (folder) of a disk. Filenames are limited to eight characters, a period, and three more characters called an extension. This is sometimes called an "8.3" name structure. Files with an extension of .EXE, .BAT or .COM are programs. You can load a program file into memory and cause the computer to execute the commands or instructions it contains by simply typing its name. You may also see files followed by the indicator <DIR>. These are called directories.

Directories are simply logical ways of organizing information stored on a computer disk. Compare a computer hard disk to a file cabinet. The entire file cabinet is analogous to the whole hard disk and the individual drawers analogous to the hard disk directories. Within each directory are files that store related information such as a word processor document or a spreadsheet. These individual files could be compared to the folders inside the file cabinet drawers.

Disk directories are organized in a hierarchical structure, somewhat like a tree, that begins with the first or main directory called the **root**. The sample in Figure 2-3 shows a typical hard disk directory.

In this directory display, a plus sign (+) beside a directory name indicates that additional directories reside within this one. You can see from this sample that directories beneath other directories are dependent on the ones higher up the line. Directories can contain files and other directories. This relationship is sometimes called a parent-child relationship, where higher directories are parents and lower (subordinate) directories are children.

CD (for Change Directory) will let you change the current directory. Type CD followed by the name of the directory you want to use, assuming the directory is immediately subordinate to the current one. Otherwise, you will have to enter a complete **path** to the desired directory. A path includes the first directory subordinate to the current one, followed by a backslash (\), then the next directory in line, and so on. If the current directory is the root or topmost directory (see Figure 2-4), for example, and you want to make current the directory Books, which is stored in the directory Data, the CD command to accomplish this would be: CD DATA\BOOKS. Note that you don't use the name of the current directory in the path.

2

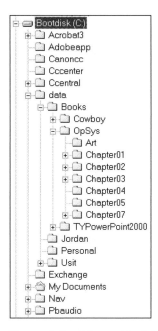

Figure 2-3   Hierarchical disk directory

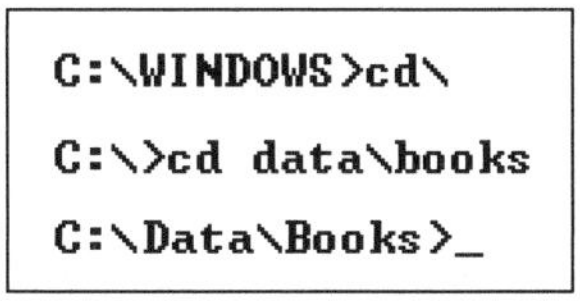

```
C:\WINDOWS>cd\
C:\>cd data\books
C:\Data\Books>_
```

Figure 2-4   Changing the directory in DOS

When you issue a DIR command after a CD command, you will see the contents of the directory. To go back to the previous directory, use CD .. (CD followed by two periods). You can see this "two-dot" directory when you use the DIR command. It refers to the directory immediately above the current one. The current directory is also listed in a DIR list. It is shown as a single dot. You can see this concept in Figure 2-5 on the next page.

To go back to the main directory on a disk, called the **root**, type CD \ (CD followed by a backslash). If you want to see the name of the directory you're in, simply type CD and DOS will tell you.

The MKDIR (Make Directory) command allows you to create a new directory. To make a directory called TEST for example, you would type MKDIR TEST, as shown previously in Figure 2-2. You can now use the CD command discussed above to make the TEST directory the current directory.

```
C:\Data\Books>dir

 Volume in drive C is BIGFOOT
 Volume Serial Number is 1851-1CCF
 Directory of C:\Data\Books

 .              <DIR>         10-24-98   9:21a .
 ..             <DIR>         10-24-98   9:21a ..
 FIXOWN         <DIR>         10-24-98   8:59p FixOwn
 OPSYS          <DIR>         10-24-98   9:21a OpSys
          0 file(s)                  0 bytes
          4 dir(s)      205,922,304 bytes free

C:\Data\Books>_
```

Figure 2-5   DIR listing

The RMDIR (Remove Directory) command enables you to remove a directory. Simply type RMDIR followed by the name of the directory you wish to remove. You will not be able to remove a directory unless it is empty, to prevent you from destroying any important files.

COPY will let you copy files from one directory to another. If you make a directory called OPSYS, you could copy files into it. Say for example that you have a file COMMAND.COM that you want to copy into OPSYS. Issuing the command COPY COMMAND.COM OPSYS would do the trick, assuming OPSYS is a directory immediately subordinate to the current directory. Otherwise, remember, you will have to use a more complete path command.

 DEL (for Delete) will let you remove files. Be very careful when you delete files! In many cases, the DEL action in DOS is final and **CANNOT BE REVERSED**!

There are many more commands built into the DOS operating system shell; there are also many external commands. External commands are simply programs that perform special functions for the operating system. They are started like other programs, simply by typing the name at the DOS command prompt. An example of an external command that is present in almost all DOS versions is the check disk command, which has the program name of CHKDSK. Running this program will give you some information about the disks and memory in your computer. There are many such commands, and new ones are added as new DOS versions are released. You'll learn new external and internal DOS commands in later chapters of this book.

Networking support is not included in MS-DOS. There are, however, extensions for the operating system, mostly created by other software vendors such as Novell, that will let MS-DOS machines function as a part of a network environment. Although there is rudimentary support for printers in MS-DOS, most of the functionality for printing has to be implemented in the application software, in much the same way that graphics are implemented.

You will find DOS in many places, from home computers to Fortune 500 companies. There are still many reasons to run MS-DOS. Industrial control applications, some financial and other specialized applications designed for a non-graphics environment, as well as many

2

applications used to access large mainframe computers need only what MS-DOS gives them. Basic DOS machines (sometimes called "DOS boxes") are also good choices for machine control applications such as manufacturing, monitoring, and security. A number of financial programs run only in DOS and many accounting professionals like it that way. DOS applications generally operate more like mainframe applications from the end-user perspective, so that people trained on early programs take to DOS-based versions of them easily. In the future, these applications will eventually be updated and require bigger, faster machines, but for now they are working with no problems on DOS machines. In general, it is not worth spending money on the hardware required to upgrade the operating system.

WINDOWS 3.1, WINDOWS 3.11, AND WINDOWS FOR WORKGROUPS 3.11

As time went by, MS-DOS with its lack of graphical user interface, printer support, memory support, and user friendliness, needed a boost. Microsoft had the answer in the form of Windows, a graphical user interface patterned loosely after the one introduced by Apple Computer in their Macintosh platform. Windows 1.0 was no more than a graphical wrapper for MS-DOS. By version 3.1, which is generally recognized as one of the first versions of Windows that was actually widely useable for some real work, Windows had more functionality.

 This book will not review Windows versions older than 3.1 as these are rarely in use. This section groups together three different versions of the Windows software that run "on top" of DOS: Windows 3.1, Windows 3.11, and Windows for Workgroups 3.11.

Windows 3.1 and its siblings run on top of the MS-DOS or PC DOS operating system on the IBM PC system architecture. Although it is possible to run Windows 3.1 on the oldest generation of this architecture, it will only run a very limited set of applications because it is running in **real mode** (16-bit mode). The limitations are mainly dictated by the way software can use memory. There are extensions to Windows 3.1 that will allow it to run 32-bit software (386 enhanced mode), and there are also some upgrades that will replace parts of the Windows system itself with 32-bit code, but at the heart of Windows 3.1 will always be a 16-bit operating system, running on top of DOS.

 Two methods are used to let applications use more than the 640 KB limit in early PCs: Expanded Memory (EMS) and Extended Memory (XMS). Expanded Memory is the earlier method. It works by switching 64 KB blocks of RAM into operation under the control of an external utility EMM386.SYS. This scheme works, but only with programs written to support the EMS standard. Newer DOS programs support EMS, but earlier ones mostly do not. Moreover, not only are you limited to 64 KB blocks of RAM, but only 16 KB can be used at a time. The XMS standard lets DOS use extended memory, RAM addressed above 1 MB. Another external utility, HIMEM.SYS, turns on XMS memory.

Windows 3.1 machines will start the DOS operating system. After the DOS shell has loaded, Windows 3.1 can be started by simply entering the name of the Windows program, WIN. In many cases, the DOS shell is instructed to automatically execute this program when it is started through the use of the AUTOEXEC.BAT batch file. (**AUTOEXEC.BAT** is a file that contains instructions that DOS executes when you start the system.) Windows will present the user with a graphical user interface, taking control of the entire screen, and providing the user with a different kind of shell. The default Windows shell is known as the **Program Manager**, shown in Figure 2-6.

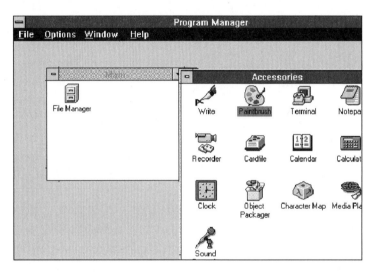

Figure 2-6   Windows 3.1 Program Manager

In this shell, programs are represented as icons, which can be started by simply double-clicking them with the mouse. The built-in commands from the DOS shell are not visible here. The interface is a lot easier than DOS for the end user, because they do not have to remember what the program names are to start them. Instead, they simply select the program icon they wish to run.

The Windows shell is very different from the DOS shell in many ways. One very noticeable difference is that this shell does not provide a way to look at directories, the contents of directories, or for that matter to delete or copy files. In Windows, these functions are performed by another part of Windows named **File Manager**, shown in Figure 2-7.

If you start File Manager from the Program Manager, you will see a graphical representation of the files and directories on your machine. As with Program Manager, there are no complicated and cryptic commands to remember. Everything you could possibly want to do with files can be done by making selections from menus and moving and selecting icons with the mouse.

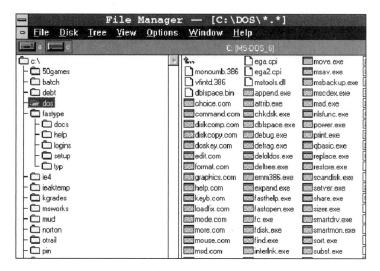

Figure 2-7   Windows 3.1 File Manager

But there is more to Windows than what you see as the user. For the application developer, Windows has a lot to offer. Whereas DOS provides only disk and file functions, with some printer functions, thrown in, Windows provides ready-to-use menus, graphics, and printer functions that can be reused by application developers. As you run Windows applications, you will find that many of them work in similar ways. The menus look and work alike, buttons behave in similar ways, and dialog boxes for saving and loading files are consistent across applications, as is the way Help is provided to the user. All of this makes life easier for the user and the program designer.

Windows also includes extensive functions to manage printer and communications functions. An application program that can draw on the screen can draw to any printer Windows supports. Many people who have installed applications on DOS systems will tell you how nice it is to not have to install new printer or modem drivers for every application. This is possible because Windows is in charge of everything that goes on behind the screens.

One question not answered is why this operating system is called Windows. The answer will lead us to one of the key features of Windows: multitasking. Windows has the capability to run many programs at once. For example, if you start the File Manager from the Program Manager, both programs will appear to be active at the same time. You were introduced to various forms of multitasking in Chapter 1; Windows 3.1 uses cooperative multitasking.

If you have many programs that can run at once, you as the user need a way to determine what program you are currently communicating with. This is where the concept of Windows comes in. The window is literally a window into the program you are running. You can change the shape and size of most of these windows, even temporarily put them away or minimize them. It will have no effect on the application running in the window. The window is merely your view on the program.

One drawback of cooperative multitasking is that all the programs and functions running on the machine must cooperate. If one of these programs is no longer willing or able to share the resources of the computer, your machine could get stuck on one such process. This can be a pretty serious situation if you have other programs that need to perform time-sensitive functions. In most cases, the cooperative multitasking system in Windows 3.1 will perform pretty well, but if many applications are making big demands on the system, you will find that system performance and stability are not always a given.

A good example of such a scenario happens when DOS programs are executed from the Windows Program Manager. Since the DOS software was never meant to run in a cooperative multitasking environment, Windows has to do some tricky maneuvers to make this scenario work. While DOS programs are running, they will slow down all other Windows applications significantly.

The features described up to this point are common to Windows 3.1, Windows 3.11, and Windows for Workgroups 3.11. To summarize, these common features include:

- 16-bit operation

- Running on top of DOS

- Program Manager graphical user interface (GUI)

- Graphical File Manager system navigation

- Consistent graphical, printer, and menu functions across multiple applications

- Cooperative multitasking

The main difference between Windows version 3.1 and version 3.11 is a large number of bug fixes, as well as additional driver support. There were no major design changes between these two versions, and for all practical purposes they are identical. However, in the internal structure of the three versions of Windows there are some distinct differences.

 One of the easiest ways to end up with a totally useless installation of Windows is to use the wrong set of installation disks to add files to an existing installation. Adding Windows 2.1 files to a Windows 3.11 installation will lead to certain disaster.

Windows for Workgroups 3.11 is the one of the three Windows versions that needs some extra attention. On top of normal Windows functions it includes a broad set of networking functions, software extensions to the operating system. At the most basic level, it can communicate with the network hardware installed in the computer. The drivers for the network hardware are partially installed as extensions to DOS before Windows for Workgroups is started. As a matter of fact, you do not even have to run the graphical Windows interface to make use of some of the networking functions available with Windows for Workgroups under DOS. The networking functions are split in two sets: client functions and server functions. The **client** functions can be used from DOS without starting Windows. These functions allow you to use disk and printer resources made available by other computers on the network. All of these functions are made available to the DOS environment by a special set of drivers, which

2

can be controlled through a new external DOS command: NET.EXE. This command is added when any version of Windows for Workgroups is installed.

When Windows for Workgroups is started, the machine can also become a **server**. This means it can make resources such as printers and disks connected to the computer available to other machines on the network. This system of being both a network client and a network server has many advantages. For one, you do not need a separate machine dedicated to being the server. There are also many disadvantages, one of which is in the very nature of Windows for Workgroups. Because of cooperative multitasking, there are some potential conflicts between how much of the computer's time is spent on local work and how much on networking functions. This system of networking where every machine can be both a client and a server, with the same possibilities on each machine, is called **peer-to-peer networking**. The idea Microsoft had when this product was developed and introduced was that it would be used in small workgroups where all people needed was to share a printer and occasionally share files. This is why the networking functions are, by today's standards, limited and not very advanced. You will find that there are many such small workgroups that work with no great problems. You will also find that in many cases where installations have gone beyond the small workgroup, say to 50 or 100 machines, certain limitations of the system will become visible, in performance and in stability issues.

The network setup for Windows for Workgroups is performed using the Windows Setup program and the Network control panel. Functions related to sharing of disks are mostly accessed through the File Manager, which was extended with a series of networking functions. The Printer control panel and printer spooler were extended to include network functions, and software to facilitate **e-mail** and group scheduling was included as well. Last of all, in Windows for Workgroups the way Windows starts changed to include entering a username and password. These are used to identify you to the other peers on the network.

 Many people initially thought the Windows for Workgroups username and password mechanism was also meant to limit access to the files on the local machines. This is not the case. A user asked to provide a username and password can access all files on the local machine.

All of these extra features may not, however, appear on all Windows for Workgroups machines. It is possible to install Windows for Workgroups 3.11 without enabling networking support, which will result for all practical purposes in a Windows 3.11 installation.

When used as a client, Windows for Workgroups also has the ability to connect to other Microsoft operating systems that can function as a server, including Windows NT and later Windows releases. Later add-ons to Windows for Workgroups 3.11 included support to function as a client in a Novell and Internet environment. Most of these extensions are not included in older versions of Windows for Workgroups 3.11, but they are all available from Microsoft.

You will find various versions of Windows 3.1, including Windows for Workgroups, in use in many corporate environments that have no need to upgrade to newer Windows versions, and that do not have hardware that will support newer Windows versions. In many cases, you will find special applications that were custom built for these environments. Many of these companies are planning to upgrade, but they are waiting until they absolutely have no other choice. You will also find Windows 3.1 in use on older home PCs and in older machines in educational environments, where money for the additional hardware needed to run newer Windows versions may be an issue.

WINDOWS 95

As the PC platform became more powerful and the Pentium architecture became more common, Microsoft recognized that it was time to step up from Windows 3.1. The idea was to create a true 32-bit operating system that would use all of the functionality of the 32-bit architecture. The task turned out to be extremely complex, because as with all versions of DOS and Windows up to this point, backward compatibility had to be maintained. Windows 95 is the first in the Windows series of operating systems that does not rely on MS-DOS to provide underlying functionality. Although there is a core operating system that lies underneath the graphical shell of Windows 95, and although this operating system looks and feels a lot like the old DOS, including the shell and the commands it uses, it is actually a totally new, 32-bit operating system. It eliminates the 640 KB memory limit and the 16-bit code. Windows 95 will therefore not run on the oldest 16-bit CPUs (8088 and 8086) of the IBM PC architecture.

The new functionality of Windows 95 requires a lot more of the hardware it runs on. As compared to Windows 3.1, this version of Windows requires about twice the memory, twice the hard disk space, and twice the processor speed to provide similar performance. (This is why many users were slow to upgrade.) But Windows 95 also includes advanced functions to help out with all sorts of hardware management, as you'll discover in the following sections.

Plug and Play

Perhaps the most exciting hardware feature of Windows 95 and later is **Plug and Play**, or **PNP**. PNP is an extension of the system architecture that lets the operating system and the hardware communicate. It enables the operating system to discover any hardware that is inside or connected to the machine, including such information as what drivers should be used to address this hardware. In turn, the hardware has some built-in functions that will let the operating system dictate how the hardware is to be configured. The end result is that in a system that supports PNP correctly, many of the tedious tasks of configuring hardware and software that previously had to be done by hand are performed automatically.

Unfortunately, not all hardware is PNP-enabled, and the PNP software is not entirely perfect. As a result, sometimes there are PNP problems, and due to the automation involved in PNP, you may find that these can be difficult to solve. Overall, however, PNP is considered a big step forward. You can find more details about Plug and Play devices later in this book.

User Interface

Once again, the shell that is presented to the user has changed from the previous operating system generation, as you can see from Figure 2-8. In Windows 95 this shell is called the desktop, and it includes a number of useful features, such as a Start button that provides direct access to system utilities and application programs. In addition, a taskbar at the bottom of the screen contains icons that represent currently running programs and other information about the operation of your system.

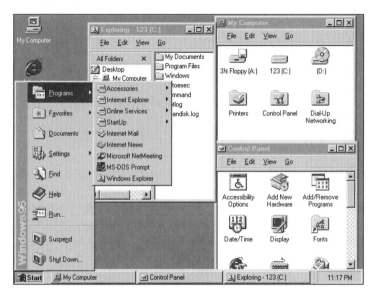

Figure 2-8   Windows 95 desktop

The user is now presented with a workspace in which the manipulation of files and the management of programs have been integrated into one seamless environment. For reasons of compatibility, it is still possible to use the old Program Manager and File Manager shells, and you will find that at times this is done to have consistency among the various machines in an environment. However, this discussion of Windows 95 deals exclusively with the new user interface model.

In Windows 95, you can use the objects on the desktop to manage your files and programs. Most file management is done with **Windows Explorer**, a feature that can also be used to access control panels, and just about anything else on the Windows 95 machine or the network to which it is connected.

ActiveX and the Component Object Model (COM)

Much of the easy manipulation of the user interface in Windows 95 is made possible by a new technology called **ActiveX**.

ActiveX, along with its parent, the Component Object Model (COM), is a standardized way for objects such as programs, files, computers, printers, control panels, windows, and icons, to communicate with each other. It is a simple, but revolutionary concept. Objects (such as folders, icons, menus and almost any other object you see on the desktop) have a series of properties. To show you a folder full of files, the operating system makes a folder, then places the file objects in the folder. The COM and ActiveX technologies enable an object to "sense" when it is interacting with other objects, such as the mouse pointer, the desktop, the trash can or the Start menu. The COM and ActiveX technologies allow you to simply drag files from one place to another. The icons you drag, through the use of COM, make it possible for the object onto which they are dragged to know what to do with them. By building this concept into the operating system, Microsoft has provided a new level of user interface consistency and program interoperability in Windows 95. You can click from a window that manages your local files, into a window that manages the files on the network, into the printer manager, or even onto the Internet without ever being aware that you are starting and stopping programs and accessing numerous resources. If you have the Active Desktop installed on your machine, the new ActiveX technology, which is part of the COM model, will be available to you as well. You will see some new features, such as the ability to drag objects in and out of the Start menu, and the ability to use more advanced features with such things as folder listings. With ActiveX objects you can have customized looks for every file folder, for example.

ActiveX and COM also have made possible the improved alternative to Program Manager and Task Manager; the icons of the Program Manager can now be simulated by placing shortcuts, small ActiveX objects, on the desktop. In addition, easy access to programs and the operating system is provided through the Start menu, which on the Active Desktop is nothing more than another ActiveX object. Overall, the use of COM and ActiveX has made Windows 95 easier to use than its predecessors, and once again has broadened the functionality provided by the operating system.

The Registry

The Windows 95 design also introduced a new concept for changing the way information is stored and managed, and how software and hardware are configured. Up to this point, such information had always been kept in files in various locations on the disk. The new design is called the **Registry**, a database that stores information about hardware and software configuration, and all sorts of other data needed to make the operating system and applications run. Although the Registry was present in a primitive form in Windows 3.1, it was not used much. In Windows 95, the Registry is the only correct way to store configuration information, as well as much of the general information that has to be shared by multiple parts of the operating system or application programs to make COM and ActiveX work. The Windows 95 Registry is similar to the one used in Windows NT 3.51 and Windows NT 4.0.

The Registry is a hierarchical database containing configuration information for Win32-based operating systems. In its current design and form, it was first introduced in Windows NT 3.1. The Registry exists as memory-mapped data that resembles a virtual directory, and provides the following for Windows 9x and Windows NT:

- OS configuration
- Service and device driver information and configuration
- Static tuning parameters
- Software and application parameters
- Hardware configuration
- Performance information

Previously, information would be stored in text files on the disk. The Registry stores all information in a set of databases. Whenever any software wants to read from or write to the Registry, it will use operating system functions to do so. This central database repository may actually extend beyond the computer on which Windows 95 is running. It is possible to share Registry data over a network, a function that can be extremely useful in situations with many users and many computers.

The Registry will be covered in greater detail later in this book. For now, you should remember that the Registry is one more place where the operating system and the software applications running on the computer are tightly associated. If there are errors in the Registry, the results can be very serious. Unfortunately, it is not uncommon to see such Registry issues, especially on machines that undergo frequent changes in the operating system setup, software setup, and hardware setup.

Multitasking

Multitasking in Windows 95 is still performed on a cooperative basis, but over the years Microsoft has greatly improved the cooperative mechanism. Apart from communications functions, which still at times can bring multitasking to a halt in Windows 95, cooperative multitasking yields mostly acceptable results. There is now a **task supervisor** that will detect tasks that seem to be stuck, and that will present you with the ability to attempt to close those tasks without having to restart the operating system. This operation does not always succeed, but at least it is an option.

The methods used for cooperative multitasking in Windows 95 are also a little more advanced than earlier methods, again largely because of the use of COM technology in many places in the operating system.

Networking and Communications Features

The networking functionality in Windows 95 has been substantially extended from earlier versions of Windows, and completely rewritten. As we mentioned previously, Windows 95 does not run on top of DOS, which means that the network drivers are a part of the actual operating system. In all but the first versions of Windows 95, all of the networking code is written as a 32-bit application. This results in a significant boost in network performance. The networking functions, as in Windows for Workgroups 3.11, consist of two parts, the client and the server. Windows 95 has significantly increased the capabilities of both. It is now possible for a Windows 95 machine to be both a client and a server for more systems than just the Microsoft proprietary network protocols.

Most popular networking systems are now a part of standard Windows 95, including client and server drivers for Novell NetWare, a networking operating system. The setup and integration of the network functions into Windows 95 is now easier and much more flexible. In Windows for Workgroups 3.11, there were many different places where various portions of the network setup were performed. PNP will now, in most cases, take care of the setup of actual network hardware in the computer. The **Network control panel** can be used to set up all client and server functions from one place. Windows Explorer is used to share network resources and attach to network resources. The Open File and Save File dialog boxes provided to application programs will let you look at all network resources available to the computer, a big step toward integrated networking functions. Even the Windows 95 Registry is network enabled. It is possible to get and save certain information to shared registries on the network. Again, you'll see this in greater detail in the chapter on Networking and Internet Connectivity.

Another important feature of Windows 95 is its integration with the **Internet**, the global network that can connect standalone workstations and networks for the exchange of information, advertising, e-mail, and many other purposes. When Windows 95 was originally released, Microsoft did not support Internet connectivity, and was instead trying to promote their own Microsoft Network. By 1997, however, Microsoft decided to embrace the Internet and integrate it into all of its operating systems. First it was an add-on option in the form of Internet Explorer in Windows 95, then an integral part of the operating system when Windows 98 was released. This has resulted in extensive Internet support in Windows 95, in the form of **Web browsers**, **Web server** software, and the ability to share computer resources over the Internet.

When it comes to communications, Windows 95 has made a giant leap forward. In Windows 3.1, there was support for communications over serial ports, but tasks such as dialing the phone or making a connection were performed by the application software. In Windows 95 the operating system takes an active role. It manages the modem and provides some pretty sophisticated communications features to the user. With the popularity of the Internet, and the need to obtain remote access to corporate networks over telephone lines, Microsoft went as far as to include network drivers that support the use of modems to obtain remote access to a network, even to the Internet. **Dial Up Networking (DUN)** can be used not only to make connections to remote networks or machines, but also to set a Windows 95 machine up as a DUN server, with the addition of the Plus!™ add-on set of utilities. A computer with a modem can be set up to answer a telephone line whenever it rings, authenticate the user who is calling, and then give them access to all the shared resources available to the computer. Many people have used DUN to gain access to their desktop machines in the office from their machines at home, or from their laptops while they are on the road.

The last new communications feature of Windows 95 is built-in fax support. Out of the box, Windows 95 can send and receive fax transmissions. The only thing required is a modem capable of sending and receiving fax traffic. This modem does not even have to be connected to the machine that wants to send or receive a fax. Through Windows 95 networking it is quite easy to use any such modem connected to any machine in the workgroup.

Windows 95 Today

During its life, Windows 95 has gone through various updates. Many upgrades have updated parts of the code from 16-bit to 32-bit, added support for new hardware, fixed bugs, and added Internet capabilities. At the writing of this book, the current Windows 95 version release is 2.5B. Because Windows 98 has been released, it is unlikely that Microsoft will do more to Windows 95 than fix serious bugs.

You will find Windows 95 on many home PCs and in many small businesses. Many larger companies and educational institutions also run Windows 95. It is the most widely used operating system at this time. Many users, especially those with many PCs, are staying with Windows 95 because it provides all the features they need, and there is no significant gain for them by upgrading to Windows 98.

WINDOWS 98

In many ways, Windows 98 is similar to Windows 95. It will run on roughly the same system architecture, and it provides roughly similar capabilities. Many of the problems people have had with Windows 95 have been solved in Windows 98, especially problems related to the Registry. If the Registry in Windows 95 got corrupted for any reason, the operating system was in most cases not able to restore it. Windows 98 now includes Registry checks and automatic Registry repair when the machine is booted. The backup mechanisms have also been greatly enhanced. The look of the Windows 98 user interface is changed, especially if you choose the Web interface settings intrinsic to Windows 98. You can see some of the differences between Windows 95 and Windows 98 by comparing Figure 2-9 with Figure 2-8 shown earlier.

Figure 2-9 Windows 98 desktop

Some of the changes from Windows 95 to Windows 98 include:

- Expanded PNP support
- Advanced power management features
- Support for new hardware standards such as Universal Serial Bus (USB)
- Improved cooperative multitasking

- Greater integration of Internet and networking features

- Extended multimedia support

Windows 98 is written as a 32-bit application, much like Windows 95. PNP support has been greatly expanded, and advanced **power management** features are now included in the operating system. These features make it possible to power down parts of the hardware that are not being used, to conserve energy. This is especially important for users of battery-operated laptop computers. Windows 98 is also updated to support many new hardware standards, such as **Universal Serial Bus (USB)**, a relatively high-speed input/output port, and updated standards for multimedia, data storage, and networking.

Windows 98 is still a cooperative multitasking system, but once again the cooperative features have been improved slightly over Windows 95. The ActiveX technology has been deployed as a standard feature in Windows 98, together with Internet integration and network functionality. This version of Windows comes equipped with a graphical shell that looks fairly similar to that of Windows 95, but this shell is now Internet enabled. It is possible to put shortcuts to Internet objects right on the desktop through the use of ActiveX technology, and these objects can even be made to update automatically. Windows 98 also includes an Internet browser, as well as programs to provide Internet e-mail and other forms of multimedia Internet communication.

It is possible to upgrade Windows 98 over the Internet. The system can automatically check whether updates are available online, and if they are, it can download and install them, either with or without user intervention. The networking functions have been slightly updated as well. Setting up dial-up connections and configuring the computer to use the Internet have been made a lot simpler. Support for multimedia applications, ranging all the way from video conferencing to high-end video production, has been greatly extended.

Most users consider Windows 98 only a minor upgrade to the Windows 95 platform. It is by no means as revolutionary as the step up from Windows for Workgroups 3.11 to Windows 95. Microsoft has openly announced that Windows 98 will be the last release in the standard Windows line. The next step from here is to Windows 2000, an updated Windows NT with an interface like Windows 98. Microsoft has made this choice because it claims that the current Windows 9x technology advanced about as far as it will go.

Because the Windows NT user interface and the Windows 95/98 user interface are nearly identical, the step from Windows 95/98 to Windows NT or Windows 2000 has now become feasible. At the same time, the hardware required to run a low-end version of Windows NT is fairly similar to that required to run Windows 98. It is generally expected that Windows 98 will be around for many years to come, much like Windows 3.1 and its siblings. Because Microsoft has announced that Windows 98 is the end of the line for this operating system, you will find that many companies are not deploying it. Instead, many choose to stick with their Windows 3.1 or Windows 95 platform until the new versions of Windows that will replace Windows 98 are available.

You will find Windows 98 on many home PCs, and also on quite a few general purpose desktop computers. Many small companies use Windows 98 to run their entire operation, including all of the networking function needed. Because many people are familiar with how

2

Windows 95 works, and because Windows 98 is nearly identical, it is generally considered easy to use. Another Microsoft Windows implementation, Windows CE, is also gaining popularity but has yet to achieve universal acceptance. It is designed for the new breed of hand-held PCs and personal digital assistants: pocket-sized, not-quite-computer devices that track names and addresses, check e-mail, and contain other applications such as scaled-down spreadsheets and word processors. By far the most popular of these devices is the Palm series from Pilot. But this machine lacks an industry standard operating system. Windows CE, on the other hand, gives users something they are probably familiar with from their desktop computers or laptops, and also the ability to support standard applications. It's yet to be determined how CE fits into the larger computer marketplace.

WINDOWS NT 3.51 AND 4.0

While Microsoft was developing the Windows line of operating systems to run on the lower end of IBM PC hardware, it was also developing a high-end operating system referred to as Windows New Technology, or Windows NT. Windows NT differs in many ways from Windows, the most significant being the system architecture for which it was developed. Over the course of its development, Windows NT has supported the IBM PC architecture, the DEC Alpha architecture, and for a while the PowerPC architecture as each of these hardware platforms gained their time in the industry spotlight. As the Alpha and Power PC moved out of the limelight, NT focus concentrated on Intel platforms. The idea was to make an operating system that could be used on some very powerful machines, with a choice of RISC or CISC processor architecture. The support for various system architectures has shifted over the years, but support for the high-end IBM PC architecture and the DEC Alpha architecture has been a constant. At this time, these are the only two architectures actively supported by Windows NT. You will find most Windows NT installations running on high-end PCs, with some setups requiring even better performance running on the DEC Alpha. Development of Windows NT began as early as 1988. Windows NT 3.1 was released in 1993 and version 3.5 was released in 1994. Windows NT was initially an extension to IBM's high-end operating system, OS/2, and was intended to support the emerging client-server networking environment. As client-server applications have gained popularity, Windows NT development—and development of applications software to use its features—has continued apace. Look for Windows NT and client-server applications to become increasingly popular among business users.

Windows NT, as with all versions of Windows, has gone through many incarnations. You will find that there are very few setups of Windows NT prior to version 3.51 still in use, because these versions were not stable and reliable. Windows NT 3.51 is still widely used. Many organizations have not yet made the complicated step up to NT 4.0. Windows NT 3.51 looks and feels much like Windows for Workgroups 3.11; the graphical interface is nearly identical, including the Program Manager, File Manager, and Control Panel.

Windows NT 4.0 looks and feels a lot like Windows 95. As a matter of fact, it is very hard to tell the difference between the Windows 95 user interface and the Windows NT 4.0 user interface. You will find all the well-known elements, such as the desktop, Windows Explorer, and the taskbar with the Start menu, as shown in Figure 2-10 on the next page. Windows 2000, yet to be released, will have a user interface similar to Windows 98.

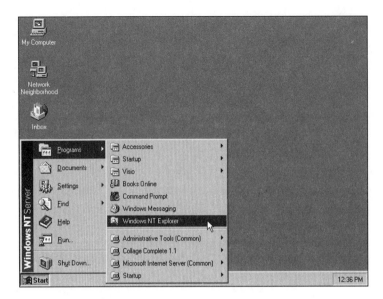

Figure 2-10   Windows NT desktop

Preemptive Multitasking

A significant improvement in Windows NT is the way it handles multitasking. Windows NT uses preemptive multitasking rather than cooperative multitasking. The advantage of preemptive multitasking is that the operating system is tightly in control of what the system will do at what time, which results in much more predictable performance. Because Windows NT was built as a 32-bit operating system from the ground up, and also because the requirement of having to run all legacy 16-bit applications was set aside, this system will greatly outperform all other Windows versions running 32-bit applications.

This performance comes at a price. Windows NT requires a faster CPU and more memory and disk space to run successfully, but it makes much better use of the resources made available to it. Windows NT 4.0 can also function very well in a hardware architecture that includes more than one CPU. Because the operating system is in very tight control of how the resources in the computer are allocated to various processes, it is able to make efficient use of multiple CPUs. Currently as many as four CPUs can be supported by Windows NT 4.0, and plans are to greatly increase this number in Windows 2000. The system architecture that is used to perform this form of multiprocessing under Windows NT 4.0 consists of a set of CPUs that has access to the main memory of the machine. The various CPUs can all carry out actions at the same time. This is known as **symmetric multiprocessing**, or **SMP**. All versions of NT 4.0 on all platforms support SMP hardware architecture; NT 3.51 does not include SMP support at all.

NT Server and NT Workstation

Windows NT is offered in two versions: Windows NT Workstation and Windows NT Server. These names are fairly indicative of the audience at which they are aimed. NT Workstation is meant to be used as the operating system on the workstation of a person who has a need for a high-end, stable, and secure graphical operating system. The code of the operating system has been optimized to provide an interactive user with maximum performance. The core of the operating system, which oversees such things as multitasking and management of memory and shared resources, is known as the **Kernel**.

In Windows NT Workstation 3.51, the Kernel is optimized for maximum performance when used to run interactive applications, such as screen updates and fast retrieval and storage of data in memory and on disk. In the NT Server edition, the Kernel is optimized to provide maximum network and disk performance. Everything the server Kernel does is aimed at serving the request of clients rapidly. This is done at the expense of speed in such things as the user interface and other interactive functions. The Kernel of the NT Server edition provides a few extra functions that are not available in the NT Workstation Kernel. All features of the NT Workstation Kernel are at this time included in the NT Server Kernel. As a result, you can run any software that runs on Windows NT Workstation on Windows NT Server, but not all software that will run on NT Server can run on NT Workstation.

The Registry, mentioned earlier in the Windows 95 and Windows 98 section, plays an equally important role in Windows NT. It is used as the central repository for configuration, hardware, software and user information.

Windows NT version 4.0 has the same Workstation and Server versions. Newly added in NT Version 4 is an Enterprise edition. The Enterprise edition supports the concept of **clustering** in addition to SMP. In a clustering setup, several separate machines running Windows NT 4.0 Enterprise edition can be interconnected in a cluster. The NT operating system on the various machines will then share the resources of the various machines as if they are all one giant machine. In an ideal world, you could simply run any piece of software on a cluster and expect it to work better. This is not yet the case.

At the time this book was written, software had to be especially developed to make use of the functionality offered in the Enterprise platform. The main reason the Enterprise platform is being deployed at this time is not so much increased performance as it is increased stability. Microsoft has announced that Windows 2000 will support as many as 16 CPUs per machine in SMP configuration, with 16 of these machines and more in a cluster providing enormous processing power.

Networking Support

The networking features in Windows NT are much stronger than in any other version of Windows. NT can be used as a serious network server that may serve hundreds of clients at a time. At the same time, NT can also be used as network client—a user workstation that can communicate with a network server—to other networking operating systems. Here again, there is a difference between NT Workstation and Server. A machine running Windows NT Workstation can be a server for up to ten simultaneous clients. A machine running NT Server or Enterprise edition can service an unlimited number of connections as long as there is enough hardware to support it. In addition to the networking protocols that are Microsoft-specific, all versions of NT support networking protocols for non-Microsoft platforms as well.

Security

Security is a significant feature of Windows NT. The operating system requires the user to log on and be authenticated by submitting a username and password to gain access to the machine. This authentication process is stronger than that of any other Windows version. Given the audience for which Windows NT is intended, this is generally considered a good thing. This strong authentication is also carried through to the sharing of resources. Every resource can be protected in many ways, based on the access rights assigned to users and the groups these users are in. Under other Windows versions, access to resources is generally arranged based on one password for read access and one password for read and write access. Windows NT uses the username as a key into a database to see which permissions a certain user has for a certain resource.

If a Windows 95 or 98 machine is a part of an NT network that uses the **domain** system, these machines will be able to use a similar kind of security to protect their resources. The domain is an integral part of the Windows security model. In every domain there will be at least one primary domain controller (PDC). The PDC machine is responsible for keeping all usernames and passwords for any user who may want to contact the domain. Any other server that is part of the domain can request password and permission information from this PDC. This is convenient when there are a large number of servers and users that need to be tracked. In addition to user and password information, the PDC can also contain system policies, which will provide general information on what certain users are and are not allowed to do on certain machines on the network, down to what function and features of the user interface should be enabled. The array of network services a Windows NT machine can provide, using optional software, extends to central database management and Internet services.

The last networking feature of Windows NT we want to mention is **Remote Access Service**, or **RAS**. Although Windows 95 and 98 machines can be used as dial-up hosts (computers that can be accessed via dial-up phone lines), security is limited because the client has access to any resources to which that machine has access. Through Windows NT RAS, the user information in a PDC can be used to grant or deny various levels of network access. This is a very powerful tool for allowing limited remote access to the resources available on the network.

Licensing

Although Windows NT is not a multiuser operating system by our definition, it can serve network resources to many users. Microsoft has chosen to provide licensing based on how many users will be accessing the machine simultaneously. When NT is installed, you can choose one of two licensing models. With the per-seat licensing model, it is assumed that there is an NT Access License for everyone who may connect to the machine. With the per-connection licensing model, it is assumed the server is licensed for a number of simultaneous connections. In either case, you have to provide user access licenses in addition to the license required to run Windows NT. These licenses must be bought separately from Microsoft for any operating system accessing the Windows NT server. The only exception to that rule is that Windows NT Workstation and NT Server software out of the box include one access license. It is possible to buy versions of NT that include more than one access license. If you try to access resources on an NT Server with a number of clients that exceeds the number of access licenses, you will find that NT will not permit this.

Organizations that grow may run into this licensing limitation many times. It is a very good idea to check on a regular basis how many users are attached to an NT machine and to ensure you do not run out of licenses. In a scenario where one user connects to more than one server, per-seat licensing is considered a more economical option. A seat (client) with an NT access license may access as many servers as they wish, so only one license per seat is needed.

Windows NT Today

You will find Windows NT Server in use on many types of servers ranging from file servers and print servers to application and database servers, in environments from small workgroups to Fortune 500 companies. Windows NT Workstation and Server have also traditionally been found in industrial control applications and in engineering environments. More and more, NT Workstation is making its way onto the desktop in offices and homes for everyday use, a trend that we expect to see continue as Microsoft discontinues development in the Windows 95/98 line. Lastly, because of its ease of use and administration, NT is becoming more and more popular as a **firewall** (controlling access from networked computers to an external network and vice versa) or Internet server, a role traditionally dominated by the UNIX operating system.

UNIX SYSTEM V RELEASE 4

The UNIX operating system comes in many different formats. Of all the operating systems covered in this book, it is the oldest, most diverse, and most complicated. This book uses Linux for its UNIX examples; **Linux** is a version of UNIX that is available to everyone free of charge. UNIX can run on almost any hardware platform; there are UNIX versions available for all platforms mentioned up to this point.

Because UNIX comes in such a wide variety of implementations, it is hard to define exactly what specifications a platform should meet to run it. In the case of Linux, almost any hardware will do to run the base operating system. UNIX is a true multitasking, multi-user operating system. This means, as we explained before, that it has the ability to fully serve all the computing needs of multiple users running multiple applications at the same time. All versions of UNIX that ship today adhere to one of the two main design standards, the **Berkeley System Distribution (BSD)** standard or the **System V Release 4 (SVR4)** standard. Examples of BSD-style UNIX include the freely available NetBSD and FreeBSD operating systems, as well as the commercially available BSDi UNIX. SVR4 versions include the freely available Linux and commercial versions such as SunSoft Solaris, and SCO UNIX. All UNIX systems include security features.

After startup, UNIX will typically present you with a request for a login, or username, followed by a request for a password. The username and password you provide determine what privileges you will be granted on the system. When your identity has been verified, you will be presented with a shell. This is another point where UNIX is substantially different from most other operating systems: by default, most UNIX versions will come with several different shells and it is up to the user to pick the shell they wish to use. Different shells provide you with different levels of functionality, but all of the shells function much like the shell in MS-DOS, with a series of built-in commands and the ability to call external commands and programs by simply typing them in at the command line.

The most popular UNIX shells are the Bourne shell (sh) and its cousin the Bourne Again shell (bash), and a version of the Bourne shell in which some of the commands are formatted to be similar to the C programming language, called the C shell (csh). Overall, these shells function in the same way: you get a prompt, you type a command, and they will do what you ask. Main commands are the same across the shells. To see the path of the directory you are in, you use the Print Working Directory or PWD command. To list the contents of the current directory, you use LS. Changing to another directory is done with the command CD, much like in DOS. When you are done with the shell, you can exit from it by using the EXIT command. Typically, this will return you to the login prompt.

Many versions of UNIX can also provide you with a graphical user interface. The most popular interface is the X11 Window System, known commonly as **X Window**. X Window is similar to other windowed systems, and makes it easier to use a multitasking, multi-user operating system such as UNIX. A unique feature of X Window is that it is network enabled. Using an X terminal it is possible to run X Window and all the application programs on a remote UNIX machine, and to interact with your applications remotely. One UNIX system can support many X terminals and users. X Window is, however, an optional part of many UNIX versions. Just as there are many different UNIX versions, there are also many different versions of X Window. Linux will generally use something called Xfree, a version that can be obtained for free. Other UNIX versions use X Window versions with added capabilities. X Window by default does not include programs like File Manager or Program Manager, but many utilities are available to provide file and application management.

All networking functions in UNIX are based on the BSD networking model, which provides support for the **TCP/IP (Transfer Control Protocol/Internet Protocol)**. This is the standard protocol in use on the Internet, and as such UNIX machines are uniquely qualified to provide numerous Internet services. The standard UNIX operating system does not provide many network functions. Most of these functions are provided by add-ons. The standard functions include login services, allowing a user to connect to the UNIX machine from another remote machine on the network, file transfers through the **File Transfer Protocol (FTP)**, and some form of e-mail service, usually the **Simple Mail Transfer Protocol (SMTP)**. Other services can be standard as well—in Linux, additional standard services include the **Network File System** (**NFS**) and support for other network systems such as those used by Microsoft, Apple, and Novell. It is also possible to add modules to UNIX to provide other services, such as World Wide Web service.

The security model in the UNIX operating system makes it a system of choice for providing many Internet functions, such as Internet server and firewall. It is possible to turn services on and off at the user's desire, and it is also possible to run services in ways that do not result in security issues for other services on the machine.

2

In addition to its role as Internet server and firewall, UNIX machines are often used as database or application servers that many users can access at the same time. You will also find UNIX machines in use for technical design and industrial control applications.

Mac OS 7.0 / 7.5 / 8.x

Apple Computer has always had a unique approach to operating systems. Their Macintosh line of personal computers revolutionized the world of operating systems. The Mac OS was truly the first operating system to have an all-graphical user interface and an all-graphical shell. Although there are subtle differences in the way Mac OS functions, you will see many similarities between it and Microsoft Windows, which many would say were designed to mimic the look and feel of the Mac OS. The current version of Mac OS is shown in Figure 2-11.

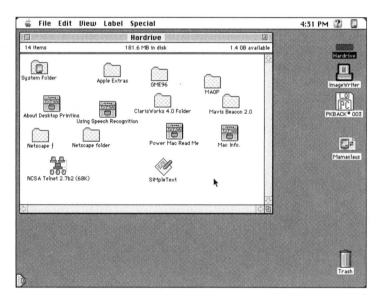

Figure 2-11 Mac OS desktop

The hardware architecture of the Mac OS is substantially different from the architecture used on most other platforms, especially because many of the graphical functions are included in the BIOS functions, located in the ROM (Read Only Memory) of the hardware. (Apple calls this "firmware.") Apple had to release a new version of the operating system (7.01) to support the newly introduced PowerBooks and Quadras (68040-based desktop Macs). Beginning with System 7.1, Apple began using system enabler files that allowed the previous version of the operating system to support new hardware. When the next version of the operating system is released, support for the most recent Macs is included so the enabler file is no longer needed for that model. The hardware architecture needed to run Mac OS is very dependent on the version of the operating system. If you run Version 7.0, you could be using any Macintosh hardware architecture, except for the PowerPC platform, which is supported as of Version 7.5. If you are running the newest generation of hardware (G3), you have to run Mac OS Version 8.1 or newer. Apple has always made the hardware and software closely interconnected, which results in strict requirements when it comes to operating system solutions.

One significant difference between the Mac OS and the other operating systems covered in this chapter is that only one company makes hardware capable of running Mac OS, and that is Apple. A few years back, Apple licensed Power Computing, Motorola, and other companies to make Mac OS-compatible hardware, but that is no longer the case. In short, using Apple software means using Apple hardware.

After the Mac is started, you will be presented with the all-graphical shell. This shell allows you to perform many operations with the mouse: starting programs, looking at the contents of directories, removing files, creating and removing folders (a folder is the Mac equivalent of a directory, a usage later adopted by most other graphical operating systems) and so on. The interface is extremely intuitive, and in many ways it is unchanged from the way it looked at its inception. The Mac makes no distinction between file management and the program start and stop functions.

Versions of Mac OS prior to 8.0 were not multitasking; they were essentially task switching with the aid of MultiFinder. Moreover, in Mac OS 8 and later, the multitasking functions are somewhat limited. While OS 8 Finder allows fairly significant multitasking operations such as emptying the trash, opening programs, and performing multiple file copy tasks simultaneously, these multitasking services are not available to other programs. It is possible to start several programs and switch between them in Mac OS 7.x, but whenever you switch from one application to another, the application you switch from will stop running. It will stay in memory until you re-activate it, at which point it will pick up where it left off. The only exceptions to this are a few pieces of the operating system, such as the print spooler, which will run while other software is in control of the machine. In Mac OS version 8.0 and newer, multitasking is a standard feature of the operating system that is available to all applications. When more than one application is active, the CPU resources will be shared among them.

The network functions in Mac OS are fairly evolved. Peer-to-peer networking, in which the machine serves both as a network client and a network server, has been a standard feature of the Mac OS since its inception. The protocol used is called AppleTalk, which originated in the Macintosh world. However, you can run AppleTalk under Windows and Linux (using the *netatalk* command). The nice thing about AppleTalk is that it has remained compatible as the new Mac OS versions arrived, and any Mac can be networked to any other Mac by simply plugging in a few cables and configuring some software. Apple implemented LocalTalk hardware with every Macintosh printer port, which uses an RS-422 interface to provide a combination networking and RS-232 serial solution in one inexpensive interface. This is, to our knowledge, the only hardware architecture and operating system combination that has consistently had these features. Through the use of optional clients, or through servers that can provide AppleTalk compatible services, many Macintoshes can also be networked easily to other networks.

Not all Macintosh hardware is equipped with standard network hardware. Many older machines only have LocalTalk, a proprietary Apple hardware standard. For these machines to be able to network with other systems, additional hardware is needed.

2

Mac OS was always meant to be a desktop operating system, and there are no extended security features to keep users from getting access to files on the local machine. For networking, Mac OS allows the user to generate user profiles. A user can be given a username and a password. Based on this combination, a user may access some of the resources made available on the network. The Mac OS can use its networking features to share printer and disk resources. In version 8.x, there are extensions that will let the Macintosh share resources using other protocols than AppleTalk, including TCP/IP, the standard Internet protocol, enabling greater flexibility in how Macs can be networked.

Throughout its history, the Mac OS has been known for its support of graphics, video, and sound capabilities. There has not been a version of Mac OS that does not support some kind of hardware that could produce sound. In this respect, Mac OS has been ahead of the industry. The same goes for sound capture, video capture and reproduction, and many other audiovisual functions. Because Apple has had tight control over both the Macintosh hardware architecture and operating system, and because it has always chosen to actively enhance the audiovisual functions of both hardware and software, you will find that the Mac and the Mac OS is favored by people in the graphics, sound, and video fields.

You will find Macintosh computers in many different environments, especially those that deal with the creative process. The Mac font management and ColorSync color matching technologies have endeared it in the graphic arts and prepress fields, while QuickTime has made the Mac popular for multimedia sound and video production. You will also find many Macs in the educational environment. The home computer market has a small, but still substantial share of machines running Mac OS. The Apple PowerBook laptops continue to be popular, even in organizations that have mostly settled on the Wintel (Windows-Intel) platform.

CHAPTER SUMMARY

This chapter provides a good foundation for the study of operating systems. This chapter discussed computer hardware and its relationship to the computer's operating system. The major features and applications for a number of popular operating systems were summarized, including MS-DOS, Windows 3.1, Windows 95/98, Windows NT, various implementations of UNIX, and the Macintosh OS.

If you have experience with only a single computer and its standard operating system, then this information on a relatively large number of operating systems may seem intimidating. However, as you move forward you will see that although each of the operating systems in this book is unique in many ways, there also are many similarities. The basic concepts and general functions of all operating systems are the same.

With the background provided in the first two chapters and the additional information in Chapter 3, you will have a solid foundation that will help you feel comfortable with all of these operating environments while allowing you to concentrate on the operating system(s) that directly interest you.

KEY TERMS

- **8086** — An early 16-bit personal computer CPU. It was released soon after the 8088 and used in machines at the same time 8088 machines were popular. The 8086 CPU was never as popular as the 8088.

- **8088** — The first popular personal computer CPU. The 8088 ran at 4.7 MHz, used a 20-bit address bus and an 8-bit data bus.

- **80x86** — A general designation for a popular line of Intel PC CPUs that started with the 80286 and continued through the 80486. There were several sub-designations within this chip line.

- **ActiveX** — An internal programming standard that allows various software that runs under the Windows operating system to communicate with the operating system and with other programs.

- **address bus** — An internal communications pathway inside a computer that specifies the source and target address for memory reads and writes. The address bus is measured by the number of bits of information it can carry. The wider the address bus (the more bits it moves at a time) the more memory available to the computer that uses it.

- **AUTOEXEC.BAT** — A system file that is part of DOS and other operating systems. This file contains lines of text that are used as commands to configure the system hardware and software as the operating system loads.

- **base memory** — The memory areas that are directly addressable by computer programs. In early PCs this was the first 640 KB of memory.

- **Berkeley Systems Distribution (BSD)** — A variant of the UNIX operating system upon which a large proportion of today's UNIX software is based.

- **cache controller** — Internal computer hardware that manages the data going into and loaded from the machine's cache memory.

- **cache memory** — Special computer memory that temporarily stores data used by the CPU. Cache memory is physically close to the CPU and is faster than standard system memory, enabling faster retrieval and processing time.

- **client** — In a networking environment, a computer that handles certain user-side software operations. For example, a network client may run software that captures user data input and presents output to the user from a network server (see **server**, below).

- **clustering** — A special computer networking configuration in which multiple computers are connected in such a way that they can share processing tasks, frequently working on portions of the same software job at the same time. In a Windows NT cluster, for example, the NT operating systems on the various machines share all of the connected resources as if they were one large computer.

- **Complex Instruction Set Computer (CISC)** — A computer CPU architecture in which processor components are re-configured to conduct different operations as required. Such computer designs require a larger number of instructions and more complex instructions than other designs.

2

- **data bus** — An internal communications pathway that allows computer components such as the CPU, display adapter, and main memory to share information. Early personal computers used an 8-bit data bus. More modern machines use 32 or 64-bit data buses.

- **Dial-Up Networking (DUN)** — A facility built into Windows 95, Windows 98, and Windows NT to permit operation of a hardware modem to dial a telephone number for the purpose of logging into a remote computer system via standard telephone lines.

- **directory** — A special disk storage location that keeps track of filenames, file types, and storage locations on a computer storage device. Also a list of these files and file information produced by a program utility that reads and reports on the disk's directory structure.

- **Disk Operating System (DOS)** — Computer software that manages the interface between the user and computer components, and among various components inside the computer. A disk operating system manages the low-level computer instructions for operation of and communication with such devices as storage hardware, a keyboard, a display adapter, and so on.

- **domain** — A logical grouping of computers and computer resources that helps manage these resources and user access to them.

- **DUN Server** — In Windows 95, Windows 98, and Windows NT, a software utility that permits a desktop machine to answer incoming calls, log on a user, and, with other software, permit the user access to the computer's resources.

- **e-mail** — Electronic mail. A method of sharing written communications and other computer data over a networked connection.

- **EMM386.SYS** — Extended Memory Manager. In personal computers running certain versions of DOS, an intrinsic utility that helps manage software access to memory above the 1 MB address.

- **external clock speed** — The speed at which the processor communicates with the memory and the other devices in the computer; usually one-fourth to one-half the internal clock speed.

- **external commands** — Operating system commands that are stored in separate program files on disk. When these commands are required, they must be loaded from disk storage into memory before they are executed.

- **File Manager** — In Windows 3.1 and Windows for Workgroups, a software utility that provides a graphical interface to the computer's files, including programs and data files.

- **File Transfer Protocol (FTP)** — In some networking environments, a software utility that facilitates the copying of computer files across the network connection from one computer to another.

- **firewall** — In a networked environment, a computer that is configured with special software to control access from networked workstations to an external network, and vice versa.

- **G3** — An Apple computer design that uses a relatively new RISC CPU, so named as a third-generation PowerPC processor.

- **instruction set** — In a computer CPU, the group of commands (instructions) the processor recognizes. These instructions are used to conduct the operations required of the CPU by the operating system and application software.

- **internal clock speed** — The speed at which the CPU executes internal commands, measured in megahertz (millions of clock ticks per second). Internal clock speeds can be as low as 1 MHz and as high as 500 MHz.

- **internal commands** — Operating system commands that load with the main operating system Kernel or command module.

- **Internet** — A global network used by individuals and businesses to connect stand-alone workstations and networks for the exchange of electronic mail, shared research information, commercial advertising, and other purposes.

- **Kernel** — In a computer operating system, the lowest level and most basic instructions.

- **Level 1 (L1) cache** — Cache memory that is part of the CPU hardware. See **cache memory**.

- **Level 2 (L2) cache** — Cache memory that, in most computer CPU designs, is located on hardware separate from, but situated close by, the CPU.

- **Linux** — An open code version of UNIX.

- **MS-DOS** — A disk operating system designed by Microsoft Corporation. See **DOS**.

- **Multimedia Extension (MMX)** — A CPU design that permits the processor to manage certain multimedia operations—graphics, for example—faster and more directly. MMX technology improves computer performance when running software that requires multimedia operations.

- **multiprocessor machines** — A computer that uses more than one CPU.

- **Network Control Panel** — In Windows 95, Windows 98, and Windows NT, a graphical user interface to network configuration settings.

- **Network File System (NFS)** — In UNIX and other operating systems, a system-level facility that supports loading and saving files to remote disk drives across the network.

- **networking** — A process for physically connecting two or more computers to permit them to share hard disk storage, printers, scanners, software, and other resources.

- **path** — In a computer directory structure, a command that specifies the complete location to a specific file or directory. Computer files are stored in files, which in turn reside in directories (folders). Directories can be stored within other directories. To access a specific file you must also specify the series of directories that must be traversed to reach the desired file.

- **PC DOS** — An operating system very similar to MS-DOS, customized and marketed by IBM.

- **peer-to-peer networking** — A computer networking configuration in which the various connected computers are essentially equal.

- **Pentium** — An Intel Corporation CPU (essentially an 80586), and often the computer system that uses this chip. Variations on the Pentium chip include the Pentium Pro, Pentium MMX, Pentium II, and others. Chip technology changes too quickly to provide a current comprehensive list.

- **pipelining** — A CPU design that permits the processor to operate on one instruction at the same time it is fetching one or more subsequent instructions from the operating system or application.

- **Plug and Play (PNP)** — In Windows 95 and Windows 98, software utilities that operate with compatible hardware to facilitate automatic hardware configuration. Windows recognizes PNP hardware when it is installed and in many cases can configure the hardware and install required software without significant user intervention.

- **power management** — A hardware facility in modern computers that permits certain hardware to shut down automatically after a specified period of inactivity. Proper use of power management facilities reduces hardware wear and tear as well as energy usage.

- **PowerPC** — A RISC CPU designed jointly by Motorola, Apple, and IBM. PowerPC chips are used primarily in Apple computer designs.

- **Program Manager** — In Windows 3.1, a software utility that provides a graphical user interface into certain components of the operating system. Program Manager displays directories and files and lets the user launch applications without resorting to DOS commands.

- **real mode** — A limited, 16-bit operating mode in PCs running early versions of Windows.

- **Reduced Instruction Set Computer (RISC)** — A computer CPU design that dedicates processor hardware components to certain functions. This design reduces the number and the complexity of required instructions and, in many cases, results in faster performance than CISC CPUs.

- **Registry** — A Windows database that stores information about a computer's hardware and software configuration.

- **Remote Access Service (RAS)** — A computer operating system subsystem that manages user access to a computer from a remote location, including security issues.

- **root** — In a computer directory system, the highest level or main directory.

- **server** — In a networked environment, a computer system designed to conduct shared operations at the request of one or more clients.

- **shell** — The operating system user interface. In MS-DOS, UNIX and some other systems, the shell interface is text-based, and command oriented.

- **Simple Mail Transfer Protocol (SMTP)** — In a networked computer environment, a software utility that manages the transfer of electronic messages among various users.

- **single-processor machines** — Computers capable of supporting only a single CPU.

- **symmetric multiprocessing (SMP)** — A computer design that supports multiple, internal CPUs that can be configured to work simultaneously on the same set of instructions.

- **system architecture** — Specific computer design features that define the computer itself, including hardware and software.

- **System V Release 4** — A version of the UNIX operating system.

- **task supervisor** — A process in the operating system that will keep track of the applications that are running on the machine and the resources they use.

- **Transfer Control Protocol/Internet Protocol (TCP/IP)** — A networking communications protocol. Used on the Internet and other UNIX networking environments.

- **Universal Serial Bus (USB)** — A relatively new serial bus designed to support up to 127 discrete devices with data transfer speeds up to 12 Mbps (megabits per second).

- **UNIX** — A popular networked, multitasking, multi-user operating system.

- **Web browsers** — Software to facilitate individual computer access to graphical data presented over the Internet on the World Wide Web, or over a local area network in a compatible format.

- **Web server** — In a networked environment, a computer that runs special software to host graphical data in a World Wide Web format. Data on a Web server is accessed with a computer running a Web browser.

- **Windows Explorer** — A graphical software utility that provides access to a computer's files and applications in the Windows operating system variants.

- **Windows for Workgroups** — A networked version of the Windows 3.1 operating system.

- **X Window** — A windowed user interface for UNIX and other operating systems.

REVIEW QUESTIONS

1. One of the main functions of an operating system is to provide an interface between _____ and _____.

2. A single-processor machine is one that
   a. can conduct only a single process at a time
   b. contains only a single Central Processing Unit (CPU)
   c. can connect in a network to only one other machine
   d. none of the above

3. A multi-processor machine can support as many as 64 CPUs. True or False?

2

4. Two general CPU designs are used in modern computers. They are Complex _____ _____ _____ and Reduced _____ _____ _____.

5. The list of commands a CPU can understand is known as the _____ set.

6. A CISC CPU design uses

   a. hardware that is software-configured to perform multiple operations

   b. hardware that is dedicated to perform specific functions

   c. hardware that requires fewer instructions than other designs

   d. hardware that requires more instructions than other designs

7. The main reason a RISC CPU is potentially faster than a CISC CPU is _____.

8. Instruction pipelining is a processing technique used by (CISC, RISC) CPUs to improve performance.

9. One benchmark of the speed of a CPU is the number of instructions it can perform with each clock cycle. True or False?

10. Modern CPUs operate with internal clock speeds around (200 MHz, 400 MHz).

11. Special memory that may reside on the CPU hardware and that can speed up computer operation is called _____ memory.

12. Describe the main difference between L1 cache and L2 cache.

13. Describe the main function of a cache controller.

14. A computer address bus is used to enable the computer to _____.

15. How many memory locations can a 16-bit data bus access? A 32-bit address bus?

16. In addition to the address bus, another internal bus is used to transfer information into and out of main memory. This bus is called the _____ bus.

17. How many clock cycles will a 25 MHz computer clock have?

18. The first widely used personal computer CPU was manufactured by Intel, their model

   a. 8086

   b. 8088

   c. 80386

   d. 68000

19. The latest Intel CPUs broke with tradition and are not designated by number. Instead they carry the name _____.

20. The first popular personal computer operating system was designed by Microsoft and was called _____.

21. The first popular graphical operating system for the PC was

    a. Windows 95

    b. Windows for Workgroups

    c. Windows 3.1

    d. UNIX

22. The operating system shell is the part of the operating system that

    a. provides access to the user through commands or graphics

    b. contains the innermost, basic commands

    c. contains only the most basic, outer level commands

    d. none of the above

23. Windows for _____ was the first graphical-oriented operating system for the PC that supported networking.

24. The most recent, graphical Windows operating system designed for business applications by Microsoft is _____.

25. Mac OS is designed by the _____ company for their line of _____ computers.

HANDS-ON PROJECTS

PROJECT 2-1

MS-DOS computer hardware and software are configured as the operating system loads. One file, AUTOEXEC.BAT, contains commands specific to a particular machine to conduct some of this configuration.

To view information in this file to help you learn about your machine's configuration:

1. Display the DOS command line prompt by restarting the machine or exiting any running application.

2. Display the root directory by typing **CD** and pressing **Enter**. Note the direction of the slash bar.

3. Type the following command: **type autoexec.bat | more** and press **Enter**. The Type command tells DOS to display the contents of the specified file one line at a time. The More command runs an external DOS program that pauses the display if the file contains more information than will fit on a single screen.

4. Note the commands contained in the file. You may recognize some of the software commands and even some hardware calls. Don't worry if these commands don't fully make sense at this point. Just remember how to display this file and familiarize yourself with the general way these commands are entered in the file.

You can look at AUTOEXEC and CONFIG data in some Windows systems, although you won't always find these files in Windows. Simply open a DOS window and repeat the steps above. If you don't find these files in a Windows system it simply means you don't have hardware or software that requires these configuration settings.

PROJECT 2-2

DOS-based computers use the command line (introduced in the previous project) to launch programs. There are internal DOS commands, external DOS commands that are really separate programs, and application programs that conduct such jobs as word processing and accounting.

To understand how DOS commands are executed:

1. Display the DOS command line prompt by exiting any running applications.

2. At the command prompt type the **dir** command and press **Enter**. You will see a list of files and possibly directories scroll up the screen.

3. Type **path** and press **Enter**. This command shows the directories that DOS will search automatically, looking for programs that can be executed when you issue a command at the command line prompt.

4. Type **mkdir mydir** and press **Enter**. This will create a new subdirectory within the current directory called mydir (you can name this new directory anything you like, as long as it contains no more than eight characters).

5. Type **dir** and press **Enter**. You should see the new directory you just created in the list of files and directories.

6. Type **rmdir mydir** and press **Enter**. This command erases the directory you just created.

PROJECT 2-3

Windows 3.1 uses a graphical interface to access programs and utilities.

To view a list of available files and directories in Windows 3.1:

1. Display the Program Manager screen by closing any open applications.

2. Click the **Main** application window to bring it to the front of the display or double-click the **Main** icon if it is not already open.

3. Double-click the **File Manager** icon to launch the File Manager.

4. Scroll through the displayed directories and files to find out what files are available on your computer.

PROJECT 2-4

Windows 95 uses an interface similar to Windows 3.1, but it is more sophisticated and, in our opinion, easier to use.

To display a list of available application programs in Windows 95:

1. Move the mouse cursor to the bottom of the screen to display the taskbar if it is not already visible.

2. Click **Start** at the far left of the taskbar and point to **Programs**. You will see the list of available applications on your machine.

3. Point to any application name that includes a right-facing arrow. This will display a supplemental menu of programs or utilities associated with this program.

4. At the bottom of the Programs list you should see Windows Explorer. Click **Windows Explorer** to open Explorer, which will display the directories (folders) and files available on this computer.

5. Note the differences and similarities between this directory display and the one you saw in the Windows 3.1 File Manager in the previous project.

PROJECT 2-5

Windows 98 is very similar to Windows 95 in its basic functions. You can use Windows Explorer as described in Project 2-4 to display files and directories.

To change the user interface in Windows 98 to use a Web-based motif:

1. Display the taskbar if it is not already visible and click **Start**.

2. Point to **Settings**, then to **Active Desktop** and choose **View as Web Page**.

3. Point to **Start**, **Settings**, then select **Folder Options**.

4. Click the **General** tab, select **Web Style** and click **OK**.

5. Note the change in your desktop display. Now you can single-click program icons to launch applications. You can also single-click program names in Windows Explorer or My Computer to launch them.

CASE PROJECTS

1. Associated Insurance is a regional insurance broker that started using personal computers shortly after they were introduced. The company uses a number of DOS and Windows 3.1-based applications to compute customer insurance needs and product costs. These programs work well, but the hardware is starting to show its age and the company wants to upgrade to a newer operating system.

   In today's environment, the upgrade most logically involves new hardware with preinstalled Windows 98. As information services manager for this company, you need to develop a plan for specifying hardware requirements and for transitioning current users to Windows 98. Hardware price and configuration are only a part of your consideration. The insurance industry applications were designed for the older operating system, so you must answer these questions:

   a. Will the software run under Windows 98?

   b. Does the company that supplied the original software offer an upgrade path to newer software that takes advantage of networking and the Windows 98 graphical user interface?

   c. How will you train employees accustomed to DOS and Windows 3.1 to use Windows 98?

2. You are PC administrator for Progressive Promotions, a large advertising agency. There are approximately 60 individual users, networked in a Windows 95 environment. Users work mostly with Microsoft Office suite software, plus some specialty layout and graphics applications. This is a technical staff who understands industry hardware and software. They would like the company to upgrade to Windows 98 and Office 2000, and to make more use of the Internet by installing a full-time networked connection.

   The majority of users are running Pentium 100 MHz computers with 16 MB of memory. What are the hardware and software considerations in upgrading to Windows 98? Consider the Microsoft stated operating system strategy, which includes stopping development of Windows 9x systems in favor of Windows NT. Remember that Windows NT is an evolving system, with version 5.0 barely on the street. What is your best short term and long term strategy for upgrading your company's hardware and software? Why?

FILE SYSTEMS

This chapter introduces the file systems of the operating systems covered in this book. A **file system** is a design for storing and managing files on disk media. As the name suggests, a file system is created to easily handle files in a systematic manner, an essential function of every operating system, used by all the programs that run on it. The file system builds a logical system on top of the physical disk organization. It organizes how information is stored on disk, and affects how users interact with the operating system to work with files.

In this chapter you'll learn the general characteristics and functions of file systems. You'll also examine the organization, specific features, typical problems, and possible solutions to those problems in specific file systems.

AFTER READING THIS CHAPTER AND COMPLETING THE EXERCISES YOU WILL BE ABLE TO:

- Understand the basic functions of all file systems
- Describe the major elements of the DOS and Windows 3.1/3.11 file systems
- Compare and contrast the Windows 95/98 file system (FAT16 and FAT32) with the older DOS/Windows 3.1 file system
- Describe the fundamental features of the UNIX file system
- Describe the basics of the Macintosh file system

UNDERSTANDING FILE SYSTEM FUNCTIONS

The file systems used by the operating systems covered in this book perform the following general functions:

- Partition and format disks to store and retrieve information
- Establish file naming conventions
- Provide utilities for functions such as file compression and disk defragmentation
- Provide for file and data integrity
- Provide storage media management functions

The overall function of the file system is to create a structure for filing data. The metaphor that is typically used for a file system is that of file cabinets, file drawers, and file folders. For example, the computer could be considered the file cabinet, and the disk drives, the drawers. Within each drawer (drive), information is organized into hanging folders (directories), manila folders (subdirectories), and individual documents (files), as shown in Figure 3-1.

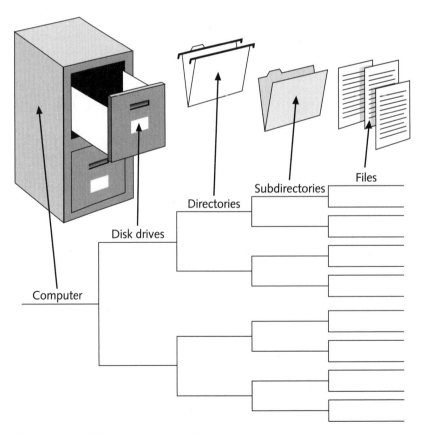

Figure 3-1   A file system metaphor

A file is no more than a set of data that is grouped in some logical manner, assigned a name, and stored on the disk. Whenever the file is needed, the operating system can be given the filename, and it will be able to retrieve the data in the file from the disk.

The data contained in files can be text, images, music and sounds, video, or Web pages for the Internet. But no matter what kind of data is stored in the file system, it must be converted into digital format—a series of ones and zeros, or "on's" and "off's"—that the computer understands. The operating system, along with the applications you use for word processing, graphics, and so on, performs this function of converting data into digital format for the computer and back into the end user format—text, pictures, etc.

Moreover, there must be a way to write digital information onto disk, to track it while it is there, update it when necessary, and call it back when the user or a program under the user's control wants it. To achieve all this, the operating system typically groups disk sectors in some logical way, creates a record of this structure, and builds a **directory** to track the type of data stored in each file. The directory connects names to the files that are stored on the disk, which makes it easy for users and programs to obtain the right data at the right time.

The term *directory* can have two meanings: the internal database maintained by the operating system to track file locations, sizes, and attributes, as well as the actual list of this information displayed and accessed by the user through the DIR command or other utilities such as the Windows Explorer.

In addition to the names of files and where to find them on the disk, directories also store information about the date and time the file was last modified and the size of the file. As you look at the individual file systems later in this chapter, you will discover what each of the operating systems stores in the directory.

BLOCK ALLOCATION

The operating systems covered in this book use a method called **block allocation** to keep track of where specific files are stored on the disk. Rather than storing absolute track and sector and head information for every sector on a disk, with block allocation the disk is divided into logical blocks (in DOS and Windows these are referred to as **clusters**), which are in turn mapped to sectors, heads, and tracks on the disk, as discussed in Chapter 2. Each hard disk platter has two sides, with a read/write head on each side. Tracks that line up on each platter from top to bottom are called cylinders, and are all read at the same time.

When the operating system needs to allocate some disk space, it does so based on a block address. Lower-level drivers translate block numbers into real disk addresses. The reference to a file in the directory and in the file allocation data is based on block numbers.

The data regarding block allocation is stored on the disk itself, using two techniques. One technique uses a fixed portion of the disk to store this data, such as the FAT file systems under DOS and Windows. The other technique uses various locations on the disk to store a special type of file that is used for directory and file allocation information, such as the NT File System (NTFS) and the UNIX file systems. As you can imagine, the areas of the disk in which allocation information and directory information are stored are of very high importance; without this data it will not be possible to access any of the files on the system!

If a system uses a specific area or set of areas on the disk to store this data, obviously this disk area will be accessed frequently. This is why many problems with disks arise as problems in disk allocation tables and directory information. Since this data also is stored in a location separate from the actual file, you could see how, when there is a problem with the disk, some of the directory or allocation data may not match the data actually stored on the disk. These occurrences are not uncommon, so it is very important to exercise proper care of disks to minimize such problems.

All operating systems have special tools that will let you check, and sometimes repair, common file system and disk problems. Some operating systems can perform checks on the file system on an ongoing basis. These tools are discussed in more detail later in this chapter.

PARTITIONS

With today's technology creating disks with larger and larger capacity, and as disks are being used in more diverse applications, sometimes it is desirable to have more than one file system on a single disk. You might install Windows 98 alongside Windows NT, for example, to accommodate various applications. This is where the concept of **partitioning** comes in. When you want to have multiple file systems on one disk, you can partition the disk so that different file systems can be installed on different disk partitions. You can also create partitions in one operating system to segment a drive into multiple logical volumes to which you can assign distinct drive letters. This technique is useful to help you segment data, and necessary when you are using older operating systems such as DOS and Windows 3.1 that don't recognize very large hard drives.

 Partitioning can typically be done only on hard disks or on large removable disks. Floppy disks and other low-capacity media do not support partitioning. There simply isn't enough room on these low-capacity disks to make partitioning practical.

The logical programming that creates disk partitions resides at an even lower level than the actual file system and it lets you divide the disk into "slices." This low-level formatting definition is stored in special sections of the hard drive itself, separate from the operating system. Obviously, the partitioning scheme must be communicated to the operating system and file system. On most disks there is a separate area that stores the partition information. This area has room to hold information about a set number of partitions. Whenever you create a partition, information about that partition is stored in this special area of the disk. On systems in the IBM PC hardware architecture, for example, there is room to store information for up to four partitions on each disk. This area is known as the **partition table** in DOS, Mac OS and Windows, or **disk label** in UNIX. In addition to the disk label or partition table, there is another piece of disk reserved known as the **boot block** in UNIX, or **Master Boot Record (MBR)** in DOS and Windows. This area holds a tiny program used to begin booting an operating system from a disk.

Not all operating systems support partitions in the same way, which you will discover in the following sections on file systems for individual operating systems. Each operating system also uses specific utilities to create partitions. When a disk partition is created, the file system is stored inside the partition. The directory structures are then built inside the file system. When files are stored on the disks, they are given some space inside the partition and data about the files is written in the directory area.

3

THE DOS/WINDOWS 3.1 FILE SYSTEM

The DOS/Windows 3.1 file system, called the **file allocation table (FAT) file system**, has been around since the early 1980s, and it has not changed much since then. FAT uses a file allocation table to store directory information about files, such as filenames, file attributes, and file location. This table structure must be searched in sequential fashion, one entry at a time, whenever users access directories or files. FAT disks contain a series of allocation units (clusters) that form a partition. An allocation unit can consist of two, four, or eight sectors on a disk.

In versions of DOS prior to 4.0, the maximum size of a file system was 32 MB. These file systems are known as FAT12. In versions of MS-DOS from 4.0 on, the maximum size of a file system is 2 GB. These file systems are known as FAT16. The FAT16 file system has been around for a long time, and many computers, even those that do not run MS-DOS, can read disks written in FAT format. Because the file system is simple there is relatively little that can go wrong, which makes this a stable file system.

 It is possible to use the FAT16 file system with Windows 95 and Windows NT. Many other operating systems support FAT12 and FAT16 as secondary file systems, which means these operating systems are able to read files from and write files to file systems of those types, something very useful when it comes to information exchange. However, using FAT with other operating systems limits the functionality offered by the native file systems of those operating systems.

Another important characteristic of FAT is its use of "8.3" filenames, which can be up to eight characters long, followed by a period and an extension of three characters, such as FILENAME.EXT. This convention led to the proliferation of many common three-letter file extensions such as .TXT for text files, .DOC for word processing files, .XLS for Excel spreadsheets, and so on. The limitations of this naming convention contributed to the development of an upgrade of FAT in Windows 95 that supports long filenames (see the section on Windows 95).

PARTITIONING

The FAT file system supports two partitions per hard drive, a primary partition and a secondary partition. The secondary partition may then be divided further into a maximum of three logical drives (see Figure 3-2 on the next page). Each of these four possible logical drives can hold an individual MS-DOS file system. Under control of MS-DOS, up to 26 logical drives (pointers to separate file systems), each with its own file system, can be active at one time. A logical drive, remember, is a software definition that divides a physical hard drive into multiple drives for file storage. A floppy disk does not support multiple file systems, since each floppy drive is allocated as one removable file system. Under MS-DOS and Windows, a CD-ROM is always treated as one file system.

 Although 26 drive definitions are technically possible, DOS reserves drives A: and B: for floppy drives, practically limiting the number of hard drives (including logical drives) to 24.

Primary Partition
It is normally active, so the system will boot
from this partition.
In most cases, this file system is referred to as
drive C:.

Secondary Partition, with logical drives

First Logical Drive Typically, drive D:
Second Logical Drive Typically, drive E:
Third Logical Drive Typically, drive F:

Figure 3-2   Sample DOS partition table structure

Each DOS file system is assigned a letter followed by a colon: A:, B:, C: and so on through Z:. This design lets you address the individual file systems easily by specifying a drive letter. Letters A: and B: are reserved for two removable file systems on floppy disk drives. Typically, C: is reserved for the first hard disk or removable disk file system (and is normally the system that contains the boot partition). All other file systems located on fixed disks that are controlled by the hard disk drivers in the operating system follow in sequential order. So, a DOS machine with two hard disks with two partitions each will have the drive letters C: for the first partition on the first disk, D: for the second partition on the first disk, E: for the first partition on the second disk, and F: for the second partition on the second disk. Disks that require special drivers, such as CD-ROM drives or removable disks, can be assigned any unused drive letter. By default, they will be assigned the next letter after the drive letter used by the last hard disk. In the example above, a CD-ROM would be drive G:.

In MS-DOS, a program called **FDISK** is used to modify partition information. The name FDISK stands for fixed disk, an alternative name for hard disk. The FDISK utility is used to look at the information contained in the partition record as well as to change it. The FDISK utility that comes with DOS is limited in that it will allow you to make partitions for the DOS operating system only.

Extreme care should be taken when using the FDISK utility. If partition information is changed or removed using FDISK, all data in the related file system will be lost permanently! You may want to consider utilities like Norton's Disk Editor, which allow you to do low-level disk editing and Master Boot Record modification.

If you start a computer in MS–DOS, you can use the FDISK utility to look at the contents of the partition record. When the FDISK command is issued, a menu appears as shown in Figure 3-3. For systems that have more than one physical hard disk, there is an additional choice that lets you select a disk other than the default first hard disk.

```
                        FDISK Options

Current fixed disk drive: 1

Choose one of the following:

1. Create DOS partition or Logical DOS Drive
2. Set active partition
3. Delete partition or Logical DOS Drive
4. Display partition information


Enter choice: [1]




Press Esc to exit FDISK
```

Figure 3-3 MS-DOS FDISK utility

You can choose option 4 to see what partitions are on the disk. This will give you a short overview, as shown in Figure 3-4.

```
                    Display Partition Information

Current fixed disk drive: 1

Partition  Status  Type   Volume Label  Mbytes  System   Usage
  C: 1       A    PRI DOS  BOOTDISK       1914   FAT16     100%


Total disk space is 1914 Mbytes (1 Mbyte = 1048576 bytes)





Press Esc to continue
```

Figure 3-4 FDISK partition information screen

In the leftmost column, you see the partition number and, if applicable, the drive letter associated with the partition. In the Status column, you see that one partition is marked A, which stands for active. When the computer is started, the BIOS looks at the partition record, finds the **active partition** (the partition currently being used to store data), and looks at the file system inside that partition to start the operating system. Only one partition on each disk should be marked active. Next is the Type, a textual representation of the Partition Type ID in the partition record. The DOS version of FDISK recognizes only a very limited number of partition types, namely those used by Microsoft operating systems in existence prior to the creation of the version of FDISK used. For example, the FDISK in DOS 4.0 will not recognize partitions made with the Windows 98 FDISK. Most versions of FDISK will show both FAT12 and FAT16 partition types as FAT. The **Volume Label** column shows the name of the file system in the partition. The Mbytes column represents the size of the partition in megabytes. System indicates what type of file system is inside the partition (in this example it is FAT). Finally, the Usage column indicates how much of the total available disk space is being consumed by this file system.

You can use the other functions of the FDISK program to delete or add partitions to the drives in your system. Once again, *remove a partition only when you are absolutely sure that's what you want to do.* When you remove a partition, all data contained in the file system inside the partition is lost. You may want to remove an existing partition to replace it with another file system, for example, or to add a file system to a disk previously configured with a single partition.

To remove a partition, select option 3 from the FDISK menu, which will present you with another menu to select which partition you wish to remove. You are then led through a series of confirmations before the partition is finally removed. You can change the active partition using option 2. Option 1 in the menu will give you the chance to create additional partitions on the disk by answering some questions.

Using FDISK option 2 (changing the active partition) can sometimes be handy to enable booting from a different partition on the disk, but great care should be taken. Setting the active partition incorrectly may make it impossible to boot your computer from the hard disk!

With a new system called **large block allocation (LBA)**, it is now possible to make file systems much larger than 512 MB under DOS. LBA translates larger logical blocks to smaller ones to allow for support of larger physical disks. However, the disk controller and disk must support LBA, and they must have been configured for LBA. The trick to LBA is that DOS is told that the sector size of the hard disk is greater than 512 bytes per sector, which results in the ability to have much larger file systems.

FORMATTING

After you have partitioned a disk, it is time to place the file system on the partition. In DOS, the file system is placed on the partition using the **FORMAT** command. This command writes all of the file system structure to the disk. In the case of a floppy disk, it uses the first sector of the disk as the boot block. This block contains some information about the disk, such as the number of tracks and the number of sectors per track, in coded form. It can also contain a very small program that enables the computer to start the operating system from the

3

floppy disk, if FORMAT is used with the /S (system) switch: FORMAT /S. As with many system level commands, FORMAT includes a number of additional switches that modify precise program operation. You can view a list of these switches by typing FORMAT /? at the DOS prompt. See Table 3-1 for a list of FORMAT switches.

Table 3-1   FORMAT Command Switches

Switch	Function
/V[:label]	Specifies the volume label
/Q	Performs a quick format
/F:size	Specifies the size of the floppy disk to format (such as 160, 180, 320, 360, 720, 1.2, 1.44, 2.88)
/B	Allocates space on the formatted disk for system files
/S	Copies system files to the formatted disk
/T:tracks	Specifies the number of tracks per disk side
/N:sectors	Specifies the number of sectors per track
/1	Formats a single side of a floppy disk
/4	Formats a 5.25-inch 360K floppy disk in a high-density drive
/8	Formats eight sectors per track
/C	Tests clusters that are currently marked "bad"

Command lines frequently use **switches** (extra codes) to change the way a particular command operates. In many operating systems these extra commands follow a forward slash and take the form of a letter, or combination of letters, such as the DIR command in DOS, which can take several switches or arguments, including /p (pause when the screen is full) and /s (include subdirectories).

The boot block is placed in the first sector on the disk. Next comes the root directory, where the system stores file information, such as name, start cluster, file size, file modification date and time, and **file attributes** (file characteristics such as Hidden, Read-only, Archive, and so on). The root directory on every partition is a fixed size that can contain a maximum of 512 entries. Behind this root directory are two copies of the file allocation table (FAT). The FAT on a floppy disk consists of a number of 12-bit entries. Each of these entries corresponds with a cluster address on the disk. When the file system performs its format operation, it divides the disk into clusters that are all sequentially numbered. In the case of a floppy disk, each cluster corresponds to a sector on the disk. Each of the two copies of the FAT has exactly one entry for each cluster.

When a file is stored to disk, its data is written in the clusters on the disk. The filename is stored in the directory, along with the number of the first cluster in which the data has been stored. When the operating system has filled the first cluster, data is written to the next free cluster on the disk. The FAT entry corresponding with the first cluster is filled with the number of the second cluster in the file. When the second cluster is full, the operating system continues to write in the next free cluster. The FAT entry for the second cluster is set to point to the cluster number for the third cluster, and so on. When a file is completely written to the disk, the FAT entry for the final cluster will be filled with all 1's, which means end of file. At this time, the directory entry for the file will be updated with the total file size. This is commonly referred to as the "linked-list" method.

Clusters are a fixed length, and if a file does not exactly match the space available in the clusters it uses, you can end up with some unused space at the end of a cluster. This is a little wasteful, and it also explains why a file's directory entry needs to include the exact file size. The operating system sets all FAT entries to zeroes when it formats the disk, indicating that none of the clusters is being used. When you write a file to disk, the operating system finds free space on the disk by simply looking for the next FAT entry that contains all zeroes. In most cases, the FORMAT command will read every address on the disk to make sure it is usable. Unusable spots will be marked in the FAT as **bad clusters**, and these areas will never be used for file storage. It will then write a new root directory and file allocation table, and the disk will be ready for use. Formatting a disk will effectively remove all data that was on the disk, because you have lost the directory and FAT data needed to get to the data. On disks that have never been formatted, the FORMAT command will write new sector and track markers on the disk. On disks that have been previously used, you can use the /Q (Quick Format) option. This tells FORMAT to dispense with the disk check, and to simply write a new root directory and FAT table. This makes the format operation a lot faster, obviously, but it also skips the detailed checking of the disk, which could cause trouble later if an application tries to write information to a bad disk location.

The format process on a hard disk is the same as on a floppy disk, with two exceptions. The first is related to the size of each entry in the FAT table, which will be 16 bits long on any disk larger than 16 MB. The second difference is in the cluster size. On a floppy disk, there are only very few sectors, and there are enough FAT entries to use a cluster size of one sector per cluster. On a hard disk, a number of sectors are combined into a cluster. Exactly how many sectors per cluster depends on the size of the hard disk, as shown in Table 3-2.

Table 3-2   Hard Disk Cluster Reference

Partition Size	Sectors per Cluster	Cluster Size
0–32 MB	1	512 bytes
32–64 MB	2	1 KB
63–128 MB	4	2 KB
128–256 MB	8	4 KB
256–512 MB	16	8 KB
512 MB–1 GB	32	16 KB
1 GB–2 GB	64	32 KB
2 GB–4 GB	128	64 KB

The largest possible partition in a FAT file system is 4 GB. Keep in mind that the smallest allocation unit is one cluster. If you store a file that is 300 bytes long on a file system that has clusters of 64 KB, you will waste a lot of space. It is for this reason that smaller cluster sizes are generally considered desirable. As a result, Windows or DOS systems using FAT with large hard disks frequently have a great number of hard disk partitions.

Each partition stores two copies of the FAT table as a backup in case one of the copies gets damaged. However, there is only one copy of the root directory on each partition. This concept is shown in Figure 3-5.

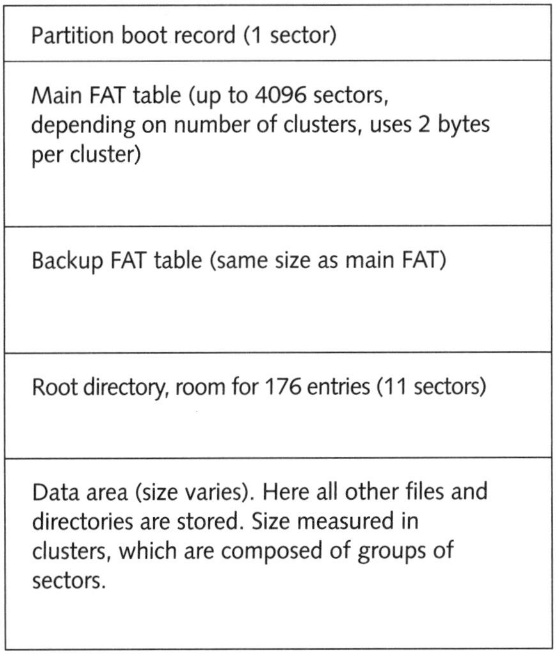

| Partition boot record (1 sector) |
| Main FAT table (up to 4096 sectors, depending on number of clusters, uses 2 bytes per cluster) |
| Backup FAT table (same size as main FAT) |
| Root directory, room for 176 entries (11 sectors) |
| Data area (size varies). Here all other files and directories are stored. Size measured in clusters, which are composed of groups of sectors. |

Figure 3-5 Typical FAT directory structure

The FAT tables and root directory are found at the beginning of each partition, and they are always at the same location. This makes it possible for the boot program in DOS to easily find the files needed to start the operating system. Other directories in the file system are no more than specialized files. They are identical to any other file in the operating system, with the exception of having the directory attribute set in their own directory entry. There can be a virtually unlimited number of directories, with a virtually unlimited number of files in each.

The FAT directory structure is simple. Each item in a directory consists of 32 bytes. In each entry, information about the file is stored, including the filename, the file change date and time, the file size and the file attributes. As mentioned earlier, the filename consists of two parts: the name, which can be up to eight characters long, and the **extension**, which contains up to three characters. All letters in filenames are stored in upper case, and the operating system treats all upper and lower case letters as if they were all upper case. In other words, the file named FILE.TXT is identical to the file named file.txt. Extensions can have a special meaning. Files with a .SYS extension are generally device drivers; files with .COM or .EXE extensions are program files the operating system can execute; while files with the .BAT extension are batch files of commands that can be executed as if they were typed on the keyboard. The filename and extension cannot contain spaces and are separated by a period.

Apart from the filename, each directory entry also contains some **status bits** that identify the type of filename contained in each entry. The status bits in use are Volume, Directory, System, Hidden, Read-Only, and Archive. The Volume bit indicates a file system volume label, or a nickname for the file system. The volume name can be set with the /V option of the FORMAT command, or by using the VOLUME command. The volume name appears at the top of directory listings, in the Windows 3.1 File Manager, and in FDISK listings. The Directory bit is used to signify that a file contains directory data, and should as such be treated as a directory by the file system. Directories may in turn contain directories, as long as the names of all directories in a path do not exceed 80 characters. You will see a directory clearly marked with a <DIR> label when you look at a directory listing in DOS, or with a file folder icon in Windows. The four remaining attributes indicate additional information about a file. Files that are part of the operating system and should not be touched by programs or users are marked with a System or S flag. Files that should not be visible to the user are known as Hidden files and are marked with the H bit. Files that should not be written to are known as Read-only files and are marked with the R flag. Lastly, files that should be backed up the next time a backup is made are said to have the Archive, or A flag set.

All in all, there are four optional flags, H, S, R, and A. The **ATTRIB** command can be used to look at these attributes, or to set them. Typing ATTRIB in a directory will show all of the attribute settings for all the files, whereas typing ATTRIB followed by a filename will show only attributes specific to that file. The ATTRIB command can also be used to set file attributes. To do this, the ATTRIB command is followed by the attribute letter, the + sign to set, or the − sign to unset an attribute, and the filename in question. To make a file named *test* hidden, for example, you would type *ATTRIB H+ test*. If you now typed *DIR*, you would not see the *test* file, but if you typed *ATTRIB test*, you would once again see *test*, with the letter H in front of it, letting you know it is a hidden file. A file with the S attribute set will also not show in directory listings, but you can view them with the ATTRIB command and you can remove the System attribute with ATTRIB as well. Table 3-3 shows the various arguments and switches you can use with the ATTRIB command.

Table 3-3   ATTRIB Arguments and Switches

Argument/Switch	Description
R	Read-only file attribute
A	Archive file attribute
S	System file attribute
H	Hidden file attribute
/S	Processes files in all directories in the specified path

DOS File System Utilities

DOS includes two programs that can be used to verify the correctness of the file system. The first one is started with the **CHKDSK** command, which checks the contents of the directories on the disk, and verifies the consistency of the FAT tables with each other and with the contents of the directories. If CHKDSK finds any problems, it displays an error message. You then have the option of letting it fix such problems by using the /F, or Fix option. The most common problems are files with 0 sizes, caused when a file is not properly closed, or chains of clusters that have no directory entries attached. CHKDSK will attempt to solve either problem by converting the parts of the damaged file it can find into files that you can read. Unless you are very lucky, these files in general will be useless to you. If you are desperately trying to recover some text data, however, try loading these files into a word processor or text editor; you may be able to recover some or all of your missing data.

SCANDISK is another utility that conducts some of the same tasks as CHKDISK, but it is a little more advanced. It has a nicer, menu driven user interface, and it can do a surface scan to determine whether you have media problems on a disk. SCANDISK can also copy to another disk the files it is about to manipulate, a useful precautionary step to help you avoid inadvertently losing files or data. Note that DOS and Windows 3.1 rely on you, the user, to know when it is time to use CHKDSK or SCANDISK; there are no automated ways to run these utilities, nor will the operating system ever suggest that you use them. If you have the option, use SCANDISK instead of CHKDSK. It is a little more sophisticated in the options it offers when it comes to file recovery, and the error messages are a little clearer.

If you find that you frequently see errors when you run either CHKDSK or SCANDISK, you should look for a bigger problem. Many times the operator is to blame. Systems that are not used properly—for example because software is not closed correctly—can cause problems on the file system. Often, disks that are about to fail will show small glitches (such as SCANDISK or CHKDSK errors) a long time before they finally fail, so be alert for possible future system failure if you see frequent errors.

DOS versions of SCANDISK and CHKDSK are limited in their ability when run directly from Windows 3.1 or 3.11. For this reason, you should always run them from the DOS prompt in those Windows versions. Windows 95, 98 and NT have their own versions of SCANDISK. It is not a good idea to run DOS versions of CHKDSK or SCANDISK under Windows 95, 98, or NT, nor should you run SCANDISK versions without FAT32 support on FAT32 file systems; serious file system problems may occur if you do.

Another DOS utility, DEFRAG, is used to **defragment** the disk, that is, to rewrite files to disk so that they are all contiguous. You run DEFRAG by typing DEFRAG at the DOS command line prompt. When DOS writes a file to disk, it looks for the first place in the first empty FAT location and uses the cluster indicated there. It continues to use the next empty cluster until there are no more clusters free immediately following the last cluster. At that point, it skips ahead to find the next open cluster. As a result, files written to disk may actually be scattered all over the disk. Imagine a scenario where four small files are written, we will call them A, B, C and D. On an empty disk, these files will occupy sequential clusters on the disk. If file A and C are removed, there will be some open clusters on the disk. If file E, which is larger than A and C combined, is written to the disk, it will start using the clusters formerly occupied by A, then use those formerly used by C, and then continue beyond the clusters occupied by D.

This is actually not a problem. The FAT can keep track of it all, but when the file needs to be written or read, the disk needs to perform more seek operations, which will result in slower access. The DEFRAG utility minimizes access times. This utility will analyze the layout of the files on the disk and reorganize them so that as many as possible are contiguous. This is a good thing for many reasons. It will speed up disk access and make it faster to write new files to the disk. There is, however, always a chance that something could go wrong in the process of moving files. A file that was once intact might be moved to a bad spot on the disk, for example, or the power may fail during defragmentation, or other catastrophes could happen. This is why great care should be taken when the DEFRAG utility is used. A crash during the defragmentation process can result in serious damage.

You should always back up your hard disk (at least data you can't replace in the event of a loss) before you use the DEFRAG utility.

The DEFRAG utility in DOS is menu driven. One of the most useful options on the menu puts all directories at the beginning of the disk. You will find that this can significantly increase access speeds to the disk. When you run DEFRAG you may see that there are certain files it will not touch. This is not a bug in the software. Any file that has its hidden or system flag set will not be touched by DEFRAG. This is because some of these files have to be at a certain location on the disk to work properly. You should not reset the system or hidden bits, as bad things are known to happen when files are moved this way.

Floppy disks typically do not need to be defragmented. The small amount of data on a floppy disk generally does not warrant the time the operation takes. Hard disks should be defragged on a regular basis, depending on the use of the machine. If you rarely use the machine, if you don't often write and rewrite existing files, and you don't install a lot of new software, then defragging your hard disk is of less importance.

As with SCANDISK, you should avoid running DOS versions of DEFRAG under Windows 3.1 and 3.11. It is best to go to a DOS prompt in these scenarios. You should also avoid running versions of DEFRAG from DOS under Windows 95, 98 or NT.

You might use DEFRAG or SCANDISK on a floppy disk if the files have become damaged and you can't read the disk. Sometimes one of these utilities can repair whatever it is that prevents you from accessing the floppy disk. You may not be able to retrieve all of the information on the disk, but you may recover enough with these utilities to make the operation worthwhile.

THE WINDOWS 95/98 FILE SYSTEM

The Windows 95 and Windows 98 file systems are essentially the same. The file system is available in two different versions, depending on the version of Windows you are running and the size of the disk you are using:

- FAT16, similar to the system used in DOS/Win 3.1

- FAT32, a new system introduced in Windows 95, release B

Both FAT16 for Windows 95/98 and FAT32 have features in common with the DOS version of the FAT16 file system, and some new features.

WINDOWS 95/98 FAT16

The way the disk is organized is identical in both the Windows 95 and the DOS file systems. In Windows 95, as in DOS and Windows 3.1, you will find a Master Boot Record, followed by two FAT tables and a root directory. The function of the FAT tables and the root directory is the same as it is in the DOS file system. However, in Windows 95 there is support for long filenames (LFNs). A filename in the Windows 95 file system:

- Can contain as many as 255 characters

- Is not case sensitive

- Can include spaces and several characters that 8.3 names cannot: " / \ [ ] : ; = ,

However, compatibility with the 8.3 naming convention of the DOS file system is maintained. This is done through a clever trick with directory entries that allows them to be converted into 8.3 equivalents. The first of the directory entries looks just like a DOS directory entry, except in place of the filename there is an abbreviated filename. This filename is obtained by taking the first six characters of the old filename, adding a tilde (~), and a number or letter behind it. You can see some samples of how DOS does this in Table 3-4.

Table 3-4   DOS 8.3 Filenames vs. Long Filenames

DOS 8.3 Filename	Expanded Filename
CIRC09~1.TXT	circ09Copyright.txt
CIRC14~1.TXT	circ14Copyright.txt
CIRC15~1.TXT	circ15Copyright.txt
CIRC40~1.TXT	circ40aCopyright.txt
COPYRI~1.HTM	CopyrightFAQ.htm
COPYRI~1.TXT	CopyrightFAQ.txt
COPYRI~2.HTM	CopyrightBASICS.htm
COPYRI~2.TXT	CopyrightBASICS.txt

This process is performed automatically when a file is written to the disk by the Windows 95 operating system. The LFN is stored by using a series of additional directory entries. Each entry can hold up to 13 characters, and the characters are stored in upper and lower case, regardless of how they are entered. Since the characters are stored in **Unicode**, a coding system that allows for representation of any character in any language, it is possible to use any character known to Windows in a filename.

Normally, letters and digits are represented by ASCII (American Standard Code for Information Interchange; pronounced "as-key") values. The problem with this standard is that it uses an entire byte to represent each character, which limits the number of characters that can be represented to 255. This is not enough to handle all the characters needed to represent world languages, including several different alphabets (Greek, Russian, Japanese, and Hindi, for example). ASCII at present deals with this problem by employing many different character sets depending on the characters you're trying to represent. The Unicode consortium, a not-for-profit organization, decided it would be a good idea to have a single, unique code for each possible character in any language currently in use. Unicode is a 16-bit code that allots two bytes for each character, which allows for 65,536 characters to be defined. It includes distinct character codes for all modern languages. To the user who communicates primarily in English, Unicode will not make a big difference, but in this age of worldwide communication, it is becoming a necessity.

The filename directory entries will not be visible to older operating systems such as DOS and Windows 3.1 when they look at a Windows 95 directory, since the attribute bits for Volume, Read only, System and Hidden are set, a combination normally ignored by other operating systems. This is a pretty neat trick, because it allows for the use of LFNs, while still maintaining compatibility with older versions of the operating system.

 Long filenames should be used and manipulated only with utilities that support LFN. DOS and Windows 3.1 utilities that support only 8.3 filenames can destroy LFN information, leaving only the 8.3 equivalents. This also happens if you move files with an older DOS utility, such as an archiving utility. Only the short filenames will appear in the archive. This is one of the common problems with files on disks that are swapped between machines that run Windows 95/98 and Windows 3.11.

As you may imagine, the use of long filenames can eat up a number of directory entries, and as you already know, the number of entries in the root directory on a disk is limited. With this naming convention, a single filename may be up to 255 characters long. In each 32-byte directory entry, only 13 characters are stored, so a filename of full length could end up using as many as 20 directory entries, one for the short name with the real file details, and up to 19 more to store the long name. Figure 3-6 shows how a file named "Filenames that are very long are stored like this in the directory.doc" would be stored. Notice that the bottom entry stores the short (8.3 equivalent) name and actual directory information, while the other six directory entries store the long name.

3

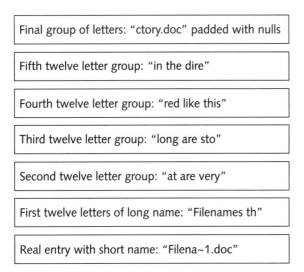

Final group of letters: "ctory.doc" padded with nulls

Fifth twelve letter group: "in the dire"

Fourth twelve letter group: "red like this"

Third twelve letter group: "long are sto"

Second twelve letter group: "at are very"

First twelve letters of long name: "Filenames th"

Real entry with short name: "Filena~1.doc"

Figure 3-6   Long filename storage scheme

This is a fast way to fill up the root directory of a disk! Luckily, only as many directory entries as needed are created, and since most files have shorter names, in many cases, a file will only have two directory entries. This is not a problem in subdirectories, as these can grow to be any size they need to be.

FAT32

To accommodate the increasing capacities of hard disks, and to get around the problem of cluster size (the minimum increment of disk space that can be allocated), the second release of Windows 95 (OSR2) introduced an improved FAT file system called FAT32. FAT32 shares characteristics of FAT16 for Windows 95 (the way the disk is organized with the double FAT structure at the beginning of the disk, followed by a fixed main directory, use of LFNs, and Unicode). FAT32, however, allows partitions of up to 8 GB; blocks can be allocated with clusters as small as 8 KB, and the maximum allowable partition size was raised to 32 GB.

To determine which version of Windows 95 you are running, go to the Start menu, select Settings, Control Panel, then select the System icon. In the General tab, you will see a System heading. The second line will tell you what version you have. Earlier releases have a version number of 4.xxxx, which does not end in a B. If the version number ends in OEM-B, B, OSR-2 or –2, you have the newer, OSR2 release released on or after August 24, 1998. The latter version has support for FAT32, whereas earlier releases do not.

FAT32 works by using a larger number of bits per FAT allocation unit, and is therefore incompatible with other operating systems such as DOS and Windows NT. It is expected that future versions of Windows NT will be made compatible with FAT32.

You can choose the FAT32 file system when the Windows 95/98 FDISK utility is run, but unfortunately the utility does not simply ask if you wish to use FAT32. Instead, you are told that the computer contains a disk larger than 512 MB, and you are asked how you would like to format it. In Windows 98, you can convert a drive to FAT32 from the Start menu by selecting Start, Programs, Accessories, System Tools, and then clicking Drive Converter (FAT32).

 DO NOT use FAT32 if you plan to access your hard disk from other operating systems. At present, it is incompatible with operating systems such as Windows NT and DOS. Use FAT16 instead. Also, do not convert to FAT32 if your drive is compressed, or you plan to compress the drive. If you do convert to FAT32, make a good backup and perform a SCANDISK prior to converting.

WINDOWS 95/98 FILE SYSTEM UTILITIES

The FDISK and FORMAT utilities in Windows 95/98 work identically to those in DOS, as does the text version of SCANDISK that launches automatically at startup if Windows detects an improper previous shutdown. There are now also graphical equivalents of these tools that you can launch from the Windows user environment, such as the Windows 95 Format tool shown in Figure 3-7.

 These and other DOS-compliant utilities are accessed in Windows using the DOS prompt (Start, Programs, MS-DOS Prompt), and entering the filename of the utility, such as FORMAT.

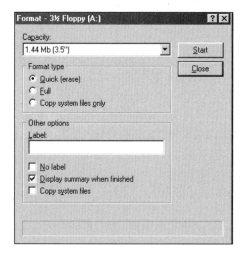

Figure 3-7   Windows 95 FORMAT utility

Although these graphical tools can be used in most cases, during initial installation and sometimes after a system crash you must use the command line or non-graphical versions.

Windows 95/98 includes the capability to create compressed disk volumes. When this option is used, a special device driver is loaded that will compress data as it is written to the disk, and uncompress it as it is being read. Disk compression was originally introduced in DOS, during a time when hard disks were much more expensive and of smaller capacity than today.

 The use of disk compression is not recommended by the authors. If something goes wrong, tools such as SCANDISK cannot be used effectively on compressed volumes, and there have been many problems with compressed volumes that resulted in loss of data.

Windows 95 also has a DEFRAG utility that can be automatically run from the **system scheduler** (a utility provided in some late versions of Windows 95 and as a standard feature of Windows 98), which can be configured to execute other programs at certain times or upon certain system events. In general, it is a good idea to defragment disks on a regular basis, whether automatically or manually. Figure 3-8 shows the Windows 95 DEFRAG utility in action.

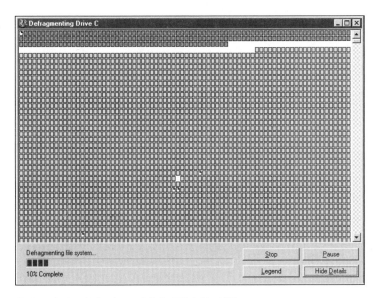

Figure 3-8   Windows 95 DEFRAG utility

 It is VERY IMPORTANT that no other programs are running while the DEFRAG program is running! Windows 95/98 is a multitasking operating system, and if any other program (including your screen saver or Solitaire) tries to access the disk while DEFRAG is running, the defrag process will restart from the beginning. Many people think DEFRAG does not work because it seems to continuously restart from the beginning. For it to operate properly, you must end all programs and make sure the screen saver will not kick in while DEFRAG is running.

Although the Windows 98 file system is essentially the same as the Windows 95 system, Windows 98 serves as a preview platform, of sorts, for the new Windows 2000, which will use the file system features of Windows NT 4 with a Windows 98 style user interface and other desirable features. Windows 2000 is targeted to meet the ease-of-use requirements of individual users as well as the security and stability requirements of business. Read the next section on Windows NT for a preview of the enhanced file system features you can expect in Windows 2000.

THE WINDOWS NT FILE SYSTEMS

Windows NT supports two types of file systems:

- The extended FAT16 system used by Windows 95
- The New Technology File System (NTFS)

EXTENDED FAT16

The extended FAT16 file system under Windows NT has the same functionality as the FAT16 system under Windows 95, and it is possible to have multiple operating systems on one disk (multiboot) with the FAT16 file system. For example, in Windows NT 3.51 and 4.0, you can select either Windows NT or Windows 95 at boot time. In addition to all the features of FAT16 mentioned when we discussed the DOS and Windows 95 file systems, FAT16 under Windows NT uses a few more bytes in the directory entry to store additional information. In addition to the last modified date of a file, Windows NT tracks the file creation date and the last time a file was accessed. This data is simply ignored by DOS and other operating systems using the directory entries, but Windows NT programs that are POSIX compliant can access this data. (**POSIX** stands for **Portable Operating System Interface**, a set of standards designed to guarantee portability of applications among various operating systems.)

NTFS

New Technology File System (NTFS) is the native Windows NT file system. NTFS has many advantages over the FAT system:

- Built-in security features
- Ability to use larger disks and larger files
- Ability to compress file and directory contents on the fly
- Better recoverability and stability
- Less disk fragmentation

From the user perspective, the security features are probably the most significant. In NTFS, parameters can be set on a per-file basis, which means that you can specify which users can have access to specific files and folders. Each file can have an owner, which is a username that is associated with the file. File and folder access can be tailored to fit the needs of an organization. For example, payroll files could be made accessible only to authorized users, or system files on a server could be protected so that only the server administrator could access them.

To add all of this information about files, of course, a lot more information needs to be stored with files in NTFS, such as explicit security settings that will indicate which users or groups of users have permissions to the file. NTFS was designed to be flexible enough to store such parameters about each file in the file system.

 When you install Windows NT you are given the choice between FAT16 and NTFS. You should use NTFS unless you need to share files with FAT16 systems.

To make an NTFS file system you will have to make a partition using the NTF disk utility, just as in previous versions of Windows and DOS. The partition in the NTFS file system may, in theory, be as large as 16 exabytes. (Table 3-5 shows the numerical equivalents of byte measurement terms.)

Table 3-5   Numerical Equivalents

Definition	Numerical Equivalent (number of bytes)
1 kilobyte (KB)	$2^{10} = 1,024$
1 megabyte (MB)	$2^{20} = 1,048,576$
1 gigabyte (GB)	$2^{30} = 1,073,741,824$
1 terabyte (TB)	$2^{40} = 1,099,511,627,776$
1 petabyte (PB)	$2^{50} = 1,125,899,906,842,624$
1 exabyte (EB)	$2^{60} = 1,152,921,504,606,846,976$
1 zetabyte (ZB)	$2^{70} = 1,180,591,620,717,411,303,424$
1 iotabyte (IB)	$2^{80} = 1,208,925,819,614,629,174,706,176$

The FAT file system allows a maximum file size of 4 GB, the size of a FAT partition. NTFS can also use an entire partition to store a file, so in theory it is possible to store a file of 16 exabytes on a file system. In practice the limit to the file size is 2 TB. Obviously, files that size are not practical and will hardly ever be seen. With an eye to the future, it is good to realize that NTFS is forward thinking when it comes to file sizes.

The NTFS system uses clusters, much like the FAT file system. Whereas the number of clusters in the FAT file system is limited to 65,546, NTFS can have as many as 1.07 billion clusters; this means that the cluster size on larger file systems can be smaller. Table 3-6 on the next page shows default cluster sizes.

Table 3-6   Default Cluster Sizes

File System Size	Sectors per Cluster	Cluster Size
512 MB or less	1	512 bytes
512 MB–1 GB	2	1 KB
1 GB–2 GB	4	2 KB
2 GB–4 GB	8	4 KB
4 GB–8 GB	16	8 KB
8 GB–16 GB	32	16 KB
16 GB–32 GB	64	32 KB
Greater than 32 GB	128	64 KB

The way NTFS keeps track of files and clusters is a little different from the FAT file systems. Rather than using a structure of FAT tables and directories, NTFS uses a **Master File Table (MFT)**. Like the FAT and directories, this table is located at the beginning of the partition. The boot sector is located ahead of the MFT, just as it is in the FAT system. Following the MFT, there are a number of system files that the file system uses to make all the features of NTFS work. Note that the MFT in itself is nothing more than a file on the file system, as are all other system files. The second file on the disk is a copy of the first three records of the MFT. This ensures that if the MFT is damaged it can be recreated. File number 5, known as $, contains the entries in the root directory, whereas file number 6, known as $Bitmap, contains data about what clusters on the disk are in use. Normally, the MFT and related files take up about 1 MB of disk space when the disk is initially formatted. As you can see, this would make it unpractical to use NTFS on floppy disks. It is therefore not possible to format floppy disks in NTFS format.

When a file is made in NTFS, a record for that file is added to the MFT. This record contains all standard information such as filename, size, dates and time stamps. It also contains additional attributes, such as security settings and permissions. If there is not enough room in an MFT record to store security settings, the settings that don't fit will be put on another cluster somewhere on the disk, and the MFT record will refer to this information. If a file is very small, there is sometimes enough room in the MFT record to store the file data. If so, NTFS may do so. If not, the system will allocate clusters elsewhere on the disk. The MFT record reflects the sequence of clusters that a file uses. The attributes can generally be repeated; it is possible to have a whole series of different security attributes for different users. It also is possible to have multiple filenames that refer to the same file, a technique known as hard linking. This is a feature sometimes used to make the same file appear in multiple directories without having to allocate disk space for the file more than once.

NTFS, when used with cluster sizes of 4 KB or less, enables you to compress files and directory contents on the fly. This is done by setting the compression attribute in the NT Disk Administrator. Disk Administrator is an NT utility that allows you to perform many disk-related functions such as partitioning and formatting disks, changing disk and partition attributes, performing disk maintenance, and even setting up RAID (Redundant Arrays of

Independent Disks). When a file is written to disk in compressed form, the system performs mathematical operations to reduce the amount of required disk space. There is a penalty in CPU time when this is done, and in most cases using compression is not advisable. However, if you want to archive a large number of files that are seldom accessed, it is a good option.

NTFS also has built-in recoverability features. When file manipulations are performed on the disk, a log is kept of changes that are made. This log is written to the disk as the operation is performed. If the system crashes during such an operation, the system will read the log on startup, and be able to undo the operations in progress, resulting in a stable file system.

After the partition has been created, the file system can be made in either of two ways. As in previous Windows and DOS versions, the command line FORMAT utility can be used, but a better choice is to use the graphical Disk Administrator utility. From this utility, you can select an available partition and create an NTFS file system on the partition.

NTFS offers quite a few features that the FAT16 system does not, but it has a few drawbacks too. On partitions smaller than about 512 MB, NTFS tends to take up more overhead than FAT. NTFS is also slightly more CPU intensive. (On partitions larger than 512 MB, the NTFS system is more efficient than FAT, and it offers all the security and recovery features mentioned above.)

The authors recommend the exclusive use of NTFS file systems on NT machines, with the exception of multiboot machines. This is because NTFS tends to better survive system crashes, has built-in security features, and it gets less fragmented than FAT systems. In today's world of large disks, it also allocates disk space more efficiently. Although Microsoft recommends a non-NTFS file system as the boot partition, and an NTFS partition for the rest of the disk, for the reasons just mentioned, we don't practice this procedure.

The standard utilities that come with Windows NT, such as CHKDSK, can be used on NTFS file systems. Windows NT systems should be defragmented on the basis of how heavily the system is used. NTFS is designed so that it needs to be defragmented less often than FAT under average use. NTFS is smart enough to allocate contiguous disk space based on the amount of space requested, resulting in less fragmentation.

Care should be taken to use only utilities designed to work with NTFS; serious damage could occur if other utilities are used. If utilities designed for use with DOS or Windows 95 or 98 are used on NTFS file systems, they may come to incorrect conclusions regarding file system layout. As a result, they may actually destroy data by managing the file system as if it were a FAT system. This can result in loss of data, damaged files, or even destruction of the complete file system and all of its contents.

One final word of caution about systems that use both NTFS and FAT16 partitions. When you copy a file from an NTFS system to a FAT16 system, the attributes of the file that are not supported on FAT16 will be lost! This may not sound like a big deal, but if you consider that all security settings to that payroll spreadsheet can be lost by copying it to a temporary file on another partition, and then back to the NTFS partition, you may change your mind.

THE UNIX FILE SYSTEM

The UNIX file system works a little differently from anything discussed up to this point. "UNIX file system" is really a misnomer. There are, in reality, many different file systems that can be used. The main difference between UNIX file systems and those covered earlier in the chapter lies in the way information is physically stored on the disk. The most popular file system across UNIX platforms is known as UFS, and that is the one we will detail here.

The UNIX file system uses a concept of **information nodes**, or **inodes**. This concept is shown in Figure 3-9.

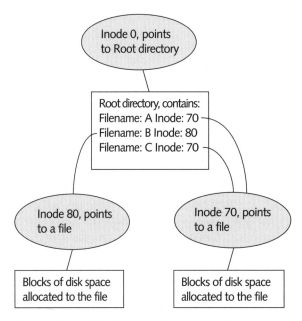

Figure 3-9   UNIX information nodes (inodes) design

Each inode can store some information about a file on the file system. The information stored on an inode identifies the inode number, the owner of the file, the group in which the file is placed, the size of the file, the date the file was created, date last modified and last read, the number of links to this inode, and information regarding the location of the blocks in the file system in which the file is stored. Blocks are typically 4096 or 8192 bytes in size, but the file system is capable of dividing these blocks if required. Groups of blocks for cylinder groups, and large files will be allocated cylinder groups at the same time. The end of files, or small files, will be stored in fragmented blocks. A block can be divided by two repeatedly until the smallest fractional block size is reached, which is typically equal to the size of a single sector on the disk. When the file system is created, a fixed number of inodes is created. Since every unique file uses an inode on the file system, the number of inodes needs to be set high enough so that the system can hold enough files. It is not possible to increase or decrease the number of inodes, so by default a very conservative scheme is used that allocates an inode for each 4 KB of disk space. Note that everything in the UNIX file system is tied to inodes. Inode 0 contains the root of the file system, the jump-off point that serves as the reference for everything else. Inode 1 contains the allocation of all bad sectors on the disk, and inode 2 contains the link to the root directory of the disk. Space is allocated one block, or a fraction of a block, at a time. The directories in this file system are also no more than simple files that have been marked with a directory flag in their inode. The file system itself is identified by the **superblock**. The superblock contains information about the layout of blocks, sectors and cylinder groups on the file system. This information is the key to finding anything on the file system, and it should never change. Without the superblock, the file system cannot be accessed. For this reason, many copies of the superblock are written into the file system at the time of file system creation. If the superblock is destroyed, you can copy one of the superblock copies over the original, damaged superblock to restore access to the file system.

Note that the inode does not contain a filename; the filename is stored in a directory, which in itself is no more than a file. In it is stored the names of the files and the inode to which they are connected. Several directory entries can point to the same inode. This implements a **hard link**, which makes it possible to have one file appear in several directories, or in the same directory under several names, without using a lot of disk space. You can see how this works in Figure 3-10.

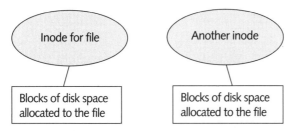

Figure 3-10   UNIX directory showing multiple entries pointing to the same inode

The inode keeps a counter that tells how many directory entries point to a file. Deleting a file is achieved by deleting the last directory entry, which will bring the inode link count down to 0, meaning the file has effectively been removed.

A UNIX system can have a large number of file systems. Unlike the DOS/Windows environment where each file system has to have a letter of the alphabet assigned to it to enable access, UNIX will mount file systems as a sub-file system of the root file system. In UNIX, all file systems are referred to by a path (see Figure 3-11 on next page).

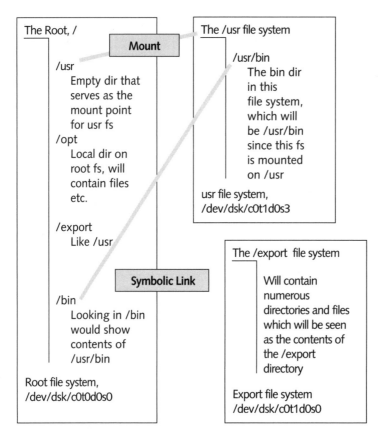

Figure 3-11   UNIX file system path entries

The path starts out with /, which indicates the root directory (inode 1) of the root file system. If other file systems are to be used, a directory is created on the root file system, for example we will call it "usr." Then, using the *mount* command, the UNIX operating system is told to map the root inode of another file system onto the empty directory. This process can be repeated many times, and there is no hard limit to the number of file systems that can be mounted this way, short of the number of inodes in the root file system. Every file in every file system on a computer is thus referred to by a long directory path, and jumping from one file system to another is seamless. The *mount* command has several options; typing it without parameters will result in a printout of the disks that are currently mounted; for each disk you will see the name of the partition and the path on which it was mounted. A typical *mount* listing is shown in Figure 3-12.

```
SunOS 5.6

login: niels
Password:

Welcome to QUAKE.USIT.NET

Last login: Thu Nov 12 21:58:23 from DOTSLASH.MYHOME.ORG
Sun Microsystems Inc.   SunOS 5.6   Generic August
1997

$ mount
/ on /dev/dsk/c2t0d0s0 read/write on Wed Nov 11
17:58:33 1998
/usr on /dev/dsk/c2t0d0s6 read/write on Wed Nov 11
17:58:33 1998
/export on /dev/dsk/c2t0d0s7 read/write on Wed Nov
11 17:58:35 1998
/opt on /dev/dsk/c2t0d0s5 read/write on Wed Nov 11
17:58:35 1998
$
```

Figure 3-12   UNIX drive mount path

Directories in the file system contain series of filenames, and directory names themselves are no more than filenames. UNIX allows you to use extremely long filenames, which may include any character that can be represented by the ASCII character set, including spaces.

 The UNIX operating system and file system treat upper case and lower case characters as different characters; a file named HELLO is a different file than one named hello, which is in turn different from one named Hello. It is therefore extremely important to type UNIX filenames exactly as they appear.

As we already mentioned, a directory is nothing more than a special file. There are several other special files in the UNIX file system. Disks themselves are, for example, referenced by a special inode called a device. There are two types of devices, **raw devices** and **block devices**. A raw device has no logical division in blocks, whereas a block device does. Every device the UNIX machine uses has to be represented by a device inode, whether it is a disk, a serial port or an Ethernet card. These devices have special parameters in the inode that enable the OS to figure out how to get to them. All partitions of all disks will appear as devices. Devices are normally kept in the /dev or /devices directory. When you look at the output of the *mount* command, you will see your disks referenced this way.

There is another special feature of the UNIX file system we should mention here, the symbolic link. As we previously indicated, it is possible to link multiple directory entries to one inode. For this to work, the inode and the directory entry have to be on the same partition. If you want to link a directory entry to a file that is on a different partition, you need to use a feature known as a **symbolic link**. This is a special file, which has a flag set in the inode to identify it as a symbolic link. The content of the file is a path that, when followed, leads to another file. Whenever one of these symbolic links is accessed, the operating system reads the contents of the symbolic link file, and interprets that as if it were the filename typed, referencing the directory entry and then in turn the inode the symbolic link refers to. Note that a hard link, when created, will have to point to a valid inode, and will therefore always be valid. A symbolic link is merely a pointer to a file. It is possible to create symbolic links that point to files that do not exist, or to remove the file to which a symbolic link points without removing the link. Doing this can result in having a symbolic link that, when looked at in a directory, appears to be a valid file, but when opened returns a "no such file" error. Another interesting effect of using links, both hard links and symbolic links, is that it is possible to create loops. You can make a directory **a**, which contains a directory **b**, which contains a link back to directory **a**. This is a feature that is nice, but can end up being extremely confusing. Links are made with the *ln* command and the *−s* option is used to make a symbolic link. The first option is the name of the existing file, followed by the name of the link you wish to create.

As with all other operating systems discussed so far, you first have to partition a disk to use the UNIX file system. The command used to partition the disk differs slightly from one version of UNIX to another. You generally will find that either *fdisk* or *format* will do the job. The utility is generally text based, and it requires you to type commands. Typing *help* at the command prompt will give you an overview of available commands. UNIX will refer to the partition information and other disk information such as the disk label. In the FORMAT utility, you can type *partition* to set to the partition screen. The *print sub* command will show you current partition information, while the other menu commands can be used to adjust individual partitions on the disk.

Great care should be taken when changing partitions! UNIX will let you make any changes you want, without the extensive warnings found in operating systems like DOS and Windows.

After making your changes, the *write* command saves the label to the disk. Most versions of UNIX allow you to write a backup label in addition to the main disk label; this is a good idea, as it can be used to restore the original label if something goes wrong with the disk. The FDISK utility is similar to the partition section of the FORMAT utility. It usually has a *print* command that shows you the contents of the partition table, and other commands to edit partition information and to write the disk label and backup label. The same caution applies here that applies to the partition editing tools in FORMAT. Linux uses an FDISK utility, Solaris uses FORMAT.

Once a partition has been made, it is time to create the file system. To do this, you will need to know the device name of the partition on which you wish to create a file system. This name can be obtained from the *print partition table* command in FDISK or FORMAT. The most convenient way to create a new file system is the *newfs* command. Simply type *newfs* followed by the name of the device. After you have confirmed that you wish to create a new file system, you will see a progress report showing you where copies of the superblocks are written, as well as some information about the cylinder group and the number of inodes. When *newfs* is completed, you can make a mount point for the new file system (remember that a mount point is nothing more than an empty directory) using the *mkdir* command. If, for example, you want to mount the new file system you just created on /dev/rdsk/c0t0d0s1 on the /test mount point, you would type *mkdir /test*. Next, you would mount the file system by typing *mount /dev/rdsk/c0t0d0s1 /test*, and now you would be ready to use the new file system. In both Solaris and Linux, *newfs* is available. The *newfs* command in turn uses the *mkfs* program to actually create the file system. In UNIX varieties where *newfs* is not available, *mkfs* should be used instead. Use of *mkfs* is less desirable, since it will require the user to specify many parameters such as the size of the file system, the block size, number of inodes, number of superblock copies and their location, and a few others depending on the version of UNIX. The NEWFS utility takes care of all these details automatically.

UNIX is very picky when it comes to file system consistency. If it finds problems on the file system in the inodes, superblock, or directory structures, it will shut down. When you save a file to disk, the system will first store part of the data in memory, until it has time to write it to disk. If for some reason your computer stops working before the data is written to disk, you could end up with a damaged file system. This is why UNIX machines should always be shut down using the proper shutdown commands, which will make sure all data is stored on disk before the machine is brought down. In normal operation, all data waiting to be saved to disk in memory will be written to disk every 30 seconds. You can manually force a write of all data in memory by using the *sync* command. When the system is properly shut down, the file systems will all be unmounted. A flag will be set in the superblock of each file system to indicate that the file system was properly closed and does not need to be checked at startup. Whenever the machine starts up, UNIX will check the file systems to make sure they are all working properly. To do this, it will verify the integrity of the superblock, the inodes, all cluster groups and all directory entries. The program that performs this operation is the **file system checker**, also known as FSCK.

 You can manually run FSCK at any time to perform file system checks after the system is up, but take great care when doing this. If data on the disk is changed while an FSCK is in progress, the results may be disastrous. The most common problems found when FSCK is run are unlinked inodes, directory entries with no associated inodes, and wrong free block counts. All of these can be a result of a system that was not properly shut down. If these errors occur frequently, hardware failure may be imminent.

Typically, UFS file systems can be up to 4 GB in size, but by using larger block sizes, the systems can be made much larger. Depending on the implementation of UNIX being used, and the exact UFS version in use, it is possible to create file systems in excess of 32 exabytes. Typically, the maximum file size is 2 GB, but in some versions of UNIX it is possible to use special libraries that allow for the creation of larger files. There are many other optional file system types, Linux for example has the Extended File System (extfs) and the Extended File System Version 2 (ext2fs), and many new file systems are being added. Check your UNIX manuals to find out more about the particular file systems your implementation supports. Most of these systems use the standard commands discussed here.

THE MACINTOSH FILE SYSTEM

The original **Macintosh Filing System (MFS)** of 1984 was limited to keeping track of 128 documents, applications, or folders. This was a reasonable limit when the only storage device was a 400 KB floppy disk drive. As larger disks became available, the need for directories and subdirectories became obvious and Apple responded with the **Hierarchical Filing System (HFS)** in 1986.

Like FAT16, HFS divides a volume (the Mac term for a disk or disk partition) into at most 2^{16} (65,536) units. On PC systems, these units are called clusters. On the Mac they are called **allocation blocks**, but the principle is the same. Interestingly, while UNIX, DOS, and Windows report file sizes in terms of their actual physical size, the Macintosh operating system typically reports file sizes in terms of logical size, based on the number of allocation blocks occupied by the file. The only way to find out the physical size is to use a third-party utility or the Mac's Get Info command (Figure 3-13). The Info screen shows logical file size, with physical file size in parentheses. The file in Figure 3-13 is on an HFS-formatted 2.9 GB partition.

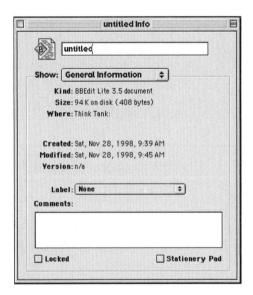

Figure 3-13   Macintosh Info dialog box

In 1998, Apple released Mac OS 8.1, which introduced a new disk format, Mac OS Extended Format, commonly referred to as HFS+. Like the Windows NT NTFS, the new format increases the number of allocation blocks per volume to 2^{32}. This creates smaller allocation blocks (clusters) and more efficient disk utilization. Systems using Mac OS 8.1 or later can format disks in either Mac OS Standard (HFS) or Mac OS Extended (HFS+) formats. However, Macintoshes with pre-8.1 versions of the OS can't read disks in Extended format. Floppy disks and other volumes smaller than 32 MB must continue to use Standard format.

The first two sectors of a Mac-formatted disk are the boot sectors, or **boot blocks** in Macintosh terminology. The boot blocks identify the filing system being used, the names of important system files, and other important information. The boot blocks are followed by the **volume information block**, which points to other important areas of information, such as the location of the system files and the catalog and extents trees.

The **catalog b-tree** is the list of all files on the volume. It keeps track of a file's name, its logical location in the folder structure, its physical location on the disk surface, and the location and size of the file's data fork and resource forks (to be discussed later). The extents b-tree keeps track of the location of the file fragments, or extents.

Macintoshes can read and write disks from other operating systems. For instance, Macs can read ISO 9660 CD-ROMs using the ISO 9660 CD-ROM driver. Macs can read all manner of DOS- and Windows-formatted disks, from floppy and Zip disks to almost any kind of SCSI device, thanks to Apple's PC Exchange control panel. Prior to OS 8.5, PC Exchange assumed that PCs used short filenames and truncated Mac filenames to 8.3 format when writing to PC-formatted media. Beginning with OS 8.5 the Mac will write files with long names to PC disks without truncation.

In terms of filename length, the Mac OS has always supported what might be called **"medium" filenames** of up to 31 characters in length. Apple is gradually incorporating Unicode support into their operating system. HFS+ (Extended format) volumes can support Unicode characters in filenames. The use of the period as the first character in a filename is discouraged, because older versions of the operating system used the period as the first character of invisible driver files (notably ".sony" for the Sony 3.5-inch floppy disk drives). Any character may be used in a filename except the colon, which is used internally by the Mac OS as a directory separator, equivalent to slashes on other OSs. It's for this reason that Macintosh paths are written as colon-separated entities like this:

Hard Drive:System Folder:Preferences:Finder Prefs

UNIX and Windows operating systems use filename extensions such as .TXT and .GIF to identify file types. The Mac uses invisible **type codes** and **creator codes**. As an example, files created with Apple's SimpleText text editor have a type code of TEXT, and a creator code of ttxt. When a user double-clicks such a file, the Mac knows it needs to open the file with an application (type code APPL) with a creator code of ttxt. SimpleText, not surprisingly, has a type code of APPL and a creator code of ttxt. Type and creator codes are normally invisible to the user, but they can be viewed and modified using Apple's ResEdit program or a variety of shareware programs.

The type and creator codes facilitate the Mac's use of icons. Documents do not store their own icons. Instead, the Mac gets the icon from the creating application. Instead of accessing the application each time the icon needs to be displayed, the Mac stores the icons and file associations in invisible files called the desktop databases. Each disk or volume has its own desktop databases. "Rebuilding the desktop" on a Macintosh rebuilds these database files, and is a common troubleshooting step when icons are displaying incorrectly. You can rebuild the desktop on a disk at startup by holding the command and option keys. For removable media, hold the command and option keys before inserting the disk.

One way in which Macintosh files are unique is that Mac files can contain two parts, or forks: the data fork and the resource fork. The **data fork** contains frequently changing information (such as word processing data), while the **resource fork** contains information that is fixed (such as a program's icons, menu resources, and splash screens). One advantage of resource forks for programmers is that they modularize the program. For instance, it becomes very easy to change the text of a warning dialog or the name of a menu item without having to change the underlying code, so customization and internationalization are easier. Most Mac documents contain only a data fork. Traditionally, Mac applications contained only a resource fork, but programs written for PowerPC-equipped Macintoshes store PowerPC code in the data fork.

One clever use of the data and resource forks is to store style information in a plain text file. The text is stored in the data fork, while the style information (font face, color, font size, italics, etc.) is stored in the resource fork. The advantage of this system is that the text file can still be read by any Mac text editing program, even if it doesn't understand the style information, and by any text editor on another operating system. This system is used by Apple's SimpleText program, America Online's text editor, and some other Mac programs.

Apple's free ResEdit utility can edit file resources. Using ResEdit, a programmer can modify a program's version number, splash screens, default memory allocation, icons, menu items, window resources, dialog text, and many other properties (see Figure 3-14). Users can also use ResEdit to modify the way programs operate.

Figure 3-14   Mac SimpleText resources, as seen through ResEdit

The fact that Mac files have invisible type and creator codes and two forks can create problems when storing files on non-Macintosh servers, or transferring files over the Internet. The need to store Mac files on non-Mac computers has led to a number of Mac file formats used on bulletin board services, online services, and the Internet. One of these formats is MacBinary, which joins the two forks into one and safely stores the type and creator codes and finder flags. For files that must be transferred through seven-bit gateways (such as Usenet news), the preferred format is **BinHex**. Like uuencode (a format used frequently in email applications to convert binary files into text files transferable in e-mail systems), BinHex transforms all files into seven-bit files using the ASCII character set. Like MacBinary, BinHex preserves the two forks, the type and creator codes, and the finder flags. BinHex files can be identified by the .hqx filename extension.

Folders can be created using the New Folder command in the Finder's File menu, and in the Save and Save As dialogs in most applications. All volumes have two special, invisible folders: Trash and Desktop. If you move a file's icon from a floppy disk to the desktop, the file still resides on the floppy disk's Desktop folder. Likewise, you can move the file's icon to the Trash can without deleting it, and it will still reside on the floppy disk's Trash folder. You can prove this to yourself by ejecting the floppy disk and inserting it in another Macintosh. The files will appear on the desktop and the Trash can will bulge!

Apple's equivalent of the UNIX link and Windows shortcut is the **alias**, introduced in System 7.0 in 1991. Files, folders, applications, and disks can be aliased. Aliased disks can be placed in the Apple menu for access to all files on the disk through the Apple menu. The system-level Alias Manager keeps track of the original, even if it is moved or renamed. The word "alias" is tacked onto the filename when the alias is created, and the filename is presented in italicized text. Beginning in OS 8.5, aliases also have small arrows on their icons, similar to shortcuts in Windows 95.

The Mac OS ships with two basic disk utilities: Disk First Aid and Drive Setup. **Drive Setup**, a replacement for the older Apple HD Setup, formats and partitions Apple IDE and SCSI hard drives. Drive Setup checks the hard drive for a ROM that is present in drives shipped with Apple computers. If the ROM is not present, Drive Setup will not recognize the drive. Third-party hard drives must be formatted with third-party utilities, such as FWB Hard Disk Toolkit or La Cie Silverlining. **Disk First Aid** repairs minor hard drive problems, and can be used on any type of disk, whether or not it has an Apple ROM.

Most versions of the Mac OS have included some sort of find file utility. Mac OS 8.5 takes this one step further with the **Sherlock** program. Sherlock can search disks for filenames and for text within files (see Figure 3-15 on the next page). These operations are extremely fast because Sherlock pre-indexes local disks, just as search engines index web pages. Because indexing takes significant processor time, indexing can be scheduled for times when the computer is not in use. Sherlock also functions as a program for querying multiple Internet search engines or the site search engines available on many web sites.

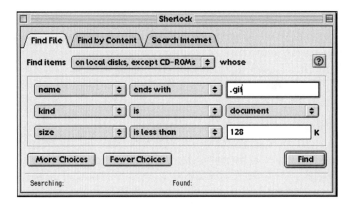

Figure 3-15   Mac OS 8.5's Sherlock search utility in file search mode

When the Mac is shut down normally using the Finder's Shut Down command, a flag is set on the hard drive. In the event of a crash or forced reboot, this flag is not set. At the next startup the Mac will see that the computer was not shut down properly and will run a disk integrity check.

The Mac is extremely versatile at booting from different devices. Like other operating systems, the Mac will boot from a floppy disk inserted during the boot sequence. If the floppy disk does not contain a valid System Folder, the Mac spits it out and continues searching for a bootable device. The Mac will also boot from various SCSI devices (Zip drives, Syquest drives, etc.) selected in the Startup Disk control panel. Macs since the early 1990s have been able to boot from a CD-ROM drive. To boot from a CD, either press the "C" key while booting up, or insert the CD, select it in the Startup Disk control panel, and reboot. Pressing the Shift-Option-Delete-Apple (SODA) keys during the boot sequence will bypass the internal hard drive and boot from the next drive in the SCSI chain.

CHAPTER SUMMARY

A file system is a design for storing and managing files on disk media. All operating systems use a particular file naming convention, and offer ways to partition and format disks, compress and defragment files, provide file and data integrity, and manage storage media.

In DOS and Windows 3.1x, the file allocation table (FAT) file system uses a file allocation table to store information about files. The FDISK and FORMAT utilities are used with these operating systems to partition and format disks, the CHKDSK and SCANDISK utilities give information about files and disks and check for disk and file integrity, and the DEFRAG utility defragments files.

The FAT32 file system was introduced in Windows 95 and is also used in Windows 98. FAT 32 gives the capability to use long filenames, as opposed to the earlier "8.3" (eight characters and a three-character extension) convention. Windows 95/98 also include FDISK, FORMAT, SCANDISK, and DEFRAG utilities.

The file system for Windows NT is called NTFS, but FAT32 is also supported. NTFS is more a more stable and secure file system than FAT, and in general can handle larger disk and file sizes. UNIX file systems use information nodes (inodes) to organize information about files. A UNIX system can have a large number of file systems mounted as subdirectories of the root. Different varieties of UNIX use different file system utilities, such as *fdisk* (Linux) and *format* (Solaris) to partition and format disks. The *fsck* (file system checker) utility is used to verify the integrity of UNIX file systems.

The Macintosh OS uses the Hierarchical Filing System (HFS). Like FAT, HFS divides a disk or disk partition (called a volume) into allocation units called allocation blocks. Unlike FAT, HFS has always allowed the use of long filenames. The HFS+ (OS Extended Format) file system was introduced in 1998 with Mac OS 8.1. Like the Windows NT NTFS, HFS+ makes more efficient utilization of disk space and supports larger disk sizes. The Mac ResEdit utility is used to edit file resources. Two basic disk utilities are Disk First Aid and Drive Setup.

KEY TERMS

- **active partition** — The logical portion of a hard disk drive that is currently being used to store data. In a PC system, usually the partition that contains the bootable operating system.

- **alias** — In the Macintosh file system, a feature that presents an icon that represents an executable file. Equivalent to the UNIX Link and the Windows Shortcut.

- **allocation blocks** — In the Macintosh file system, a division of hard disk data. Equivalent to the Windows disk cluster. Each Macintosh volume is divided into 2^{16} (65,535) individual units.

- **ATTRIB** — A DOS command that is used to review or change file attributes.

- **bad clusters** — On a hard disk drive, areas of the surface that cannot be used to store data safely. Bad clusters are usually identified by the FORMAT command or one of the hard drive utilities such as CHKDSK or SCANDISK.

- **BinHex** — In the Macintosh file system, a seven-bit file format used to transmit data across network links.

- **block allocation** — A hard disk configuration scheme where the disk is divided into logical blocks, which in turn are mapped to sectors, heads, and tracks. Whenever the operating system needs to allocate some disk space, it allocates it based on a block address.

- **block devices** — In the UNIX file system, devices that are divided or configured into logical blocks. See also raw devices.

- **boot block** — In a Mac-formatted disk, the first of two important system sections on the disk. The boot blocks identify the filing system being used, the names of important system files, and other important information. (See also volume information block, the second system section).

- **catalog b-tree** — In the Macintosh file system, a list of all files on a given volume. Similar to a directory in the Windows file system.

- **CHKDSK** — A DOS external command (utility) that analyzes a specified disk drive to determine drive configuration and to locate and repair, where possible, bad disk locations.

- **creator codes** — Hidden file characteristics in the Macintosh file system that indicate the program (software application) that created the file.

- **data fork** — That portion of a file in the Macintosh file system that stores the variable data associated with the file. Data fork information might include word processing data, spreadsheet information, and so on.

- **directory** — A special file on a disk drive that is used to store information about other data stored on the disk. A directory typically records a filename, a physical starting and ending point on the disk, file type, and file size.

- **Disk First Aid** — A Macintosh utility program that analyzes a Macintosh hard drive and files. It is useful in overall maintenance of a Mac hard drive.

- **Drive Setup** — A Macintosh file system utility that helps configure Macintosh hard drives.

- **extension** — In DOS, that part of a filename that typically identifies the type of file associated with the name. File extensions traditionally are three characters long and include standard notations such as .SYS, .EXE, .BAT, and so on.

- **FDISK** — An external DOS command (utility) that is used to partition a hard disk drive or to change or review existing partitions.

- **File Allocation Table (FAT)** — A file management system that defines the way data is stored on a disk drive. The FAT stores information about file size and physical location on the disk.

- **file attributes** — File characteristics stored with the filename in the disk directory that specify certain storage and operational parameters associated with the file. Attributes are noted by the value of specific data bits associated with the filename. File attributes include hidden, read only, archive, and so on.

- **file system** — A design for storing and managing files on a disk drive. File systems are associated with operating systems such as UNIX, DOS, and Windows.

- **file system checker (FSCK)** — In UNIX, a program utility that checks the integrity of the file system.

- **FORMAT** — A program utility in DOS, UNIX and other operating systems that is used to prepare a disk drive for data storage. The FORMAT utility usually removes any existing data, checks the disk for bad storage locations and can optionally install some operating system files.

- **hard link** — In Windows NT, a file management technique that permits multiple directory entries to point to the same physical file.

- **Hierarchical Filing System (HFS)** — An early Apple Macintosh file system file storage method that uses hierarchical directory structure. Developed in 1986 to improve file support for large storage devices.

- **information node (inode)** — In UNIX, a system for storing key information about files. Inode information includes the inode number, the owner of the file, the file group, the file size, the file creation date, plus the date the file was last modified and last read, the number of links to this inode, and information regarding the location of the blocks in the file system in which the file is stored.

- **large block allocation (LBA)** — In DOS, a technique to allow the creation of files larger than 512 MB. With LBA, DOS is told that the sector size of the hard disk is greater than 512 bytes per sector, which results in the ability to have much larger file systems.

- **Macintosh Filing System (MFS)** — The original Macintosh filing system, introduced in 1984. MFS was limited to keeping track of 128 documents, applications, or folders.

- **Master Boot Record (MBR)** — An area of a hard disk that stores partition information about that disk. MBRs are not found on disks that do not support multiple partitions.

- **Master File Table (MFT)** — In Windows NT, a file management system similar to the FAT and directories used in DOS and Windows. This table is located at the beginning of the partition. The boot sector is located ahead of the MFT, just as it is in the FAT system.

- **medium filenames** — In the Macintosh file system, the 31-character filename length that Macintosh OS has supported from the beginning.

- **Mkdir** — An operating system utility program that is used to create a new directory.

- **New Technology File System (NTFS)** — The 32-bit file storage system that is the native system in Windows NT (Windows NT also supports the DOS FAT system).

- **NEWFS** — A program utility in UNIX used to create a new file system.

- **partitioning** — A hard disk management technique that permits the installation of multiple file systems on a single disk. Or, the configuration of multiple logical hard drives that use the same file system on a single physical hard drive.

- **Portable Operating System Interface (POSIX)** — A UNIX standard designed to ensure portability of applications among various versions of UNIX.

- **raw devices** — In the UNIX file system, devices that have not been divided into logical blocks.

- **resource fork** — In the Macintosh file system, that portion of a file that contains fixed information such as a program's icons, menu resources, and splash screens.

- **SCANDISK** — A DOS and Windows utility that is used to locate bad disk drive storage locations and to mark and repair these areas.

- **Sherlock** — In the Macintosh file system Version 8.5, a file search utility that can find filenames or text within files.

- **SimpleText** — A Macintosh utility program for text editing.

- **status bits** — Bits used as part of a directory entry to identify the type of filename contained in each entry. The status bits in use are Volume, Directory, System, Hidden, Read-Only, and Archive.

- **superblock** — In the UNIX file system, a special data block that contains information about the layout of blocks, sectors and cylinder groups on the file system. This information is the key to finding anything on the file system, and it should never change.

- **switch** — An operating system command option that changes the way certain commands function. Command options, or switches, are usually entered as one or more letters separated from the main command by a forward slash (/).

- **symbolic link** — A special file in the UNIX file system that permits a directory link to a file that is on a different partition. This is a special file, which has a flag set in the inode to identify it as a symbolic link. The contents of the file is a path that, when followed, leads to another file.

- **system scheduler** — A Windows utility program that can be configured to execute other programs at a specified time or at the completion of other system events.

- **type** — In the Macintosh file system, embedded file information that denotes what applications were used to create the files. Mac OS type codes are used in much the same way as Windows file extensions that identify file types with .TXT, .DOC and other extensions.

- **Unicode** — A 16-bit character code that allows for the definition of up to 65,536 characters.

- **volume information block** — In a Mac-formatted disk, the second of two system sectors (see also boot block, the first sector). The volume information block points to other important areas of information, such as the location of the system files and the catalog and extents trees.

- **Volume Label** — A series of characters that identifies a disk drive or the file system it is using.

REVIEW QUESTIONS

1. A file system is sometimes compared to a conventional office filing cabinet. Explain how the various components of a filing cabinet—cabinet, drawers, folders, and documents—relate to a computer file system.

2. For a computer file system to manage information, the data must first be converted to _____ format.

3. Software applications that use data on a disk in this special format must conduct one crucial operation when using this information. What is the process that application programs conduct to make stored data useful?

4. A special file on each disk drive stores information about other files on the disk. This special file is called the disk _____.

3

5. File systems manage disk files with a scheme called block allocation. Logical blocks are divided into other data structures, including (give all that apply)

   a. Sectors

   b. Sections

   c. Heads

   d. Tracks

   e. Ports

6. Disk allocation tables are used to

   a. Allocate certain portions of a disk drive for the use of specific software applications.

   b. Allocate certain portions of a disk drive for the use of specific users.

   c. Track the location of data stored on the disk and facilitate storing and retrieving data from the disk.

   d. Allocate different disk drives in a hardware system to different file systems.

7. A technique for managing hard disks that enables the installation of multiple file systems on a single physical drive or that lets you configure multiple logical drives is called

   a. Disk partitioning

   b. Disk allocation

   c. Disk formatting

   d. None of the above

8. A DOS/Windows file system can support up to _____ disk partitions.

9. One DOS/Windows disk partition can be used to store up to two more _____ partitions.

10. In a DOS/Windows system, physical and logical disk drives are designated by what special characters?

11. A DOS file system reserves the first two drive designations for what kind of storage device?

12. The graphical Windows 95 operating system has a very different file system design from the all-text-based DOS file system. True or False?

13. If you create filenames in Windows that contain more than eight characters, you won't be able to see them or access them in the DOS 8.3 file system. True or False?

14. For years computer character data was represented in ASCII format. What do the letters ASCII stand for?

15. A newer text standard called Unicode is now used by many operating systems. What is the main difference between ASCII and Unicode?

16. Newer operating systems support long filenames (LFNs), a useful user feature. However, LFNs take up a large amount of directory space. Explain why.

17. With later versions of Windows 95, Microsoft introduced a new file system called FAT32. What are the main advantages of this new design? Disadvantages?

18. Windows 95 and other operating systems include disk compression utilities that can provide up to twice as much storage on existing hard drives. List some of the disadvantages to using disk compression to increase storage space.

19. The Windows NT NTFS file system has some similarities to FAT32, but it also offers some desirable enhancements. Discuss a few of the major differences.

20. The Windows NT system that tracks directory entries is known as

   a. Master Boot Record (MBR)

   b. Master File Record (MFR)

   c. Master File Table (MFT)

   d. File Table Master (FTM)

21. Microsoft recommends that Windows NT systems be configured with a 16-bit boot partition and the rest of the hard drives configured in the 32-bit NTFS system. Your authors recommend against this practice. Discuss the advantages and disadvantages of the Microsoft-recommended configuration.

22. The UNIX file system uses a file system concept called

   a. Information node (inode)

   b. UNIX nodes (unode)

   c. Directory List Notation (DLN)

   d. None of the above

23. The UNIX file system can cause multiple directory entries to point to the same physical file. True or False?

24. A special link in UNIX permits directory pointers across partitions. This link is called a _____ link.

25. The practical size limit on UNIX files is a maximum of _____ MB.

26. A later Macintosh file system that addressed hierarchical directory structures was the _____, abbreviated as _____.

27. DOS and Windows file systems use disk clusters as one data organization design. In the Macintosh file system this disk subdivision is called _____.

28. Macintosh files contain two structures, or forks. These are the data fork, which contains variable information and the _____ fork, which contains fixed data about individual files.

29. In the Macintosh file system, file type codes are used to _____.

30. In the Macintosh file system, file creator codes do what?

Hands-on Projects

Project 3-1

The DOS utility FDISK is used to partition one or more hard drives. FDISK sets the file system type and sets the size of each system by type. However, FDISK also can be used to help you understand the existing structure of your hard drive or drives.

To view existing partition information on a DOS or Windows file system:

1. Start up DOS or open a DOS window (**Start**, **Programs**, **MS-DOS Prompt**) in Windows.

2. At the DOS prompt type **FDISK** and press **Enter**. If you have a hard drive larger than 512 MB, you may see the screen that asks if you wish to enable large disk support.

3. Choose **Y** from this screen if you have a large disk drive to display the main FDISK screen, otherwise press **N**.

4. Choose menu item **4** to display current partition information. You may see only a single partition if you have only one disk drive and it is configured as one large partition. However, if you have a hard drive larger than 4 GB you probably will see at least two partitions. Can you think why? What would you have to do to increase the partition size beyond 4 GB?

5. Press **Esc** twice to exit FDISK without making any changes.

DO NOT CHANGE YOUR HARD DISK'S PARTITION INFORMATION! If you do, you may have to re-install your operating system and all applications. Be sure to press Esc to exit the FDISK program.

Project 3-2

You learned earlier in this book how to use CHKDSK to find out key information about your hard drive. CHKDSK also can repair certain hard disk problems. However, later versions of DOS and Windows include a better utility, SCANDISK, for finding and repairing disk problems.

To use SCANDISK to look for hard disk problems:

1. Exit all other running programs while SCANDISK is running. Do you remember why?

2. Point to the **Start** menu in Windows 95 or Windows 98.

3. Point to **Programs**, **Accessories** and then **System Tools** and click **Scandisk** from the menu. The SCANDISK screen appears.

4. Choose the hard drive you want to scan. In most cases you can accept the program's suggested drive.
5. Click to check **Automatically fix errors** if you want the program to correct errors it finds automatically.
6. Click the **Start** button to begin the disk scanning.
7. Watch the progress reporting screens as the program runs through its fairly extensive checklist. The feedback you see on this screen gives you a good idea of what SCANDISK does, and it also shows you size and cluster information about your hard drive.

PROJECT 3-3

Windows 95 and 98, NT and UNIX systems include automatic checking routines to help avoid data loss or file damage. These utilities will run automatically any time you fail to shut down your computer in the proper manner. You may already have seen how these programs work, but you can force them to run so you can see how these operating systems automatically handle potential problems.

To force your operating system to launch some automatic diagnostics:

Caution: This is basically a safe test. Even though it is not recommended that you shut down a computer in this way, it is doubtful that you will damage any data. However, don't do this test with a UNIX machine unless you are very familiar with UNIX in general and the configuration of the test machine in particular.

1. Close all running programs.
2. Make sure no other users are attached to the computer you are about to test. If so, ask them to log off temporarily.
3. Push the system hardware reset button or simply turn off the power.
4. If you turned off the power, wait about 15 seconds and turn the power back on. If you pushed the reset button, the system will automatically restart.
5. Monitor the boot process. At a certain point you will see a screen informing you that the computer was not shut down properly. A disk scanning utility will be launched and the drive and programs tested before the computer reboots.

PROJECT 3-4

Unlike DOS, Windows, and UNIX file systems, the Macintosh file system uses two separate file units to define file type and contents. These units are the data fork and the resource fork. Normally only applications interpret this information. It is transparent to the user. A free

Macintosh utility called ResEdit lets you view this information and even change it if you like. You can view file information with ResEdit and learn a lot about the way the Macintosh tracks file data.

 We don't recommend that you make changes to information you see in ResEdit, unless you have a fair amount of experience and in no case unless you have made a backup copy of the file you are changing.

To open ResEdit and study file information:

1. Locate the ResEdit application icon on your Macintosh desktop, hard drive or system folder.

 If you don't find a copy of ResEdit in your operating system utilities, you can download a copy from Apple. Point your Web browser to *www.apple.com* and search for ResEdit. You will be referred to several download sites where you can secure your own copy of this interesting utility.

2. Double-click the **ResEdit** icon to launch the application. You will see a jack-in-the-box opening screen with the program version number and other data.

3. Navigate to a folder that contains the application program or file you want to view in ResEdit.

4. Click the program name to select it and click **Open**. You should see a screen of resource icons.

5. Double-click one or more of these icons to view their contents. You will see different items depending on the type of file you are viewing. Among the items you might see are program startup icons, menu screens, sound icons, and so on.

PROJECT 3-5

 Aliases are among the more useful Macintosh file system features. Like shortcuts in Windows, aliases let you create custom icons and names to place on your desktop, menus or elsewhere to point to other applications. Aliases give you multiple ways to access the same application, and let you easily place these access points at various locations to help you get to them when you need them.

To create a program alias in the Macintosh file system:

1. Click once on an application icon to select it.
2. Choose **File**, **Make Alias** from the menu.
3. Type an alias name and other information you want on the Make Alias dialog.
4. Drag the alias icon to the location where you want it to reside.

Although an alias only points to the actual application, you can treat an alias like an application. For example, you can drag a file onto an alias icon to open the file with the application to which the alias points. You can also create an alias for a folder instead of an application. This will let you save files into a folder by choosing its alias. You can also create an alias from a network connection so you can open the server it represents by simply double-clicking the alias icon wherever it resides.

CASE PROJECT

1. As network administrator for Action Software Inc., you have successfully convinced your system planners and budget masters that the network must be expanded to include two new Windows NT machines and a UNIX workstation. The new machines will serve as network Web, database, and e-mail servers and for platform-specific program development. The company's chief technical officer (CTO) has instructed you to use the NTFS file system on the Windows NT machines, and as part of the overall system upgrade, to convert your existing Windows 95 and Windows 98 machines to FAT32 file structure. You agree in principle with this decision, but you disagree with the CTO's request to create multiple partitions on each of the 9 GB hard drives that came with the new computers. You are drafting a memo arguing for keeping a single partition on all drives.

   a. What are the advantages to keeping a single disk partition on large drives such as these?

   b. Are there different issues in dealing with FAT32 as opposed to NTFS?

   c. Are there any compatibility issues with the UNIX workstation when all of the machines are connected in a network?

   d. Can you think of any disadvantages to keeping a single large partition on the new machines?

   e. Assuming you agree to multiple partitioning, can you think of designs that might be better than others? In other words, would you create two 4.5 GB partitions on each drive, or would you arrange the drives in another scheme?

INITIAL INSTALLATION

This chapter looks at what is involved in the initial setup of various operating systems. An overview of the installations is given in the text portion of the chapter, and you can step through actual installations in the Hands-on Projects at the end of the chapter. By the end of the chapter, you will know what to expect when you sit down at a machine to perform an operating system installation, what to watch for, and what to avoid during operating system installation. It is beyond the scope of this book to cover all possible options and settings, so only typical installations are covered.

AFTER READING THIS CHAPTER AND COMPLETING THE EXERCISES YOU WILL BE ABLE TO:

- Understand the overall process of operating system installation
- Prepare for operating system installation
- Install the MS-DOS operating system
- Install Windows 3.11 for Workgroups and understand the differences between this and the MS-DOS installation
- Install Windows 95 and Windows 98 and understand the various options presented during the installation
- Install Windows NT Server and Workstation, understand options presented during the install, and understand the differences between these versions of Windows NT
- Install UNIX variety Linux and understand the basic differences between this installation and those of other operating systems covered in this chapter
- Install Mac OS version 8.5 and understand some of the options you have during the installation

Installing an Operating System

The process of installing operating systems varies from operating system to operating system, but there are certain features common to all installations. Operating system installation can be divided into three general stages: preparation for installation, the installation itself, and any required or optional steps following installation.

Preparing for installation involves the following:

- Checking that the computer(s) on which you will install the operating system meet or exceed the hardware and/or software requirements for the operating system

- Ensuring that all equipment (computer and peripheral devices) is powered on and operating correctly

- Having the appropriate floppy disks or CDs on hand, including disks or CDs for operating system installation, and any floppy disks needed during the installation to create startup disks

- Understanding the general features of the operating system you are installing so you can decide which modules to install and which to omit

- Having the most up-to-date device drivers for your CD-ROM, SCSI devices, printers, etc.—usually from the manufacturer's disk that came with the device, or downloaded from the manufacturer's Web site

- Having pertinent information available about your computer and peripheral devices

During the installation, you may have to provide some or all of the following information:

- Where (in which directory or path) to install the operating system

- What type of installation you wish to perform (typical/default, portable, compact, custom, etc.)

- Information about you, your company, and your computer (your name, company name, computer or workgroup name)

- Licensing information (usually a license key or ID number), verifying your right to install the OS

- Which components of the operating system you want to install

Some operating systems (Windows 95 and 98, Mac OS) can automatically detect and configure devices such as printers, mice, network cards, video cards, and sound cards. In other operating systems (DOS, UNIX), these devices must be configured manually.

Installation programs can be primarily text-based, (MS-DOS and UNIX), use a combination of text-based and GUI (Windows 3.1, Windows NT), or use an automated "wizard" to step you through the process (Windows 95/98 and NT, Mac OS). Operating systems can be installed from floppy disks or CD-ROM, and in many cases can be installed over a network. (Network installations are not covered in this book.)

The installation itself consists of some or all of the following general functions:

- Loading/running the installation program

- Gathering system information

- Determining which elements of the operating system are to be installed

- Configuring devices and drivers

- Creating a floppy disk used to boot the operating system in an emergency

- Copying operating system files onto your computer

- Restarting the system and finalizing configuration of devices

Not all of these functions are performed in every operating system installation. For some operating systems, devices and drivers are installed after the operating system installation (MS-DOS), for others, device/driver configuration is part of the OS installation. Windows 95 and 98 have a feature called **Plug and Play** that automatically configures internal and external devices as part of the installation, and at startup whenever a new device is added.

After the operating system is installed, you may have to configure memory for optimum performance, or configure devices to work with the operating system.

For example, if your machine contains a CD-ROM drive, you will need to install a CD-ROM driver before you can use the CD-ROM in DOS. In the following section you will learn how to prepare for installation. After that, each operating system installation will be covered in more detail.

PREPARING FOR INSTALLATION

Before you can install any OS, you need to make a few advance preparations. First, and most important, the machine must be working correctly. If you have defective hardware, such as a disk drive, CD-ROM drive, or a bad section of memory, the operating system installation can be extremely difficult. Most operating systems interface with the hardware on many levels. Many of the operating systems covered in this book try to detect the hardware connected to your computer automatically; the result of non-working hardware can be a failed installation.

CHECKING THE HARDWARE

Before you begin an installation, you should be sure that all hardware is actually turned on and ready for use, including the computer and any external peripheral devices such as SCSI devices, tape drives, disk drives, and scanners.

 It is recommended that you remove any tapes or removable media that contain important data from tape and other drives. In general, an operating system installation will not destroy data on tapes or removable media, unless it is specifically instructed to do so. However, if important data is backed up, and removable media are out of the drives, the chance of losing anything is nil.

You should also have information available about your hardware. This means that you should know how many hard disks you have, what size they are, and how they are connected to the machine. You should also know how much memory you have in your machine. For any expansion cards, such as your video card, network card, sound card, and SCSI cards, you should know the make and model. If you have a printer, modem, scanner, plotter, or other device, you should have the device driver disks handy, and you should know what types they are. Table 4-1 is an example of how you might organize this information to have it available during installation.

Table 4-1   Hardware Component Information

Component	Description/Setting
CPU (type)	The system BIOS knows this information and the operating system should adjust anything required accordingly and automatically.
Amount of RAM	Your operating system should detect the amount of RAM your system has automatically. However, guidelines supplied with your OS will tell you how much RAM is recommended. You should know how much you have to make sure the OS will install and operate properly.
Type of buses	You'll need this information if you are installing new expansion cards.
Hard disk(s)	Type, size, connection. Most newer hardware includes BIOS routines to detect automatically the type of hard drive installed as well as critical drive settings. It also is a good idea to write down hard drive statistics, such as number of cylinders, capacity, number of heads. This information may be available in your owner's manual or on the case of the hard drive itself.
Keyboard	Unless your keyboard has special features that require custom drivers, the type of keyboard you have should not be a factor during OS installation.
Mouse	Standard, three-button, wheel mouse? Is a custom driver required?
Video card	Most modern operating systems will detect your video card and include required drivers automatically. However, special features of your video card may become available only with the use of a special driver provided by the manufacturer.
Floppy drive type	This information will probably be detected automatically by your OS.
Sound card	Some operating systems include drivers for common sound card hardware. If your card isn't one of the really popular models, make sure you have the required drivers supplied by the card's manufacturer.
NIC	Windows 95, Windows 98, and Mac OS probably will detect your NIC automatically. However, it may still be a good idea to use the manufacturer's custom drivers for best performance.
Printer	You should have custom drivers from your printer manufacturer.
Modem	Use manufacturer drivers or those supplied with your operating system. You should know at least the manufacturer of your modem's basic chip set in case you have to choose it during installation. If you have custom driver software that came with your modem, use it.
Other input/output devices	If your OS doesn't detect other hardware during the installation, you'll need to understand hardware basics and have available any custom drivers required to make it function properly with your OS.

Chapter 6, "Output, Input, and Storage Devices," gives more detailed information on devices and device drivers.

Many cards installed in the machine have settings on the card. In the Intel PC architecture, these cards often need to be configured to interface with the computer in a certain way. Windows 95 and later Windows products use the Plug and Play system to do this. If you are installing a Plug and Play operating system, card configuration will be automatic. If you are not using a Plug and Play operating system, or if your machine does not support the Plug and Play system, you could be in for a few surprises. Many Plug and Play cards have a utility (usually included on the manufacturer's disk with the drivers) that will let you configure them to work in non Plug and Play mode. Currently, only Windows 95 and Windows 98 support true Plug and Play mode. There is support in Windows NT 4.0 for something that looks like Plug and Play, but it is not truly Plug and Play! Windows NT 4.0 can detect some hardware features, but not as reliably as Windows 95/98. Windows 2000 (the latest release of Windows NT) will include sophisticated Plug and Play features. Interface cards in the Macintosh architecture usually don't need any special configuration for the hardware to work properly.

 With newer hardware there may be BIOS settings that can turn on or off Plug and Play compatibility. Plug and Play should be enabled by default. If it isn't, check your computer's BIOS documentation to find out how to turn it on before installing a new operating system.

CHECKING DRIVERS

Many devices such as CD-ROM drives, software-driven modems, and input devices such as scanners require special drivers to work correctly. In general, drivers will be on the disks that come with the devices, but often these disks do not include drivers for all possible operating systems, or the most up-to-date drivers. Also, your device may not be in the list of drivers that come with the operating system, which can result in some installation problems.

If you install drivers that came with your hardware, the hardware should operate properly. However, in some cases (particularly with modems) you may experience significantly better performance by installing later drivers that you secure from the manufacturer. There are a few strategies to obtain the latest drivers for your particular device and operating system. If you have access to the Internet, simply go to the Web site of the manufacturer of your hardware for drivers and support information. Or, contact the manufacturer and ask for the latest driver disks for your device. You don't want to have to abort an installation because of a lack of driver files.

Even though you may have driver disks in hand, it is best to get the most recent drivers, because updates often fix bugs in older driver versions.

You should also check the documentation that came with any hardware you want to use with your new OS. In many cases the manufacturer will include a disclaimer indicating which operating systems are certified for use with particular hardware.

ENSURING HARDWARE COMPATIBILITY

Because of the wide range of hardware available today, you will find that many operating systems have certain minimum hardware requirements. These are usually listed on the box or in a section of the manual. More advanced operating systems will often include a **hardware compatibility list (HCL)**; this is usually a list or book that contains brand names and models for all hardware supported by the operating system. Windows NT, and some UNIX systems, for example, will include an HCL. Unless you request it separately, you probably won't have an HCL with lower-level operating systems such as Windows 95 and Mac OS. Separate technical documentation may provide this information.

If you have hardware that is not on the HCL, all is not lost. If the hardware comes with appropriate drivers for the operating system you are about to install, you are usually in good shape. However, if you have no drivers and your hardware is not on the HCL, you may be asking for trouble.

If the hardware you are planning to use is a clone, or OEM (original equipment manufacturer) version of hardware that is on the list, proceed as if it is the hardware in question. If your hardware is not on the list of compatible hardware, or you have no drivers, beware. The installation of the OS could fail, or the OS could become unstable after installation. Stick with compatible devices and drivers.

Regardless of the detail offered with your hardware, the OS manufacturer is usually very minimal in its hardware recommendations. Many "minimal" recommendations are so small that you might be able to install the OS, but you probably won't be able to use it. Consider a 2 GB hard drive and 32 MB of RAM as the bare minimum to install any modern operating system, no matter what the OS manufacturer recommends.

MAKING TIME TO DO THE JOB

Last of all, make sure you have enough time to complete the operating system installation. Nothing is more frustrating than not being able to finish an install because you have some other obligation at an inconvenient moment. Having to come back to the process later can often turn out to be extremely confusing.

INSTALLING MS-DOS

MS-DOS is still popular, especially in the corporate world. You will need from 20 minutes to an hour to get DOS up and running, depending on what devices you are installing and the speed of your hardware. The only drivers you should need for a basic DOS installation are those for a CD-ROM drive, and even these are installed after the basic MS-DOS install completes. However, you likely will need driver software from the hardware manufacturer to complete the installation.

During installation, you can choose to use a floppy disk to save uninstall information. This is a good practice, so you should have one or two blank, formatted floppy disks handy. A single 3.5-inch floppy disk may suffice, but if you are using an older system with 5.25-inch floppy drives, two disks may be required.

HARDWARE REQUIREMENTS

The list in Table 4-2 shows recommended hardware for the installation of modern versions of MS-DOS.

Table 4-2   MS-DOS Hardware Requirements

Hardware	Minimum	Recommended
CPU	80386	80486 or better
RAM	2 MB	4 MB
Storage	5 MB	10 MB or more

The MS-DOS system is distributed on floppy disks. Installation is started by turning off the computer, inserting MS-DOS disk 1 in the floppy drive, and turning the power back on. (Complete steps for installing MS-DOS version 6.22 are in Hands-on Project 4-1 at the end of this chapter.) The machine boots from the floppy disk; you will see the message Starting MS-DOS after only a few seconds. You will then see the initial setup screen, followed by the main menu as shown in Figure 4-1 on the next page. You press Enter to start setup.

Your setup and installation screens may differ slightly from those shown here, depending on the version of DOS being installed.

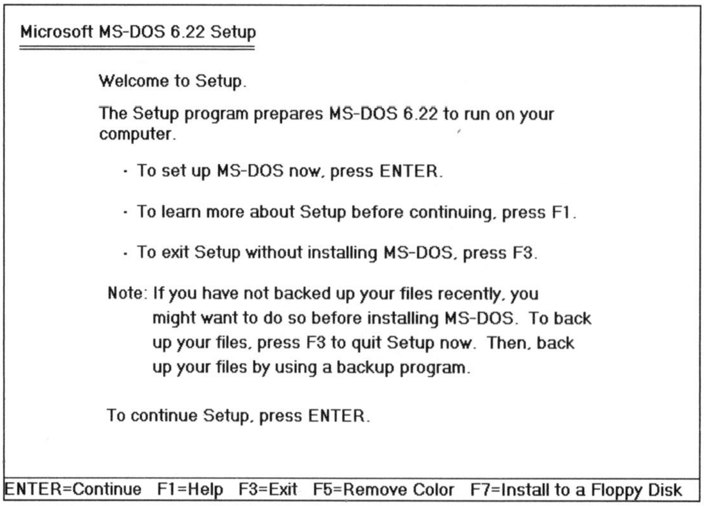

```
Microsoft MS-DOS 6.22 Setup

     Welcome to Setup.

     The Setup program prepares MS-DOS 6.22 to run on your
     computer.

          · To set up MS-DOS now, press ENTER.

          · To learn more about Setup before continuing, press F1.

          · To exit Setup without installing MS-DOS, press F3.

     Note: If you have not backed up your files recently, you
           might want to do so before installing MS-DOS.  To back
           up your files, press F3 to quit Setup now.  Then, back
           up your files by using a backup program.

     To continue Setup, press ENTER.



ENTER=Continue  F1=Help  F3=Exit  F5=Remove Color  F7=Install to a Floppy Disk
```

Figure 4-1   MS-DOS config screen

On the setup screens you enter configuration information about the country in which you live, your keyboard layout, the correct date and time, and which directory you wish to use for DOS. Use the default directory C:\DOS, since many programs look for DOS there. The MS-DOS files are then copied to the specified directory, and you will be prompted to insert subsequent installation disks. When the copy process is completed, you will be prompted to remove all disks from the drives and press Enter. The machine will restart from the hard disk. You now have a basic MS-DOS setup. There are no applications installed at this point, and you may still need to install drivers for CD-ROM drives, printers and other hardware, but you do have a bootable operating system with basic DOS utilities.

There are cases in which you may have to vary this process: for example, if the machine will not boot from the floppy disk, or if you are trying to do a new install with an upgrade version of DOS. Those special cases are covered in the following two sections.

SETTING DISK BOOT ORDER

If your machine will not boot from the floppy disk, it may be because the BIOS has been set to boot from another drive. To reset the boot disk order, press a designated key (such as F2 or Del; check your screen or consult your computer manual) to get into BIOS setup while the Power On Self Test (POST) is running, or you can use the Diagnostics disk that comes with the computer to enter BIOS setup. In the setup, in the basic CMOS or Extended Bios Setup section, you will find an option for boot sequence. Before you make any changes, note the current settings! The boot order for the purpose of installing DOS should be drive A: (or your floppy drive), then drive C: (or your boot hard drive). With this change made, follow onscreen instructions to get back to the point where the machine reboots, and make sure the DOS disk 1 is still in drive A:.

USING AN UPGRADE VERSION OF MS-DOS FOR A NEW INSTALL

If you are trying to do a new install using an Upgrade version of MS-DOS, after the DOS disk 1 boots, you will be told that upgrading will not work, and you will be notified to get other disks and try again. (If you already have MS-DOS on the machine and want to upgrade to a newer version, see Chapter 5 on upgrades.) If you have the legal right to perform this install, for example because an older version of DOS that was once licensed on this machine is simply no longer installed, there is a way around this problem, but you will have to start from scratch. Follow these steps:

1. Keep your DOS floppy in the drive and restart the machine (this can be done by holding down **Ctrl** and **Alt**, then pressing **Delete**).

2. When the machine restarts, pay close attention. The moment you see the words *Starting MS-DOS*, hold down the **left Shift** key. Moments later, you will see an MS-DOS command prompt.

3. You can now run the FDISK utility from the DOS floppy disk by typing **fdisk**. (See Chapter 3 for more detailed instructions on how to partition your disk.)

4. When this process is completed, you will be prompted to insert a boot disk and press Enter to reboot. Leave the DOS disk in the drive, press **Enter**, and again, when you see the words *Starting MS-DOS*, hold the **left Shift** key until the DOS prompt appears.

5. Now use the FORMAT command to format the partition on which you wish to install DOS. You should use the options U, for Unconditional format, and S to transfer System files. So, assuming you will be installing to drive C: you would type **format C: /S /U** and press **Enter**. When the format is complete, you simply restart the installation as described above. When you get to this point in the installation, you may be presented with a new dilemma, which is also the second error message you are likely to see.

6. At this point, you may be prompted with a screen that tells you a version of DOS is already on the hard disk. The installer will recommend that you stop your installation here, restart your computer from the hard disk, insert the floppy in the A: drive, and then run Setup. DO NOT DO THIS! Restarting the computer will cause any and all drivers that you normally load to be loaded and they will be present in memory during the install process. This is not a good idea, so choose the option from the menu to continue with setup as is. A similar set of messages may appear if you have the OS/2 operating system from IBM installed on your machine. In this case, you should read the section in the DOS manuals on OS/2 before continuing.

INSTALLING ADDITIONAL HARDWARE AND OPTIMIZING MEMORY

After the basic installation of MS-DOS, you generally need to install drivers for additional hardware, such as your CD-ROM drive, mouse, and sound card. We will not address the installation of sound card drivers, as this process varies from brand to brand, and instructions shipped with the card are usually fairly good. CD-ROM drives can be a different story! Most come with a disk containing only a single driver, and rely on you to figure out what to do from there. Hands-on Project 4-2 steps you through the process of installing CD-ROM and mouse drivers in DOS.

For the CD-ROM driver, you copy the device driver to your hard disk, and then edit two DOS files to tell DOS where and how to access the driver: CONFIG.SYS and AUTOEXEC.BAT. **CONFIG.SYS** is a file that is read whenever the system starts. It contains instructions on how to configure specific parts of the operating system, and what additional drivers to load. You add a line to CONFIG.SYS to load the device driver for the CD-ROM. **AUTOEXEC.BAT** is a file that contains a series of commands that is run when the operating system starts. You add a line to this file, an extension that can deal with the CD file system called the **Microsoft CD Extension**, or **MSCDEX** for short. It will link the CD-ROM file system extension with the device driver. You also add a line for a mouse driver to AUTOEXEC.BAT if you wish to use such a pointing device. AUTOEXEC.BAT and CONFIG.SYS are text files, and are edited with the DOS Editor.

Finally, you may want to optimize memory configuration. If you are using a machine equipped with a 486 or better CPU, and more than 1 MB of RAM, not all of the memory will be used in the most efficient way possible. MS-DOS includes a program called MEMMAKER, which will optimize the way the operating system and device drivers use memory. This process is nearly automatic, and can be run at any time after MS-DOS installation (see Hands-on Project 4-3). Usually, the result of running MEMMAKER will be more efficient use of the memory available on your machine, which will in general translate to higher execution speeds and more flexibility to deal with large data files.

 It is a good idea to run MEMMAKER after you have installed any new device drivers, so it can find the most optimum memory solution for your configuration.

INSTALLING WINDOWS 3.1x

There are three different flavors of Windows 3.1: "pure" Windows 3.1, Windows 3.11, and Windows for Workgroups 3.11. Windows 3.1 is not widely used; it is full of bugs, and should not be installed anymore. The version of Windows you should install in environments that need Windows 3.1x is version 3.11. This version comes in the standard 3.11 and in Windows for Workgroups 3.11. The significant differences between the two were addressed earlier in this book; in this chapter you will notice that when it comes to installing, the only difference is the installation for network support. You will get a chance to install Windows 3.11

for Workgroups in Hands-on Project 4-4 at the end of the chapter. Table 4-3 shows basic hardware requirements for Windows 3.1x.

HARDWARE REQUIREMENTS

Table 4-3 Windows 3.1x Hardware Requirements

Hardware	Minimum	Recommended
CPU	80386	80486 or faster
DOS	V. 5.2	V. 6.2
RAM	1 MB	4–16 MB
Storage	10 MB	60 MB

You also need drivers for any special hardware you have; this includes your network card, video card, printer, mouse, and sound card. Note that most network and sound cards make extensive use of IRQs, I/O ports, and DMA channels. You will need to know how the hardware on your cards is set up so that you can match the software settings to your hardware. The list in Table 4-1 will help you get started with a hardware inventory.

Windows 3.1x has no way to figure out what the hardware settings are, and it will take a stab at putting in default values for you. Unless you know the correct settings, you could end up with an installation that does not work. The documentation with the cards should tell you the default settings, and the person who installed the cards may remember the current settings. However, you may end up guessing the settings. If you expect this will happen, take a moment now to find the information on card settings. You cannot pull a card during an install, so be as prepared as you can. If you are installing Windows 3.1x from CD-ROM, you will need a working CD-ROM drive under DOS; as described in the previous section and in Hands-on Project 4-2.

Although it is possible to run Windows 3.1x at very low resolution, at least 640 × 480 pixels is recommended, with at least 16 colors. However, 800 × 600 in 256 colors would be much better. It is also possible to run Windows 3.1x without a mouse, but you will do much better if you have a mouse attached when you start this installation process. Depending on the speed of your computer and the components you choose to install, your installation can take between 15 and 120 minutes.

The standard Windows 3.11 is installed from floppies; the Microsoft Developer software kit includes Windows 3.11 on CD. With floppies, you will be asked throughout the install process to swap disks, a time-consuming process. To save time, install from a CD-ROM in a fast CD-ROM drive.

The Windows 3.11 installation offers a choice of Express or Custom installation. The Custom install gives you the advantage of more control over how Windows is set up, particularly in terms of the swap file. (A **swap file** is a file on disk used when there is not enough memory to hold all data.) The Windows defaults for the swap file under the Express install are inadequate. This is one reason to choose the Custom install, which you will do in Hands-on Project 4-4. However, if you have only basic hardware, minimum experience with operating systems, and don't plan on much future expansion, the Express install will be just fine.

 As with a DOS installation, it's best to accept the default directory for the Windows 3.1x operating system, in this case C:\WINDOWS.

A difference between the DOS installation and that of Windows 3.1x is that Windows goes through a hardware and software detection phase, although it doesn't always correctly identify hardware and software, and will display a screen listing the hardware and software it detects. The results of this screen may be wrong, so you should especially check the hardware settings carefully. If you have special drivers for your video card, or for any other device on the list, you can change the settings at this phase of the installation.

When you are done with the selection of hardware, you can select other components and files to be installed, and the drivers and files are copied to the hard disk. If you are installing Windows for Workgroups, you can set up networking. You can also add or remove networking protocols. In our hands-on example, we use **NetBEUI**, the default networking protocol in Windows environments. If you are operating in a Windows/DOS only environment, you may also want to remove the **IPX/SPX protocol** (default protocol for versions of Novell NetWare prior to version 5). You do not need this protocol unless you will be connecting to a Novell network. A third protocol choice is **TCP/IP** (Transfer Control Protocol/Internet Protocol), the protocol used on many networks and on the Internet.

NETWORK NAMES IN WINDOWS FOR WORKGROUPS

An important part of setting up networking in Windows for Workgroups is specifying network names: the user name, workgroup name, and computer name. The user name is the default user name that will be filled in at Windows login. This is the name you will be using on the network to identify the user who will be using this machine, and it can be anything you want it to be. The workgroup is a very important setting; in Windows for Workgroups, only computers that are in the same workgroup can share resources with each other, so you should make sure that this name is the same on all machines you want to be able to share resources with each other. The default workgroup is WORKGROUP, and you can leave it that way if you want. This way, all new machines will automatically be in the correct workgroup by default, and all will be able to communicate with each other.

In environments with large numbers of computers, it is customary to have several workgroups. One could be named SALES, one could be named FINANCE, another MARKETING, and so on. This way, people in various departments can share data with each other, without sharing it with other groups.

Finally, there is the computer name. This name *must* be unique on the network to which the computer will be connected. It can be whatever you want, but it makes sense to pick logical names, up to 15 characters. You can use spaces and special characters such as underscore, but again, use a logical name convention that you can remember.

Computer names are in many cases set to the name of the person that uses the machine. This is not such a great idea. If the person for whom the computer is named leaves the company, and that computer is sharing resources, it can be a real chore to change the machine name, and then have to change all the other machines that use resources from this machine.

You should use short and meaningful names. PRINTSRV for the machine with the printer, or FILESRV1 and FILESRV2, or RECEPTION are good names because they will not likely change, and they tell you something about what the machine does or where it is. In large network environments, it can be helpful to name machines after office numbers, say office number 280 would be OFF280. Avoid using spaces in machine and workgroup names, and try to keep both as short as possible. The maximum length for a computer name or workgroup name is 15 characters; the user name can be no more than eight characters.

CHANGES TO THE CONFIG.SYS AND AUTOEXEC.BAT FILES

The Windows 3.1x installation automatically makes some changes to the CONFIG.SYS and AUTOEXEC.BAT files, and there is an option during installation to review and edit changes yourself. To automatically start Windows 3.1x when the computer starts, you can add the command **WIN** as the last line in the AUTOEXEC.BAT file.

Typically, Windows for Workgroups will add the command *net start* to AUTOEXEC.BAT. This is what starts the network functionality. Any version of Windows 3.11 will change the MSCDEX version that is used, if you have a CD-ROM drive, and the path will typically be modified. In the CONFIG.SYS file, the HIMEM.SYS driver from Windows instead of DOS is used, and Windows adds a line that tells DOS to make more memory available for scratch usage, usually STACKS=9,256. If you install Windows for Workgroups, you will also see the **IFSHLP.SYS** device driver added; this driver is used to support the disk sharing features of Windows for Workgroups. Windows 3.1x also stores copies of your old CONFIG.SYS and AUTOEXEC.BAT files, which can be handy to have if your computer will not start properly.

During the setup of the Program Manager graphical interface, you can specify where Windows should look for installed applications. You should use the Path option, which means Windows will look only in the active execution path to find applications that should be added to Program Manager. There is an option to view a short tutorial, and you can choose to exit to DOS or restart the computer. It's best to restart the computer, because the drivers added and changes made to CONFIG.SYS will not take effect until you reboot. At this point Windows 3.1x is installed.

ADJUSTING MEMORY

After Windows 3.1x is installed, it is a good idea to adjust the Virtual Memory settings as follows:

1. Start Windows, open the **Control Panel**, and choose **Enhanced**.

2. Click the **Virtual Memory** button.

3. In the Virtual Memory screen click **Change**. You will see the Virtual Memory Control Panel shown in Figure 4-2.

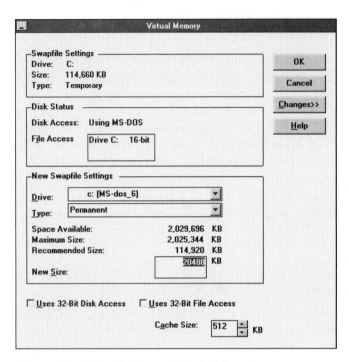

Figure 4-2   Virtual Memory Control Panel

 You will notice that the top swap file setting says the swap file is temporary. As mentioned earlier, the swap file is a disk file that is used when there is not enough memory to hold all data. If this file is temporary, it can get seriously fragmented, as it needs to be re-created every time it is used. It would be better to have a permanent file that does not have to be re-created every time. The drawback is obviously that the file will always take up disk space, whether it is used or not. Note that the swap file, if it is made permanent, must be on a contiguous block of disk space. You may want to run the DOS Defrag utility before you make a permanent swap file.

4. Assuming you have the disk space to spare, set the **Type** to **Permanent**, if necessary. You will see a recommended size in this window. This is the maximum amount of space that will be used on the file! Making the file larger than the recommended size will only waste disk space. The bigger the file, the more memory Windows will have to work in, so make the file as big as you can, but not bigger than the recommended size.

5. On many machines, there will be a set of check boxes at the bottom of this window to use 32-bit disk access and to use 32-bit file access. If these boxes are available, you are using an IDE drive, and your machine is a 486 or better.

Select the boxes that are available to you. Depending on how much memory you have, you may wish to use quite a bit of it for cache. On a machine with 16 MB of RAM, use about 2 MB for disk cache if 32 file access is turned on, or about 512 KB if it is not.

6. When you've made your selections on the Virtual Memory Control Panel, click **OK**.

7. Confirm that you wish to make changes, and once again you will have to restart your computer.

Ideally you won't need much virtual memory at all. Virtual memory is much slower than real RAM, of course, but if you don't have enough RAM, virtual RAM is necessary and a workable alternative.

As with a DOS installation, you can run MEMMAKER with Windows 3.1x installations. It is a good idea to run MEMMAKER after the installation at this point, and make sure you use the Custom setup. MEMMAKER can help you wring the most out of the RAM you have by placing some DOS components into upper memory, for example, and making the most out of lower memory. When you get to the Advanced Options screen, set the Optimize upper memory for use with Windows to Yes. You will now be asked to identify your Windows directory, and then the MEMMAKER process will continue as usual. Note that when MEMMAKER reboots your machine, you will not see Windows! This is normal; MEMMAKER will fix this when it is done. After MEMMAKER is done, reboot the machine so all changes will take effect. Your Windows 3.11 is ready to go.

INSTALLING WINDOWS 95

Windows 95 comes in various versions or releases. You may see these referred to as Service Releases identified by number. Updates to the basic operating system may be referred to as Service Packs. The differences in installation are minor from version to version. Newer releases have increased device support, and fewer bugs. Also, newer versions have more 32-bit code, and they include copies of Internet Explorer (the Microsoft Web browser) and the Active Desktop. You can get Windows 95 on floppy disks or on CD-ROM. The version on floppy disk spans 26 disks, so it certainly pays to have a version you can install from CD-ROM. Included with the CD-ROM is a Windows boot disk; it starts the Windows 95 command-line-only version from floppy, loads the CD-ROM drivers, and then runs the Setup program. You can practice installing Windows 95 in Hands-on Project 4-5 at the end of this chapter.

If you have lost the Windows 95 boot disk, and you have a machine that runs DOS, you can simply use the FORMAT A: /S command to make a system floppy, on which you can then install the driver for your CD-ROM drive and the MSCDEX extensions as described in the Installing DOS section of this chapter. You then have to make a CONFIG.SYS file and an AUTOEXEC.BAT file to run these programs (also described in the DOS section).

If you have to make such a floppy, put the FORMAT.COM and FDISK.EXE utilities on it, as you may need them. If you have the original Windows 95 boot floppy, these utilities will be on the disk. Just make sure that you don't mix utilities from different versions of DOS on this disk. You can't use most DOS 6.22 utilities on a Windows 95 system, for example.

You can make a boot disk from inside Windows 95, of course. Open the Control Panel (point to Start, then Settings and choose Control Panel), choose Add/Remove Programs, and click the Startup Disk tab, then click Create Disk and follow the instructions.

HARDWARE REQUIREMENTS

To run Windows 95 you will need at least the hardware suggested in Table 4-4.

Table 4-5 Windows 98 Hardware Requirements

Hardware	Minimum	Recommended
CPU	486 DX 66	Pentium 166 or faster
RAM	8 MB	16 MB or more
Storage	190 MB	500 MB

The installation should take between 30 and 120 minutes, depending on whether you install from floppy disk or CD, and the speed of your machine. On a machine with a CD-ROM drive, 30-50 minutes seems to be about average.

The hard disk on your machine must already be formatted and have a partition made (see Chapter 3; you can use the FDISK and FORMAT utilities on the Windows 95 boot disk for these purposes).

 Review Chapter 3 on file systems before you decide to install a FAT32 file system on your machine!

 The FAT32 system is available only with the OSR2 release of Windows 95.

If you are installing from CD-ROM, you should have the correct CD-ROM driver on your floppy, and it should load and activate the MSCDEX driver as well. When you prepare your hard disk, copy the CD-ROM driver, the MSCDEX utility, and the CONFIG.SYS and AUTOEXEC.BAT files needed to your hard disk. This is important because the Windows 95 installer will count on them being there and working correctly. The procedure for doing this is described in the Installing MS-DOS section of this chapter. Some CD-ROM manufacturers have done their homework, and their Windows 95 installer will do all of this automatically when you install the CD-ROM driver, but now you know how to do it yourself. If you use the floppy disk version of Windows 95, this is obviously not an issue.

WINDOWS 95 INSTALLATION OPTIONS

Windows 95 can be installed from either CD-ROM or floppies. The setup program begins with a graphical user interface welcoming you to Windows 95. Clicking Continue and accepting the Software License Agreement initializes the Setup Wizard, an interactive utility shown in Figure 4-3 that guides you through the setup process.

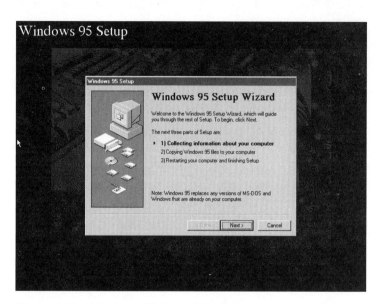

Figure 4-3   Windows 95 Setup Wizard

There are four setup options for Windows 95. The Typical (default) installation will install the most popular Windows components for desktop computers. It will perform most of the installation steps without much input from you; you need to confirm the installation directory and whether to create a Startup disk. The Portable option provides support for options on portable computers such as **PCMCIA** (Personal Computer Memory Card International Association) cards (expansion cards used in laptops and desktop machines), and support for **LCD** (liquid crystal display) screens. This option is useful for mobile users with portable computers, and installs the Briefcase and support for direct cable connections. The Compact option will perform an absolute minimum installation of Windows 95. This is for users with a limited amount of hard disk space. The Custom option allows you to choose the installation options you want.

   If you want to install mail and fax support, you must use the Custom option.

As with other Microsoft operating systems, we recommend that you use the Custom option, so you can exercise control over what will get installed. You should install all of the Disk tools; by default Backup is not selected! If you have plenty of disk space, it would not hurt to install all operating system components.

You can also choose whether to use the Windows 95 interface, which is the default selection, or to use the Program Manager (Windows 3.1) interface, if for some reason it is important to retain the look and feel of Program Manager.

Windows 95 will ask if you want to create a **startup disk** (a bootable disk that can start the operating system if there is a problem with the hard disk). You should always create this disk; it will help you fix problems if you are unable to boot from the hard disk. This disk will be formatted, so any existing data on it will be lost.

During installation, you can choose to configure networking, printers, and modems, or you can bypass these options and set them up later from the Windows 95 Control Panel. After the installation is completed, unlike MS-DOS and Windows 3.1x, there is no need to tweak any memory. The full steps for installing Windows 95 are given in Hands-on Project 4-5.

INSTALLING WINDOWS 98

The Windows 98 installation is quite similar to the Windows 95 installation; this section addresses the elements that are different in Windows 98. It comes on either CD-ROM or a large set of disks. Use the CD-ROM for speed and ease of installation.

HARDWARE REQUIREMENTS

To run Windows 98, you will need at least the minimum hardware listed in Table 4-5.

Table 4-5   Windows 98 Hardware Requirements

Hardware	Minimum	Recommended
CPU	486 DX 66	Pentium 166 or faster
RAM	8 MB	16 MB or more
Storage	190 MB	500 MB

You will need one blank disk to make the system recovery disk, and the installation will take somewhere between 40 and 180 minutes.

As with Windows 95, you will need a startup disk that has working CD-ROM support. This disk comes with your Windows 98 bundle, but if you do not have it, you can make one yourself, as described in the Installing Windows 95 section of this chapter. You will also need to have a partitioned and formatted hard disk; a process detailed in Chapter 3. Note that you will need to use a Windows 95 OSR2 or a Windows 98 boot disk to format your hard disk with the FAT32 file system.

If there is not an operating system currently installed on your computer, you will have to use the Windows 98 startup disk. Insert the startup disk, turn on your computer, and then insert the Windows 98 installation CD-ROM. If you already have an operating system installed, simply insert the Windows 98 installation CD-ROM. At this point, the Windows 98 Setup

Wizard appears to step you through the installation. You can practice installing Windows 98 in Hands-on Project 4-6.

 It's a good idea to choose the option to save your existing operating system files, which will enable you to later uninstall Windows 98 and return to the prior operating system configuration.

If you are trying to use an Upgrade version of Windows 98 to do a full installation, you may see the Upgrade Compliance window. If so, simply insert disk 1, or the CD, of an older Windows version, and you should get past this point with no problems.

You can choose from the same four types of installation as in Windows 95: Typical, Portable, Compact, or Custom, as shown in Figure 4-4. As usual, choosing Custom is the best option.

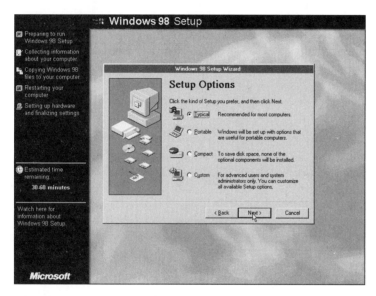

Figure 4-4   Windows 98 Setup Wizard

When you are able to select the components you wish to install, there are some options not included in Windows 95: Internet tools, Microsoft Outlook Express, Multi Language Support, online services, and WebTV support. It is recommended highly that you add the Backup program to System tools.

During the installation of Windows 98, the left side of the screen contains an outline of what portions of the installation process are still to be completed, and the estimated remaining install time. Don't make appointments based on the time estimate; it can be inaccurate.

In Windows 95, there is quite a bit of interaction required to configure devices after the basic operating system files are copied; in Windows 98 nearly everything is automatic up to the point of final configuration. Several restarts will occur automatically, whereas in Windows 95 you have to be there to perform them. After the first restart, Windows 98 performs hardware detection, a process that may take a few minutes. Your machine will start once again, and the drivers will be installed. Remember, no human interaction is needed for any of this to happen, so you could be doing something else while this is happening. This is one of the biggest advantages of the Windows 98 installation.

 There are no questions about drivers or network cards, printers, or monitors during the Windows 98 installation; if these are not detected during installation you have to set them up after the installation.

When you perform a Windows 98 installation, it will help a great deal if you have Internet access. This OS has a facility to access the Internet and download fixes and updated software, installing it automatically. As this book is written there are close to 100 additions and fixes available! Additional information on Windows 98 upgrades is available in Chapter 5.

INSTALLING WINDOWS NT

Windows NT comes in two different configurations; Server and Workstation. The division of Windows NT into Workstation and Server occurred in 1994, with the release of version 3.5. Both NT Server and NT Workstation are designed as network operating systems, and either can be used for servers or workstations. The primary difference between them is the number of supported users that can be connected while the operating system is in server mode (NT Workstation is designed for no more than 10 simultaneous users, while NT Server supports several thousand), and the features for network management (NT Server has more extensive features). Windows NT 4.0, released in 1996, offered a new desktop interface, enhanced networking, Internet, and directory services, and a more automated installation. This section will focus on installing Windows NT 4.0, but it will be noted where Windows NT 3.51 installation differs.

There are several ways to install Windows NT: from a combination of floppy disks and CD-ROM, over the network, or using an answer file, a batch file that provides responses to questions that come up in the installation (sometimes called "unattended" installation). This chapter covers only installation from floppy disks and CD-ROM (see Hands-on Project 4-7).

HARDWARE REQUIREMENTS

Although Windows NT will run on many platforms, this chapter covers installation on the PC platform. The installation on all platforms is nearly identical; just some specifics regarding hardware are different. You will need at least the hardware recommended in Table 4-6.

Table 4-6   Windows NT Hardware Requirements

Hardware	Minimum	Recommended
CPU	486 DX 66	Pentium 100
RAM	16 MB	32 MB
Storage (Server)	200 MB	500 MB
Storage (Workstation)	150 MB	400 MB

4

Your install time will be somewhere between 45 and 120 minutes.

The hardware requirements for NT 3.51 are identical, although NT 3.51 is supposed to run on a 386; however, this is not recommended. Windows NT 3.51 cannot be booted from CD-ROM on a PC, so you will have to have boot disks.

Windows NT comes with an HCL (hardware compatibility list). Of the operating systems discussed so far, NT is the most picky about what hardware it will support.

To save yourself a headache, make sure that your hardware is on the HCL, or that you have Windows NT 4.0 drivers for the hardware you want to install. You cannot use any drivers with Windows NT 4.0 other than drivers made specifically for NT 4.0. Using unsupported hardware and drivers can have disastrous results! However, given the rising popularity of Windows NT among vendors and users alike, you should be able to secure any drivers you require.

Although the HCL on your distribution CD-ROM may be out of date, you can update this list on the Internet. Point your browser to *www.microsoft.com* and search for "HCL" or "Technet". When you register for Technet you can download the latest NT HCL and find other recent information about Windows NT.

STARTING THE INSTALLATION

Windows NT 4.0 Server and Workstation come with an installation CD-ROM and three installation floppy disks. The disks can be used to start the installation on an Intel platform. If you have lost the disks, you can make a set using another computer as follows:

1. Load the NT CD-ROM in a working machine running DOS, Windows 3.1x, 95, 98, or NT. Have three, blank formatted floppy disks on hand.

2. From the MS-DOS prompt, navigate to the **\i386** directory on the CD-ROM. (This directory contains installation files for 80486 and Pentium computers using Intel, Cyrix, or AMD processors.)

3. Run **WINNT /OX**.

4. Follow the prompts and you will end up with the startup disks for Windows NT.

Other platforms, such as the PowerPC, DEC Alpha, and RISC-4000, do not need the floppy installation disks; they will boot from the CD-ROM. Newer Intel machines generally also include an option to boot from the CD-ROM.

Note that Windows NT does not require that a hard disk partition already be created and formatted. The NT Setup program will partition and format the drive(s) for you. Unless you need to retain a FAT partition (such as if you want to leave a portion of the disk for MS-DOS or Windows 95), you can install Windows NT on an NTFS file system, which is discussed in Chapter 3 on File Systems. This is the default file system created by the NT installer. You should make the NT partition at least 500 MB and preferably 1 GB. The maximum FAT partition space is 4 GB; you can create much larger partitions with NTFS.

Windows NT installation is divided into two parts. The first part is character-based, and focuses on detecting hardware and loading installation files. The second part uses a graphical display with Windows-based dialog boxes focusing on configuring the server or workstation.

If you are installing the Server version, you have two licensing options, depending on what you have purchased. **Per-seat licensing** (a license for each workstation) makes sense in larger settings where you have more than one NT server, as one client can be connected to multiple servers with only a single per-seat license. In most smaller settings with only one server, however, **per-server licensing** with a single server and a set number of workstations may make more sense.

If you are installing NT Server, you will have to specify how this machine fits in the domain structure. A **domain** is a group of computers that share a common security database. If you are installing a single NT server and do not plan to have other servers, or if you want it to participate only in a workgroup or exist as a stand-alone server in an existing domain, you should choose the Stand-alone server option during installation. If you will have multiple NT servers, and want to keep user and permission information consistent among all of them, you will put them all in a domain. There is only one primary domain controller (PDC) per domain, which is the main source for information about users and security rights for all the servers in the domain. Each domain has one PDC. There can then be multiple backup domain controllers per domain. More about domains can be found in Chapter 8 on Networking.

Windows NT also gives you the choice to create a startup disk, called the Emergency Repair Disk. It is strongly recommended you make one. You will need one blank floppy during installation to make your Emergency Repair Disk. This disk is unique to the machine on which you are installing, and you should make an Emergency Repair Disk for every NT computer you have.

 Never use the Emergency Repair Disk from another computer! Doing so is likely to result in loss of data, and in many cases require a new installation of Windows NT!

If your computer is connected to a network, you will need to answer questions about network connections and protocols. You can also install Remote Access Services (RAS) either during or after the NT installation; RAS setup is covered in greater detail in later chapters.

You can also confirm or change **network bindings**, which are part of the NT Server system used to coordinate software communications among the NIC, the network protocols, and network services. Setup automatically configures network bindings for the highest performance.

If you're installing NT 3.51, insert disk 1 and boot the machine. After a while, you will be prompted for disk 2, and the installer will start. You have two choices here, Express install or Custom install. As always, you should choose Custom install. You will now be told the Mass Storage Device check will begin when you press Enter, and then you will be asked to insert disk 3.

The rest of the detection sequence works exactly as described previously for NT 4.0. You will next be prompted to install from floppy disks or CD. If you choose to install from floppies, you will be asked to change disks during the install... about 51 times! Use CD-ROM installation for obvious reasons. From this point on, the installer is identical to Windows NT 4.0, up to the point where the graphical interface and Setup Part II start. One note about Part II: In Windows NT 4.0, there are Back buttons on nearly every screen. If you make a mistake, click Back and you can usually fix it. Windows NT 3.51 is not equipped with this feature; a wrong change means you'll have to do the install again from scratch.

INSTALLING THE SERVICE PACKS

With the basic installation of NT completed, you can fix several bugs and problems in the operating system. Microsoft releases NT service packs, known as SPs, to fix problems in the OS. When we wrote this book, the latest service pack was SP4. In general you should always apply the latest service pack right after you install NT.

 Before installing a service pack, always make a backup of your machine!

You can either download service packs from the Internet, or you can order a CD from Microsoft. If you have Internet access, go to *http://www.microsoft.com/windows/downloads/default.asp*, and select Windows NT Server 4.0. You will see a list of the service packs and upgrades available. Pick the service pack you want, and on the bottom of the page you will find a download option. Choose this option to download the service pack, and then follow the instructions to get it installed. When you are done with the service pack installation, you should make a new Emergency Repair Disk. The latest service pack can be quite large, so downloading with a conventional modem connection could take awhile. Unless you have a high speed connection you probably should consider ordering the service pack on a CD.

INSTALLING UNIX: LINUX

And now for something completely different: UNIX. This section discusses installing one UNIX version, Linux, on the Intel PC platform. There are numerous other versions of UNIX designed for different hardware platforms. If you understand how Linux installs on the Intel platform, however, you should have no problem installing other versions of UNIX. Some UNIX flavors, such as **Solaris**, a version of UNIX developed by Sun Microsystems, are available for a variety of hardware platforms. Solaris was initially designed to run on many other platforms, including one based on Motorola 68000 CPUs and SPARC processors. A version for the 386 was introduced many years ago, but it was not a great success. Now, functionally similar versions are released on both SPARC and Intel platforms.

INSTALLING LINUX

Linux is available in many shapes and forms. This section focuses on installing a commercial version of Linux, although there are shareware versions around. In the business environment, most companies will choose to use operating systems for which they can get support. Using a commercial version of Linux will guarantee there is someone to support it. Red Hat Linux 5.1 is the most recent commercial version as this book is written.

Linux Hardware Requirements

This operating system requires at least the hardware shown in Table 4-7.

Table 4-7 Linux Hardware Requirements

Hardware	Minimum	Recommended
CPU	386 DX 40	Pentium 100
RAM	8 MB	32 MB
Storage	40 MB (minimal install)	700 MB (full install)

You will get a boot floppy and a set of CD-ROMs in the package if you buy Red Hat Linux, or you can download the files from the Internet. For information on Red Hat Linux, point your browser to *www.redhat.com*. You can also search for "linux download" (use any Web search engine) to find many sites where you can download versions of Linux.

Install Red Hat from CD-ROM. If your machine can boot from the CD-ROM drive, you will be able to boot Red Hat from the CD. You will need between 15 minutes and an hour to install Red Hat Linux. You do not need to make partitions or format your disk ahead of time. Step-by-step instructions for installing Linux are included in Hands-on Project 4-8 at the end of this chapter.

The Linux operating system comes with the complete source code for the Kernel, all the drivers, and most of the utilities. This can be very nice if you are a computer programmer who wants to change code to make it do exactly what you want. This is probably the strongest point of Linux; because thousands of people the world over are doing this kind of development, you will find a very wide variety of programming tools and toys on the Internet. How well they work, and how well they are supported, is a different story. Linux is not for everyone!

INSTALLING MAC OS

The installation of Mac OS 8.5 (the current version of the operating system as of this writing) uses a graphical interface and a Setup Assistant that functions similarly to the Microsoft setup wizards. Mac OS 8.5 is the first version of Mac OS to require a Macintosh with a PowerPC processor chip. It also requires at least 16 MB of RAM, and around 150 MB of hard drive space.

Unlike most of the other operating systems covered in this chapter, the Mac OS installer does not require booting from a floppy disk, and can be installed from CD-ROM or over an AppleTalk network. The easiest way to install Mac OS is directly from the CD. The installation process has three parts: booting the CD, running the installer, and restarting from the hard drive. Complete, step-by-step instructions for installing Mac OS 8.5 are given in the Hands-on Project 4-9 at the end of this chapter.

BOOTING FROM THE CD-ROM

A Macintosh will boot from the CD-ROM drive only if you tell it to. This may be done either by selecting the CD icon in the Startup Disk Control Panel, or by holding down the C key on the keyboard at the very beginning of the startup process (put the CD into the machine, restart, and immediately hold down the C key). You will know you have started from CD when you see the desktop pattern, which will be tiled pictures of CDs.

At the end of the boot process, the CD icon will appear in the upper-right corner of the screen, just below the menu bar, and the Mac OS 8.5 window will open, showing you the contents of the CD, as shown in Figure 4-5.

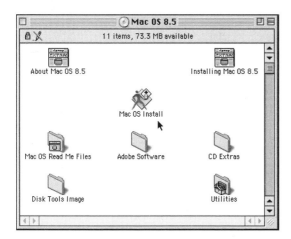

Figure 4-5   Mac OS 8.5 CD boot initial screen

 You may want to read the Mac OS Read Me files before starting the installation.

RUNNING THE INSTALLER

To proceed with the installation, just double-click the Mac OS Install icon. The installer will launch, and you will be presented with the opening screen, which lists the steps for the installation (Figure 4-6).

Figure 4-6   Mac OS 8.5 installation steps

During this phase, you will select a destination drive, read important information, agree to the software license, and then the installer will copy operating system files to your hard drive. Copying files will take anywhere from about 6 minutes on a fast G3 to about 45 minutes on a 6100/60.

RESTARTING FROM THE HARD DRIVE

When the installer finishes copying files, you will be prompted to restart the computer. If you've done a clean install, the operating system software that's appropriate for your Macintosh will be on your hard drive, along with AppleTalk and TCP/IP networking software, and drivers for almost all Apple-brand printers. If you chose to install over existing system software, the installer may leave out printer drivers that do not match ones already on your system.

When you restart, the first thing you will be presented with is the Mac OS Setup Assistant, shown in Figure 4-7.

Figure 4-7   Mac OS Setup Assistant

If you cancel this, you will be able to use your computer right away, but it's a good idea to go through this final section of the installation, to set up your AppleTalk networking settings and select your printer. You will also be asked to decide on your preferred nationality, to tell the computer your name and organization, to set your clock, to pick a city in your time zone so the computer will correctly store times and dates, and to decide if you want to put the computer into a simplified mode for novice users. The Assistant will then proceed to the networking questions, allowing you to name your computer and set a file sharing password (Figure 4-8), ask you if you would like to have a guest access folder, and let you specify your printer (Figure 4-9 on the next page).

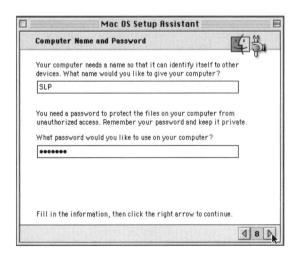

Figure 4-8   Naming the computer and setting the file sharing password

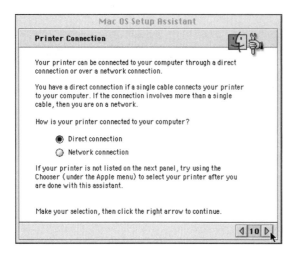

Figure 4-9   Configuring the printer

Once you have finished this and given the Assistant the go-ahead to set up everything, you will be presented with the Internet Setup Assistant, shown in Figure 4-10.

Figure 4-10   Mac Internet Setup Assistant

The Internet Setup Assistant is the easiest way to get your Macintosh connected to the Internet, though its settings may require some manual adjustments if you are on a LAN. You will first be asked if you want to set up your computer to use the Internet, and you can choose an existing Internet account or set up a new Internet account.

If you're going to be connecting to the Internet with a modem, you'll need a user name, a password, and a phone number to dial. You will also need to know your DNS numbers and your IP address if you have a static one. If you have a network connection, you also need to know if you are connecting directly to a TCP/IP network, or through MacIP, which is TCP/IP over an AppleTalk network.

The most common installation is a modem connection, with a dynamically assigned IP address, so that's what is illustrated here. The first thing you'll be asked for is a name for the configuration, as shown in Figure 4-11.

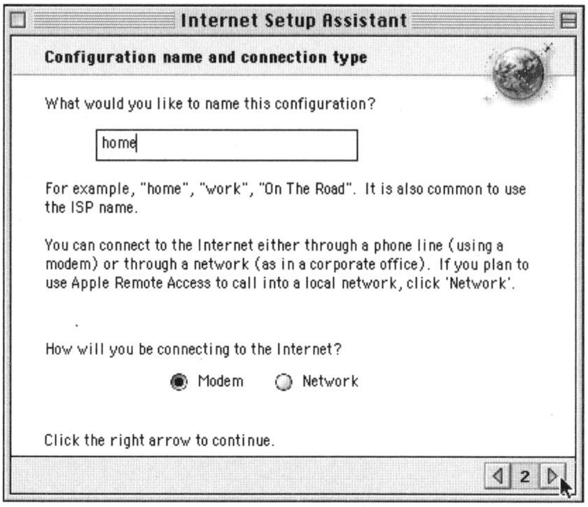

Figure 4-11   Naming the modem configuration

The name can be anything you like, and the Assistant even offers a few suggestions. Next, you will be asked to select your modem, choose the port it is connected to, and to specify tone or pulse dialing. The next screen asks for the phone number, user name, and password (Figure 4-12).

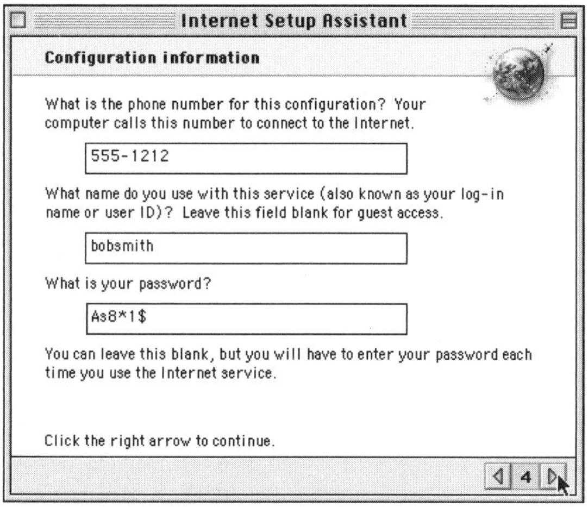

Figure 4-12   Entering the user name and password

You will be given a choice to use a connection script, and asked if you know your IP address. Then, input your DNS numbers (you are allowed to have up to ten separate DNS servers listed here) and a default domain name for the configuration, as shown in Figure 4-13.

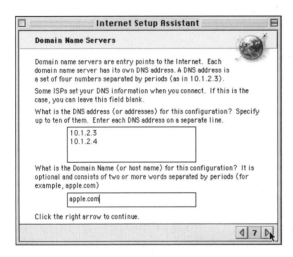

Figure 4-13 Entering DNS and domain information

This is enough to get you connected, but the Assistant will proceed to ask you for an e-mail address and password, an e-mail account (allowing you to specify a mail server that is different from your e-mail address) and a news server for your usenet news. It will also set up any proxy servers you might need if you are going to be behind a firewall. It then gives you the option to proceed with the configuration, and defaults to connecting immediately when finished.

If you are not using a modem, you will probably want to double-check the settings that the Assistant chose for you. These settings are controlled directly in the TCP/IP Control Panel, and the Internet Control Panel. Your modem connection settings are also going to use the Modem Control Panel and the Remote Access Control Panel.

Mac OS Installation Options

Up to this point, we've covered a basic installation. You can access additional installation options by clicking the Options or the Customize buttons on the last screen before starting the install, as shown in Figure 4-14.

Figure 4-14   Click Options or Customize before starting the installation

The Options button gives you the option to not update your hard disk drivers, which should be updated unless you know with absolute certainty that the existing drivers are more recent than the version included with the operating system installer, and the option not to create an installation log.

The Customize button allows you to control which components you want to install, down to the specific drivers to be installed. Use it if you know you don't want to install such pieces as Personal Web Sharing, or know that you don't need to connect to the Internet. Unchecking components here is safe enough, unless you uncheck the Mac OS installer itself. Three components are unselected by default: QuickDraw GX, English Speech Recognition, and Multilingual Internet Access. Most users won't need these. QuickDraw GX is only required for a few applications, speech recognition is fun to play with, but doesn't really do anything useful, and multilingual Internet access is only needed if you can read Web pages written in non-Roman alphabets.

Selecting the customized installation option of any of these components will generally bring up many choices within the individual sections, and is not recommended unless you know exactly what you are doing.

CHAPTER SUMMARY

This chapter provides an overview of the installation process for the operating systems covered in this book. You have seen how to prepare for operating system installation by checking hardware and gathering information about your system, and you have surveyed basic installations of MS-DOS, Windows 3.11 (including Windows for Workgroups), Windows 95, Windows 98, Windows NT (Server and Workstation), the Linux variety of UNIX, and Mac OS 8.5.

In addition, you learned how to configure networking and other hardware with each of these operating systems, and what hardware and software issues to watch for during operating system installation.

The key to making the most out of the information in this chapter is to try the hands-on exercises that follow and to practice installing various operating system functions. Nothing can replace experience in performing these installations. It takes about 20 hours to install all the operating systems as described in this chapter twice; so be warned, it will take some time. However, it will be time well spent as you will develop a broad understanding of general operating system theory as well as the specifics of installing and configuring some of the most popular ones.

KEY TERMS

- **AUTOEXEC.BAT** — A text-based configuration file in DOS (and Windows versions that use a DOS-based platform). This file automatically runs batch files and other executable files as one of the final operations during the bootup process.

- **CONFIG.SYS** — A text-based configuration file in DOS (similar to AUTOEXEC.BAT). The commands in CONFIG.SYS are executed early in the bootup process and normally are used to configure memory, to load special drivers, and so on.

- **domain** — A group of computers that share a common security database.

- **Hardware Compatibility List (HCL)** — A list of brand names and models for all hardware supported by an operating system. Adherence to the HCL will ensure a more successful operating system install. HCLs can often be found on OS vendors' Web sites.

- **IFSHLP.SYS** — In Windows for Workgroups, one of the final files to load during the bootup process and which helps facilitate the network component of Windows 3.1x.

- **IPX/SPX protocol** — In various Windows versions, a networking protocol that is compatible with Novell networking. A Microsoft client running this protocol as part of its networking configuration can communicate with Novell clients as well as Microsoft clients.

- **LCD** — liquid crystal display, the display technology in some laptops and other electronic equipment.

- **Microsoft CD Extension (MSCDEX)** — In Microsoft Windows, a software driver that enables CD-ROM hardware support.

- **NetBEUI** — The default networking protocol in Microsoft Windows environments.

- **network bindings** — Part of the NT Server system used to coordinate software communications among the NIC, the network protocols, and network services.

- **PCMCIA** — Personal Computer Memory Card International Association, standard for expansion cards used in laptops and desktop machines. Now usually shortened to PC Card.

- **per-seat licensing** — A software licensing scheme that prices software according to the number of individual users who install and use the software.

- **per-server licensing** — A software licensing scheme that prices software according to a server configuration that permits multiple users to access the software from a central server.

- **Plug and Play system (PNP)** — In Windows 95 and later Windows products, a protocol and hardware standard that permits the operating system to automatically recognize and configure compatible hardware.

- **Solaris** — A Sun Microsystems operating system based on UNIX.

- **startup disk** — A bootable floppy disk that includes the basic operating system, key disk utilities and drivers (such as for the CD-ROM drive). This disk can be used to start the system in the event that the hard drive or its operating system are damaged.

- **swap file** — A hard disk file that is used by the operating system to swap out portions of running programs when RAM memory resources become low.

- **TCP/IP** — Transfer Control Protocol/Internet Protocol, the networking protocol used on many networks and on the Internet.

- **WIN** — In Microsoft Windows, the command that launches the Windows operating system. WIN is an executable program.

REVIEW QUESTIONS

1. Windows 3.1x and DOS are completely independent and separate operating systems. True or False?

2. DOS—and operating systems based on DOS—uses two configuration files to help set up the operating system during booting. These two files are _____ and _____.

3. A DOS-only system uses what type of user interface?

4. What are the main differences between the user interfaces in DOS and Windows systems?

5. A Plug and Play operating system eliminates the need to understand operating system hardware requirements and limitations before installing the system. True or False?

6. Software driver requirements change as you add new hardware or install new software. Perhaps the best resource for updated drivers for any manufacturer's hardware is _____.

7. There is a potential problem in installing DOS or Windows on a DOS-based machine if the distribution software is supplied on CD-ROM. Describe this potential problem and offer one possible solution.

8. You can bypass the installation of files included in the CONFIG.SYS and AUTOEXEC.BAT files during DOS system bootup by pressing a special key as soon as you see the message "Installing MS DOS." What is this special key?

9. By default, MS-DOS installs in what directory on your hard drive?

10. A special driver file supplied with MS-DOS and all DOS-based programs permits you to configure a CD-ROM drive. This file is named _____.

11. The DOS program MEMMAKER is used to

    a. Install more physical memory on your computer.

    b. Configure existing memory on your machine for maximum efficiency.

    c. Make additional memory available for your Windows programs.

    d. None of the above.

12. To install Windows for Workgroups from a CD-ROM disk, you will need access to two hardware components in DOS first. They are

    a. A mouse and a CD-ROM drive.

    b. A TV monitor and a printer.

    c. Speakers and a sound card.

    d. A keyboard and a sound card.

13. Three of the following protocols are routinely installed as part of a Windows networking setup. Choose the entry below that is not part of the standard Windows networking setup.

    a. NetBEUI

    b. TCP/IP

    c. IPX/SPX

    d. NetCxn

14. A swap file is used to supplement RAM while programs are running. Windows will set up a dynamic swap file for you during operating system installation. For what reasons would you configure a permanent, fixed-size swap file instead?

15. The FDISK utility is used for what purpose?

16. When you set up a networking operating system, you must first make components of each local computer available to other computers on the network. This process is known as device _____.

17. Windows 98 and other operating systems frequently have update files to fix bugs and add enhancements. In today's computing environment there is a single source that is the best resource for obtaining operating system updates. What is it?

18. Windows NT is supplied in two configurations. What are they?

19. One advantage of Windows NT is that it can automatically create disk _____ during the installation process.

20. Windows NT has two popular versions today, 4.0 and 3.51. Each is analogous to products in the consumer Windows environment. What consumer products would you liken each of these NT versions to?

21. Sun Microsystems offers a popular UNIX version known as _____.

22. Another popular UNIX configuration is available as shareware and also as a commercial product. This UNIX is called _____.

23. The windowed interface for users of Linux and other UNIX systems is most commonly called _____.

24. The HCL helps ensure that you have the proper hardware available during some Windows NT and UNIX installs. HCL stands for what?

25. The Linux operating system is different from most other current popular operating systems in what regard?

26. Among the methods you can use to install Mac OS are (choose all that apply)

   a. Floppy disk

   b. CD-ROM

   c. AppleTalk network

   d. Over the Internet

27. Choosing the Customize button during Mac OS install allows you to

   a. Select which operating system you will install.

   b. Choose the install location.

   c. Choose various OS components you want to install.

   d. None of the above.

HANDS-ON PROJECTS

Be sure to read the text sections on installing these operating systems before attempting the Hands-on projects. The text contains important background information, such as hardware requirements, that you will need to know before attempting the installations.

PROJECT 4-1

In this activity you install MS-DOS version 6.22. Installations of other DOS versions will be similar, but some specifics may differ. You will need the MS-DOS installation floppy disks, as well as a blank, formatted floppy disk to save uninstall information, if necessary.

To install MS-DOS version 6.22:

   1. Power off the computer and insert MS-DOS version 6.22 disk 1 in the A: drive (this exercise assumes that your floppy drive is A:).

2. Power on the computer. It should boot from the floppy disk. If it doesn't, follow the instructions in the text for Setting Disk Boot Order to boot from drive A:.

3. You will see the message "Starting MS-DOS", as the operating system loads. Loading the operating system from floppy disk takes a lot longer than loading it from hard disk, so be patient. After a while, you will be presented with the initial setup screen, followed by the main menu as shown earlier in Figure 4-1.

4. Press **Enter** to start setup.

If your hard disk has not yet been partitioned, the installer will tell you this, and it will start the FDISK program to give you a chance to make a partition. (Refer to Chapter 3 on creating partitions in DOS.) If you are using an Upgrade version for a new install, please refer to the section on this topic in the text of the chapter, and follow the instructions there.

5. On the appropriate screen, specify the country you live in, your keyboard layout, and the correct date and time. If the default setting for USA is correct, simply press **Enter**, unless you need to change the date and time. If you do, simply choose the time zone that matches yours.

6. Next, you will be asked which directory you wish to use for DOS, which will be C:\DOS by default. Although it is possible to change this directory, it is not a good idea. Many programs meant to run under DOS assume the operating system and its utilities are in C:\DOS, and unless you have a special circumstance that makes this impractical, you should not change this option. Press **Enter** to accept the default directory, and MS-DOS will be copied to your machine. You will see the progress bar while files are being copied, as shown in Figure 4-15. (Your screen may vary slightly depending on your hardware and software configuration.)

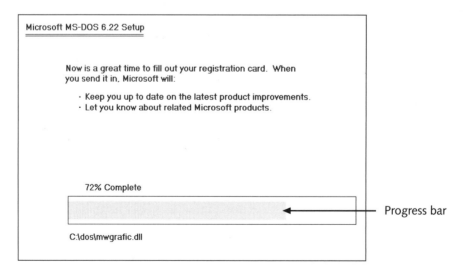

Figure 4-15   MS-DOS installing files screen

7. Insert subsequent floppy disks and press **Enter** when prompted.

8. When the copy process is completed, you will be prompted to remove all disks from the drives and press **Enter**. You will be prompted to restart your computer. Press **Enter**. The machine will restart from the hard disk.

9. If you made any changes to the Extended BIOS (i.e., changing the boot disk order), now would be a good time to undo the changes you made.

10. You now have a basic MS-DOS setup. Installing CD-ROM and mouse drivers, and optimizing memory are covered in Hands-on Projects 4-2 and 4-3.

PROJECT 4-2

In this project you install CD-ROM and mouse drivers for the DOS operating system you installed in Project 4-1.

To install CD-ROM and mouse drivers:

1. Locate the driver for your particular CD-ROM hardware on the disk that came with the CD-ROM. Copy this driver to a directory on your hard disk; the root directory would be a good place. Assuming your driver is called CD.SYS, and it is on the floppy in drive A:, you would type the command **COPY A:\CD.SYS C:** and press **Enter**.

2. Now tell the operating system about the driver; you do this in the CONFIG.SYS file using the DOS Edit utility. At the command prompt, type **EDIT C:\CONFIG.SYS** and press **Enter**. This brings up the text of the CONFIG.SYS file.

3. Go to the end of the file, and add the line **DEVICE=C:\CD.SYS /D:CD0**. This line instructs DOS to load the device driver. DEVICE= tells DOS this is a device driver, C:\CD.SYS tells DOS what file to load and run, and /D:CD0 tells the driver what name to use to reference the CD-ROM drive. Remember this name, as you will need it in a minute. D:CD0 is a common and convenient name for the initial CD-ROM drive you install. You can use other names, but we recommend this one.

4. Choose **File**, **Save** to save the changes to CONFIG.SYS, then **File**, **Exit** to exit the DOS Editor.

5. The line you added to CONFIG.SYS will load the driver when your system boots, but you also need to add a line to the AUTOEXEC.BAT file to deal with the CD file system, the Microsoft CD Extension or MSCDEX. To edit AUTOEXEC.BAT, from the command prompt, type **EDIT C:\AUTOEXEC.BAT** to display the contents of the file in the DOS Editor.

6. Somewhere above the line that starts with SMARTDRV, add the line **C:\DOS\MSCDEX /D:CD0**. Save the file and exit the DOS Editor as indicated in Step 4.

7. Restart the machine by pressing **Ctrl+Alt+Del**, and if all goes well, you should see some new messages, one of which should be that your CD-ROM drive has been assigned drive letter D:, or something similar. This means you now have successfully loaded the CD-ROM drivers. Time to pop in a CD and make sure everything works!

8. You will also need to add a mouse driver if you wish to use such a pointing device. DOS ships with a driver called MOUSE, which you will find in the DOS directory. To enable mouse support for all DOS programs that support the use of a mouse, open AUTOEXEC.BAT in the DOS editor as described in Step 5, and add the line **C:\DOS\MOUSE** to your AUTOEXEC.BAT file.

If you are installing a mouse driver from a vendor-supplied disk, Step 8 is probably unnecessary. The installer software should insert the required information for you.

If you receive a "Bad command or filename" error after you restart your machine, your mouse driver may not be in C:\DOS (the default directory for DOS drivers). Check your C: drive for another mouse-related directory, such as C:\MSMOUSE, and substitute that directory for C:\DOS\MOUSE in Step 8. If you can't find a mouse driver, you may have to install a mouse driver from the manufacturer's distribution disk, or contact the vendor for a driver.

9. Save the file and exit the DOS Editor as described in Step 4.

If you make a mistake in editing the CONFIG.SYS or AUTOEXEC.BAT files, you may see some error messages flash by when the machine starts. Often they go by too quickly to read, or they are not specific enough to tell you what caused them. When you restart the computer, press the F8 key as you see the Starting MS-DOS message appear. DOS will ask you to confirm every line in CONFIG.SYS and AUTOEXEC.BAT before it is run. This gives you the chance to see which lines caused the error messages.

If you hold down the left Shift key (or F5) while the Starting MS-DOS message appears, you will drop onto a clean command prompt, without CONFIG.SYS and AUTOEXEC.BAT being executed. This can be handy when you have corrupted drivers that prevent the operating system from starting.

PROJECT 4-3

In this project, you optimize the memory configuration of the DOS you installed in Hands-on Project 4-1.

Before you start MEMMAKER, make copies of the CONFIG.SYS and AUTOEXEC.BAT file and put them in a safe place. There are instances when you will be glad you have them.

To optimize DOS memory configuration:

1. From the MS-DOS command prompt, type **MEMMAKER** and press **Enter**. You will be guided through the various MEMMAKER selections; use the **Custom** option when asked to select how you wish to run MEMMAKER. When running with the Custom option, you can indicate whether you will at some point in the future be running MS Windows 3.11 on this machine. In this way, you can optimize your machine for future Windows usage.

2. Respond to the MEMMAKER prompts. MEMMAKER will restart the computer two or three times during the optimization process; the prompts and progress are fairly self-explanatory. When MEMMAKER is done, an overview screen appears, like the one shown in Figure 4-16.

```
Microsoft MemMaker
_____

MemMaker has finished optimizing your system's memory. The following
table summarizes the memory (in bytes) on your system:

                            Before      After
Memory Type                 MemMaker    MemMaker    Change
_____

Free conventional memory    606,520     632,896      26,376

Upper memory:
  Used by programs                0      29,504      29,504
  Reserved for Windows            0           0           0
  Reserved for EMS                0           0           0
  Free                            0     129,540           0

Expanded memory:            Disabled    Disabled


Your original CONFIG.SYS and AUTOEXEC.BAT files have been saved
as CONFIG.UMB and AUTOEXEC.UMB. If MemMaker changed your Windows
SYSTEM.INI file, the original file was saved as SYSTEM.UMB.

TER=Exit  ESC=Undo changes
```

Figure 4-16   MEMMAKER overview screen

PROJECT 4-4

In this project you install Windows for Workgroups 3.11 on a computer that already has DOS (preferably version 6.2 or higher) installed.

To install Windows for Workgroups 3.11:

1. To start the process from floppy disks, begin at the DOS prompt, insert the Windows for Workgroups disk 1 and type **A:\SETUP** or **B:\SETUP** (depending on whether your floppy is in drive A: or drive B:). To start from CD-ROM, type **D:\SETUP**, where D: is substituted for the letter that identifies your CD drive. You will see a screen that looks similar to Figure 4-17 on the next page.

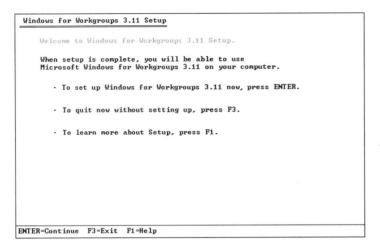

```
Windows for Workgroups 3.11 Setup

   Welcome to Windows for Workgroups 3.11 Setup.

   When setup is complete, you will be able to use
   Microsoft Windows for Workgroups 3.11 on your computer.

      · To set up Windows for Workgroups 3.11 now, press ENTER.

      · To quit now without setting up, press F3.

      · To learn more about Setup, press F1.




ENTER=Continue   F3=Exit   F1=Help
```

Figure 4-17   Initial Windows for Workgroups installer screen

2. Press **Enter** to install Windows. A screen appears asking what kind of installation you wish to perform. You have two options, the Express or Custom install. Choosing the **Custom** install allows you more control over how Windows is set up.

3. The install program will next ask for the path in which you want to install Windows. As with DOS, it's best to accept the default, in this case **C:\WINDOWS**. Although most Windows applications have intelligence built in to know where to find the Windows directory even if it is in a different place, there is usually not a reason to put it anywhere else.

4. Press **Enter**, and after a short wait while hardware and software is being detected, the next screen reveals the hardware and software that was detected. Check the results on this screen carefully against your device information and documentation, since the settings Windows assigns may be wrong. If you have special drivers for a video card, for example, or for any other device on the list, or if you need to change a wrong setting, use the up and down arrow keys to highlight your selection, then press **Enter**. Scroll to the bottom of the menu of options and choose **Other**. (You may have to scroll the list. This is not obvious as there are no scroll bars.) You will be asked for the path to the driver for that device. Type in that path, press **Enter**, and the drivers will be loaded. See the manual that came with your hardware for more details.

On machines with SuperVGA video cards, the Windows 3.11 installer will normally detect a VGA card. It is a good idea to select one of the listed drivers, or to use the VGA driver disk from the hardware vendor. If you have repeated installation failures and you are using a SuperVGA driver of some sort, try installing Windows with the plain VGA driver. You can change these hardware preferences later, once installation is completed.

5. When you finish with the selection of hardware, press **Enter** to continue. If necessary, insert appropriate disks when prompted. Windows files copy to the hard disk, and then Windows is started. At this time, you will see a screen that tells you that the computer may crash. Assuming the machine does not crash, you will next see a notice in

Windows that tells you your network card is being detected (if you are on a network), again warning you the machine may hang.

6. Next you will be asked for your user information; full name, company name, and product number. The product number can be left blank since it is not used for anything. You should enter your name and company name. Press **Enter** and the confirmation screen appears. If you made any mistakes in entering your information, click the Change button to change them. Otherwise, press **Enter** to continue, and you will see the Windows Setup window, as shown in Figure 4-18.

4

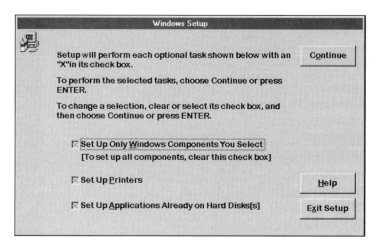

Figure 4-18   Windows 3.11 Setup window

7. From the Windows Setup window, you can choose to set up all Windows components, to install printers, and to let Windows find applications already on your hard disk. If you have a printer, install it at this time. You can allow Windows to find the software already installed on your machine. If you do not have a printer, or if you do not want to detect installed software, uncheck those two options. Click **Continue** to go to the next screen, which lets you elect which optional components of Windows you wish to install.

8. The bottom three selections on this screen, Games, Screen Savers, and Wallpapers, are optional, and they can be unselected if hard disk space is at a premium. It's best to install the **Accessories** and **Readme** files, but if hard disk space is at a premium, you can choose the Accessories you need. To do this, click **Select Files** next to Accessories, and pick the files you want. If you do not need the Microsoft Mail Client, the Schedule+ program, and the Fax software, you can save quite a bit of disk space by unselecting these items. (Note that at the bottom of this screen there is an indicator for disk space required for the selected component. This is the *additional* disk space, on top of the space already required for Windows.) When done selecting components, click **OK** to return to the Windows Setup screen.

9. Click **Continue**, and Windows will install all the files specified. Depending on the speed of your computer and on whether you install from CD or floppy disks, this may take only a minute or so, or it can take as long as 20 minutes.

10. Next, if you chose to install a printer, you will be presented with the Printer selection screen; you can choose a printer from the list. If you have a driver disk for your printer, or if your printer is not listed and you have a driver disk, you can choose the **Install Unlisted** or **Updated Printer** options. Selecting one of these options, then clicking **Install** will prompt you for the location of the printer driver. If you select a printer, it will by default be set as Connected to LPT1, the first printer port. If this is not correct, select the printer in the top list, then click **Connect**, and change the port to which the printer is connected. Specific details about the printer, such as paper source, which tray to use and other details, can be set by selecting the printer and clicking Setup. When you are done with printer setup, click **Continue**.

11. The Network Setup screen (Figure 4-19) will appear (Windows for Workgroups only). Click **Advanced** on this screen to see more details.

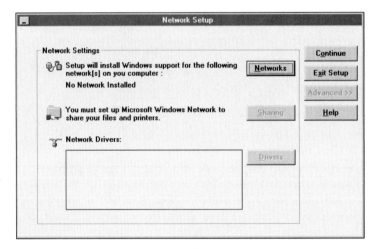

Figure 4-19   Windows for Workgroups Network Setup screen

12. Click **Networks**. You need to select the network type you wish to support. Chapter 8 deals with networking in more detail; for now we will show you how to set up the most popular network for use with Windows for Workgroups, the Microsoft Windows Network. To do this, select **Install Microsoft Windows Network** and click **OK**.

13. Click **Sharing** from the Network Setup window. The Sharing window appears. This is where you can specify whether this machine should be a server on the Windows for Workgroups network. Being a server in addition to a client will take some additional resources, and obviously you should turn this feature off if you do not wish to share files or printers with others. For this installation, leave this option selected. Click **OK**.

14. Click **Drivers** on the Network Setup screen to bring up the Network Drivers window. You will see a list of the adapters detected in your machine, if any. If you have a

network card that was not detected, you can click **Add Adapter** to show a list of available adapters. At the top of this list, you can once again select the option to use a custom driver from a disk you provide. Click **OK** to return to the Network Drivers window. At this point you should determine whether the settings selected for your adapters are correct. Select the adapter from the list, then click **Setup**. A window appears which allows you to identify the adapter to the computer. If these settings are incorrect, your adapter will not work! You should be aware that in many cases, Windows does *not* complete these settings correctly, so you should always check to make sure that what is in this window is indeed the way your hardware is set up. When you're finished, click **OK**.

15. After you have an adapter installed, you can choose to add and/or remove network protocols. For this example, select **Microsoft NetBEUI**, the default networking protocol in Windows environments, and click **Set as Default Protocol**.

16. Close the window, and click **Continue** in the Network Setup window. The Microsoft Windows Network Names window will appear.

17. Enter the user name, workgroup name, and computer name (refer to the chapter for hints on naming). When you have made your entries, press **OK** to continue. Windows Setup will now copy the network drivers.

18. You have the option of letting Windows automatically make modifications to your CONFIG.SYS and AUTOEXEC.BAT files, or to review and edit changes, before modifications are made, or to make the modifications later. You should choose to **review and edit changes**. When you do, you will see what your AUTOEXEC.BAT and CONFIG.SYS files will look like before and after the proposed changes. Windows usually makes all changes correctly, but it is educational to see what has changed. After a while, you will recognize changes that are wrong and correct them. Typically, Windows for Workgroups will add the command *net start* to the AUTOEXEC.BAT file. This is what starts the network functionality. Any version of Windows 3.11 will automatically change the MSCDEX version that is used, if you have a CD-ROM drive, and the Path statement will typically be modified. Click **Continue**.

19. If you would like to automatically start Windows when the computer boots, go to the bottom of the AUTOEXEC.BAT file, and add the command **WIN**, the command that launches the Windows operating system. When you are done with AUTOEXEC.BAT, click **Continue** or press **Enter**.

20. You will now see the CONFIG.SYS file, where a few lines have also changed or been added. In Windows for Workgroups, you will see the IFSHLP.SYS device driver added to support device sharing. If you have no other changes for AUTOEXEC.BAT or CONFIG.SYS, click **Continue**.

Windows will tell you where copies of your old CONFIG.SYS and AUTOEXEC.BAT were saved; you might want to write this down since it could be handy to access these files if your computer will not start properly.

21. Next, the Program Manager is set up, a process that may take a while. Then the Setup Application window appears; here you tell Windows where to look for installed applications. Use the **Path** option, which means Windows will look only in the active execution path to find applications that should be added to Program Manager. Click **Search Now**, and all applications that Windows recognized will be shown, with an option to choose how they should appear in Program Manager. When the search is completed, select the applications you want to see in the Program Manager and close this dialog box. After you have completed this, installation is complete.

Be careful when picking an application; there are some background settings that are changed based on the application you select from the pop-up list. If the application is not listed, click **None of the above**. Never select the wrong application.

22. Now you can choose to view a short tutorial that introduces Windows basics, or you can skip the tutorial. Next, you will be shown the Exit Windows Setup window. You have two options here: Return to DOS or Restart the computer. Remove any floppies and click **Restart Computer** so that the new drivers and changes to CONFIG.SYS and AUTOEXEC.BAT will take effect. MS-DOS should start as always. If you added the WIN command to the end of your AUTOEXEC.BAT file, Windows will start immediately. If you are on a network, and the network card was set up correctly, you will be prompted to log in to the network, and your installation is complete.

If you get an error message saying your network is not working properly, click OK through all the error messages, then from Program Manager's Main window select Windows Setup. Open the Windows menu and choose Network. From the Network window double-click Network Setup. The same window you saw during Setup will appear, and you can make the changes needed. When you make changes, you may be notified that your CONFIG.SYS and AUTOEXEC.BAT files have changed, and that your machine will be rebooted.

23. After installation is complete, you may want to adjust the Virtual Memory settings and run MEMMAKER as detailed in the section entitled "Adjusting Memory" in the Windows 3.1x section of this chapter.

PROJECT 4-5

Most of us will probably never install an operating system from scratch. Usually when you buy a computer an operating system is already installed. If you want to change the operating system you probably purchase an upgrade—a version of the software that won't work by itself; it requires the presence of an earlier version of the operating system to function properly. (Chapter 5 covers upgrade installations.)

However, if you build a computer yourself, or if you install a new boot hard drive, then you'll need to install a full version of an operating system. With modern operating systems the process is very similar to installing an upgrade, however, there are some differences. For example, you will have to install a printer for the first time, you'll need to install and configure communications components, and so on.

In this project you install a full version of Windows 95 from a CD-ROM distribution medium. We assume the new hard drive already is installed, that you have used FDISK to create a DOS partition and that you have used FORMAT to prepare it to receive the new operating system.

To install a full version of Windows 95:

1. Obtain or create a bootable floppy disk. You'll need a bootable DOS disk, a Windows 95 boot floppy, etc. Also make sure this bootable floppy includes support for your CD-ROM drive. Your installation will be easier if you have also installed DOS-level support for a mouse. However, the setup routine itself also looks for a mouse and probably will install the drivers needed for it if your mouse is a standard device Setup can recognize.

2. Insert the floppy disk into the **A:** drive and boot the system.

3. Insert the Windows 95 CD-ROM into the CD-ROM drive. Type **d:setup**, where **d:** is the drive letter of your CD-ROM drive. You will see an information message that says "Setup is now going to perform a routine check on your system. To continue press Enter. To quit Setup, press ESC."

4. Press **Enter**. Setup runs the SCANDISK utility to verify the integrity of your hard drive. When SCANDISK is finished, you will see a message that says, "Copying files needed for setup." Next you will see a dialog box titled Windows 95 Setup with the message "Welcome to Windows 95 Setup."

5. Click **Continue** or press **Alt+C**. You will see a message that says "Now preparing the Windows 95 Setup Wizard" and you'll see a progress bar in the Setup window while Setup copies files to your hard drive.

6. When the Software License Agreement dialog box appears, read the agreement, and click **Yes** to continue the Installation Wizard. The next dialog box summarizes the next steps the wizard will complete in the installation process: Collecting information, Copying Windows 95 Files, and Restarting the system. The first choice is displayed in bold face, indicating this is the next step. You will see this dialog box twice more during the installation process as each section of steps is completed.

7. Click **Next** to continue.

8. Choose the directory where you want Windows installed. The default directory is C:\Windows. This is the best choice.

9. Click **Next**. You will see a Preparing Directory dialog box, then the Setup Options dialog box will be displayed. The choices on this dialog box are:

   - Typical — Recommended for most computers
   - Portable — Files required for portable computers
   - Compact — A minimal install that includes no optional components
   - Custom — Allows you to customize all installed components

   Although the onscreen prompt indicates the Custom option is recommended only for advanced users, programmers, or system administrators, it is recommended that all users choose this option. If you choose Typical, the Setup Wizard determines which components to install for you. Later, as you install other software, you may be required to locate your Windows 95 CD and add more components. It is usually easier to install everything the first time. The rest of this project assumes you have chosen the Custom installation option.

10. Click the **Custom** option button to select it and click **Next**. You will see a Certificate of Authenticity dialog box. Enter the CD-key number, which may be printed on the cover of your Windows 95 manual, on a separate piece of paper supplied with the software, or on the back of the case in which the CD was shipped. If you are installing a version of the software that was shipped with your computer, this number takes the form:

xxxxx-OEM-xxxxxxx-xxxxx

If you purchased the operating system outright from another outlet, you won't see the OEM designation as part of the CD-key.

11. Enter whatever key was provided with your version of the operating system and click **Next**. A User Information dialog box is displayed.

12. Enter your name and company name, if applicable, in the fields provided and click **Next**. The Analyzing Your Computer dialog box opens. It asks whether you want Setup to scan for available hardware or if you want to manually install everything. You should choose the default, to scan the system.

13. Click **Next** to view a hardware list. This is a quick list of hardware Setup already knows about, such as a sound card, network interface card, and so on.

14. Click the check boxes beside the hardware you want to install. In general this should be all of the hardware displayed on this dialog box.

15. Click **Next** to continue scanning the system for additional hardware. A progress bar in the middle of the dialog box shows how far along you are in the process. This part of the installation will take several minutes until finally the Select Components dialog box is displayed. You should choose all possible options on this dialog box. Notice that in the list of components there are check marks beside some, no checks beside others. In addition, some of the boxes with check marks are gray and some are white. Setup has selected a subset of available components as a starting point.

16. Click any empty check boxes to select them. If a check box is gray, click Details to display a list of available components under that main heading. Check all of the options in this list and click OK to return to the main Select Components dialog box. Repeat this process until all available components are chosen.

17. Click **NEXT** to select the options you have chosen and continue the installation.

18. If you have a network adapter installed you should see a Network Configuration dialog box. The default choices are:

- Client for Microsoft Networks
- Client for NetWare Networks
- Dial-Up Adapter
- IPX/SPX-compatible Protocol
- NetBEUI

If you aren't using a network with this computer right now, or if you want to configure networking later, simply click **Next**.

19. If you aren't using a Novell network, you don't need the Novell networking components, so click IPX/SPX-compatible protocol and click Remove. Setup will remove
this entry as well as the Client for NetWare entry. This leaves everything you need to
network in a Microsoft Windows environment as well as sets the stage for dial-up
networking, such as connecting to the Internet.

20. If you will be using the Internet or if you are networking in a UNIX environment,
you need to install the TCP/IP protocol. We will assume you want to install the
TCP/IP protocol.

21. Click **Add** and choose **Protocol** from the list of available options. Click **Add**.

22. At the Select Network Protocol prompt, click **Microsoft** in the manufacturer list (left
side of the dialog box) and then click **TCP/IP** from the Network Protocols list on
the right side of the dialog box.

23. Click **OK**. TCP/IP appears in the Network Configuration dialog box.

24. Click **File & Print sharing** to display the File and Print Sharing dialog box.

25. Click in the boxes that turn on Share printers and/or Share files and click **OK**.

26. Click **Next** to display the Identification dialog box.

27. Type a name for this computer.

28. Type a workgroup name. It is best if this is a relatively short, easy to use name. But
remember that all computers on the network that you want to communicate with
each other should be in the same workgroup.

29. Type a description in the Description field. This can be anything that describes this
particular computer.

30. Click **Next** to display the Computer Settings dialog box. This is a recap of the configuration settings you just specified.

31. Review the settings and click **Next** if everything is okay. To change an item displayed
in this screen, click Back instead of Next.

32. The next window asks if you want to create a startup disk. You should click **Yes** and
then click **Next**.

33. The Start Copying Files dialog box is displayed. Click **Next**.

34. The next screen asks for a disk on which to copy the startup files. Insert a blank, formatted disk and click **OK**. A progress bar shows the file copy progress.

35. When you see "Setup has finished creating startup disk," remove the disk from
the drive and click **OK**. Setup continues by copying more files to your hard disk.
Promotional and tip dialog boxes are displayed to introduce you to the Windows 95
environment.

36. When all files are copied you should see the Finishing Setup dialog box. Click **Finish**.
Setup will restart your computer. After the reboot you will see "Getting Ready to
Run Windows 95 for the First time." Setup is finishing the final Windows configura-
tion, which may take several minutes.

37. Finally you will see a user name and password dialog box. Type the name you want to use to log into Windows and your network, then click in the Password field and enter a password (if you are using a password; otherwise leave the Password field blank).

38. Press **Enter** or click **OK** and you will see the Set Windows Password dialog box. This is a crosscheck to make sure you haven't mistyped the password. Enter the password again and press **Enter** or click **OK**. You will see the Setting up Hardware and Plug and Play dialog box.

39. Set the system clock when you see the Date/Time Properties dialog box, then click **Close**.

40. If you included Windows messaging in your component choices at the beginning of this process, you will see a dialog box asking whether you have used Windows messaging before. Since this is a fresh install, the correct answer is **No**. Click **Next** to display the Inbox Setup Wizard opening dialog box.

41. Click the check boxes beside the services you want to use and click **Next**. You may be asked for your area code and other information as part of dial-up networking configuration. Enter the requested data and click **OK**.

42. Continue with the Inbox Setup Wizard, answering questions specific to your particular installation and clicking **Next** on each Wizard screen to move on to the next step.

43. You will be prompted to let Windows find and configure your modem, or you can manually set up the modem yourself. You should let the computer scan the system to find your modem and set it up for you.

44. If you included fax services as part of your original configuration specification, you will next see a dialog box asking whether you want the Fax server to answer every incoming call. Unless you have a dedicated telephone line for fax services, choose No here.

45. Click **Next** to display the Microsoft FAX dialog box. Enter your full name, country, and fax number with area code at the prompts.

46. Click **Next** to move to the next wizard screen where you can enter the path to your post office. This information is required only if you will be using LAN-based e-mail. If you are using only Internet e-mail, you can bypass this option by entering a bogus directory (C:\ is a good choice), and accepting the entry when Windows warns that it can't find the post office. Otherwise, check with your LAN administrator for the correct location of the post office files.

47. Type a mailbox name and password. (Consult your LAN administrator or enter bogus data. You can correct it later if necessary.)

48. Click **Next**, then click **Finish** to complete the Inbox configuration process. The Add Printer Wizard launches.

49. Click **Next** and choose Local or Network printer from the next dialog box, depending upon which type of printer you are installing.

50. Click **Next** and choose a printer from the list or select the network host printer you want to use.

51. Click **Next** and click **OK** when Setup says it wants to restart your computer.

52. After the reboot, enter your user name and password (the same combination you chose the first time the system rebooted). The startup process continues and final setup is complete.

> If Setup didn't install or configure all of your hardware—your CD-ROM drive or sound card, for example—click on Start, point to Settings, choose Control Panel, and select Add New Hardware. Let Windows scan your system for new hardware or manually configure the missing pieces.

4

Project 4-6

In this project you install a full version of Windows 98 from a CD-ROM distribution medium. We assume the new hard drive already is installed, that you have used FDISK to create a DOS partition and that you have used FORMAT to prepare it to receive the new operating system.

The installation of Windows 98 is very similar to that of Windows 95. However, you will notice quickly that Windows 98 is more sophisticated. The Setup program does more of the work for you and there is less necessity for user intervention; for example, you don't have to keep clicking Next to continue the process. Once you have chosen the basic components you want, and specified the directory where you want Windows 98 to reside, the rest of the installation process is mostly automatic. Please read the section on Installing Windows 98 in this chapter before completing this exercise.

To install a full version of Windows 98:

1. Obtain or create a bootable floppy disk. You'll need a bootable DOS disk, or a Windows 95 boot floppy disk. Also make sure this bootable floppy includes support for your CD-ROM drive. Your installation will be easier if you have also installed DOS-level support for a mouse. However, the setup routine itself also looks for a mouse and probably will install the drivers needed for it if your mouse is a standard device Setup can recognize.

2. Insert the floppy disk into the A: drive and boot the system.

3. Insert the Windows 98 CD-ROM into the CD-ROM drive. Type **d:setup**, where **d:** is the drive letter of your CD-ROM drive. You will see an information message that says "Setup is now going to perform a routine check on your system. To continue press Enter. To quit Setup, press ESC."

4. Press **Enter**. Setup runs the SCANDISK utility to verify the integrity of your hard drive. When SCANDISK is finished, you will see a message that says, "Copying files needed for setup." Next you will see a dialog box titled Windows 98 Setup with the message "Welcome to Windows 98 Setup."

5. Click **Continue** or press **Alt+C**. You will see a message that says "Setup is preparing the Windows 98 Setup Wizard" and you'll see the progress bar in the Setup window while Setup copies files to your hard drive. On the left of your screen is a menu that shows the steps that will be completed with the current step highlighted. You'll also

see an estimate of the time remaining. At this stage, with a medium speed CD-ROM and reasonably capable computer, you will see a time remaining of 35–40 minutes.

6. Click **Next** and choose the directory where you want Windows installed. The default directory is C:\Windows. This is the best choice. However, if you want to change the directory, click the option button beside the Other Directory prompt.

7. Click **Next**. You will see a Preparing Directory dialog box, and messages that say "Checking for installed components" and "Checking for available disk space." In a few moments you will see the Setup Options dialog box. The choices on this dialog box are:

   ■ Typical — Recommended for most computers

   ■ Portable — Files required for portable computers

   ■ Compact — A minimal install that includes no optional components

   ■ Custom — Allows you to customize all installed components

   Although the onscreen prompt indicates the Custom option is recommended only for advanced users, programmers, or system administrators, all users should choose this option. If you choose Typical the Setup Wizard determines which components to install for you. Later, as you install other software, you may be required to locate your Windows 98 CD and add more components. It is usually easier to install everything the first time. The rest of this project assumes you have chosen the Custom installation option.

8. Click **Custom** option button to select it and click **Next** to select available components. As with Windows 95, you should select every available option during this initial installation to avoid having to repeat any of the installation process later.

9. Click **Next** to display an identification screen. Enter a computer name, the workgroup and a computer description.

10. Click **Next** to display the Computer Settings dialog box. This will show you a brief list of basic computer hardware, such as the keyboard layout and regional settings. You should accept the defaults on this screen (however, you can click Change to make any modifications you want to this list).

11. Click **Next** to view the Establishing Your location Location dialog box. Accept the default or choose from the list (United States, United Kingdom, Turkey, etc.).

12. Click **Next** to display the Startup Disk dialog box. When prompted, insert a blank floppy disk into the drive.

13. Click **OK** and Setup begins copying files to the floppy disk. A progress bar shows how much is left to do. Eventually you will see a message that says "Setup has finished creating your startup disk."

14. Remove the disk and click **OK** to continue. You will see a dialog box that reports "Start Copying Files." This is an informational dialog box and Setup waits on this screen for you to click **Next** to continue the installation.

15. Click **Next**. The Welcome to Microsoft Windows 98 dialog box is displayed. You are invited to "Sit back and relax while Windows 98 installs on your computer." Note the time remaining at the lower left of the screen. At this point it should be about

30 minutes. As more files are copied you will see informational messages in the middle of the screen: promotional material, tips, progress reports.

16. In the User Information dialog box, fill in your name and the company name, if applicable. Click **Next** to continue.

17. When the Software License Agreement appears, read the agreement, and click the button beside the **I accept** prompt and then click **Next**.

18. Setup then asks for the CD product key. It is located on documentation that came with your software or on the back of the case in which the CD itself was delivered. The Windows 98 CD key takes the form:

XXXXX-XXXXX-XXXXX-XXXXX-XXXXX

You will enter a combination of letters and numbers to fill in all of the blanks. The Key is not case sensitive, so enter the letters in either upper or lower case. Click **Next**.

Eventually you will see a message that indicates that Windows is setting up hardware and Plug and Play devices. One or two more dialog boxes tell you that hardware is being detected. Windows 98 does a pretty good job of detecting the hardware you have installed and of configuring it. However, you must make sure to have all printers, scanners and other devices installed on the system and turned on before reaching this stage of the installation to ensure proper detection and configuration. You are 13 to 15 minutes away from finishing the installation at this point.

19. Set the system clock when you see the Date & Time Properties dialog box, then click **Close**. You will also see a dialog box that says, "Windows is now setting up the following items:" followed by a list of remaining tasks, including Time Zone, Control Panel, Programs on the Start Menu, and more. Additional dialog boxes will show progress with each of these steps as they are completed.

20. Finally you will see a dialog box that asks for your user name and password. Type the name and password you want to use to log into Windows and click **OK**. The password in Windows 98 is not case sensitive. A Building Driver Information Database dialog box is displayed, then you will see various dialog boxes as Windows 98 finds your hardware components and installs the drivers they require.

21. Then you will see a large Welcome to Windows 98 dialog box with the following options:

- Register Now
- Connect to the Internet
- Discover Windows 98
- Maintain Your Computer

22. Click the X at the upper-right corner of this dialog box to close it.

23. If you want to install dial-up networking, double-click **My Computer**.

24. Choose **Dialup Networking** to launch the Dial-Up Networking Wizard. Follow the on-screen instructions, clicking **Next** at each stage to move on to the next step. (For more information on setting up dial-up networking, see Chapter 7.) You have successfully completed the installation of Windows 98!

PROJECT 4-7

Please read the section on Installing Windows NT in this chapter before completing this exercise. You will need one blank floppy disk during installation to make your Emergency Repair Disk. This installation should be performed on a "clean" machine, one with no prior operating system installed.

To install Windows NT Server 4.0:

1. Power off the computer.

2. If your machine can boot from CD-ROM, insert the Windows NT CD-ROM, and turn on your computer. If not, insert Setup disk 1 into drive A: and turn on the machine, and then insert the CD-ROM into the CD-ROM drive. This method automatically starts WINNT.EXE, and the first screen of the installer appears.

3. Setup checks the system configuration and requests you to insert Setup disk 2 and press **Enter**.

4. The NT Server Setup options appear. Press **Enter** to continue the installation.

5. Setup attempts to automatically detect mass storage device controllers, such as ESDI, IDE, and SCSI. This process requires Setup to load device drivers from many hardware vendors, contained on Setup disk 3. Press **Enter** and then you are prompted to insert disk 3. As requested, insert disk 3 and press **Enter**.

6. If Setup has problems detecting SCSI adapters for hard drives or CD-ROM drives, you might need a supplementary driver disk from the manufacturer to install these drivers. Press S if you need to manually select a driver from those suggested by Setup, or to install a driver from a manufacturer's disk.

 If Setup does not detect a SCSI adapter that is non-critical for the installation, such as a tape drive, you can install it later using the Windows NT Server Control Panel.

7. Press **Enter** to continue.

 If you receive a message that your hard disk may actually be larger than the size for which it is currently configured, press Enter to continue.

8. You will now see the license agreement. When finished reading, press **F8** to agree to the terms of the license.

9. If there is already a version of Windows NT loaded, you will see an upgrade choice. If there is an earlier version of Windows NT installed, press **Enter** to upgrade.

10. Setup lists information about your computer, such as type of PC, display, keyboard, etc. If a change needs to be made, use the arrow keys to highlight the selection and press **Enter** to view the alternatives. If the information is correct, highlight **No Changes: The above list matches my computer** and press **Enter**.

11. The detected disk drives and partitions are displayed, and Setup asks you where you want to install Windows NT. If you already have created a partition that you want to use, pick it from this list, and press Enter. Figure 4-20 shows two partitioned disks, drives C: and D:. Choose the partition on which you want to install Windows NT, and press **Enter**.

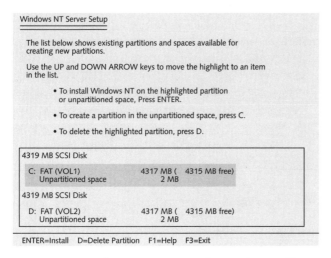

4

Figure 4-20   Selecting a partition for NT Server files

 You could also choose to press D to delete the FAT partition, and later repartition the drive for NTFS. You don't need to do this, because Setup gives you an opportunity to convert the partition to NTFS in the next screen. Also note that deleting a partition permanently erases all data on the partition!

12. Setup confirms the drive location for the NT Server partition and lists these choices: Format the partition using the FAT file system, Format the partition using the NTFS file system, Convert the partition to NTFS, or Leave the current file system intact (no changes).

 If you decide to use NTFS instead of FAT, you can either format the partition for NTFS or convert the partition to NTFS. Either choice works. However, if you want to leave a partition for MS-DOS or Windows 95, choose to leave the current file system intact.

13. Highlight a selection (such as **Convert the partition to NTFS**). Then select **C** to confirm your choice. Press **Enter** to continue.

14. A screen may appear that shows the minimum and maximum partition size. Select the size for the partition; we recommend at least 500 MB, preferably 1 GB for NT Server. Press **Enter** to continue.

15. If you choose to format the drive, a confirmation screen appears so you can confirm that the correct drive is selected. Press **F** to continue.

16. Setup shows the default path and name for the NT Server files. As before use the default values by pressing **Enter**. However, you can enter another directory path and name if you need to change it.

17. After selecting the path, Setup asks to check your hard disks. Press **Enter** to proceed with the check, which may take a few minutes. Upon completion of the test, a message appears that shows the NT files are being copied to the hard disk.

18. When the copy process is completed, remove all disks from the floppy and CD-ROM drives. Press **Enter** to restart the machine. This is the end of the text-based portion of the installation. Your computer may restart one or more times.

19. As prompted, insert the NT CD-ROM, and the GUI part of the installation, the NT Setup Wizard shown in Figure 4-21, will load. It shows the next three steps in setup: Gathering information about your computer, Installing Windows NT Networking, and Finishing Setup. Click **Next**.

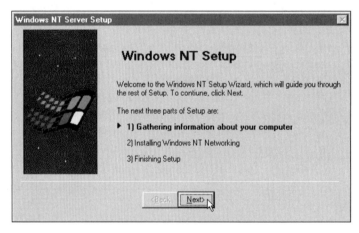

Figure 4-21   Windows NT Setup Wizard

20. Follow the prompts onscreen to enter your name and your organization's name, click **Next**, then enter the CD-key code from the sticker on the back of the NT Server CD-ROM case and click **Next**.

21. Next you see the license screen. Select the appropriate licensing option (Per Seat or Per Server) and click **Next**.

22. Enter the name of the server. This name must be unique on the network. Click **Next**.

23. Specify the server type, such as Stand-alone server or primary domain controller (PDC) and click **Next**. If you are installing a single NT server and do not plan to have other servers, choose Stand-alone server. If you will have multiple NT servers, and wish to keep user and permission information consistent among all of them, you might assign the first one as the primary domain controller (PDC), and other servers as member servers.

24. Enter the Administrator account password. Enter the password again in the confirmation box, then click **Next**.

This password is extremely important; without it you will not be able to manage your NT server. If you forget this password, the only way to get access to your server is to re-install it!

25. Select the option to create the Emergency Repair Disk (ERD), if desired. If you choose this option, the ERD will be created toward the end of the installation.

26. Specify the software components to add at the time of installation. Setup automatically marks the most commonly used components, as shown in Figure 4-22. To accept the components listed, click **Next**. (You can install other components after installation if you need them.)

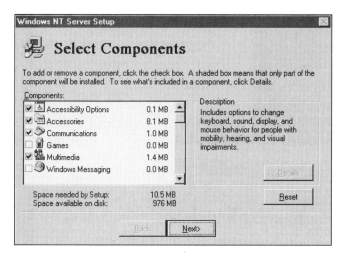

Figure 4-22   Selecting NT Server components to install

27. The Windows NT Setup screen appears, showing you are entering Setup Step 2. Click **Next** to continue.

28. Now, specify network connection options. Indicate whether the server is directly connected to the network, used for dial-up access, or both. If you have a network interface card, click **Wired to the network**. If a modem is installed, you might also click the Remote access to the network option, which enables you to later set up Remote Access Service (RAS). RAS is covered in greater detail in Chapter 8.

29. Select the option to install the Microsoft Internet Information Server (IIS), if desired, and click **Next**.

30. If you chose the Wired to the network option, click **Start Search** to have Setup automatically detect the network card. If the card is not detected, you can click Select from List to manually choose the card, or click Have Disk to use a driver from the NIC manufacturer's disk. Once the NIC is identified, click **Next**.

31. Select the protocol or protocols to be installed and click **Next**. You may select all protocols or only one, such as NetBEUI. You should select all three, TCP/IP, IPX/SPX, and NetBEUI. If you select TCP/IP, you will need to enter the IP

address information (get this from your instructor or network administrator) in another dialog box.

32. The networking services that will be installed are listed, as shown in Figure 4-23. The list will vary according to which protocols and network options you have selected. The checked services are required; you will not be able to unselect them. You can select other services by clicking Select from list, but adding services after installation is better. Click **Next** to confirm the default selections.

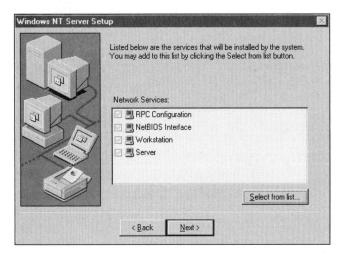

Figure 4-23 Selecting network services in Windows NT

33. Click **Next** to start the installation of network components by automatically detecting system settings for the NIC. Confirm the settings or change any as needed.

34. Setup is ready to install selected components. If you installed a network card and the TCP/IP protocol, you may be asked whether there is a DHCP server on your network. Consult your network administrator for the answer. Once you click **Yes** or **No** to the DHCP question, the networking files will be copied.

35. Confirm or change the network bindings as desired. It is best to go with the defaults and make any necessary changes later. Click **Next** to accept the selections made by Setup.

36. If you elected to install TCP/IP, you will see the TCP/IP Properties window. You must provide the IP address, subnet mask, and gateway information at a minimum. (Consult your instructor or network administrator on how to fill in this dialog box.) Make sure your server is connected to the network, and click **Next**. (*Note:* If you chose Yes for the DHCP option in Step 34, you may not see the TCP/IP Properties window. Proceed to Step 37.)

37. Click **Next** to start the network. The next windows you see depend on whether you chose to install a stand-alone server or if you are installing Workstation; you can choose to be part of a domain or a workgroup at this time. Enter the name of the domain or workgroup and click **Next**. Setup checks for any identical domain or workgroup names on the network. Click **Finish** if instructed to do so. A short message tells you that the software is configuring the server.

38. If the Microsoft Internet Information Server (IIS) 2.0 Setup screen appears, choose any IIS components you wish to install and click **OK**.

39. The Install Drivers screen appears. Choose an appropriate driver and click **OK**.

40. Adjust the date, time, and time zone in the Date/Time Properties dialog box, if necessary. Click **Close**. (The time, date, and video settings can also be reset from the Control Panel after NT is installed.)

41. Click **OK** to verify the display settings for the video card and monitor. (It's best to accept the defaults here. You can install new drivers after setup.) Click **Test** and then click **OK** to check that the color and resolution are accurate. Click **Yes** to continue.

42. Click **OK** in the Display Settings dialog box, and click **OK** in the Display Properties dialog box.

43. Setup informs you that it is installing program shortcuts, security, and messaging services. When these tasks are done, it prompts you to insert a blank disk for the Emergency Repair Disk in Drive A:. Insert the disk and click **OK**.

44. The last screen tells you the installation is complete. Remove any floppy disks and click the **Restart Computer** button. The server is rebooted into Windows NT Server.

45. When the new server restarts, a logon screen appears with a message to press the Ctrl+Alt+Del keys at the same time. This combination is used to start the logon screen and does not reboot the server. Press **Ctrl+Alt+Del**, enter **Administrator** as the account, and enter the Administrator password you supplied during installation. The NT Server desktop appears.

PROJECT 4-8

Please read the section on installing Linux earlier in this chapter for important hardware requirements.

To install the Red Hat Linux operating system:

1. Boot the system either from CD-ROM or from the included floppy disk; you will shortly see the installer option screen.

2. Choose one of several installation methods shown here; install or upgrade a system running Linux 2.0 or later by pressing **Enter**. Press **F3** to get the expert install, which will give you more control over the installation of hardware drivers; the normal installer will probe the system and find what hardware you have without your input. If you have configuration files for a custom setup, you use the Kickstart option. Use the standard Install by pressing **Enter**. After a while, you will be welcomed to Red Hat Linux.

3. Click **OK**. Select a language, then a keyboard type. Click **OK**.

4. Select the installation medium you want to use. CD-ROM is recommended, but there are a large number of options here to install from resources on a network. For more details about these options, look in the excellent installation section of the Red Hat manual. These options are very useful if you have to install a large number of machines that are on a network. For single machines, the CD-ROM install is recommended.

5. If you choose CD-ROM, you will be prompted to insert the CD. Click **OK**.

6. Select whether you wish to install a new system, or upgrade an existing system. For this example, choose **Install new system**.

7. You are now asked whether you have SCSI adapters. If so, they will be found at the next step in the process; you will get a chance to pick which driver you wish to use, and then you can choose whether you wish the system to find the adapter for you, or whether you wish to specify the parameters to use. When this section is completed, it is time to partition disks.

8. Red Hat will let you use Disk Druid or FDISK to partition your disk. We recommend that you use Disk Druid.

You should make at least two partitions; one for root (/), and one for swap. Make your root partition the first one on the drive, your Swap the second. Your swap partition should be about twice the amount of memory you have. The root should be big enough to facilitate the operating system. At least 1 GB is recommended; as much as 4 GB is better.

9. To make the root partition, click **Add**. The Edit New Partition window appears.

10. In the Mount Point text box, enter **/** (a forward slash).

11. In Size in Megs, choose the partition size in megabytes. (The growable option makes partitions that can later be extended; you may not want to use this option, as some errors have been reported because of it.)

12. Choose **Linux Native** as the type for your root partition. Select **Allowable Drives** and click **OK**.

13. Add a swap partition, then add any extra partitions you want on other mount points.

14. When you're done, click **OK** to continue.

 You can also delete a partition here. Be extremely careful if you do, as all data in that partition will be lost permanently!

15. If you made any changes, you will be asked if you wish to save changes. Click **Yes** if you do. Next you will select which partition you wish to use for swap space.

16. Select the **Check for bad blocks during format** option, so that the partition will be guaranteed good. Click **OK**. The swap space will then be formatted, a process that may take a while.

17. You will next be asked which partitions you wish to format; during install you should format all partitions that do not have data on them.

18. Select the **Check for bad blocks during format** option; it will take a bit longer but may save you a lot of trouble later. Click **OK**.

19. Now you select what package you wish to install. You should install the packages selected by default, and add functionality you may need. Printer support, network file system support, and Web server are the most useful in our experience. If you will be compiling programs, also select C Development, Development Libraries, and C++ Development. If you click Select Individual Packages, you will be able to go into very great detail as to what you do and do not wish to install. Keep in mind that it is possible to unselect packages you should not unselect, so it's better if you do not go down to that level of detail. Click **OK**.

20. A screen appears stating that a complete log of the installation will be kept. Click **OK** to continue.

21. The installer will now build the file systems on your hard disks, after which the installation process will begin. It will take several minutes to copy everything onto your hard disk, depending on the method of installation you choose, the speed of your machine and the number of packages you are installing. It could take up to an hour. When the installer has copied all files, the system will do a hardware probe if you chose to install the X Window System.

22. The installer likely will identify your mouse correctly, and you should choose **OK** twice.

23. Next, your video card will be identified. Again you should be able to just choose **OK**, or if the wrong card is picked, you can select the correct card from the list.

24. The appropriate monitor selection is up next; simply follow the on-screen prompts.

25. If you see a Screen Configuration dialog box asking if you want your video card probed, choose the default, **Don't Probe**.

26. Choose the amount of video card memory.

27. When prompted for a clock chip choice, use the recommended settings.

28. Click **Probe** to probe for clocks.

29. Next, pick the screen resolution you want to work in. At least 800 × 600 is recommended.

30. If you have a network card, LAN installation is next. The machine either finds your card for you, or lets you pick from a list of options if it cannot. If you pick from the list, you will next need to provide hardware parameters for your card.

31. When this is completed, choose whether you want to manually specify IP settings, or use BOOTP or DHCP. (We assume you are choosing the Static IP option at this point.) If you choose Static IP, you will be asked to provide the IP Address, Netmask, Default Gateway, and Primary nameserver.

32. The next window will ask for your domain name and host name, as well as any additional name servers. Remember: The host name is everything before the first dot in your Internet name, the domain name is everything thereafter.

33. You are now ready for the final Linux installation steps. The next window that appears will be the Clock setting; here you pick the local time zone from a list.

34. On the services screen that appears next, you can choose which services you wish to start. You should leave the defaults, but unselect *dhcpd* if you will not be using this machine as a DHCP server, *lpd* if this machine will not be a print server, *named* if this machine will not be a name server, *nfs* and *nfsfs* if this machine will not be a fileserver and *snmpd* in all cases. (If your selections vary from these, check with your instructor about which services to select.) Click **OK**.

35. You can next configure a printer, but you should do not do this during installation.

36. You will now be asked to enter the root password. Enter the password again and click **OK**.

37. Next, you will be given the option to create a boot disk for your system, an option that is recommended. Make a different boot disk for each system you install; they are unique.

38. You now have to choose where to install the boot record. If Linux is the only OS on this machine, choose the Master Boot Record, otherwise choose the first sector of the partition. Click **OK**.

39. If you see a Lilo Installation screen at this point, simply accept the default settings.

40. The next question is about boot options; you can leave this option blank. The boot loader will be installed, and installation is complete.

41. After the system reboots, you should go to *http://www.redhat.com* and look at the errata section, to find any patches and updates you need to install. Carefully follow online instructions at the site.

42. When Linux starts, you will see a text login. After you login as root, you can type the **startx** command to start the X Window system.

PROJECT 4-9

Please read the section in this chapter on Installing Mac OS before completing this project.

To install Mac OS 8.5:

1. With the machine powered off, insert the Mac OS 8.5 CD-ROM into the CD-ROM drive, restart the computer, and immediately hold down the **C** key to boot from the CD-ROM. You should see the CD icon in the upper-right corner of the screen, just below the menu bar, and the Mac OS 8.5 window shown earlier in Figure 4-5 will open, showing you the contents of the CD.

2. If desired, double-click **Mac OS Read Me Files** and read them.

3. To begin the installation, double-click the **Mac OS Install** icon. The installer launches, and the opening screen appears, as shown earlier in Figure 4-6.

4. Click **Continue** to take you to the first step, selecting the drive for the installation. Select the drive you want to hold the operating system. This is usually your internal hard drive.

Clicking Options will allow you to select a "clean" installation, which will rename the System Folder currently on the drive to Previous System Folder. It will then create a new System Folder, and install the operating system there. Creating a clean installation is a good idea if you aren't sure that all the extensions currently on the machine are compatible with the new OS, but it does require you to manually move the extensions and preferences from the old folder to the new one if you want to keep any of them.

5. Choose **Select**, which takes you to one of the Read Me files. If you haven't already read it, do it now. Otherwise, click **Continue**.

6. Next, you'll have to agree to the license agreement for the software: click **Continue**, and then click **Yes** to agree.

7. Click **Start** (shown earlier in Figure 4-14) to begin copying the installation files. This may take between 6 and 45 minutes.

8. When the installer finishes, restart the computer. The operating system loads from the hard drive, and you will see the Mac OS Setup Assistant, shown previously in Figure 4-7. Click the right arrow to continue.

9. Specify your preferred nationality, your name, and organization.

10. Set the clock, and pick a city in your time zone so the computer will correctly store times and dates.

11. Specify if you want to put the computer into a simplified mode for novice users.

12. Continue to configure networking, printers, and Internet features as described in the text of the chapter in the section entitled, "Restarting from the Hard Drive," under Installing Mac OS.

PROJECT 4-10

Your hardware system BIOS controls many basic functions of your computer. This chapter discusses the need for being able to boot from a CD-ROM disk. You can find out how your system BIOS handles CD-ROM booting by displaying the Setup or Configuration screen in your computer.

To display your current booting options by looking at your BIOS:

1. Display your computer's BIOS setup screen. How you do this varies with the machine, but common techniques are to press the **Del** key during the system bootup process, or press the **Ctrl+Alt+Esc** keys simultaneously. If neither of these work, study your computer's documentation or read carefully all screens during system boot.

2. Look for settings for boot order. This usually involves using the cursor keys to position the cursor over a field, then using space or Page Up/Page Down to step through the settings.

3. Step through the choices available on your machine.

4. If available, choose a CD-ROM boot and save and exit the Configuration screen.

5. Insert your operating system CD-ROM disk and re-boot the computer. Did the CD boot your computer? What error messages did you see, if any?

6. Can you re-configure your system to boot from your hard disk drive?

CASE PROJECTS

1. Your supervisor at Acme Insurance has asked you to investigate the feasibility of installing several UNIX servers on your relatively large network. You are authorized to purchase one new computer—as large as you need, within reason—but the remaining UNIX installs must be done on existing hardware. With this background, answer these questions:

   a. What minimum hardware configuration would you recommend for the new UNIX network server?

   b. How would you go about evaluating existing hardware to judge its feasibility for conversion to a UNIX box? Keep in mind such concepts as hard drive capacity, existing applications, memory size and other storage devices.

   c. What are the major software considerations in converting an existing machine with a different operating system to UNIX?

   d. Cost is important; you can't go over the specified budget. What product might you consider in lieu of the standard commercial UNIX offerings? Why?

   e. Think about what might be involved in converting some of the computers on an existing network to another operating system. What are the major issues? How might you avoid the major problems?

2. Your company's computers are stand-alone machines without benefit of network connection. Most run Windows 3.11, with a few new machines that use Windows 98. You have just learned about the built-in networking features of Windows 98 and figure the benefits of networking your machines would be worth the effort. Study the individual networking sections in this chapter to answer these questions:

   a. Given that your budget won't allow a system-wide upgrade to Windows 98 machines, what additional hardware and/or software will be *required* to enable you to network all of the existing machines? Is it possible to network the older machines with the new ones?

   b. What additional hardware and/or software will be *desirable* to make it easier to network the existing machines?

   c. What software upgrades will be required to complete this networking project?

   d. What would be the best methodology for networking these machines? Consider the operating systems in use and the level of your knowledge about networking. (Remember, the criteria above suggest that you have only recently learned about networking Windows 98 machines.)

UPGRADING TO A NEWER VERSION

This chapter looks at the steps involved in upgrading an operating system from either an older version of the same operating system, or from a different operating system. Many of the upgrade procedures are similar to those required for an initial installation, so it is a good idea to complete Chapter 4 on Initial Installation before reading this chapter. This chapter covers general upgrade considerations, backup and safety procedures, and finally the specific steps (and possible pitfalls) involved in upgrading several operating systems.

AFTER READING THIS CHAPTER AND COMPLETING THE EXERCISES YOU WILL BE ABLE TO:

- Prepare for an operating system upgrade
- Understand the importance of testing system upgrades before implementing them
- Understand how and why to make backups before upgrading your operating system
- Successfully upgrade the operating systems covered in this text

PREPARING FOR AN UPGRADE

Before you upgrade, the first thing to consider is whether an upgrade is actually necessary. If you are certain that an upgrade is necessary and desirable, then you need to ensure that you have the necessary hardware and software (including device drivers) to perform the upgrade, as well as information about your system that may be needed during the upgrade. You should also make a complete backup of your current system and data before upgrading. If you are upgrading more than two or three machines at once, you may want to perform a test upgrade on one or two machines before doing a complete upgrade. These and other general upgrading considerations are covered in the following sections.

DECIDING TO UPGRADE

When new versions of operating systems are released, promising new features, bug fixes, enhanced capabilities, and more speed make it tempting to jump immediately on the upgrade bandwagon. However, before taking such a step (especially in a large production environment) you should carefully consider (1) whether you need to upgrade, and (2) whether this is the right time to upgrade. Although newer versions of operating systems promise great new features, you should ask yourself whether you actually need the new functionality. Objective analysis of the situation may show that an upgrade may not be cost effective. In many cases, upgrades to operating systems have little immediate effect on the functions performed by the computers you are responsible for. You may also find that software or hardware that ran just fine on the older version of the operating system will not run on a newer version. Check with your software and hardware vendors before attempting an upgrade, to ensure that the software and hardware will be compatible with the upgrade. Do not assume that all of your current software and hardware will work flawlessly with the upgrade.

Experience has also shown that it is best not to upgrade shortly after a new operating system is released. If you can put an upgrade off for several months, maybe even a year, you will have the benefit of the experiences of thousands of other users, solving problems that might have been yours. You will have access to many patches and bug fixes not available for early releases. If you feel you must upgrade soon after a new version is released, consider using the test upgrade strategy covered later in this chapter.

Never upgrade production machines to a beta version of an operating system! **Beta software** is software in the final test stages before release. It can have many bugs and may be unstable. A production machine is any machine used to perform real work, and which, if it were to become unusable for any reason, would cause an inconvenience or hinder workflow.

CHECKING HARDWARE AND SOFTWARE

Before you continue with any upgrade, you should always carefully check the machines you wish to upgrade against the requirements of the new operating system. In many cases, newer operating systems require more hardware: increased memory, disk space, CPU speed, and sometimes even improved display properties. Take special note of the hardware installed in the machine, such as network cards, scanners, sound cards and other devices that require special drivers. (You can use a form such as Table 4-1 in Chapter 4 to record this information.)

Before you upgrade to a new operating system, you should also make sure that the current drivers for input and output devices and storage media (see Chapter 6) work with the new version, or that there are drivers available for these devices for the new operating system. It is a good idea to contact vendors of hardware to get some assurance that their devices will continue to work properly after the upgrade. Do not leave this to chance; older or discontinued hardware may not be supported in newer operating system versions.

Before you start an upgrade, make sure that you have all the device drivers needed for the hardware available on floppy disk or CD-ROM. If there are drivers that exist only on the hard disk of the machine, make sure to copy them to a floppy disk or to some other safe place. Otherwise, if the upgrade were to fail, you would not have the drivers you need to get the machine back to work! As suggested above, look for drivers for the new version of the OS, and have those handy, as well as copies of the drivers you are currently using. This will enable you to reinstall the old operating system if for some reason you are unable to complete the upgrade.

It is also a good idea to keep detailed records of custom software settings—changes in the defaults for the operating system and other software—so these custom settings can be restored if necessary after any operating system or other software upgrade. For example, it is not uncommon for users to modify display or other settings after they have run an operating system for a while; they may use an automated backup program, run special disk tools on a regular basis, or have customized network settings. Upgrade installations may reset some settings to their defaults, which may not be what you want. The sections on individual operating systems discuss some of these issues in greater depth.

CONDUCTING A TEST UPGRADE

It is wise to test any upgrade before you apply it in the real world. If you only have one or two machines to upgrade, this may not be an option. But when you have five or more machines to upgrade, it can be beneficial to perform an upgrade test on a sample machine or machines.

The purpose of an upgrade test is to simulate what would happen in a real upgrade. You can discover any problems that might occur, either with the upgrade itself, or with running hardware and software after the upgrade. To do this, you need a working machine that closely resembles the machines you will be upgrading. Choose a machine that resembles the "lowest common denominator" of the machines you are upgrading in terms of the amount of memory, the speed of the CPU, the size of the hard disk, and any devices connected to the machine. You should also install all software that would typically be found on a production machine in your situation. If you are in a network environment, connect the machine to the network and make sure everything is fully functional. You should be able to use this machine as if it were a production machine. At the beginning of the test, this machine will be running the old version of the operating system, the version you are currently running on your production machines.

If the test machine is also a production machine—one you are using for real work day-by-day—it is important also to back up any data files stored on this machine. Operating system upgrades can destroy application configuration files and data during the upgrade. See the backup section later in this chapter for more information.

When this machine is fully functional, you can perform the upgrade. During this first upgrade, it is very helpful to take exact notes describing the steps of the installation and any problems that arose, and what you did about them. Also note any questions you had about the installation, and any information you had to look up to complete the installation. Write down any drivers you needed. These notes will serve as a guide in later installations.

It is not uncommon to upgrade machines over a period of time, so having notes on the exact steps of the upgrade process will help you remember the information you need and what problems you found.

When you have completed the upgrade on the test machine, and noted and dealt with any software issues that came up immediately, test the machine yourself for a couple of days. Perform tasks that you would normally perform, and take note of anything that has changed in the way the machine, and in particular the user interface, works.

If you find no major problems, the next step is to let another person who is fairly computer literate, and whose machine is on the list to be upgraded, use this machine for day-to-day work for a few days. Again, you should keep in close communication with this person, taking note of problems they may be experiencing and of things that do not work properly. After any software upgrade, one of the first things to check is whether all application software still functions correctly. It is not uncommon after upgrades for certain functions in software packages not to work, or to work differently. This is why you should let someone else work with this machine for a while, doing real-world work. If there are problems, chances are that they will not surface until a user tries to access a certain function that you would never have thought to test.

You should also double-check that the upgrade of the operating system has not changed any settings, or moved, or in some cases even removed, files or programs.

If you do encounter major problems with hardware or software not working up to this point, you should hold off on the full upgrade until these problems are resolved. Just as a beta test may find many major problems with new software design, an upgrade test like this can uncover conflicts between the new operating system software and your particular system configuration.

After resolving any problems, repeat the test installation process starting with a **clean machine** (a computer from which all unnecessary software and hardware have been removed). Install the old OS, then all software, then upgrade the OS (using your initial set of notes), and make the changes you think will cure the issues you encountered before. As before, first test the machine yourself for a couple of days, then let a user test the upgraded machine. In this way, you have another chance to test the upgrade and your installation notes.

These pre-upgrade tests can be time consuming; you may need a week or longer to get through them. In some cases you may perform many test installs before you get every detail worked out. Or, you may decide after repeated tries that the upgrade is not going to work, and decide not to upgrade. Either way, the test results, when carefully documented, will tell you what to expect from your upgrade. Obviously it is better to find out in a test situation that an operating system upgrade won't work for you. Your test results can also be used as a tool to explain to employees and management why an upgrade should or should not be carried out. If you decide the upgrade should proceed, you will know the steps, you will know what to expect, and you will be efficient in performing the upgrade. A test upgrade is well worth your time.

5

MAKING BACKUPS BEFORE UPGRADES

Making backups of software and data is a very important part of day-to-day computer operation: hard disks crash, files accidentally get deleted, lightning strikes; in short, unexpected things happen. As operating systems and computers get more complicated, failures can even happen for unexplainable reasons during normal machine operation. If you use computers long enough, eventually you will lose critical information. Backups are essential to recovering from such a loss.

It is essential to have a complete backup of your old operating system and essential software and data before beginning an actual upgrade. Some operating systems, in particular the Windows series, can change large numbers of configuration files, even those not used exclusively by the operating system. As a result, some applications may not be able to locate data. There have also been cases in which operating system installers destroyed parts of application programs altogether.

As you learned earlier in the book, the operating system is responsible for, among other things, the management of files and disks, and at the same time it provides numerous services to application software. With this level of complexity, a change in even one file during an upgrade can drastically change the way the new OS works.

 If a program is lost, you may be able to simply reinstall it. But when data files are lost, the damage may be hard to repair. For this reason, make a full and complete backup prior to upgrading to a new operating system.

Here are some points to consider when backing up your information:

- Make sure that you have the software needed to restore the backups under both the old and the new operating systems. There is nothing more frustrating than having a backup, and being unable to restore it. Even though you have tested the backup and restore software with the old operating system, there is no guarantee that it will work properly with the new one. Before you perform an upgrade, you should test the restore software, preferably by making a backup and restoring it to a computer that has already been upgraded to the new operating system.

- Make sure that you are actually making a full backup. Sometimes important files are not included in the backup process because of program error or human oversight. In addition, you should make a backup of all the contents of all fixed disks connected to the computer, not just the boot drive. If a disaster happens, it can save you a lot of time. You would only need to restore backup tapes instead of having to hunt all over the place to find installation disks for software programs.

- If you are upgrading to a new version of backup software on your new operating system, make 100% sure, preferably by a test you carry out yourself, that the new system will be able to read your backup without problems.

Some machines you upgrade will not have a built-in drive that is suitable to make a full backup of the machine. If the machine is connected to a network, you may be able to use another machine on the network, which is equipped with an appropriate backup device, to make your backup. Alternately, backup devices such as tape drives or large removable disk drives are now fairly inexpensive; almost all operating systems will support easily moveable external drives that connect to the parallel printer or SCSI port on a computer. It is usually worth the money to have one of these devices handy to make full backups of machines before an upgrade installation.

Upgrading an operating system can be very simple; it may take only 20 minutes, and you may never need those backup tapes that took two hours to create, or that test upgrade that took two weeks. However, if that 20-minute job turns into a 3-week project, if you have to give up the upgrade and start from scratch, you will be very happy to have the backups. And the time spent doing a test upgrade can prevent many headaches and problems with your larger system upgrade.

UPGRADING SPECIFIC OPERATING SYSTEMS

This section covers information specific to upgrades to and from the operating systems covered in this book: DOS, Windows 3.1x, Windows 95/98, Windows NT, UNIX, and Mac OS. The major differences between the upgrade installation and the full installation of these operating systems will be described.

UPGRADING DOS

Upgrading from an older to a newer version of DOS can be a fairly simple process. You need your installation disks for the new DOS version, and you may need one or two blank disks, depending on the DOS version you are installing. In this example you are upgrading to DOS version 6 or 7 from a previous version of MS-DOS.

A warning about DOS backups applies here. All versions of MS-DOS have a backup program that will let you make backups to floppy disk, and versions after 5.0 have a program that will let you make backups to tape. You should be aware, however, that not all of these backup programs are compatible with each other! If the upgraded version of DOS has the same basic version number as the original (you are upgrading from DOS 6.0 to DOS 6.2, for example), the backup programs are compatible. If the basic versions differ (for example, upgrading from DOS 6.2 to DOS 7.0), the backup programs probably are not compatible. You certainly will not be able to read backup disks written in DOS 5 from a restore program in DOS 6, for example. Even worse, when you try to run the restore utility that came with DOS 5 under DOS 6, you will get an "incorrect DOS version" error. This problem can be remedied using a utility called SETVER, available with all DOS versions after 5.0.

You *can* run older DOS programs under newer DOS versions, however. To do this, add DEVICE=SETVER.EXE to your CONFIG.SYS file, and then from the command prompt, you will type SETVER RESTORE.EXE *x.x* where *x.x* is the DOS version associated with the **RESTORE** program. Make sure you make a copy of the old restore program to a floppy disk; it will be replaced during the installation of the new DOS version.

If you are on a network, you can use any of a number of third-party network-based backup programs (such as Cheyenne Software's ARCServe) that will work on many DOS versions.

You should boot your computer into the current version of MS-DOS before you start the DOS upgrade. Although this is not specified, let your current DOS version start as you always do, and do not bypass any configuration files at DOS startup. If you have your system configured to support multiple configurations, selectable at startup, start DOS with the configuration that loads all of your available device drivers. This is important, as the DOS installer may make changes to your configuration files, and it will look at the drivers that are loaded to determine what changes should and should not be made.

When the computer is started, begin the installation process by inserting the first installation floppy in the disk drive and running the SETUP program. Installation proceeds as described in the previous chapter, with the exception that you are asked a few additional questions. The first new question regards your previous MS-DOS files; the installer has an option to save these files to a location on your hard disk so that it is possible to uninstall the new DOS version at a later time. It's best to use this option; you can always delete these files later.

Second, you are prompted to provide one or two **uninstall disks**. Make sure you have some formatted floppies handy for this purpose. Apart from this, the install should be as described in the last chapter. When installation is complete, be sure to run through the post-installation steps mentioned in the previous chapter. With new and changed device drivers you want to go through optimization again, and you will want to make sure your CD-ROM device is still set up correctly. At this time, you should make sure your application programs work as expected. Note that there are some subtle differences in the way DOS works internally from version to version, in particular when it comes to memory management. Some applications that use memory modes enabled by HIMEM.SYS and EMM386.SYS may not run properly after the upgrade. A check of the CONFIG.SYS files in the old and new versions should tell you what has changed; usually changing things back to the way they were will fix most problems. (The old CONFIG.SYS file can be found on the first recovery disk the installer made.)

UPGRADING TO WINDOWS 95

Before upgrading to Windows 95 from either DOS or Windows 3.1x, you need to make a backup of your current operating system and data files. However, the backup programs provided with DOS make backups that cannot be read with Windows 95. The Windows 3.1 backup program writes backups that cannot be read with the Windows 95 RESTORE program. In addition, the Windows 3.1 RESTORE utility cannot be used after an upgrade to Windows 95. For these reasons, use either of the two following strategies for making backups when upgrading from DOS or Windows 3.1 to Windows 95:

- The least expensive solution is to use the backup utility provided by the DOS version on your machine; after the upgrade, you could boot into DOS and use the RESTORE utility for your DOS version to restore files if needed. Remember to copy that RESTORE utility onto a floppy since it is removed by some Windows 95 installers during the upgrade.

- The second option is to find a third-party backup program that will write files from Windows 3.1 or DOS, which can be read from Windows 95. If you are in a networked environment, you can use a networked backup solution such as ARCServe from Cheyenne Software.

An upgrade from DOS to Windows 95 is almost identical to a fresh install of Windows 95. The Windows 95 installer runs as described in Chapter 4 on Initial Installation.

Microsoft does not consider the shift from DOS to Windows 95 to be an "upgrade," so you will either need to use the full version of Windows 95 (see Chapter 4), or you will have to provide the first disk of an older Windows version as proof of ownership during the install of an upgrade-only version of Windows 95.

In an upgrade from DOS to Windows 95, make sure that your CD-ROM drivers are working correctly prior to starting installation, if you will be installing Windows 95 from CD-ROM. These drivers must load without your intervention when your computer starts, because the installer will be relying on them during the installation. When the installation is complete, you will find that Windows 95 works exactly as it would if you had done a clean install. However, if you press the F8 key when the "Starting Windows 95" text message appears during initial boot, you will find that the boot selection menu has one additional option. This option enables you to boot the previous version of MS-DOS. This can be a useful feature since you may have older software that doesn't run correctly under the Windows 95 version of DOS. By booting from the older DOS version, you may be able to use utilities and other software that would be totally unavailable in a Windows-only environment.

An upgrade from Windows 3.0, 3.1, 3.11 or Windows for Workgroups 3.11 to Windows 95 is almost the same as a clean install, but here again the version of Windows 95 you are using can cause a bit of a problem. For example, if you are attempting to upgrade from Windows 3.1x to Windows 95 with a full version, you may not be able to do so. The installer may refuse to run, telling you this is not an upgrade product. You may have this same problem in upgrading from one version of Windows 95 to another. This is part of the Microsoft copyright protection scheme. The company wants to make sure you aren't indiscriminately installing versions of Windows on multiple machines. Presumably an upgrade is okay, but placing a full install on a machine with an operating system licensed only for new computers, for example, may be disallowed. You can solve this problem by renaming the WIN.COM file in your old Windows directory to something else, for example WIN.3. The installer will try to adopt as many of your old Windows settings as it can; as a result you will see that some questions in the installer will have preselected answers that are a little different from those that you may expect.

You may see some questions during installation that ask you whether you want to overwrite a file with a newer version. This happens when a file Windows 95 is trying to install is already on the hard disk, and the version on the disk is newer than the version Windows is trying to install. Make a note of all files where this happens; be sure to write down the exact name, including the extension, and the version number and data information of the old and new file. Be aware that these may be shared files that are used by applications. These files may install with Windows, but later when you install an application, the application installer may replace the original with one of its own. Now when you upgrade Windows, the Windows installer "knows" that the file placed there by the application isn't the same one being installed with the Windows upgrade. You can see that if you replace the application-specific file there is a possibility that the program won't run properly.

Nevertheless it's best to let Windows install the file it wants to install; note that in most cases this is not the default option. If after installation is complete, you find that some software will not work, you can locate the file on your hard disk and replace it with the original file from your backup. Note that when you do this, you should always keep a copy of the file you are replacing. Windows 95 will sometimes not respond kindly to this kind of trickery, and you may find yourself in a situation where you have to restore the Windows 95 file to make everything work again.

There is one group of files that you should never replace with an older version: files that contain the **Microsoft Foundation Classes (MFC)**. MFC is a series of core routines used by almost all applications on your Windows 95 machine; the files will be named MFC*xx*.DLL, where *xx* is a numeric expression such as 32, 30, or 42. You can learn more about MFCs in Hands-on Project 5-6 at the end of this chapter.

Make sure you never replace any of the MFCs with an older version; doing so will seriously corrupt your operating system. In many cases you may be unable to boot the machine again!

When the installation of Windows 95 is complete, you should see that all of your old Windows 3.1x programs have been moved into the Start menu, or the Program Manager if you chose to use that interface.

You may find that some of your programs do not work quite as you expected. Some Windows 3.1x programs simply will not work under Windows 95 due to system incompatibilities. This is why performing a test installation is a good idea.

One reason that some Windows 3.1x programs may not work under Windows 95 is that they rely on entries that are no longer in the WIN.INI or SYSTEM.INI files; the information in them has been moved to the Registry. In some cases, you can edit the SYSTEM.INI and WIN.INI files to make these programs happy. Another major problem with some upgrades to Windows 95 is caused by the use of older device drivers. If Windows 3.11 device drivers are used under Windows 95, they can cause problems with power management and performance. Although the drivers may work, they generally do not support 32-bit operation, which can result in poor performance. With network or hard disk drivers, this can be quite a drain on system performance.

Since Windows 3.1x did not provide for standardized power management, none of the Windows 3.1x drivers supports Suspend mode, and machines will not be able to use all of the Windows 95 power management functions. The common solution for this problem is to obtain new, Windows 95-compliant drivers for the devices that don't work properly after the upgrade. These drivers can be installed according to instructions provided with the drivers after the initial Windows 95 upgrade is complete.

Note that in an upgrade from Windows 3.1x to Windows 95, file systems will not be converted to Windows 95 FAT32 system. This can possibly be a disadvantage since FAT16 won't achieve maximum use of larger hard drives and FAT16 also offers slower disk I/O performance, in many cases. Also, all of your old Windows 3.1x files will be left on the disk. You will notice this because during the installation you may be prompted whether you wish to replace certain files.

One approach to avoiding these upgrade problems would be to make a backup of all data on a computer, format the hard disk with the old operating system (DOS or Win 3.1x), and then do a clean install. Try an upgrade first. Then, if you have serious failures that cannot be solved by installing new drivers, re-installing software, and installing Windows 95 updates, make sure all hardware in the machine is supported by Windows 95. If it is, and you have all the latest drivers, try a clean install. Be prepared to install all software, so make sure you have access to all software needed before you do this. Also triple-check that your backup is working before trying this step!

UPGRADING TO WINDOWS 98

The only upgrade path to Windows 98 is from Windows 95, and luckily the Windows 98 backup program will read Windows 95 backups. The step from Windows 95 to Windows 98 is in many ways not as big as the step from Windows 3.1x to Windows 95, so this upgrade generally works well. Nevertheless, make a backup and make sure your backup works before starting this upgrade (see Hands-on Projects 5-1 and 5-2 at the end of the chapter). Whatever you do, make sure you make copies of the Windows 95 Registry. Most backup software offers an option to back up the Registry, which you should use. If your backup software does not allow you to back up the Registry, you can back it up yourself by copying the SYSTEM.DAT and USER.DAT files, both of which are hidden files in the Windows directory. You can copy these files from the DOS command line, even though you won't see them if you display a directory list of the Windows folder. You can also use Windows Explorer to back up these files if you first turn on hidden files view, as shown in Hands-on Project 5-3.

To upgrade to Windows 98, start Windows 95, and make sure to close all other running programs. (The installer may crash if other software is running concurrently.) Then insert your Windows 98 upgrade CD in the CD-ROM drive. When Autorun starts the CD, you are notified that the CD contains a newer version of the Windows operating system, and you are asked if you wish to upgrade. Click Yes, and you are on your way. The complete steps for the upgrade are in Hands-on Project 5-6 at the end of this chapter.

During the installation, you may be asked about certain files that are already installed on your computer, because there is a version of the file on your computer that is newer than the version on the CD. As with Windows 95, keep notes on these filenames, and let Windows 98 install the versions provided with the upgrade CD for all files. If applications do not work after the upgrade, simply install the original versions from your backup. If applications don't run after an upgrade, you'll probably see an error message that tells you which file is missing or incompatible. This is the file you want to restore. If you don't get a message that includes a filename, you may be able to determine which files need to be replaced from the name of the program executable file. Study the filenames in the directory in which the application is installed. Do any match names you noted during the upgrade?

Under no circumstances should you replace any MFC file in Windows 98 with an MFC file from Windows 95. Doing so will result in a non-functional operating system installation!

Towards the end of the installation, if your Windows 95 machine is connected to the Internet, Windows 98 may use the Internet connection to look for newer drivers and components. As long as you have a reasonably fast Internet connection, it should be no problem. Toward the end of the setup process, the Windows 98 installer will attempt to set up drivers for all possible devices. When this is done, the installer will look at all the devices installed on your Windows 95 machine for which you have not yet removed the drivers. For example, if you once had a certain network card, and you removed the card without removing the drivers for it, the Windows 98 installer will try to determine whether or not those drivers should be installed in Windows 98. Although this is a good thing, it may take a while. You may have to wait for as much as half an hour or more, even though the installation "clock" shows only a minute or two to go!

It is important that you do not interrupt this driver detection process. However, if nothing happens for more than an hour, something probably went wrong and you should restart the installation.

If you previously upgraded the same machine from Windows 3.1x to Windows 95, you may still have some older 16-bit drivers on the machine. The same problem that was discussed in Windows 95 may occur in Windows 98: you may end up with some devices that will not work properly with power management features, and system performance may be less than optimal. Although this problem is much less frequent with Windows 98, since it will replace all drivers for which it has newer versions, you will find that devices for which Windows 98 does not have drivers will still cause these problems. The answer is to obtain new drivers (from the manufacturer or the manufacturer's Web site). If updated drivers are not available, you can either live with the problem or replace the hardware in question.

When your installation is complete, use the Windows Update feature (your computer must be able to access the Internet) as follows to get the latest patches and upgrades:

1. After you have completed installation, click **Start** and choose **Settings**, then select **Windows Update**. You will be connected to the Internet if you are not already connected. (Chapter 8 covers setting up an Internet connection.) Your Web browser starts, and you see the Microsoft Windows Update Web page.

2. From the Windows Update page, select **Product Updates**. If you are asked to download a component, click **Yes**. You are asked for permission to scan your machine. If you click **Yes** your computer is scanned for installed software, and you are presented with a list of all the patches you should install, as well as a list of available new software. It's helpful to at least pick every item on the list tagged as Critical Updates.

3. Click **Download**, located at the top or bottom of the page. Figure 5-1 shows how the page looks.

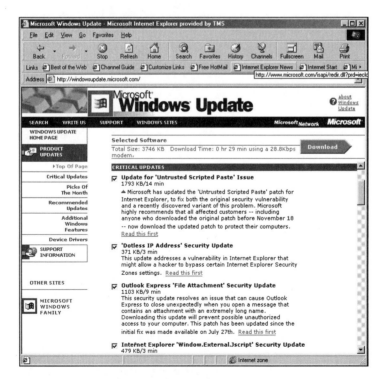

Figure 5-1 Windows Update page

4. After you click Download, you will see the next screen contains the patches you have selected, how long it will take to download them, and a link to some instructions. Click **Start Download**. You receive one more warning (click **Yes** to continue), and the download will begin.

5. After a while, you may be asked to restart your machine. Restart the computer as specified. Your Windows 98 will now be up to date.

If you have permanent Internet access, you can set up Windows 98 so that it will perform these updates periodically, and install all software automatically. Some people see this last option as a security risk; you can periodically use the Windows Update feature to look at what is offered for installation rather than setting up automatic updates.

5

UPGRADING TO WINDOWS NT 4.0

The Windows NT 4.0 upgrade can only be performed from a version of Windows NT 3.51. (If you are using Windows 98 or any other operating system, you'll have to do a full installation of Windows NT 4.0 as described in Chapter 4.) Windows NT Workstation can only be upgraded to NT Workstation, and Windows NT Server can only be upgraded to Windows NT Server. The setup program will check certain Registry keys to assure that this rule is obeyed, and the program will not work if it finds a problem in this area.

Before starting the upgrade, a backup of the system is of critical importance. The NT 4.0 Restore program is not capable of reading NT 3.51 backups. Try using a third-party backup program that will work on both platforms, such as Cheyenne Software's ARCServe. Make sure the backup software can back up the Registry, and has support for NTFS.

There is no uninstall feature in the Windows NT 4.0 installer. If you decide this upgrade does not work, you will need to rely on your backups to restore the NT 3.51 system.

The software driver model used in Windows NT 4.0 is quite different from that used in Windows NT 3.51. The other versions of Windows were able to use older drivers that were already installed; in an NT 4.0 installation this is not the case. You will need drivers specifically for NT 4.0 for the hardware that is installed in your machine. Although there is a collection of drivers that comes with NT 4.0, it is far from complete, and quite out of date for some drivers.

Before upgrading to Windows NT 4.0, it is a good idea to check with the vendors of your hardware to see if there have been any problems with upgrades to NT 4.0 for your devices. Vendors may be able to provide updated drivers and/or workarounds for such problems before they occur.

For example, a SCSI card and a network card installed in an NT 3.51 machine might not function properly during the upgrade to NT 4.0. The vendors for those devices might be able to provide the drivers you need, that are not on the NT CD-ROM, to get past this problem.

The NT 4.0 upgrade is started from the 3.51 version of Windows NT, and proceeds as follows:

1. Make sure that no users are trying to use the resources made available from this machine.

2. Insert the NT 4.0 Upgrade CD, and choose the SETUP32 program from the i386 directory on the CD. The setup program copies all files to the hard disk, and after the machine is restarted, the setup process continues as described in Chapter 4.

The NT 4.0 upgrade installer is identical to the non-upgrade (full) version installer. However, you should be aware that some questions are already filled out according to your preferences from the previous install of the earlier operating system version.

During the installation, you can choose to convert some or all of your FAT file systems to NTFS. This process, if interrupted, will leave disks beyond repair, thereby making your reliance on a backup much greater. You probably should not use this option unless you are very certain your backups are perfect. You can choose to update to NTFS at a later date, if you wish.

The networking setup has changed significantly from NT 3.51 to NT 4.0, and you should pay special attention to the section of the installer that deals with the setup of your network hardware, addressing, and protocols. In many cases, the installer will configure the devices and fill in the information about them correctly, but especially in machines that have multiple network cards with a mix of protocols on each card, care should be taken to ensure that the information entered for all devices is correct.

When setup is complete, follow the instructions given in Chapter 4 on the post-install setup of Windows NT. At the least, apply the appropriate Service Packs.

UPGRADING UNIX SYSTEM V

There are many backup programs that can be used with UNIX. These programs are standardized; that is, it is possible to make backups in one version, and read them in many other versions, whether older or newer, from the same vendor or from someone else. The standard UNIX backup utility is called a **dump** (*dump* in Linux and *ufsdump* in Solaris). Backups can be made to local devices or across a network. In Solaris, there is a backup program with a graphical user interface called *tapetool*. Since tapetool uses *dump* to make a backup, it too will be compatible with almost any UNIX version.

 It is especially important to make backups of all the system configuration files on UNIX machines; if for some reason the upgrade does not work, you will have to do a full, fresh operating system installation. Having configuration files to fall back on can save a lot of time and trouble. You should make a backup of the contents of the entire /etc directory, so that you have copies of all system configuration files. This can be done using the *tar* command. For example, to copy the contents of /etc to a file called *myetc.tar* in the root directory, you would go to the root directory by entering *cd /* and then enter *tar –cvf /myetc.tar etc*. You may also want to back up your /usr/local/etc directory, as shown in Hands-on Project 5-4.

The configuration files found in the /etc directory include the various *rc* startup scripts, the *inittab* file which helps your system start, and the *disktab* or *vfstab* files, which help you mount your file systems. They also include various service configuration files, such as the *hosts* file, which contains information needed to set up networking, the *host.** files, which help configure the machine at startup, and the *syslog.conf* file, which tells *syslog* what to do and how. Depending on what services your machine runs there may be additional configuration files; you will probably also want to back up your password and group files.

If you have installed any special kernel or device driver files, you should make backups of these as well. You may also want to back up your Web and other configuration files; these are generally found in /usr/local/etc. Exactly which files you should back up depends on your installation. Backing up both /etc and /usr/local/etc will ensure that you have copies of any configuration files you may need.

In the other operating system installations covered in this chapter, if upgrade installation fails, you simply restart it, and it will either start from the beginning, or it will detect that an error occurred, and will try to resume the upgrade from the point where it left off. In the world of UNIX, however, if an install or upgrade fails in the middle, you must reinstall the operating system as if nothing was on the disk. Again, *if you attempt a UNIX upgrade that fails, you cannot just restart the upgrade; you will have to do a new install.* This is a weakness in UNIX that various vendors are trying to address. Meanwhile, you should be very certain your backups are in tip-top shape before starting an upgrade.

There are many flavors of Linux; for this book we are using the RedHat edition. The upgrade process described here is based on the RedHat Linux 5.2 installer. Although the installers have changed significantly in appearance over the years, the functionality has not changed much. Upgrades from any version of Linux to this version should work, but in many cases the installer will not be able to determine the exact features installed on the previous version of Linux. It's recommended that you upgrade to RedHat Linux 5.2 only from RedHat version 3.0 or up. If you have used a different Linux version, you should back up your data and perform a clean install, then restore your data.

Under Linux, the upgrade process works a lot like the installation process. You will start the installation as described in the previous chapter, then choose to perform an upgrade. The installer will ask for some basic system information to help it determine what hard disks to use for the installation. It will then get most system information from the hard disk, and prompt you with questions that have been pre-answered. The appropriate system files will be replaced, and the installer will work identically to the full install. Note that many libraries and programs will be replaced, and if you added software to the machine, you should check carefully to ensure that everything still works the way you think it should when installation is complete.

One big caveat in UNIX upgrades is that many configuration files are overwritten during the upgrade. The mail system, the printing system, the X11 window system, and other network services such as FTP and World Wide Web server may be reconfigured. You should double-check configuration files on these services to make sure they have not changed.

As with other upgrades, backing up these files could make recovering from problems easier if things go wrong after the upgrade. The /etc/services and /etc/inetd.conf files are also known to change; many times you will find new services added or some of your custom services removed, so a careful check of these files should be made. Also, the *inittab* and the *startup* files should be checked to ensure that they still start the things you expect them to start.

Solaris, like Linux, comes in many versions. If you are comfortable with upgrading Linux as described here, you should have no problems conducting a Solaris upgrade.

UPGRADING MAC OS

Before attempting to upgrade the Mac operating system, you should always perform three basic steps:

1. As with other operating systems, you must perform a backup of all data and configuration files on the hard drive. That includes the entire System Folder, which may contain the user's browser bookmarks and Eudora address book and mail files.

2. Check the disk for errors, using a utility such as Norton Disk Doctor (part of Symantec's Norton Utilities for Macintosh) or Apple's own Disk First Aid. Otherwise, the installation could aggravate existing directory damage and cause new problems, including data loss. Newer versions of Apple's installers perform a basic check automatically.

3. Always upgrade the hard disk drivers. Skipping this step can also result in a loss of data if the old disk drivers are incompatible with the new OS. If you are using an Apple drive formatted with an Apple driver, newer versions of the installer will take care of this automatically. For third-party drives, contact the publisher of your disk-formatting utility for new disk drivers. If new disk drivers have not shipped, postpone the upgrade until the necessary software is available.

CLEAN VERSUS DIRTY INSTALLS

There are two ways to install or reinstall the Mac OS: "dirty" and "clean." In a dirty install, the OS is installed on top of the previous System Folder. Files with the same name will be overwritten, but older, obsolete components that don't have a modern equivalent will be retained. Likewise, the dirty System Folder will contain all of the third-party software that was present in the old System Folder, including software that may not be compatible with the current OS. Any time you upgrade or reinstall the Mac OS on a volume that contains an existing OS install, you are performing a dirty install.

In a clean install, a fresh new System Folder is created. Clean installs are always the safest option. The technique for performing a clean install depends on the operating system version, as follows:

■ Systems prior to 7.5: rename the old System Folder to something else ("System Folder Old," for instance). Move the Finder from the old System Folder to another location.

- System 7.5: in the main installer window, press Command+Shift+K. A dialog box will appear, giving you the option to install a new System Folder.

- OS 7.6: in the Software Installation window, click Options and choose the "Create new System Folder (clean installation)" check box.

- OS 8.0/8.1: choose the Perform Clean Installation check box in the Select Destination window.

- OS 8.5: in the Select Destination window, click Options and put a check next to Perform Clean Installation, as shown in Figure 5-2.

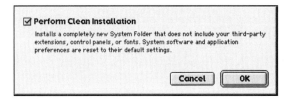

Figure 5-2   Choosing a "clean" install of Mac OS

MERGING THE OLD AND NEW SYSTEM FOLDERS

Once you test the system to make sure it is functioning correctly, you need to recover certain files from the old System Folder. For instance, you need certain extensions and control panels that are necessary for the operation of printers, disk drives, and other peripherals, as well as third-party fonts and application preferences files. If the preferences files are lost, you will have to reenter the serial numbers for some commercial programs. The serial numbers may be printed on manuals or installation disks that have been scattered to the four winds. Likewise, the Control Panels, Extensions, and Fonts folders may contain critical files whose installer disks can no longer be located.

When transferring these files, especially extensions and control panels, exercise caution. Some of those files may not be compatible with the new operating system. For instance, RamDoubler and SpeedDoubler are almost guaranteed to require maintenance upgrades to be compatible with a new version of the operating system, because of the intimate way those programs interact with the OS. If you are reinstalling the OS because the computer has been crashing, be especially wary. The crashes may be caused by a buggy extension or control panel, or by a corrupted font or preferences file. Keep that in mind when moving files into the new operating system. It's a good idea to transfer a few files at a time and restart to make sure everything is working okay.

When merging the old and new System Folders, you should concentrate on five folders and two subfolders: the Apple Menu, Control Panels, Extensions, Fonts, and Preferences folders, and the Modem Scripts and Printer Description subfolders inside the Extensions folders.

Modem Scripts are modem configuration files used with Apple's Apple Remote Access, PPP, and Remote Access. Printer Descriptions are PostScript Printer Description (PPD) files.

Files can be moved manually from the old System Folder to the new a few at a time. Files that exist in the new operating system (such as the Date & Time Control Panel) don't have to be moved. You'll mainly be moving third-party files. Again, it's a good idea to move a handful of files at a time, restart, and verify that the files are not causing problems. (There is third-party software, such as Cassady & Greene's Conflict Catcher, that can merge the old and new software at the touch of a button. Conflict Catcher can also diagnose extension and control panel conflicts, and is a useful addition to the system administrator's toolbox.)

CHAPTER SUMMARY

The process for upgrading an operating system is very similar to that for installing a new operating system, as discussed in the previous chapter. However, you should take certain steps in preparing for an upgrade.

Before upgrading, you should be sure that an upgrade is necessary. If you decide to upgrade, check that your hardware meets the requirements for upgrading, as well as ensuring that you have the correct, most up-to-date drivers for the various devices on your system.

It is essential to make a backup of the current operating system and data before upgrading, and to check that you can run the backup program from both the current and upgraded version of the system.

It is also a good idea to test system upgrades before you implement them. Although it can be time-consuming, the test results will tell you what to expect from your upgrade, and give you a chance to resolve any problems.

There are major issues and considerations involved in upgrades to specific operating systems, whether you are upgrading to a new version of DOS, upgrading to Windows 95 from an earlier version of Windows, upgrading to Windows 98, or to Windows NT 4.0 Server and Workstation. It's important to realize when upgrading various UNIX versions that there are critical differences between a UNIX upgrade and a conventional Windows or DOS upgrade. Likewise, when upgrading your Mac OS to a later version you must choose between a "clean" and "dirty" install.

This information, coupled with the more detailed data on original operating system installation covered in the previous chapter, should give you a strong foundation for installing your operating system on virtually any platform.

KEY TERMS

- **beta software** — During software development, software that has successfully passed the alpha test stage. Beta testing may involve dozens, hundreds, or even thousands of people and may be conducted in multiple stages: beta 1, beta 2, beta 3, and so on.

- **clean machine** — A computer from which all unnecessary software and hardware have been removed. A clean machine is useful during software upgrade testing since a minimum number of other software and hardware elements are in place, making it easier to track down problems with new software.

- **Microsoft Foundation Classes (MFC)** — A series of core routines used by almost all applications on a Windows 95 machine.

- **RESTORE** — A software utility available as part of many operating systems that permits the copying of backed up data from the backup medium to the computer hard drive.

- **uninstall disks** — A set of operating system disks that contain information from a previous version of the operating system. These disks are used to restore the original operating system in the event the user wishes to remove an upgraded system.

REVIEW QUESTIONS

1. Each operating system upgrade is somewhat unique, but there are some general steps you should conduct with every upgrade. Select all that apply:

   a. Test the upgrade on a non-production machine.

   b. Back up all data and applications before starting the upgrade.

   c. Test backup and restore software before committing to the new software version.

   d. Remove the old operating system completely before starting the upgrade.

2. Why should you avoid upgrading to a beta version of operating system software?

3. Why is it important to back up existing files before you start an operating system upgrade?

4. You only need to back up application files, since an operating system upgrade won't touch your data files. True or False?

5. During an operating system upgrade you may need two versions of your backup and restore software because _____.

6. To ensure that you can successfully restore backed up data, you should (select all that apply)

   a. Restore the data to your main production computer

   b. Restore the data to a secondary machine

   c. Restore the data using both old and new operating systems

   d. Not perform any special testing, because backup devices are reliable today

7. If you decide to test an upgrade before implementing it in a production environment, a single test install is sufficient if you take careful notes during the process. True or False?

8. You may not need a second restore program if you are upgrading within the same system level (DOS 6.0 to DOS 6.2, for example). True or False?

9. Describe the function and importance of uninstall disks during an operating system upgrade.

10. When you upgrade to a completely different operating system, it is unlikely that the original restore programs will work properly to replace backed up files. Describe how you might prepare for this eventuality to ensure that you can retrieve backed up data if necessary after an upgrade.

11. Attempting an operating system upgrade with a full version of the install software may fail because _____.

12. If an upgrade in Windows fails, what is one technique you might use to convince the installer to recognize properly your previous installation?

13. A core group of files called MFCs are used by most Windows 95 applications. MFC stands for

   a. Microsoft Foundation Classics

   b. Microsoft Foundation Classes

   c. Machine Function Codes

   d. Master Foundation Codes

14. Older applications may not function properly after a Windows upgrade because some configuration information has been moved to the system _____.

15. You may be able to restore proper application functionality after an upgrade from Windows 3.1x to Windows 95 by editing which files?

16. The only upgrade path to Windows 98 is from _____.

17. Some installers automatically back up the system Registry. You also can back up the Registry manually by making copies of the _____ .DAT and _____ .DAT files in the Windows directory.

18. During the installation of some versions of Windows the installer may access the Internet. What is the purpose of this access? Is it desirable or should you stop this process in the interests of local system security?

19. Describe how to upgrade a Windows NT Workstation to Windows NT Server.

20. What operating systems can be used as the basis of an upgrade to Windows NT 4.0?

21. If a Windows NT installation fails you can use the intrinsic uninstaller to back out of the install and restore the previous version. True or False?

HANDS-ON PROJECTS

PROJECT 5-1

You should back up system and application files prior to conducting an operating system upgrade.

To back up specific directories or files in Windows 98:

1. Click **Start** and point to **Programs**.

2. Point to **Accessories**, then **System Tools**.

3. Choose **Backup** from the System Tools list. (If the Backup program does not detect any backup hardware installed on your machine, it will ask if you want AutoDetect to try to find it. If this occurs, click No.)

4. On the opening Backup screen, choose **Create a New Backup Job** and click **OK**.

5. Choose **Backup selected files, folders and drives.** You can use this choice to back up to floppy disks or a removable high-density disk such as a Zip or Jazz drive. If you have a tape backup system, choose **Backup of My Computer** to back up everything on your hard drive. Click **Next**.

6. Navigate to the folder(s) or file(s) you want to back up and click the check box beside the entries you want to back up.

7. Click **Next** and choose **All selected files** from the following dialog box.

8. Click **Next** and specify the backup location. This is where you choose the destination drive for the backup files. Note that you can back up to a network hard drive or even to a file on a local hard drive if you wish.

9. Click **Next** to continue the backup wizard and choose whether you want to use file compression.

10. Click **Next** and name the backup job. This will let you repeat this process later, or modify the job for later backups.

11. Click **Start** to complete the backup process. A dialog box informs you when the operation is complete. Click **OK**.

12. Click **OK** in the Backup Progress window and then close the Microsoft Backup window.

5

PROJECT 5-2

No data backup is useful if the restore software or the backup media fail. Many critical failures occur during data restoration because of bad media and incompatibilities between the restore software and new system software. That's why backup and restore testing is critical during operating system upgrades.

To test the backup created in Project 5-1:

1. Click **Start** and point to **Programs**.

2. Point to **Accessories**, then **System Tools**.

3. Choose **Backup** from the System Tools list.

4. From the opening Backup screen choose **Restore Backed Up Files** and click **OK**.

5. Choose the source for the restored data from the next wizard screen. Click **Next**.

6. Choose from the list of backup sets displayed on the next dialog box. Click **OK**.

7. Click the check box beside the items within the backup set to select individual items to restore and click **Next**.

8. Choose a restore location from the next dialog box. During testing you should choose a destination other than the original in case you encounter problems. Click **Next** to continue the wizard.

9. Choose the type of restore operation if the program finds existing files at the destination location. You can tell the program not to replace existing files, to replace files only if the ones on your computer are older, or to always replace existing files.

10. Click **Start** to begin the restore. You will be prompted for the backup media originally used. Insert the requested disk and click **OK**.

11. Click **OK** in the Operation Complete dialog box, then click **OK** in the Restore Progress dialog box. Close the MSBackup window.

12. Test the restored data to make sure everything was restored properly.

PROJECT 5-3

You can manually back up the Windows 98 Registry data by copying the SYSTEM.DAT and USER.DAT files, which are hidden files in the Windows directory. This exercise shows how to view the hidden files and copy them to a floppy disk using Windows Explorer.

To manually copy Windows Registry files to a floppy disk:

1. Point to **Start**, then to **Programs** and choose **Windows Explorer**.

2. Click **View** on the menu and choose **Folder Options** (for Windows 95, choose **Options**). You will see a display similar to the one in Figure 5-3 for Windows 98 (in Windows 95 you will see the Options dialog box).

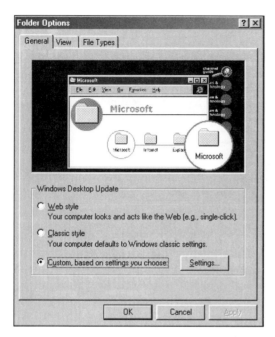

Figure 5-3   Windows 98 Folder Options dialog box

3. If necessary, click the **View** tab.

4. Make sure the Show all files option button is selected, as shown for Windows 98 in Figure 5-4.

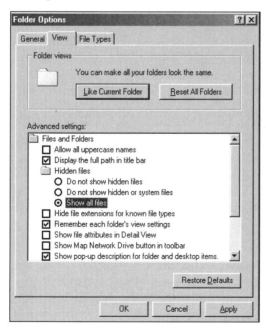

Figure 5-4   Show all files selection on View tab

5. Click **OK** to close the Folder Options (or Options) dialog box.

6. Label a blank, formatted floppy disk "Registry Backup" with today's date, and insert it into the floppy drive.

7. In Explorer, browse to and click the **Windows** folder to display its contents.

8. In the right pane, browse to and click the **System.dat** file. Browse to and **Ctrl+click** the **User.dat** file, so that the two files are highlighted.

9. Click the **Copy** icon, or press **Ctrl+C** (Windows 95) to copy the two files to the Clipboard.

10. In the left pane of Explorer, browse to another directory on your hard drive (or to another hard drive if you have one available) and click to select it.

11. Click the **Paste** icon or press **Ctrl+V** to copy the files to the floppy disk.

12. Click **View**, **Refresh** on the Explorer menu and check that the two files have been copied to the floppy disk.

13. Remove the floppy disk and close Explorer.

PROJECT 5-4

Before you upgrade to a new version of UNIX, it is crucial to make a backup of important UNIX configuration files, so that it will be easy to restore your old system if necessary. Many systems have important files in the /etc directory, and also in the /usr/local directory.

  To complete this exercise, you must have root privileges on the system.

  To back up UNIX configuration files:

1. To make a backup to a disk:

   a. Use the *df* command to find a partition that has enough space to hold your backup. Simply type **df**, and locate a directory on your file system that has enough space. DO NOT use the TEMP or root (/) directory!

   b. Use the *tar* command to create a compressed format backup file. The syntax for *tar* is *tar -[command][options][parameters]*. For example, to back up the /etc and /usr/local directories and all their subdirectories to a file called *archive.tar* in the /home directory, you enter

   tar −cvf /home/archive.tar /etc /usr/local

   The command *c* is to create a new tar file, the *v* and *f* options are for verbose and file (to show you what is happening and to indicate that what follows next is the path and filename of the file to be saved), and the parameters include the file or directory name(s) you are backing up.

2. To make a backup of /etc and /usr/local and all of their subdirectories to a tape drive using built-in compression:

   a. Load an empty tape in your tape drive.

   b. Enter the command **tar –cvf /dev/rmt/0c /etc /usr/local**
   (If necessary, replace "rmt/0c" with the proper designation for your tape drive.)

PROJECT 5-5

Your computer came with an operating system installed. It probably works fine for most things. Periodically, however, operating system manufacturers release new versions of their product. These new versions may correct flaws in an earlier release and certainly will add new functionality. You may also want to update a much older version of an operating system to a new one—upgrading from Windows 3.1x to Windows 95, for example.

To upgrade to Windows 95 Service Release B on a computer with the MS-DOS or Windows 3.1x operating system:

1. Start up the computer.

2. Insert the Windows 95 Release B CD-ROM, and put the Windows 95 boot floppy in the A: drive; or for the floppy version, put Windows 95 disk 1 in the A: drive and restart the computer. The steps will illustrate a CD-ROM installation; but will indicate where there are differences for older versions or for installation from a floppy.

If you made your own boot floppy as detailed in Chapter 4, the installer will not start by itself. To start the installation, at the DOS prompt type **D:** and press **Enter** (where D: is your CD-ROM drive), type **CD WIN95** and press **[Enter]**, then type **Setup** and press **[Enter]**. A message tells you your system is about to be inspected. Press **[Enter]**. The system is briefly inspected, and if your hardware does not support Windows 95, you will be told at this time. You will also be told about an option to bypass the check of your disks, but you should be aware that if the hardware does not pass the test, it will probably not work well with Windows 95.

If you are upgrading from Windows 3.1x, at this point you see a message that you need to start the existing version of Windows and run Setup from there. Click **Cancel**, then open **File Manager** and run **Setup**.

3. The Setup program will start the installation process by copying some files, then you will be welcomed to Windows 95. Click **Continue** and the Setup Wizard will be initialized, after which the software license agreement appears. Indicate your agreement with the license by clicking **Yes**, and the Setup Wizard will appear.

4. Click **Next**.

At this point, you may be told that this is an upgrade version of Windows. If you have a right to run this version, you can get past this screen by providing disk 1 of your old Windows version as verification that you own a license to an older Windows version. This older version may be an upgrade version itself.

5. You will be asked where you wish to install Windows. Select the default directory C:\WINDOWS. After you click **Next**, Windows will check the directory, and present you with the setup options for Windows 95 (Typical, Portable, Compact, or Custom).

6. Choose the **Custom** option, and click **Next**.

7. Enter the license key (sometimes called CD key or Product ID), a long alphanumeric number usually including the letters "OEM" on a label on your Windows 95 CD case, or on the Certificate of Authenticity in the documentation. You should not lose this key, as you cannot install Windows 95 without it. Enter the alphanumeric key and press **Enter**.

You can use a magic marker to write the license key on the back (printed side) of the CD or on the label of disk 1; this way it cannot get lost unless the CD or disk 1 gets lost.

8. Enter your name and the company name, if applicable. The company name may be left blank, but you must enter a personal name. Click **Next**, and Setup will show you a window titled Analyzing your Computer. In this window you have the choice of letting the wizard detect your hardware, or modifying the list of hardware to be detected. Let the wizard analyze all hardware for you by clicking **Yes**. This may take a little longer, but the result is that you will discover potential hardware problems. After selecting Yes, click **Next**.

9. If you have a network adapter and/or a sound adapter, click the appropriate boxes to have the wizard analyze them, then click **Next**. Setup Wizard will analyze your computer. This may take as much as 10 minutes, so be patient.

The Setup Wizard has been known to crash during analysis; if that happens, turn your computer *off* and restart the Windows installation. Any time you receive error messages during computer operation it is best to turn the machine off rather than just conducting a warm boot. Memory and other hardware devices may retain erroneous settings during a warm boot; removing power to all hardware ensures that everything returns to default during the OS reboot. Windows will detect that you have interrupted installation, and pick up where it left off. It is important that you actually turn off the power, and not reboot with Ctrl+Alt+Del or the Reset button. This will ensure that all memory locations have been cleared of old information. You want the new operating system to load completely when you restart.

10. After the wizard analyzes your computer, the Select Components screen appears. This is where you pick what optional parts of the operating system you wish to install. A gray check box means that some components under that option have been selected. To make specific changes, you can click the check boxes next to the options you wish to install. If there is no checkmark in Disk Tools, or it is grayed, click **Disk Tools**, then click **Details** to see additional options. Click **Backup** to select it. Click **OK**. When you are finished selecting operating system components, click **Next**.

 If you unselect a gray box, then reselect it, it will turn white; this is the quickest way to turn on all options in a group.

11. If you have a network card in your machine, or if you selected the communications options, the Network Configuration window appears. This is one of the areas where Windows 95 is much more advanced than Windows 3.11, as can be seen in Figure 5-5.

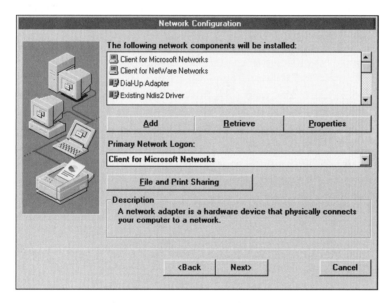

Figure 5-5 Windows 95 Network Configuration window

12. If you have a network card and it was not detected, you can click **Add**, select **Adapter**, click **Add**, and pick your card from the list.

13. If you want to be a server on a peer-to-peer network, you need to install file and printer sharing. To do this, click **File and Printer Sharing**, and select the check boxes in front of file sharing and printer sharing (or one of the two, depending on your needs).

14. If you will not be using a modem with the computer, you should delete the Dial-Up Networking Adapter at this time. (If you have not installed a dial-up adapter, skip this step.) To do this, select it, then click **Remove**.

15. When you click **Next**, you are asked for identification information; you should provide the computer and workgroup names. (See Chapter 4 for more details on computer and workgroup names.) Click **Next** again. If your network adapter was automatically detected, and it was a Plug and Play device, this will complete the network setup. If it was not, you will be asked if you wish to provide additional details about your adapter now or later. Do this now, by clicking **Continue Setting Up Network Adapter**, then **Next**. You will be prompted with a screen that asks information about your adapter; simply fill in the correct settings and click **Next** to continue.

16. The Setup Wizard now displays the settings it has determined are correct for your machine. You can click on an individual setting and change it if you wish, but if all has gone well so far, everything should be correct. Some devices you have may not yet be listed; this is normal, they will be detected later. Click **Next**.

 If you scroll all the way to the bottom of the list, you will see an option called User Interface. If you select Change, you will see you have an option to use the Windows 95 interface, which is the default selection, or to use the Program Manager (Win 3.1x) interface. If for some reason it is important to retain the Program Manager look and feel, this is an option.

17. Next you are asked if you want to create a Windows 95 startup floppy disk. You should always create this disk; it will help you fix problems if you are unable to boot from the hard disk. Click **Yes**, then click **Next**. Have a blank, formatted disk ready. Click **Next**. Insert the blank disk when prompted and click **OK**, and the startup files are copied to the disk. This may take a few minutes. Keep this disk in a safe place.

18. After you create the startup disk, the Windows 95 files copy to the hard disk. Only the files needed to install the components you have specified are copied. This may take a while, depending on whether you install from floppy or from CD, and also depending on the speed of your computer.

19. After all files are copied, the Finish Setup window appears. Remove any floppy disks and click **Finish** to restart the computer. You can leave the CD in the CD-ROM drive. The restart will start your system with the new Windows 95 drivers.

20. After your machine reboots, you will see the Windows 95 logo and you will return to the Setup Wizard. If you have not configured your network adapter correctly, you will receive a warning about it at this time (you can correct that issue later). If you installed any Windows networking components, you are asked to enter your username and password. If you do not wish to use a password, just enter a name and leave the password blank. If you did not install any Windows networking components, this question will be skipped.

21. Next, Windows goes through the Plug and Play setup to automatically detect all hardware in the machine that is capable of negotiating settings with Windows. This may take a few minutes. Then various software elements, such as the Control Panel, are installed.

22. Select your time zone when prompted to do so.

23. If you installed Microsoft Exchange, a wizard appears for installing Microsoft Network (MSN), MS Mail, MS Fax, and other settings. You can follow the simple on-screen prompts to configure the services you wish to use, or click Cancel to configure these at another time.

24. If you installed dial-up networking, you are asked whether you wish to use a local modem or a network service. If you choose a network service, you need to select the server you wish to use.

> If you are not prompted for this information you can bring it up later from the Control Panel. This is also true of many of the features described in the following sections.

25. If you use a modem, you can set it up at this time. The Modem Wizard appears; choose to let it detect your modem. In many cases, it will figure out what modem you have connected to what port, and install it for you. All you have to do is click **Next** a few times. The Fax Wizard returns, and if you're using a local modem, you are asked whether the Fax program should answer incoming calls. Next, provide the information that identifies you when you send a fax. The wizard then asks you to pick a location for your personal address book and your personal mailbox. If possible, leave these values unchanged.

26. Now the Printer Wizard runs. If you have a network connection set up, you can choose to install a network printer or a local printer by selecting the appropriate option. If you wish to use a network printer, it's best to install it later. To install a local printer, choose the **Local printer** option, then select from a list of printer makes and models. Pick the make of your printer from the left, then the appropriate printer model from the right. If you have a driver disk for your printer, click **Have Disk** and follow the options.

27. After you select a printer, you are prompted to pick the printer port.

28. Name the printer at the prompt; either leave the default name or give the printer a meaningful name, such as where it is located.

29. Finally, you are asked if you wish to print a test page. This is a good idea, as it will confirm that the printer works correctly.

30. With the printer installation completed, you are prompted to restart the computer one more time. This is necessary for all of the final configuration changes to take effect. If something went wrong with your printer install, you may get a warning about print jobs that will be lost if you restart Windows. (If this happens, click OK.) When Windows 95 restarts, it updates settings, and may install additional drivers depending on what hardware you have.

31. Windows 95 should be ready to go! Unlike MS-DOS and Windows 3.1, there is no need for memory tweaking after the upgrade is completed.

PROJECT 5-6

To upgrade to Windows 98 from Windows 95:

1. Insert the Windows 98 installation CD-ROM. A dialog box appears, indicating that the CD-ROM contains a newer version of Windows than you are presently using.

> If you don't see a message within a few seconds of inserting the CD-ROM disk, your CD-ROM drive doesn't support Autorun. You can launch the Windows 98 setup routine by pointing to the Start menu, choosing Run, and typing **d:\setup** in the Run field of this dialog box, where *d:* is the drive letter of your CD-ROM drive.

2. Click **Yes** to upgrade your computer to Windows 98. The Windows 98 Setup screen appears.

3. Click **Continue** to start the installation. The license agreement appears. Read and accept the agreement by clicking **I accept the Agreement** and click **Next** to continue.

4. When prompted, enter the Product key from your installation CD or documentation. Windows creates a directory for system files.

5. Click an option to specify if you want to save your existing operating system files (recommended). Click **Next** to continue.

6. While Setup saves system files, click **OK** to accept the default location for uninstall files.

7. Select your country from the list displayed. The wizard uses this information to provide Web channels (specially designed Web sites that Windows can deliver automatically to your computer) it considers to be of interest to people in your country. Click **Next** to continue.

8. Setup now creates a startup disk to use if you have trouble starting Windows 98. Click **Next** to continue.

9. You are prompted to insert a floppy disk for the startup disk. Label the disk **Windows 98 Startup Disk**, insert it in drive A: (or your floppy drive), and click **OK** to continue. You will see a message when Setup finishes creating the startup disk. Remove the floppy disk from the drive and click **OK** to continue.

10. Now Setup displays the Start Copying Files screen. If you want to go back to a previous step to change your answers, you can click Back. Otherwise, click **Next** to continue. It may take several minutes to copy all the files to your computer.

11. When all files have been copied to your computer, you will be prompted to restart the computer. Restart your computer. After it restarts, the wizard restarts your computer a second time and begins the final phase of installation. It sets up any hardware devices and Plug and Play devices it finds on your computer. If your computer has a network card, you may be asked to enter a password. If this happens, type your password and then press **Enter**. (If you used a password with the previous version of Windows, you can use the same password with Windows 98.) After the computer updates its settings, it may restart a third time.

12. Windows 98 starts and the Welcome to Windows 98 dialog box appears.

PROJECT 5-7

MFC Files (Microsoft Foundation Classes) are important files that may be used by many applications. These files are installed with your operating system and also by some applications software.

To view MFC files currently installed on your computer:

1. Open a DOS session. Click **Start**, point to **Programs**, and choose **MS DOS Prompt**.

2. Type **CD** and press **Enter** to make the root directory the current directory.

3. Type **dir mfc*.dll /s** and press **Enter**. You will see a list of directories and MFC files. Some of these will be in the Windows directory; others may be within the directories of application software.

5

CASE PROJECTS

1. As this book is written, Microsoft is preparing to release Windows 2000, the NT-based networking business operating system. The look and feel of Windows 2000 is similar to Windows 98 but the underlying features are more NT-like, with enhanced security, networking, and communications support. Suppose you manage a small network of about 10 machines, running a combination of Windows 95, Windows 98, and Linux. You want to assess the feasibility of upgrading all or part of the network to Windows 2000. Based on the procedures outlined in this book, answer the following questions:

   a. What additional hardware, if any, should you consider purchasing prior to making a switch to Windows 2000?

   b. What is the first step in evaluating such an operating system upgrade?

   c. Why might you want to install Windows 2000 on all machines in your network? Why not?

   d. How can you ensure that all existing data will be available after a systemwide upgrade?

   e. Could you make such an upgrade with all production machines in place? Why or why not?

   f. Describe some of the potential problems involved in changing the Linux machines over to Windows 2000.

   g. How can you use the existing network infrastructure to help you back up data?

2. As a single user of one computer and one operating system, you probably take one of two approaches in maintaining your system: you adopt the "bleeding edge" approach and install every new feature or update as soon as it is available, or you run your original operating system until you install a new computer. For corporate users decisions to upgrade are much more difficult, and making the right decision is much more important.

Imagine that you work for a medium-sized company with about 100 computers installed. In addition to internal LAN communications, most employees also access the Internet via a high-speed LAN connection, and you have some shared accounting and sales tracking applications used by most employees.

The company has a mix of older Pentium 100s, a few Macintosh computers, and some newer Pentium IIs with various memory and storage capacities. You are a power user, someone with a fair amount of computer experience, but you are not managing the network.

At your request, the network administrator agrees to install a newer, more powerful computer to replace your aging Pentium 100 running Windows 95. Your new machine is installed, but you are disappointed to discover that instead of getting the latest Windows 98 release, your new machine is still running Windows 95 and your Microsoft Office is two versions old.

a. From a LAN manager's viewpoint, can you think of reasons why new machines are installed with an older operating system?

b. What arguments could you make in favor of getting an upgrade to Windows 98?

c. Can you foresee any problems if you were to upgrade to the latest release of the Microsoft Office suite? (This issue isn't explicitly discussed in this chapter, but consider the implications of multiple users running different versions of production software, whether it is word processing, a spreadsheet, or a graphics production package.)

d. You personally own a multiuser license for Windows 98, but your company won't allow you to install it on your machine at work. Why do you think they take this stance?

e. Can you devise a reasonable upgrade strategy that will get everyone in the company up to speed with Windows 98?

OUTPUT, INPUT, AND STORAGE DEVICES

Regardless of what you do with your computer, you need to input commands and data (whether text, sound, or visual), and produce output (for example as the video display on your computer monitor, as printed hard copy, or as sound through your computer's speakers). In addition, you need to be able to save information to disks or other storage devices so that all of your changes are not lost when you power down the computer, and so that you can make backup copies of important data. This chapter describes how major input, output, and storage components work, including installation and configuration considerations, and how various operating systems work with them.

AFTER READING THIS CHAPTER AND COMPLETING THE EXERCISES YOU WILL BE ABLE TO:

- Review how operating systems interface with input, output, and storage devices
- Understand the need for software drivers for specific hardware output devices
- Discuss software driver installation within major operating systems
- Describe popular printer technologies, connections, and methods of installation
- Discuss general display adapter design, types of adapters, and hardware installation
- Identify important considerations when installing and using a variety of input devices
- Understand basic disk drive interface technologies

OPERATING SYSTEMS AND DEVICES: AN OVERVIEW

As you may recall from Chapter 1, one of the primary functions of any operating system is to provide basic input/output (I/O) support for application software, that is, to translate requests from application software into commands that the hardware can understand and carry out. For example, the operating system must:

- Handle input from the keyboard, mouse and other input devices

- Handle output to the screen, printer, and other output devices

- Control information storage and retrieval using various types of disk drives

- Support communications with remote computers

There are two ways that an operating system accomplishes these tasks: through software (device driver code within the operating system itself, as well as accessing third-party device driver software) and hardware (controllers and adapter boards for specific input or output devices) that is controlled by the operating system. Device drivers perform the actual communication between the physical device and the operating system (such as CD-ROM or hard disk drivers), and adapters are circuit boards that plug into a slot on the motherboard of the computer (such as display adapters to produce video output, or sound cards to produce audio output). The particular configuration of device drivers and adapters varies from operating system to operating system, but they function in the same way in each operating system.

Likewise, setting up or installing input, output, or storage devices involves two general steps across operating systems:

1. Installing any software drivers that are required

2. Setting up the hardware

SOFTWARE CONSIDERATIONS

As necessary and common as printers, display adapters, and other devices are today, it may seem strange that you need a custom driver for each item you install—but it is true. The operating system provides the basic input/output support for the parallel, serial, bus, or other ports your printer and other hardware use, but it doesn't support specific features of individual devices you may connect to these ports. For that you need a driver, which may be supplied by the hardware manufacturer or supplied by the producer of the operating system. (See the discussion of driver software in Chapter 1.)

Many hardware manufacturers supply with their product a floppy disk or CD-ROM with drivers for current operating systems. In general, you should use the manufacturer's driver, if available, instead of the driver supplied with your operating system. Although many operating system drivers for specific hardware were developed by the hardware manufacturer in cooperation with the operating system producer, they may be generic—designed to support a range of hardware models—or they may be older than the specific hardware you are installing. Using the driver shipped with your particular printer or other device gives you a better chance of having the latest version designed for your specific hardware.

Even if your hardware is brand new, it is good practice to check with the manufacturer for newer driver software. Drivers usually are designated by version number and sometimes with a date. Drivers with later version numbers and dates may contain fixes for problems identified with earlier releases, and they sometimes enable or improve the performance of some hardware features. The best source of new driver software is the World Wide Web. Check the documentation that came with your hardware for a Web site for new drivers, or simply point your browser to the manufacturer's main Web site and look for downloads, product support, software updates, or pages with a similar title.

For example, to find drivers for a broad range of Epson printers, point your browser to *http://prographics.epson.com* and choose Downloads. You'll find a range of printer drivers for Epson's high-end printer models and, typical of many hardware manufacturers, Epson also offers you a patch for third-party software, including PageMaker 6.5 to enable PageMaker to work better with their printers. Use *www.epson.com* to choose a specific Epson product line and browse for support software. Here are some other examples of Web support addresses, as this book is being written:

- *www.hp.com/cposupport/eschome.html* Choose a specific Hewlett-Packard printer or plotter model, then Download to obtain the latest drivers

- *www.lexmark.com* Choose Drivers and select the product or model from the drivers page

- *www.creativehelp.com/home.html* Navigate to the Creative Labs (Soundblaster) knowledge base to submit questions and find drivers

- *www.matrox.com/mga/drivers* Choose a particular Matrox display product and navigate to more information or to download the latest drivers

Remember that you can usually guess the home page for major companies. Simply type *www.companyname.com* in the address line of your browser, where *companyname* is the actual name of the manufacturer of your hardware product. If you don't find the page you want, try a variation of the company name. If this doesn't work, go to *www.search.com* and search for information about a particular company or product.

The procedure for installing drivers varies slightly with the source of the driver and the operating system you are using. If you download a new driver from a manufacturer's Web site, you'll probably have to uncompress the file before you can use it.

For example, many PC users use the **PKZIP** or **WINZIP** compression/decompression utilities. Many software producers distribute software that has been bundled and compressed with the PKZIP/WINZIP format. Compression software not only reduces the size of the supplied files by removing redundant information, it also groups multiple files into a single distribution file or archive. Distribution files may be supplied in self-extraction format, an executable file that will decompress the archive and expand individual files. PC executable files normally use an .EXE file extension. If you download a driver archive that includes this extension, it is a **self-extracting file**. If the file includes a .ZIP extension, on the other hand, you'll need a program such as PKZIP or WINZIP to expand the archive before you can install the driver software.

 If you don't have the PKZIP or WINZIP software, you can download it from the Internet at a variety of sites. There also are other programs that perform similar functions. One resource for a wide variety of shareware, freeware, and low-priced software is: *http://tucows.usit.net*. Enter this Web address as shown, without the usual *www* prefix.

Macintosh users can use ZIP-format archives, but a more common format is **StuffIt**, a utility similar to PKZIP that also bundles multiple files into a single distribution archive. StuffIt files can be self-extracting or you can use StuffIt Expander or another utility to expand the archive into its individual components. If you don't have this utility, you can download the shareware StuffIt Expander from Aladdin Systems at *www.aladdinsys.com*. Even if you work primarily in Windows, you might want to retrieve this utility for your PC. It also supports ZIP format and it lets you retrieve compressed or archived files from Macintosh users. For a small fee you can purchase the full-blown StuffIt software so you can create archives for Mac and Windows environments. The ZIP utilities available for the Mac don't always produce files that are compatible with Windows systems. The StuffIt Expander software, on the other hand, works both ways quite well.

UNIX system users may retrieve drivers and other software in a *tar* format. **Tar** files also are archives that group multiple files into a single distribution file. *Tar* doesn't compress the files; it merely groups files to make it easier to copy and distribute multiple files together. You may find that a *tar* archive is also zipped. You can use a UNIX version of unzip to expand the compressed *tar* archive into an uncompressed file, then you issue a UNIX *tar* command to extract individual files from the archive.

Once you have located the driver you want to use, you generally have two choices for installation, depending on the source of the driver: you'll either use your operating system's install utility or you'll run an install utility provided by the hardware manufacturer. Procedures are slightly different among different operating systems, and precise steps differ with different equipment (a printer installs slightly differently than a sound card, for example), but the general process is very similar. This section steps you through an operating system printer install, which is representative of how various operating systems handle hardware driver integration.

MANUFACTURER DRIVER INSTALLATION

When you use a hardware manufacturer's install utility, the process is usually fully automatic and well documented. In fact, newer printers, plotters, and other devices frequently come with extensive support material on CD-ROM. You might be presented with video or animated training material to teach you how to install or use the device, for example. Certainly you shouldn't have to know much about the way your operating system installs drivers or interfaces with the device you're installing because the manufacturer's installer routine will handle it all for you. And, since each manufacturer has a different procedure with different devices and different operating systems, it is difficult to document each system and device type.

In general, however, the procedure is to insert a floppy disk or CD-ROM into a drive and either wait for a program to start automatically, or run a setup or install utility. Then, simply follow onscreen prompts. If you run into problems, look for a disk-based tutorial or go to the manufacturer's Web site to search for more information. Some software suppliers also include .TXT files on their install disk to present new information or tips for the installer. You can use Notepad or any text program to look for these files and read them.

DOS Driver Installation

If your computer experience is limited to Windows or Mac OS, then the concept of installing drivers and configuring hardware from the command line or by editing system-level configuration files may be a little strange. Chances are, with today's technology, you won't have to concern yourself much with DOS-only installations anyway, but it couldn't hurt for you to at least be somewhat familiar with the process.

DOS applications and hardware, as with Windows, may include automatic driver installation routines. If yours doesn't, there should be information with the device for installing and configuring the required drivers yourself. In general, DOS drivers are installed and configured by adding statements in two system-level files, CONFIG.SYS and AUTOEXEC.BAT, as discussed in Chapter 4. Although these are system-level files, they are simple text files that contain operating system commands executed when the system starts. You can edit these files with any text editor. The intrinsic DOS EDIT utility is a good choice that is always available.

Since these files control the operating of your DOS-based applications as well as your operating system, they are different for each computer. What you see in these configuration files depends on how you have your operating system configured and what applications you are running. However, the files shown in Figures 6-1 and 6-2 (on the next page) demonstrate typical contents of the CONFIG.SYS and AUTOEXEC.BAT files, respectively.

```
dos=high
command=c:\DOS\command.com
files=20
buffers=20
device=c:\dos\emm386.sys
device=c:\dos\mouse.exe
device=c:\setver.sys
```

Figure 6-1   Typical DOS CONFIG.SYS file

```
c:\windows\Net Start
A:\SMARTDRV.EXE
echo off
call pmpt
set compspec=c:\command.com
loadhigh c:\mouse\mscmouse /a5
loadhigh doskey
doskey dir = dir $1 /p /on
PATH C: \WINDOWS;c:\;c:\dos;c:\wp51
SET TEMP=C:\WINDOWS\TEMP
loadhigh mode con: rate=30 delay=1
doskey cls=c:\utility\melt
doskey dir = dir $1 /on /p

date
time
```

Figure 6-2 Typical DOS AUTOEXEC.BAT file

The CONFIG.SYS file loads first. It includes commands to load low-level drivers and to configure memory. For example, the DEVICE command in CONFIG.SYS lets you specify files (that are not actually part of DOS) that will load into memory and function like part of the operating system. The DEVICE command loads drivers for a CD-ROM drive, a memory management utility such as EMM386.EXE, and so on. Each driver requires different commands, but the general format for the CONFIG.SYS file is:

device=<path> filename

where *<path>* is the path to the folder (directory) that holds the device driver and *filename* is the actual name of the driver to be installed. Table 6-1 shows a partial list of commands you can use in CONFIG.SYS.

Table 6-1 CONFIG.SYS Commands

Command	Purpose
break	Sets or clears extended CTRL+C checking. You can use this command at the command prompt or in a batch file.
buffers and buffershigh	Allocates memory for a specified number of disk buffers when the computer starts. The buffershigh form causes reserved memory to be taken out of the upper memory area. You can use these commands only in CONFIG.SYS.
country	Enables the operating system to use country-specific conventions for displaying dates, times, and currency; for determining the order by which characters are sorted; and for determining which characters can be used in filenames. You can use this command only in CONFIG.SYS.
device	Loads the device driver you specify into memory. You can use this command only in CONFIG.SYS.
devicehigh	Loads the device driver you specify into upper memory. You can use this command only in CONFIG.SYS.

Table 6-1   CONFIG.SYS Commands (continued)

Command	Purpose
dos	Specifies that the operating system should maintain a link to the upper memory area (UMA), load part of itself into the high memory area (HMA), or both. You can use this command only in CONFIG.SYS.
drivparm	Defines parameters for devices such as disk and tape drives when you start the operating system. You can use this command only in CONFIG.SYS.
fcbs or fcbshigh	Specifies the number of file control blocks (FCBs) that the operating system can have open at the same time. The fcbshigh form causes reserved memory to be taken out of the upper memory area. You can use these commands only in CONFIG.SYS.
files or fileshigh	Specifies the number of files that the operating system can access at one time. The fileshigh form causes reserved memory to be taken out of the upper memory area. You can use these commands only in CONFIG.SYS.
include	Includes the contents of one configuration block within another. You can use this command only in CONFIG.SYS.
install	Loads a memory-resident program into memory. You can use this command only in CONFIG.SYS.
lastdrive or lastdrivehigh	Specifies the maximum number of drives you can access. The lastdrivehigh form causes reserved memory to be taken out of the upper memory area. You can use these commands only in CONFIG.SYS.
menucolor	Sets the text and background colors for the startup menu. You can use this command only within a menu block in CONFIG.SYS.
menudefault	Specifies the default menu item on the startup menu and sets a time-out value, if desired. You can use this command only within a menu block in CONFIG.SYS.
menuitem	Defines up to nine items on the startup menu. You can use this command only within a menu block in CONFIG.SYS.
numlock	Specifies whether the NUMLOCK setting on the numeric keypad is set to ON or OFF. You can use this command only within a menu block in CONFIG.SYS.
rem	Enables you to include comments (remarks) or prevent commands in a batch program, or CONFIG.SYS from running.
shell	Specifies the name and location of the command interpreter you want Windows 95 to use. You can use this command only in CONFIG.SYS.
stacks or stackshigh	Supports the dynamic use of data stacks to handle hardware interrupts. The stackshigh form causes reserved memory to be taken out of the upper memory area. You can use these commands only in CONFIG.SYS.
submenu	Defines an item on a startup menu that, when selected, displays another set of choices. You can use this command only within a menu block in CONFIG.SYS.
switches	Specifies special options. Used only in CONFIG.SYS.

6

AUTOEXEC.BAT functions at a higher level. As with all .BAT (batch) files, AUTOEXEC issues DOS commands as if they were typed at the command prompt. In fact, you don't need AUTOEXEC.BAT at all, if you don't need to configure or run specific software or if you are willing to type the commands from the keyboard at the command line. You use commands in AUTOEXEC.BAT to launch external programs, applications that run outside DOS. If you are running an early version of Windows, for example, you might include in AUTOEXEC.BAT a command to start Windows automatically, instead of booting and leaving you in DOS where you have to type the WIN command from the keyboard. You can launch any application in this way. Suppose you are using a DOS-based application that is your primary program, the real reason you are using this computer. You can load the program with an AUTOEXEC.BAT command and never see the DOS prompt.

Other AUTOEXEC.BAT commands can conduct final configuration of the system as it boots. You can see this in Figure 6-2. The first command launches the local area networking utility that is part of Windows for Workgroups, for example, and the two LOADHIGH commands in the middle of the figure launch utilities for mouse management (MSCMOUSE) and to add command functions to DOS (DOSKEY).

 One way to debug a series of AUTOEXEC.BAT commands is to type the commands individually from the keyboard at the DOS prompt. You can easily discover problem commands or programs that don't work properly when you issue the commands one at a time.

Commands in the AUTOEXEC.BAT file are a little harder to generalize about than CONFIG.SYS commands, since different devices will require different levels of customization; different manufacturers choose to automate more of the process, others leave the user with more freedom for personalized installations.

However, the process is the same: you load the AUTOEXEC.BAT file into a text editor, type the command or commands required by your hardware, and save the file.

With either of these files you need to be aware of the order of commands. Some commands won't work unless prerequisite drivers have been installed first, for example.

WINDOWS DRIVER INSTALLATION

Whereas installing a driver from a supplied floppy disk or CD-ROM usually involves interactive instructions from the install routine, when you install a driver with the operating system's routines, you may need to be a little more savvy. This section shows you the basics of installing drivers in the Windows environment, illustrated with sample printer installations. Following sections cover the procedures for other operating systems.

Windows 3.1x

The path to installing most hardware in Windows 3.1x starts in the **Control Panel**, which you will find in the Main window on the Windows desktop. Note that in Windows 3.1x the various objects may be open on the desktop so you can see individual elements, or they may be closed and represented only as icons. Figure 6-3 shows a typical Windows 3.11 desktop with the Main window shrunk to an icon. This condition frequently causes problems for users of this operating system. If you don't see the application window you want open on the desktop, look for it as an icon at the bottom of the screen.

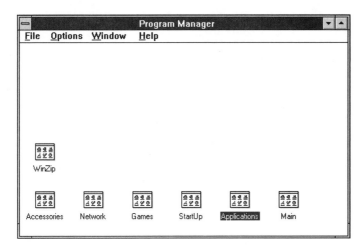

Figure 6-3   Window 3.11 desktop/Main window as icon

To open the Main window, simply double-click it, then double-click the Control Panel icon inside the Main application window to open the Control Panel. Inside the Control Panel is a Printers icon, as Figure 6-4 shows, which represents the currently installed printers and also lets you choose routines for installing a new printer.

Figure 6-4   Windows 3.11/open Control Panel window

You may already have one or more printers installed, or you may be installing the first printer. Either way, the process of adding a printer is the same. Double-click the Printers icon inside the Control Panel to open this window. Your display will look something like the one in Figure 6-5 on the next page.

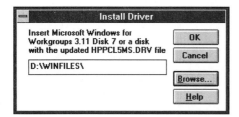

Figure 6-5   Windows 3.11 Control Panel/open Printers window

At the left of this dialog box you will see a list of installed printers—if there are any installed. At the right is a series of buttons that let you connect a printer, set up (configure) a printer, remove a printer, and add a new one.

 If you have not previously installed a printer in this operating system, your display will be slightly different from the one in Figure 6-5. Many of the choice buttons are grayed out, and you should see a list of available printers to install.

If you have not previously installed a printer, choose a printer from the list and click Install at the right side of this dialog box. You are prompted to insert one of the Windows 3.11 disks so the appropriate driver can be loaded.

Insert the requested disk and click OK, or click Browse to locate the required driver at another location. When you navigate to the new location, choose the drive or directory and click OK. You'll see the dialog box in Figure 6-6.

Install Driver

Insert Microsoft Windows for Workgroups 3.11 Disk 7 or a disk with the updated HPPCL5MS.DRV file

D:\WINFILES\

OK   Cancel   Browse...   Help

Figure 6-6   Windows 3.11 Install Driver dialog box

If you have previously installed a printer, then you can add another printer simply by clicking on the Add button shown in Figure 6-5 to display the dialog box shown in Figure 6-7.

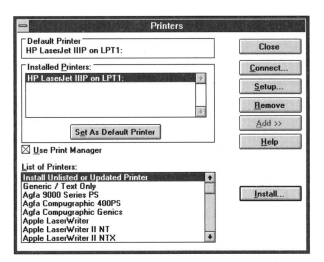

Figure 6-7   Adding a printer in Windows 3.11

The Add button opens up another section of the Printers dialog box that you saw previously. At the bottom of the expanded dialog box is a list of available printers. This list is based on manufacturers and models that were available when your operating system was installed, and will depend on the version of the operating system you are using. Notice the first entry in this list: *Install Unlisted or Updated Printer*. Choose this if you have a disk or CD-ROM from the printer manufacturer. When you choose this option and click Install at the lower right of this dialog, you are prompted for a disk. The default is the A:\ drive, but you can change the path in this window to anything that is valid for your machine. Once you enter the correct path to the manufacturer's installation disk, you should be able to follow relatively simple instructions to complete the installation.

 This is the procedure you'll use if you are installing only a driver from a manufacturer's disk. However, many manufacturer disks contain other utilities and also will complete this part of the installation for you. Instead of using the Control Panel as shown here, you might try running an Install or Setup routine on the manufacturer's disk. The process could be easier and there may be additional utilities for use with your printer that you won't get if you use the drivers-only install routine in the Control Panel.

To use the drivers available in Windows, scroll down the list of available manufacturers and models, select the one you want to install, and click Install. You will be asked to insert one of the Windows distribution disks (or CD-ROM if this version of Windows was installed from a CD instead of floppies). Simply insert the requested disk or CD-ROM and follow the instructions. You may be asked to reboot the computer when the driver installation is complete. Then you should be able to use the new printer within any applications you're running on this machine.

Windows 95/98

Installing hardware in Windows 95 and Windows 98 is very similar. The Windows 98 perspective is shown here. If you're using Windows 95 some of the icons may look slightly different, but the process is essentially the same.

A nice thing about Windows 98 (and to a slightly lesser degree, Windows 95) is its Plug and Play feature. You can install a new printer in Windows 98 very quickly with these steps:

1. Shut down the system by choosing Shut Down from the Start menu.

2. Turn off the power.

3. Connect the printer to the computer's printer port.

4. Plug the printer into a power outlet and turn it on.

5. Turn on the computer.

When the operating system boots, it will recognize that a new piece of hardware is attached to the printer port and will try to locate the drivers for it. If this device is something Windows already knows about, it will find the drivers on the Windows distribution disks or CD-ROM. Otherwise you'll need to insert the manufacturer's disk or CD-ROM into an appropriate drive when Windows asks for it.

If Windows doesn't recognize the new hardware, or if you simply want to conduct an install from scratch, you will use the Printers dialog box, accessible through the Control Panel or directly from the Start menu. To display the Printers dialog box in Windows 98 or Windows 95, click Start on the taskbar, point to Settings and choose Printers from the supplemental list. You will see a window similar to the one in Figure 6-8.

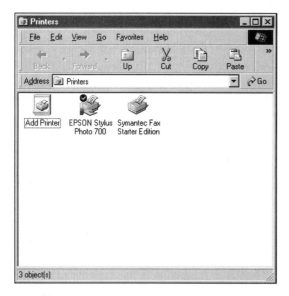

Figure 6-8   Windows 98 Printers window

Choose Add Printer from the Printers window to display a series of wizard screens that help you complete the installation. In the wizard screens, you answer questions about whether you want to set up a local or network printer, and specify the manufacturer and printer model, as shown in Figure 6-9. If you have a disk supplied by the manufacturer, you can click the Have Disk button and specify the path to the driver disk or CD-ROM.

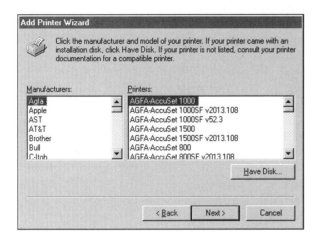

6

Figure 6-9   Choosing a printer manufacturer and model in Windows 98

You will also choose the port to which this printer is connected, and give a name that you want to use for the printer. You can probably accept the suggested printer name. However, if this is a networked printer and you have more than one printer of the same model from the same manufacturer on this network, you'll need to give the printer a unique name so everyone who uses it will know what printer to use. You also need to specify whether you want Windows to use this new printer as the default printer.

Next you can choose to print a test page. This is a good idea when you first install a new printer, to ensure that the physical connection to the printer is OK and that the drivers have been properly installed to create at least basic text and graphics images. After printing a test page, check to see if it printed correctly.

At the end of the installation, you will see the Printers screen with the new printer you just installed listed along with any others that were previously installed.

You can now use this new printer from any applications you have installed by selecting the printer from the Print dialog box of individual applications.

Windows NT

Many Windows NT 4.0 screens look very similar to Windows 95/98 screens. In fact, with many screens you have to look closely to be sure which operating system you are using. The process of installing a new printer in Windows NT is also quite similar to installing a printer in Windows 95/98.

To install a new printer in Windows NT 4.0 or later, click Start, choose Settings, and open the Control Panel. Double-click the Printers icon in the Control Panel to display the Printers dialog box shown in Figure 6-10.

Figure 6-10   Windows NT Printers dialog box

Double-click the Add Printer icon in the Printers dialog box to start the Windows NT Add Printer Wizard shown in Figure 6-11.

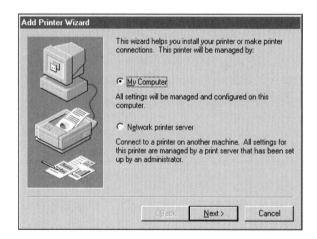

Figure 6-11   Windows NT Add Printer Wizard

As with Windows 98, in the Add Printer Wizard you choose whether the printer you are installing is connected directly to your computer or installed already somewhere else on the network, select the port (if this is a local printer, or the previously installed network printer if the printer you are installing already exists somewhere on the network), choose the manufacturer and printer model, and enter the name you want to use for this new printer.

Then you specify whether you want to share this printer with other users on a network, as shown in Figure 6-12. If you choose Yes, you will be asked to enter a Share Name. This is the name other users on the network use to locate and connect to your printer.

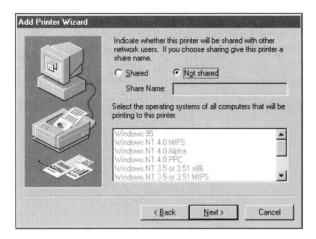

Figure 6-12   Windows NT shared/not shared dialog box

Additionally, if you are networked in a mixed environment where Windows 95/98 or other systems might need access to your printer, say so by choosing the appropriate auxiliary operating systems from the list at the bottom of this dialog box.

On the next screen, you can choose to print a test page. Remember, it is always a good idea to print a test page when you install a new printer. This is especially true if you are installing a network printer.

Unless you have installed this printer before, Windows NT also needs to retrieve the drivers required for this printer. You may be asked to insert the Windows NT distribution disk or CD-ROM. When you're done, you'll see a new printer icon that represents the just-installed printer in the Windows NT Printers dialog box.

MAC OS DRIVER INSTALLATION

The Mac OS installation includes drivers for almost all Apple-brand printers. Unless you have chosen a customized installation of the operating system, and intentionally removed the printer drivers, you will already have the Apple drivers on your system.

If you do have an Apple printer, and the printer is not listed in the Chooser (Apple's tool for selecting the printer, found in the Apple menu) you should first check to see if the currently installed drivers are compatible with your printer. For example, if you have a Color StyleWriter 2400, the current version of the driver is actually called Color SW 2500. If you have a StyleWriter or StyleWriter II, you should use StyleWriter 1200. In general, if your printer isn't listed, you should try the next higher-numbered printer in the Chooser before installing software that is included on disk with the printer.

If you aren't sure that you have all of the Apple printer drivers installed, you may need to install them. This requires re-running part of the Mac OS installer.

To begin this process, launch the installer (there is no need to boot from CD-ROM to do this, just put the CD in) and go through the install process as described in Chapter 4 until you reach the last screen. Before you click Start, click the Customize button, as shown in Figure 6-13. Remove the checks from everything but Mac OS 8.5, then change the installation mode by clicking the Customized Installation selection, as shown in Figure 6-14.

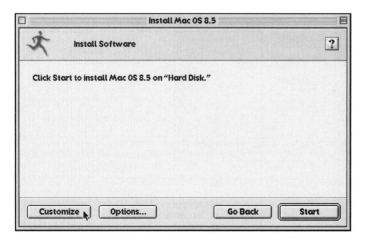

Figure 6-13   Customize button in Mac OS install

Figure 6-14   Customized Installation selection

A second window will open. Check Printing, then click OK (see Figure 6-15).

Figure 6-15   Choose Printing installation

On the next window (Figure 6-16), click the Start button. When the installer finishes, restart and pick the correct driver and port using the Chooser.

Figure 6-16   Click Start to launch the printer driver installer

If you have a printer not manufactured by Apple, you will need to follow the instructions provided with that printer, though it might also be a good idea to check the printer manufacturer's Web site. Many printers include driver versions significantly older than the currently available downloadable versions, and these older versions can cause problems when used with the latest version of Mac OS.

UNIX DRIVER INSTALLATION

The concept of drivers in Unix is slightly different than in other operating systems. The central portion of the UNIX operating system, known as the Kernel, is where most of the

UNIX device drivers are loaded. Device drivers are either in the form of kernel modules, which are pieces of code that have to be linked into the Kernel, or loadable modules, similar pieces of code that are not linked into the Kernel but are loaded when the operating system is started. Device support in most UNIX versions is limited compared to other operating systems; manufacturers of devices will often provide drivers for their special hardware which are then linked or loaded into the Kernel.

Since UNIX is a multi-user, multitasking operating system, it uses a print queue. When a print job is sent from an application, a **print queue** or **spooler** temporarily stores the print job, from which it is sent to the printer. In order to configure a printer on a UNIX system, you first have to define the printer parameters and define the print queue. All definitions of printers and queues are kept in the file /etc/printcap. This file is maintained in plain ASCII text and could be edited by hand. However, there are UNIX utilities to make this job easier; take advantage of these tools. Hands-on Projects 6-4 and 6-5 step you through the process of setting up printers in Linux and Solaris, using the *printtool* and *admintool* utilities, respectively.

You need Root privileges to perform most UNIX printer maintenance.

The UNIX operating system provides a standard mechanism for network printing; a printer connected to one computer can be used to print jobs from another computer. Every machine that wants to use a printer, whether remotely or locally, must first create a print queue for that printer. If there is one machine with the printer connected, and three other UNIX machines that want to use the printer, a print queue for that printer must be created on all four machines. When a print job is submitted, it is queued in the local print queue. From there it will be submitted to the print queue of the machine to which the printer is connected, and then it will be spooled to the printer.

The UNIX platform has traditionally used PostScript printers; for this reason PostScript printers have the most trouble-free installations in UNIX.

Now that you're familiar with the basic process of installing device drivers in various operating systems, it's time to survey the various types of input, output, and storage devices you might want to install.

PRINTERS

A printer is an important part of nearly every computer installation. The following sections outline the most popular types of printers and printer connections.

The installation of printers in various operating systems was covered earlier in the chapter, in the Software Considerations section.

PRINTER TYPES

The following types of printers are the most popular today:

- **Dot matrix printers**, which produce characters by slamming a group of wires (dots) from a rectangular grid onto a ribbon and then paper to produce characters (thus the designation, "impact printer"). Dot matrix printers tend to be noisy, and the quality of the characters is not as good as laser and ink-jet printers. Although dot matrix printers are declining in popularity, you'll still find them behind sales counters to support point-of-sale (POS) computers, in hospitals, at airline counters, in insurance companies—anywhere a computer is used to fill out forms or where multiple copies of the same document are needed simultaneously.

- **Ink-jet printers**, another printer that creates characters from dots by squirting tiny droplets of ink directly onto the page. Whereas impact dot matrix printers may be capable of printing a few hundred dots per inch, some ink-jet designs can lay down more than 1,400 dots in an inch. And, of course, full color—even near-photographic quality—printing with ink jets is quite common today. Ink-jet printers are popular personal printers in many offices and have the bulk of the printer market for schools and homes. Small, quiet, and inexpensive, these printers are perfect for relatively low-volume letter-quality text and even graphics output. Models that support color and high resolution are used for proofing by graphics designers and printers. And, with the rising popularity of digital electronic cameras, high-resolution ink-jet printers are used increasingly to produce photograph-like output on heavy, slick paper much like photographic paper stock.

- **Laser printers** use an imaging technology similar to copiers to produce computer output, and are probably the most popular printer design for business text and graphics. A typical laser printer contains its own CPU and memory, since printed pages are first produced electronically within the printer. Laser printer prices have declined sharply over the past several years, so that even small businesses can afford to have them.

In early dot-matrix printers, the operating system, the printer driver, and application software manage the printer at the character level; that is, directions are given for positioning the print head wires for every character. In later models, the printer itself may contain software that can receive basic character information from the computer, and adjust quality level of the output by making multiple passes over the characters.

Early ink-jet printers also depend on character-by-character instructions from the operating system via the device driver, but later models include internal electronics and programs that can take more general formatting information from the operating system and device driver and translate it into output.

With laser printers, the printer's own CPU conducts most of the print processing in the memory of the printer itself. The operating system and applications software sends basic character and graphics information to the printer and the printer handles the formatting, font and font attributes, and so on. The printer drivers interpret application output and convert it to a series of commands based on the printer programming language. These commands tell the printer how to format the output, but the actual formatting is conducted inside the printer.

Aside from these three major printer types, there are some other printer designs that are used in specialized arenas:

- **Line printers**, one of the earliest impact printer designs, print an entire line at a time rather than a character at a time. Line printers are fast but extremely noisy, as the "line" is actually a metal chain. They use some form of tractor feed or pin feed. Line printers are rare these days; you may see them in government agencies, colleges or universities, or other venues that require large amounts of paper output, particularly paper output with multiple copies. Impact printers of this type are still the best way to produce multiple pages of the same document or form. You would have to repeatedly print the pages on a laser printer to achieve multiple copies.

Vestiges of the line printer still remain: The main printer port on a PC is designated **LPT1**, which stands for Line Printer 1. It is doubtful that very many PCs ever were connected to a true line printer, but this big machine terminology stays with us.

- **Thermal-wax transfer** printers. Two basic thermal wax transfer designs exist. One uses rolls of plastic film coated with colored wax, which is melted onto the page, one primary color at a time. A second type, known as phase change, melts wax stored in individual colored sticks and sprays the molten, colored wax onto the page. These printers generally produce very high quality color output, but they also are relatively slow since they must pass the print head over each printed line once for each color. In addition, these printers frequently require special paper, which adds to the cost of the printed output.

- **Dye sublimation** (sometimes shortened to dye sub) printers. The dye sublimation design takes the concept of atomizing waxy colors onto the paper a step further. Dye sub printers don't just melt pigments and spray them onto the paper, they vaporize them. This colored gas penetrates the surface of the paper to create an image on the page. Dye sub printers produce high quality output. Moreover, they can mix and blend colors to produce output at near photographic quality. Thermal-wax transfer and dye sublimation printers are used in many graphics applications where very high quality, color printed output is required. Graphics design shops, for example, use them to produce proofs for book covers, brochures or other graphical material that ultimately are produced on high quality printing presses.

- **Imagesetter** printers, high quality output devices frequently used in the printing industry to produce final output or to produce page masters for offset printing. Imagesetters frequently produce output directly to film rather than paper. The film is used in a printing press to produce the final output. In color printing, a separate piece of film is produced for each of the colors cyan, magenta, yellow, and black.

In addition to traditional printers, another printer-like device called a **plotter** is popular in engineering, architecture, and other fields where hard copy output (such as blueprints) won't fit standard paper sizes or can't be produced by standard character or graphics printers. Plotter design is even more complex than printers, using pen and control mechanisms. As with printers, plotters require special drivers to enhance the operating system's intrinsic capabilities, but the process of installing plotter hardware and software is similar to that for printers. Likewise, plotters can be installed on a computer's parallel and serial ports in much the same way as printers (see the next section on Printer Connections).

PRINTER CONNECTIONS

In the early days of computing, nearly all printers were connected to a **serial port**—the same port where you may connect your modem or mouse today. A serial port manages communication between the computer and devices in a one-bit-after-the-other (asynchronous) stream. Today, the most common PC printer connection is a **parallel port**, which manages communications between the computer and peripherals in which data flows in parallel streams. Because more data can be sent at the same time (synchronously) in a parallel connection, it is generally a higher-speed connection than a serial connection. The parallel port is sometimes called a **Centronics interface**, after the printer manufacturer that made it popular. The original Centronics interface used a 36-pin connector. Current PC platforms and most UNIX machines use a 25-pin (**DB-25**) connector, since some of the original Centronics lines aren't necessary.

Some printers are designed with both parallel and serial interfaces so you can connect either way, depending on current needs.

 In general, a parallel printer connection is best, since it provides a faster data path and better two-way communication between the computer and the printer. However, if you need to locate the printer more than 10 feet or so from the computer, a serial connection is the better choice. You can place a printer up to 50 feet from the computer if you use a serial connection.

Printer manufacturers are increasingly offering alternative connection methods. Printers designed for corporate environments, for example, frequently have a direct network connection option that lets you place the printer virtually anywhere on a LAN where it can be shared among all of the computers also attached to the LAN. If a particular printer doesn't include a networked option, you can purchase a network printer interface from a third party. These interfaces have one or more network ports plus one or more printer ports. You connect the network on one side and plug in the printer on the other. It is generally more efficient to use a direct network-attached printer rather than a printer attached to a computer on the network. Using a printer attached to a computer can be a drain on that computer's resources when others are using the printer, and a network interface is always on, making the printer always available to network users.

The new **Universal Serial Bus (USB)** interface is gaining in popularity. Although not common as this book is written, printers with a USB interface should start to appear as this interface matures. External disk drives, cameras, scanners, modems and other devices are already using this interface. Printers with USB connections surely can't be far behind. New Apple computers are supplied with USB connectivity, but older Apple machines used a slower but similar technology, the **Apple Desktop Bus (ADB)**. The ADB is used for keyboard, mouse, printer and other device connections in much the same way as the newer USB interface.

In the Macintosh world, serial connections through a **DIN8M** plug are common if you're using an Apple printer. Of course, networked and parallel connections also are possible with the Mac.

DISPLAY ADAPTERS

Once wildly diverse in design and features, display adapters today are reaching a common ground across operating systems and hardware platforms. The general industry acceptance of the PCI bus standard (see Chapter 2 for a discussion of computer buses) has enabled adapter manufacturers to supply one hardware product or a line of hardware products to a variety of hardware platforms.

BASIC DISPLAY ADAPTER TECHNOLOGY

If you are using a PC with a monitor, you have a display adapter card already installed in your machine. The display adapter is part of a standard computer package. No matter what computer platform you are using, the basic display (and the baseline standard in most cases) consists of 640 pixels horizontally and 480 pixels vertically. A **pixel**, remember, is a picture element, actually a small dot of light that represents one small portion of your overall screen display. Top-end display adapters today are easily capable of displaying 1280 × 1024 pixels or even 1600 × 1280 in some cases.

In general, as you display more pixels on the screen, you'll need a larger monitor to read the displayed data comfortably. It should be obvious that while higher resolution displays can present more data at a time on the screen, for a given size of screen the information will be presented in a smaller format. A 1024 × 768 display on a 15-inch monitor works okay; but better on a 17-inch monitor. And if you need 1280 × 1024 or higher resolution you should consider at least a 19-inch monitor (a 21-inch monitor is a better choice).

Current operating systems support devices with the full range of resolution, so the major considerations in choosing adapters are the adapter's resolution capabilities, the amount of memory included onboard the adapter (more memory on the adapter generally means faster performance when rendering screen images), type of video processor (display adapters may have their own CPU or accelerator to speed things up for you), and cost. As noted previously, you should also consider what kind of monitor you need as you decide on the screen resolution you need to use. DOS systems generally don't support the same wide range of display formats as Windows, but some manufacturers have designed boards and driver software to fill this gap.

There's another aspect of screen resolution that isn't often discussed: the density of the displayed image, or bit depth. A resolution of 640 × 480 (the default resolution on PCs, Macs, and most other computers) simply means that images are displayed with 640 dots of light from left to right and 480 dots of light top to bottom. However, there is a third dimension to this display, the bit depth, or how many of these dots of light can be crammed into an inch of display. All computer displays have a bit depth of 72 dots per inch (dpi), and this is probably why so many books and articles about computer graphics ignore this important aspect of image display. When you consider graphics programs (such as PhotoShop or CorelDraw) or as you choose a digital camera or other image source, then this aspect of resolution becomes important. A high quality photograph, for example, may contain 4,000 dots per inch. Books are printed at 133 lines, but to ensure good quality, files are usually produced at 300 dpi or greater; brochures may be printed at 1,200 dpi.

When you view graphics on your computer monitor you are seeing only 72 dots per inch, because that's all your monitor is capable of showing. However, your printer may be able to reproduce 600 dpi, 1,200 dpi, 1,440 dpi or even 2,400 dpi for some applications. It is important to know this third dimension when you spec printers, plotters, scanners, digital cameras, video editing software, and graphics programs.

Although 640 × 480 is the basic Video Graphics Array (VGA) resolution, the majority of new computers are being shipped with 800 × 600 set as the default. Larger monitors also are the norm. Whereas 14-inch monitors were the norm just a few years ago, 15-inch displays are shipped with even the lowest-end computers today. With a 17-inch monitor (included in many packaged systems), you can probably routinely set a resolution of 1,024 × 768 and still see everything you need to see.

Standard VGA adapters also have standard color rendition capabilities that range from 16 colors at the very low end to millions of colors at the top. At the mid range is a 256-color setting that will let you reproduce color material with reasonably good quality; that setting is compatible with the broadest range of display adapters. World Wide Web page designers frequently design their images for 256 colors to ensure the broadest possible compatibility with computer hardware in use by Web browsers. A 256-color setting is pleasing, but still very low quality compared to higher settings.

INSTALLING DISPLAY ADAPTERS

Unless you're building a computer from scratch or you want to upgrade your existing machine's video capabilities, there should be no reason for you to install a display adapter yourself. The computer should come from the manufacturer with an adapter pre-installed. If you designed your computer when you purchased it for the type of work you will do with it, the original adapter should last for the life of the computer.

However, there can also be good reasons for upgrading display hardware. Technology changes, software changes, and our personal needs change, all leading to potential upgrade situations.

By far the majority of display adapters are supplied as PCI cards. The PCI bus has become a popular standard among computer hardware manufacturers, including Intel-based machines, Macintosh computers, and workstations designed for UNIX, Sun Solaris, and other systems. As with printers and other hardware, display adapters are installed in two phases, hardware and software.

Today's computer hardware is pretty rugged. You can drop it, twist it, mash it and probably it will survive. Still, perhaps the biggest enemy of the devices supplied on circuit boards is static (high-voltage, low-current charges that can exist between any two devices, including human bodies). Static discharges are obvious when the voltage is high enough to cause a spark to jump between objects or from an object to your finger. However, you can damage delicate computer parts with voltage levels below this sparking level.

You need to avoid the possibility of static discharge damage by observing these cautions:

1. Keep the expansion card in its factory packaging until you are ready to use it.

2. After you unwrap the card, hold it in one hand and touch the metal case of the computer power supply or chassis with the other hand to discharge any static buildup.

3. Continue touching the computer frame with one hand (or even your elbow or forearm) as you work the new board into place.

To avoid damage to circuit boards during installation, follow these simple guidelines:

- Leave the card inside its protective plastic cover until you are ready to install it.

- Prepare the computer by removing the case and any slot covers for the slots you will use.

- Position the card, inside its plastic cover, near the computer.

- Touch a grounded part of the computer. The power supply case is a good choice. Now, without removing your hand from the computer, open the plastic bag and remove the card you are about to install. If you have to, swap hands as you move the card into position, just be sure you keep touching the computer case. This is easier than it sounds. You can use your elbow, wrist, the back of your hand, and so on, to maintain contact with the computer as you handle the card.

- Insert the card carefully into the chosen slot and press it firmly into place. It is helpful to wiggle the card into position, pressing first one end, then the other until it is firmly seated. You'll quickly get the hang of it as you work with more cards. Just remember that the card itself is quite rugged. Except for static discharge, it isn't likely that you'll hurt a modern computer card during installation.

Installing any bus card is similar. And, thanks to the industry's adoption of the PCI bus standard and similarities among computer case designs, you shouldn't have problems adapting any hardware install procedure you learn for one platform to any other platform.

SOUND CARDS

Until recently, computer support for sound and other multimedia devices was rare. Today there's hardly a computer that doesn't include some pretty high-end audio support. Multimedia, sound output and even quality recording capabilities have become more important to a broader range of users. Businesses use sound as part of their documentation or training, as part of sales presentations, and even for music and motion video productions.

You'll find that support for a sound card is automatic with newer machines. The sound card comes pre-installed and the operating system includes integral support for sound input and output. However, there are drivers for individual pieces of sound hardware that must be installed as described in the earlier overview section. Also, if you format your hard drive (or replace it with a new one), you'll need to install the proper drivers for your sound hardware for everything to work properly.

Sound devices are of two general types: bus cards and hardware integral with the motherboard. Increasingly you will see sound cards built into the motherboard. This provides the easiest installation because the hardware is always there and all you might need to do is install or configure drivers. The downside to motherboard sound hardware, as with built-in disk controllers, video adapters, and other devices, is that it may be harder to update or change the hardware.

6

OTHER OUTPUT DEVICES

In today's computer marketplace there are so many output options that it would be impossible to cover them all here. Digital video, for example, is becoming a popular consumer and professional computer-based feature. Adapter cards that let you capture and output digital video to a camera or VCR are available, coupled with capable and low-cost video editing software to help you use it.

Enhanced sound output has also become reasonably priced. Instead of living with analog output, for a few dollars more you can output (and input) a digital audio stream to minidisk or DAT (Digital Audio Tape) recorders. Multi-port sound cards are available today that permit a computer to serve as a fully digital, multi-channel recorder for sound studio applications.

As you interact with a variety of computer systems and read specifications for products from a variety of industries, be aware of what hardware and software may be driving the features you are using or reading about. And, be aware that there's probably some specialty software required to make everything work as it should.

STANDARD INPUT DEVICES

There are two standard and universal computer input devices: the keyboard and the mouse. The keyboard is the single most important input device, and the second most important is the mouse (or one of the mouse alternatives such as a track ball, stylus, touch pad or pointing stick). As universal as the mouse is today, it is a relatively new addition to the average user's computer hardware. Macintosh computers have used the mouse from the beginning, of course, but it was several years later before Microsoft-based machines routinely were supplied with a mouse. Today you wouldn't consider computing without a mouse—even if your preference is UNIX; that is if you're in a networked environment where the X-Window graphical interface is pretty much the norm on these platforms. If you're using an older DOS machine, chances are there is no mouse support. However, some DOS applications software may offer a Windows-like user interface and install a mouse driver to support it.

MOUSE AND KEYBOARD DRIVERS

Because the input/output routines for the mouse and keyboard are highly standardized across operating systems, it is unlikely that you as an end user will need to interact with the operating system to set up these devices. Although mice and keyboards do use device drivers, unlike printers and other output devices, these drivers are standard and included as part of the operating system in most cases. The operating system provides only general support for output devices like printers (it includes routines to send data out a parallel port, for example, and to receive data sent to the computer from a device connected to this port, but has no intrinsic routines to support specific printer brands, models or capabilities). For keyboards and mice, however, most operating systems contain intrinsic routines to handle these devices.

The mouse and keyboard use ports—serial ports, basically—in a way similar to the way a printer uses a parallel port. Like a printer or other output device, the keyboard and mouse also need additional software to support specific functionality. However, the main difference between your mouse and keyboard and another device you may connect to your computer is their virtually universal standardization. You can plug in a keyboard supplied with your computer, use a cheap replacement from a discount store, or pay the difference for a high quality custom design, and in most cases you won't need any drivers beyond what is supplied with your operating system. For the most part, individual differences among keyboards are handled inside the keyboard itself. All the operating system cares about is the set of standard signals presented to the keyboard port when individual keys or key combinations are pressed. Different keyboards may include different hardware designs—switches or membranes for the keys, for example, and unique electronics for processing keystrokes. Some keyboards even include specialty keys that replace complex keystroke combinations or sequences. As long as these special keys send standard keystroke sequences to the keyboard port, the operating system doesn't really care how the codes are generated. These key closure codes or encoded sequences are captured at the port by intrinsic operating system routines and passed to higher-level operating system applets and to applications (word processing, spreadsheet, etc.) running under the operating system. No special drivers are required; the ones that install as part of your standard operating system will work just fine.

Newer operating systems include fairly sophisticated keyboard driver routines and custom configuration utilities, such as the one from Windows 98 shown in Figure 6-17.

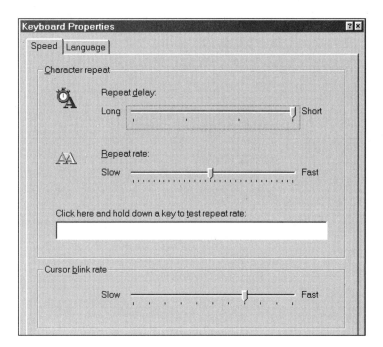

Figure 6-17   Windows 98 Control Panel keyboard configuration utility

As you can see from this illustration, the degree of user-specified configuration is minimal. This simply points out the standard nature of the keyboard itself and of the drivers that support it. Earlier operating systems—particularly non-Windows systems—may have even more limited keyboard configuration options. You plug it in and it either works or it doesn't.

A mouse consists of a ball that rotates as you move the mouse across a desk or mouse pad and one, two, or three buttons on top. As the ball rolls it moves two **potentiometers** (variable resistors) positioned at 90-degree angles to each other. As this movement changes these resistor values, the operating system records the direction of movement, the distance moved and even the speed of movement. The top-mounted buttons are connected inside the mouse housing to **micro-switches** that close when the buttons are pressed. Operating system drivers capture this switch closure and send the information to other operating system routines and to applications programs for interpretation.

As with the keyboard, the intrinsic operating system mouse drivers may offer minimal customization options to the user. Mouse options for Windows 98 are shown in Figure 6-18 on the next page.

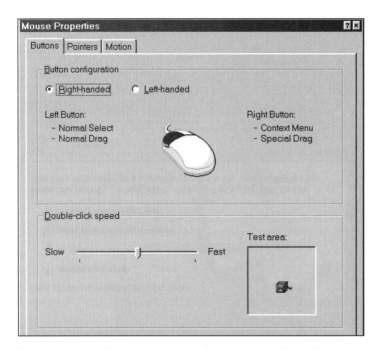

Figure 6-18   Windows 98 intrinsic mouse configuration

Configuration routines such as this let you set the double-click speed, perhaps calibrate mouse movement and direction (based on how you hold the mouse as you roll it around the desk), and perhaps some other basic features. Again, because of the basic nature of the mouse functionality and the standard interface used, you can't do all that much and you don't need to.

However, this does not mean you will never need custom drivers for a keyboard or mouse. Many companies build in special features that aren't supported by the standard drivers. Consider the relatively new **wheel mice** popularized by the Microsoft IntelliMouse design. In addition to the standard ball and buttons, the IntelliMouse (and other wheel mice designs from such companies as LogiTech) includes a wheel on top of the mouse that rotates front-to-back, parallel to the buttons. The wheel can be programmed for several application and operating system functions, but by default it replaces the vertical scroll bars used on many dialog boxes. In addition, a micro-switch mounted beneath the wheel is set by default to let you scroll horizontally by moving the mouse body itself after pressing the wheel downward to engage to switch. Other mice designs include trackballs and programmable keys.

You can use these enhanced mice designs without special drivers, but you will be limited to standard functions. If you want to use their extended features, you'll need special drivers supplied by the manufacturer. These drivers usually are installed separately from the operating system in much the same way as you would install any other application software (by inserting the manufacturer's disk and running a setup program from it). In addition to adding special features to the function of the mouse itself, such manufacturer's drivers also usually provide additional levels of user configuration, as you can see from the IntelliMouse configuration interface shown in Figure 6-19.

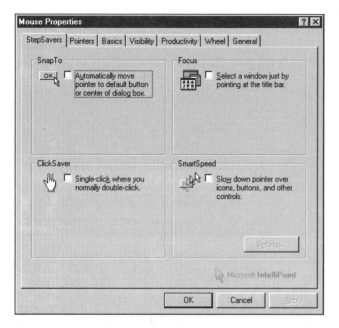

Figure 6-19   Microsoft IntelliMouse configuration dialog

One thing most PC users notice about the Macintosh right away is the single mouse button. The Mac mouse has one button whereas the PC mouse has at least two and in many cases three. In Windows you right-click a lot, which means you click with the right-most button on your mouse. That's something a Mac user has never done; the right button doesn't exist. Mac users use keyboard shortcuts for most of the same functions that the right-click serves in the PC world. Additionally, Apple has added contextual menus to Mac OS 8 that are strikingly similar to the PC's properties menus. If you want second-button functionality on a Mac you can add a third-party two-button mouse, or you can use a trackball or joystick with two or more buttons. Generally these extra buttons are programmable with software that ships with the hardware.

OTHER INPUT DEVICES

The keyboard and mouse are ubiquitous and standard. If your computing needs stop with fairly common business applications such as word processing, spreadsheets and databases, you probably won't need anything more. On the other hand, if you do graphics design, Web page development, digital photography, or movie or sound editing, then you will use one or more specialty input devices, such as digital tablets, scanners, joysticks and gamepads, digital sound input, or digital picture and video input. The following sections introduce these devices.

DIGITAL TABLETS

A **digital pad** or **tablet** is really a different kind of mouse. A mouse is an excellent input tool for fairly gross operations: choosing from a menu, selecting an icon or other graphic object, dragging text or graphics to a new screen location. However, when you need to draw pictures, sign your name, color a detailed graphic image, or conduct other tasks that require a high degree of manual dexterity, then a digital pad or tablet is a useful addition to your computer hardware.

A digital pad plugs into your computer via a standard or custom serial port or through the USB or ADB (Macintosh) ports. After you have installed custom drivers—usually supplied by the pad manufacturer—then you can use the pad to conduct usual mouse operations such as selecting menu items or moving objects. But in addition you can use the pad's electronic stylus for finer tasks such as object drawing, capturing signatures, or manipulating specialty graphics programs such as CorelDraw or Photoshop. If you've ever tried to use even a simple drawing program with a mouse as your only input device, you can appreciate the value of a digital pad that lets you write and draw in much the same way you would with a pen or pencil.

The digital pad, like the mouse, can range from fairly standard, simple hardware, to specialty devices that include LCD display panels that mirror your computer's video display. Even the simplest pads require some custom software and a unique installation process. Refer to the previous chapter for general information on installing drivers (operating system support software) for specialty devices such as the digital pad.

SCANNERS

A **scanner** is like a printer in reverse, or maybe like an office photocopier that "prints" to your computer instead of onto plain paper. Instead of accepting digital data from the computer and converting it to hard copy like a printer does, a scanner starts with hard copy—a photograph, negative or slide, newspaper article, book page, even a solid object—and creates a digital image of it, which is then transmitted to the computer. Once in the computer this digital image can be saved in a variety of graphics image formats, edited, merged with other images or text, transmitted over the Internet or other network connection, or, of course, printed.

Most scanners use some form of SCSI hardware interface, or, for newer designs, the USB port. Some scanners are supplied with their own SCSI card, but you don't have to use this interface. If you have any standard SCSI interface already installed in your computer, then chances are your scanner can use it. You will need drivers to enable the scanner to use any SCSI port. Interestingly enough, whereas the Mac OS has supported SCSI ports from the earliest days, Windows still doesn't support SCSI ports without custom drivers. One reason is the fact that different SCSI interface manufacturers implement the standard SCSI protocols in different ways, making it impossible for the operating system to support all versions. If you're using a USB scanner with Windows 98, installation and configuration should be automatic.

For the most part, you'll install custom drivers and in many cases custom interface software supplied by the scanner manufacturer when you install the hardware. In many cases the driver software—usually a driver with user interface and scanner control—links automatically with a variety of graphics software. If you're using PhotoShop, for example, the scanner may show up as an add in; if you're using a Microsoft product such as Publisher or Photo Editor, you'll see a scanner icon on your toolbar. When you click the icon the custom scanner software will load so you can use your scanner. These drivers and the user interface interact with the operating system to control the SCSI port (or whatever port your scanner uses) and capture data supplied by the scanner.

Windows and other operating systems generally ship with a number of SCSI drivers—in much the same way as they ship with printer drivers—and you can probably find an intrinsic driver that will enable input and output through your SCSI port. However, to get the best and most reliable performance from any SCSI interface you should install the drivers supplied by the manufacturer of the device itself. Again, you should check the vendor's online site to determine whether there are later versions of the required drivers for your hardware. This is true even if you just bought the hardware. Chances are the manufacturer has posted on their Web page the very latest driver versions, which you can download over the Internet and install on your computer.

JOYSTICKS AND GAME PADS

If your computer application is strictly business, you'll have no need for joysticks and game pads. If, on the other hand, some part of your computer experience includes an occasional game, then one of these alternative input devices could be part of your hardware collection.

A joystick is more like a mouse than a digital pad. Like a mouse, the joystick uses a mechanical device to rotate one or more potentiometers. Changing resistance tells the joystick driver what value to feed to the operating system and any associated applications software. You use the joystick for three-dimensional movement of an on-screen cursor or other object such as a car, airplane, or cartoon character. Just as the digital pad makes it easier to input handwriting, picture retouching and the like, the joystick offers a lot more control than a mouse when it comes to detailed movements of graphical screen objects. Although games are the primary application for joysticks, Mac users sometimes use them to supplement the mouse functionality. Joysticks can be used for virtually any application input task, given the proper driver.

In addition to the three-dimensional movements of the vertical joystick, this input device usually includes one or more push button switches that can be associated with gun firings, boxing swings, menu selection, and so on. Like the digital pad, the joystick can use a conventional serial port, including the Mac's ADB or the PC's USB. Potentiometer settings or switch closures are sent through the I/O port as positive/negative pulses or as variable values on a scale. The operating system's basic port I/O routines grab this basic data, then it is up to the associated application—a game, for example—to interpret this data in a meaningful way.

Game pads come in a wide variety of designs. As the name suggests they are primarily designed for interaction with games and include multiple buttons, wheels or balls to effect movement of a variety of onscreen objects. As with the joystick, the game pad sends standard signals to a serial port where the operating system I/O routines grab the data and pass it off to an application program or custom driver for interpretation.

DIGITAL SOUND INPUT

Almost every Mac, PC, and even workstation computer is supplied with some kind of analog sound card for sound input and output. For most of us this sound capability is used pretty frivolously: software startup sounds, beeps when email arrives, playing music CDs. There are more serious applications for sound hardware, however. You can connect a microphone to an input port on your sound card and record voice mail that you can include with electronic mail, for example, or for narration of slide presentations. You can record custom sounds or music for use within software applications from a CD player or tape deck. Voice input to word processing and other programs is important for those unable to use a keyboard or mouse.

For more professional applications, such as editing music or voice for electronic journalism or training applications, you may want to add a digital I/O card. This lets you capture digital sound from a DAT recorder or digital camera directly into the computer without having to convert to analog in the process. A digital card lets you copy digital audio directly from a recorder to your hard drive in much the same way as you would copy digital information from one hard drive to another. There is no loss of quality, you can edit the sound files in native digital format, then copy the finished files back to tape or burn them onto a CD for distribution or presentation.

There are multiple professional audio I/O standards, both optical and copper. Which one you use depends on the external hardware you will be interfacing with your computer. Some DAT machines and digital cameras include more than one digital I/O port, so you can choose which format to use based on personal preference, your need to interface with other users, or which interface you can find. Most cards require custom driver software. And, like scanners, these cards usually can be controlled and accessed from inside application software such as digital audio or video editing packages. Once the driver is installed, you can transfer audio information through the digital sound card from inside the application you are using to manipulate the audio files.

Most digital audio interfaces plug into the computer's internal bus—PCI most commonly—but there also are some devices that use a USB port. If you need to transfer audio into multiple computers, the USB interface is a good choice, since USB is self-configuring for the most part and most USB devices are external to the computer. By installing the required drivers on a second machine, you can easily add digital audio I/O capabilities.

DIGITAL PICTURE AND VIDEO INPUT

Digital picture and video I/O works similarly to digital audio I/O. You'll need a digital I/O interface and drivers to allow your operating system to recognize and use the card. And, as with digital audio, you will import digital images into whatever application software you are using for picture or video editing. In some cases you will use a utility supplied by the interface manufacturer to import the digital image, then launch another application—such as Adobe Premier or PhotoShop, for example—to conduct the actual editing. On the other hand, some card manufacturers include the ability to link their hardware drivers directly into editing software so you can import and export digital files from an external camera and edit the video or still images, all from the same application.

COMPUTER STORAGE OPTIONS

Another kind of computer input/output device is disk storage. Storage devices are somewhat different from the other devices discussed so far in this chapter, but they also are an integral part of a functioning computer system and its associated operating system. This section briefly discusses various storage technologies and relates their function to general operating system theory.

Today most computer systems are supplied with a single 3.5-inch floppy drive, perhaps a high-density floppy or Zip disk, one or more internal, fixed hard drives, and a CD-ROM or DVD drive. These storage devices are mounted in the computer case and connect to the computer hardware through an electronic interface and a cable system.

Floppy and hard disk drives include internal electronics and an external interface to connect the drive to the computer. In modern computers, the floppy drives and the hard drives may plug into the same bus interface card, which includes separate connectors and separate controllers that share some common components. The operating system acts as an interface between this controller and the rest of the computer, and application software that needs to read from and write to the drive. There are many controller designs, but when they comply with the standards required by the operating system, what goes on inside the hard drive itself, or even in the hard drive controller that connects to the computer, is not significant in terms of the user or the operating system.

The most popular hard drive interface in the Intel PC architecture is the **Integrated Drive Electronics (IDE)** interface. This interface is often built into the main board of the computer, or is otherwise present in the form of an interface card. A single IDE interface can support two devices, one so-called **master** (the first or main drive) and one **slave** (secondary storage device). In general, devices have to be set up to be a master, which is the only device on a cable. The cable usually has three 40-pin header connectors. One connector plugs in to the IDE card or to the appropriate connector on the main board. The other two can be used to connect to the IDE devices.

IDE has many subtypes, which control the speed of data transfers between the devices and the computer. An advantage of IDE is that the controller and the devices are able to determine which of the various substandards they support, and as a rule of thumb, you as the user do not have to worry about the details. The newest IDE standard, **Extended IDE (EIDE)** Mode 3.0 will support transfer speeds as high as 33 megabits per second! And, today's computer systems generally include dual IDE controllers, usually built into the system motherboard. The primary controller interfaces the boot drive to the system. The secondary controller may be used for a CD-ROM drive, a second hard disk, and so on.

The last type of drive, which can be used in all PC platforms mentioned in this book, is the type that uses the **Small Computer System Interface (SCSI)**. SCSI is one of the more confusing standards, partially because there are so many different SCSI designs, each with its own set of cables and rules. You are most likely to encounter SCSI-1, SCSI-2 and Fast SCSI-2, which all use 50 pins in the cable. Each of them can address up to 8 devices per SCSI controller. One of these devices is the controller, usually device 7. This leaves device numbers 1 through 6 open for disks.

The disks are connected to each other and to the controller by a single cable. This cable, when it is run inside a computer, is a ribbon cable with 50 wires and header connectors. SCSI cables can have as little as one, or as many as eight of these connectors. There is a limitation in the length of the overall cable, it should not exceed 18 feet. Each end of the cable has to be electrically terminated to prevent echoes and ghost signals on the cable. Termination is done with terminator resistors. Since one end of the cable usually is terminated in the SCSI controller, you will find that in most cases one of the terminators is built in to the card. Either a disk drive or an external terminator typically terminates the other end of the chain. In the case of a drive, sometimes you will simply set a jumper on the drive to turn termination on or off. In other cases you will actually plug **terminator resistor packs**, or **TRPs**, into the drive to set up termination. If SCSI drives are external to the computer, something you will find quite often, an external SCSI connection is used. This connection can take many forms.

SCSI-1 normally uses either a DB-25 connector (often used in the Apple Macintosh architecture, but now also popular in many Intel PC architecture designs), or a 50-pin Amphenol or Centronics connector, the format that is more standard.

The DB-25 connector needs to be treated with care. On the Intel PC it looks identical to the connector used for the printer port. Plugging the printer into a SCSI port or vice versa may lead to serious hardware damage.

SCSI-2 and Fast SCSI-2 are typically brought out on either a DB-25 or a Mini DBC-50 connector. The Mini DBC-50 is the most popular connector format. It snaps in place and can easily be removed. The pins in this connector are spaced very closely, and connectors can be damaged easily by inserting them with too much force. Terminators for SCSI-1 and SCSI-2 come in a few variations. For SCSI-1 and SCSI-2, you should use passive terminators. These terminators consist of simple resistors, and in many cases they will work fine. For Fast SCSI-2, which uses a higher clock speed and is therefore faster than SCSI-2, the requirements put on the terminator are stricter. As a result, Active Terminators are often used for Fast SCSI-2 installations. These terminators contain electronics that can actively change the characteristics of the terminator, resulting in cleaner signals on the line.

The two most common problems you will see in SCSI installations are related to the terminators and the total cable length. SCSI-1 is an 8-bit wide bus; SCSI-2 is 16 bits wide. SCSI-1 runs at a speed of 10 MHz, as does SCSI-2. Fast SCSI-2 runs at a speed of 20 MHz. The newest, and currently very popular Fast Wide SCSI-3 format is different in a few ways. It has a 32-bit data path, it supports 15 devices per cable, and runs at a speed of 20 MHz. The drives used for Wide SCSI are more expensive; the cables are slightly different. Internal cables are 68-pin Micro Header connectors, external cables are Mini-D 68-pin connectors. All terminators in this scheme are Active. The most frequent problems with this type of SCSI are cable length, which may not exceed 15 feet, followed by termination problems. Interface speed of the various SCSI drives varies widely; SCSI-1 will typically be able to transfer about 1 MB per second, SCSI-2 will transfer about 2 MB per second, Fast SCSI-2 will transfer as much as 4 MB per second, and Fast Wide SCSI-3 will transfer as much as 8 MB per second.

The number of platters, heads, tracks and sectors per track varies widely from hard disk to hard disk. For the computer and operating system to interact successfully with the disk, in most cases the user needs to configure the computer and the operating system with details about the disk. This information is often stored in an area of non-volatile memory in the computer. In addition, many operating systems keep a table somewhere on the disk that describes the disk in great detail. IDE and SCSI provide ways for the controllers to communicate with the electronics on the disk, which enables the controllers to figure out this information. However, this exchange of information does not always work correctly, and it is a good idea to have the information about a disk on hand. This data is known as the **disk geometry**. Many operating systems impose limitations on the geometry they will support; most will not support disks with more than 1023 tracks, 255 heads or 63 sectors per track. (In Chapter 3 on file systems you learned how operating systems, in cooperation with the hardware, get around these restrictions.)

Storage capacity of a single hard disk can be anywhere from a few megabytes to several gigabytes. Hard disks are fast and allow the user to store large amounts of data and programs. In many machines, they are used to store the operating system, the application software and all the data.

Because of the delicate mechanisms inside the disk, it is not uncommon for a hard disk to fail. When a floppy disk fails, only a small amount of data is lost. Because floppies fail often, users do not usually rely on floppies as their only data storage. Hard disks seem much more stable, and many users do not make copies of data stored on hard disks. As a result, hard disk failures are often catastrophic for a user. Backing up data on hard disks is an essential practice.

RAID ARRAYS

Although hard disks can store large amounts of data, are relatively fast and fairly reliable, there is room for improvement on all three points. To address some of these issues, a group of researchers at the University of California in Berkeley introduced the concept of a **Redundant Array of Inexpensive Drives (RAID)**. They defined various levels of RAID technology; a brief discussion follows. (A more detailed discussion of RAID levels is found in Chapter 10.)

RAID arrays are used to serve three purposes: increased reliability, increased storage capacity, and increased speed. Different levels of RAID focus on different purposes, and there is no RAID level that can be declared superior for all situations. Because RAID array implementation tends to be costly, they are used primarily on network servers, with network operating systems (NOSs).

RAID is implemented as a combination of hardware and software. The hardware can consist of simply a few hard disks connected to one controller, or something as complicated as a very large set of hard disks connected to a number of disk controllers equipped with processors to assist in running RAID software. The RAID software is typically a low-level device driver that works with any RAID hardware and provides an interface to the operating system to provide access to the special RAID features offered. Some systems are presented to the operating system as if they were a simple drive; the RAID hardware interacts with the OS as if it were a hard disk.

CD-ROM AND DVD

This section compares the **compact disc read-only memory (CD-ROM)** to its newer sibling, the **digital versatile disc (DVD)**.

Compact Disc (CD) Technology

CDs are very important in today's operating system environment, because most software and documentation is distributed on these media. These disks are different from floppies and hard disks for many reasons, including the way data is stored. Instead of using a system of tracks and sectors like floppy and hard disks, CDs use a big "spiral" that starts at the inside of the disc and winds itself slowly toward the outside of the disc. Whenever data is needed from the disc, a laser pickup is pointed at a part of the disc surface.

The disc itself is rotated by a precision motor that keeps the disc speed exact. The optical pickup is typically moved by yet another motor under computer control. Extreme precision is required when moving the pickup, and there is a wide variety of mechanisms that connect to stepper motors and to the pickup. Most modern drives use a direct drive mechanism, where the motor moves a little rod that pulls the head to the correct position. Optical encoders are often used to make sure the head is positioned correctly. Older drives use worm wheel drives, and these drives tend to develop mechanical problems after intense use.

When a disk is read, laser light is emitted by the CD-ROM head and reflected off the disc surface onto an optical pickup. The surface of the disc is covered with little indents, which shift the position of the reflected laser light as it is returned to the pickup. Depending on the size of the dents, ones or zeroes are returned. You are probably familiar with the CD disc itself, a silver disc about four inches in diameter. The surface of the CD reflects light during a data read operation. Although CD discs are extremely reliable, the large number of dents make this surface very sensitive to scratches and other kinds of damage that could hinder optical readout.

Because it is almost inevitable that the CD surface will become damaged through frequent use, the CD-ROM drive and disc are equipped with extensive mechanisms to protect the user from critical data errors. The data on the CD has CRC bits encoded in it as other disks do, and it also has error correction bits encoded on the disk. As long as there is not too much damage to the disc surface, the reading mechanism will recover from reading errors. Parity bits, which are interlaced in the data stream, are used to reconstruct any missing or damaged data before it is passed to the operating system. Although the CD is one of the more delicate media, its built-in error detection and correction make it one of the most reliable.

The storage capacity of a CD-ROM is fairly high. About 650 MB of data can be stored per disk. CDs are single-sided disks. The typical transfer speed of a single-speed CD-ROM drive is roughly 150 KB per second, with an average seek time of about 150 milliseconds. CDs were originally invented for use as an audio storage mechanism to replace the old LP, and the single-speed nomenclature originates from this use. A single-speed CD-ROM player will spin the disc and read the data at the same speed as an audio CD player.

For many purposes, that speed is quite acceptable, but as always, faster is better. Not long after introduction of the single speed CD-ROM came faster models. The main difference between the single-speed and multispeed CD-ROM drives is the speed at which they can spin the CD, and the speed with which they move the optical pickup heads from one place on the spiral to another. Rotational speeds can range from as little as twice the normal audio speed, or 2X, to as high as 36 times that speed (36X).

High speed CD-ROM drives can reach data transfer rates of several megabytes per second, some as much as about 6 MB. The seek times vary widely. Many are in the 50 to 70 ms range; some of the fast ones are in the 20 to 30 ms range. This kind of performance is very close to what you would expect from some hard disks, but in most practical situations CD-ROM drives appear to be a lot slower.

Digital Versatile Disc (DVD) Technology

The digital versatile disc, or DVD, works a lot like the CD-ROM. It is also a totally optical drive, and has the data written on the disc in the form of a spiral of blocks. All data is read from the disk with the use of a laser and an optical pickup. The storage capacity and data transfer rate of the DVD are much higher, but the size of the disc is the same. Almost all DVD drives can read CD as well as DVD discs. This is important because there is minimal DVD software—movies, high-density data, software distribution—available. A computer equipped with a DVD drive must be able to read CDs for versatility. There is a physical similarity between the DVD and CD-ROM discs and drives.

The DVD disc can have two sides with up to two layers per side. The concept of layers is relatively new. All data on a hard disk, floppy disk, or CD is stored on one layer of material. On the CD, when laser light hits the layer, it is reflected. On a DVD, the same thing happens, but in addition to the first layer, which is a spiral that moves from the middle of the disc to the outside like a conventional CD, the DVD disk has a second layer. This layer is read by using light that hits the disk at a different angle. The second layer is also a spiral, this one written from the outside of the disk to the inside. At this writing, each side of a DVD disk may contain up to two layers, and each layer can hold about 5.4 GB of data. The result: on each DVD, you can store roughly 22 GB of data. Although many applications have absolutely no use for this kind of storage at this time, the trend toward more graphics and multimedia as part of operating systems and application programs is certain to make DVD a very popular format in the near future.

DVD drives are typically multispeed drives. The 1.0X (single speed) benchmark for a DVD drive is the speed at which most DVD drives used for video applications retrieve video data.

Typical computer DVD drives are in the 2.0X to 4.0X range, with faster drives to come in the future. When these drives read CD-ROM discs, they do so at about 24X speed. DVD has even better bit error correction than the CD format, but, like a CD-ROM, is very sensitive to damage to the disc surface.

As with most CD-ROMs, DVD discs are read-only. The data transfer rate of DVD is anywhere from about 1.3 MB per second to about 5 MB per second. The average seek time is anywhere from 5 milliseconds to about 30 milliseconds. The switching sides or layers tends to take a little longer, sometimes as much as about two-tenths of a second. For most applications, this performance is very acceptable. DVD is fairly new, and as mentioned, not much software is currently available.

Look for much more DVD software in all forms in the near future. DVD is fast enough to run applications directly from the DVD disc as you would from a hard disk. This could change the way application software is used and could increase significantly the number of applications at your disposal at any given time.

CD and DVD Interfaces

CD and DVD discs are typically connected to the computer using a hard disk interface. Many PCs use the IDE interface with SCSI as a close second. Because these discs have a distinctively different organization than hard disks, and because they cannot be written to, typically an operating system will require a special driver to read from them. The latest generations of PCs have drivers for CD-ROM drives built into the ROM BIOS, which allows them to use CD-ROM drives without special drivers. This enables them to boot an operating system directly from a CD-ROM. MacOS, Windows NT 4.0, and many flavors of UNIX can boot an operating system directly from the CD-ROM for initial installation. This is not generally true for DVD drives at the present time, but look for that to change as DVD hardware becomes more widely distributed.

CONNECTING DRIVES

All of the drives discussed in this chapter connect to the computer in much the same way as hard disks do, typically through an IDE or SCSI interface. The drivers needed for many of these drives are often quite specialized. It is very important to make sure you have the drivers required for the operating system with which you want the drives in question to function. Do not assume that any drive can be used with any operating system. When it comes to specialty drives like the ones discussed in this chapter, always make sure they are supported for your operating system.

REMOVABLE DISKS

Removable disks in most cases are hard disks with a twist. These also come in many shapes, sizes, and formats, and we will briefly take a look at some of the more popular drives and disks available today. The first group of drives are those that use flexible magnetic disks, in particular the low capacity **SuperDisk (LS-120)** and **Zip disks**, and the high capacity

Jaz drive. The second group consists of drives that use hard platters, much like a hard disk. Bernoulli and SyQuest are examples of these technologies.

Removable Large-Capacity Floppy Drives

The SuperDisk, also known as the LS-120 floppy disk, uses a drive much like a 3½" floppy. As a matter of fact, the drive is able to read from and write to 3½" HD floppies. The SuperDisk looks a lot like a 3½" floppy, however the shutter mechanism is slightly different. The storage capacity of a SuperDisk is 120 MB. There are several types of SuperDisk drives: some connect to the computer's printer port, others replace an internal floppy drive, and others connect to the IDE or SCSI interface of the machine. This format is fairly new at the time this book is written, but it seems to be taking the market by storm. Software drivers for this format are currently available for the various versions of Microsoft Windows and for Mac OS. UNIX drivers are expected shortly.

The higher storage capacity (higher than floppy capacity, that is) on the SuperDisk is achieved by using a higher density magnetic storage medium. The speed when using floppies is similar to that of a 3½" disk drive. The medium is relatively cheap, so this seems to be a good alternative for exchanging moderate amounts of data. Note that there is physical contact between the heads and the disk, which make this disk sensitive to wear, much like floppies.

A competitor to the LS-120 floppy is the Zip disk, designed by Iomega. The Zip drive is addressed by the system like a hard disk, and offers a storage capacity of 100 or 200 MB. Zip drives are available in both external and internal varieties with printer port, SCSI, or IDE connections. The newest generation of external Zip drives has a port that will connect to either a printer port or a SCSI port. It automatically adapts to the port to which it is connected. The Zip disk was initially plagued by mechanical problems, but newer models seem to be quite reliable. The disk consists of a cartridge that contains a magnetic disk. The medium is much like that of a floppy, and the size is similar to that of a 3½" floppy. Unlike the LS-120, the Zip drive cannot read or write 3½" floppy disks. The Zip drive was the first affordable, compact, medium storage capacity removable disk to hit the market, and is a quite popular option. When connected to a native disk interface such as SCSI or IDE, most operating systems do not need to have any special drivers to use a Zip drive. It is generally recognized as yet another hard disk connected to the system. There are, however, special drivers for the Zip drive, which will enable some additional functions. As is generally the case with removable drives, some of the features the special drivers offer are related to change notification. This means that the operating system is notified when the disk is inserted or removed. Operating systems such as DOS and Windows 3.1 generally do not care about disk changes, but more advanced operating systems will typically store some information about the disk in memory. It may be as little as the table of contents, or as much as some of the data stored on the disk.

If the operating system is not told when a disk is swapped, the results can be rather disastrous. For example, the operating system could blindly write data to an area on a disk that it assumes to be empty, but if a disk has been swapped without the operating system being notified, some of the data may be damaged beyond repair.

 It is possible to use Zip drives with many operating systems without any special drivers, but *not recommended*, particularly with operating systems that cache part of the disk such as Mac OS, UNIX, Windows 95, Windows 98, and Windows NT.

Zip drives are available for many platforms. Some commercial machines, even some laptops, now have a built-in Zip drive. The media is slightly more expensive than that used in the LS-120 drive, but the market penetration at the time this book was written is much greater.

You can connect Zip and LS-120 drives to a computer's printer port, which is a great feature. In many cases, a Zip disk can hold enough information to install an entire operating system from one disk. This is convenient for fixing problems on computers that do not have a CD-ROM drive. In addition, disks that connect to the printer port can be easily connected and disconnected, and used on more than one computer.

The price you pay for this convenience is speed. When connected to the printer port, the speed at which the disk can be accessed is greatly reduced. Throughput may go down to as little as 140 KB per second. In addition, much of the CPU time may be used in making the drive work.

An alternative with much higher capacity is the Jaz drive, also made by Iomega. Jaz drives come in internal or external models, which are connected to the computer using either a SCSI or EIDE interface. The cartridge is slightly bigger than the Zip cartridge, but works much the same. Inside you will find a flexible plastic disk covered with a magnetic layer on which the data is stored. This disk also stores data much like a floppy disk. The heads are in continuous contact with the disk as data is being read or written. There are two versions of the Jaz drive, a 1 GB and a 2 GB model. These drives will be recognized by any operating system as a hard disk, but as with Zip disks, there are special drivers for many operating systems that enable them to work correctly when disks are swapped.

Removable Rigid Cartridges

The second class of removable disks have a disk made out of a solid material inside the cartridge, much like the platters found in a hard disk The heads in these systems, much like the heads in a hard disk, are not in contact with the disk surface. Instead, they float above the surface at a very close distance. This has some advantages and some disadvantages. A very big advantage is that there is no mechanical contact between the heads and the disk, which means that both the heads and the disk will last a lot longer. They suffer no wear and tear from the read/write head. A big disadvantage is that it is not easy to make a head float very close to a platter in a system where the platter is in a removable cartridge.

Bernoulli drives are semi-rigid removable cartridge hard drives based on the Bernoulli aero-dynamic principle. They can be used on desktop or laptop computers and provide relatively high speed, high capacity storage. **SyQuest** makes a series of removable drives that are used with many operating systems. The drives work similar to the Bernoulli drives in that they use a hard platter, much like the one in a hard disk, which is housed inside a hard plastic cartridge. The platter is also spun at high speed, and has heads floating above it to read and write data. However, the principle of an air cushion and positive air pressure is not used. The distance between the disk and the heads is slightly greater. A different technique is used in the heads that makes it possible for them to be a little further away from the disk surface. The SyQuest Sparq drive is among the newest SyQuest removable hard disk designs, and used in many offices that require high density, removable storage. Unfortunately, the Sparq model has been discontinued. However, this design should be around for some time, due to the relatively good penetration of the device in the user marketplace.

6

CHAPTER SUMMARY

This chapter provides a conceptual overview of how operating systems interface with input, output, and storage devices, and how such devices usually require both hardware and software setup. It is impossible to provide detail about every input, output, and storage device, since each one is different and, moreover, works differently with different operating systems. You've learned the general steps to install required driver software, and special considerations of specific operating systems as they relate to some devices. This chapter covered various printer technologies, and discussed other output devices such as sound cards and display adapters.

Basic keyboard and mouse technologies are available to users of all operating systems, and there are general considerations that are important when installing and using a variety of input devices, including digital pads (tablets), digital cameras, and digital scanners.

Popular computer storage technologies include hard disk drives, CD-ROMs and DVD drives. You saw how these storage devices interface to the computer hardware and learned basic operating system considerations in using them.

KEY TERMS

- **Apple Desktop Bus (ADB)** — A serial bus common on the Apple Macintosh computer. ADB is used to connect the Macintosh keyboard, mouse, and other external I/O devices.

- **Bernoulli** — A semi-rigid hard drive based on the Bernoulli principle. These high-capacity, removable cartridge drives provide reasonably high-speed, high-density add-on storage for desktop and laptop computers in data-intensive applications such as graphics.

- **Centronics interface** — An industry standard printer interface popularized by printer manufacturer Centronics. The interface definition includes 36 wires that connect the printer with the computer I/O port, though all of these pins aren't always used, particularly in modern desktop machines.

- **compact disc read-only memory (CD-ROM)** — A non-volatile, digital data storage medium used for operating system and other software distribution.

- **Control Panel** — In Windows operating systems, an application window that contains utilities for system configuration, such as the modem settings, mouse, printers and so on.

- **Cyclic Redundancy Check (CRC)** — An error correction protocol that determines the validity of data written to and read from a floppy or hard disk.

- **DB-25** — A 25-pin D-shaped connector commonly used on desktop computers, terminals, modems, and other devices.

- **digital pad** or **digital tablet** — An alternative input device frequently used by graphic artists and others who need accurate control over drawing and other data input.

- **digital versatile disc (DVD)** — A high-capacity CD-ROM-like hardware device used for high quality audio, motion video and computer data storage.

- **DIN8M** — An 8-pin connector common on Macintosh computers for printer connections.

- **disk geometry** — Critical information about a hard drive's hardware configuration. This information is often stored in an area of non-volatile memory in the computer.

- **dot-matrix printer** — A character printer that produces characters by arranging a matrix of dots. Dot matrix printers can be impact, ink jet or other technologies.

- **dye sublimation** — A printer technology that produces high quality, color output by creating "sublimated" color mists that penetrate paper to form characters or graphic output.

- **extended IDE (EIDE)** — A more modern, faster version of IDE.

- **Imagesetter** — A high end printer frequently used for publishing. Capable of producing film output.

- **ink-jet printer** — A character printer that forms characters by spraying droplets of ink from a nozzle print head onto the paper.

- **Integrated Drive Electronics (IDE)** — A storage protocol popular in today's desktop computer systems. IDE is significant because it simplifies the hardware required inside the computer, placing more of the disk intelligence at the hard drive itself.

- **Jaz** — An Iomega company removable hard disk design capable of storing 1 or 2 GB of data, depending on the model.

- **laser printers** — A high quality page printer design popular in office and other professional applications.

- **line printer** — A printer design that prints a full line of character output at a time. Used for high speed output requirements.

- **LPT1** — The primary printer port designation on many desktop computers. Also designated Line Printer 1.

- **master** — In an IDE drive chain, the main, or first drive. Most IDE interfaces can support two drives. One is the master (Drive 0) and the second drive is the slave. See *slave*.

- **micro-switch** — A small electronic switch used in a computer mouse, gamepad, or joystick to connect and disconnect electronic circuits. These openings and closings can be monitored by driver software to enable certain software features or functions.

- **parallel port** — A computer input/output port used primarily for printer connections. A parallel port transmits data 8 bits or more at a time, using at least 8 parallel wires. A parallel port potentially can transmit data faster than a serial port.

- **pixel** — Short for picture element. The small dots that make up a computer screen display.

- **PKZIP** — A utility program that archives files and compresses them so they require less disk storage and can be transmitted over a network faster.

- **plotter** — Computer hardware that produces high-quality printed output, often in color, by moving ink pens over the surface of paper. Plotters are often used with computer-aided design (CAD) and other graphics applications.

- **potentiometer** — A hardware device used to vary the amount of resistance in an electronic circuit. In computer I/O hardware this variable resistance can be used to monitor mouse movement, joy stick positioning, and so on.

- **print queue (print spooler)** — A section of computer memory and hard disk storage set aside to hold information sent by an application to a printer attached to the local computer or to another computer or print server on a network. Operating system or printer drivers and control software manage the information sent to the queue, responding to printer start/stop commands.

- **Redundant Array of Inexpensive Drives (RAID)** — A relatively inexpensive, redundant storage design that uses multiple disks and logic to reduce the chance of information being lost in the event of hardware failure. RAID uses various designs, termed Level 0 through Level 5.

6

- **removable disks** — A class of relatively high capacity storage devices that use removable cartridges. These devices are used for data backup, for long-term offline storage, and for data portability among multiple computer systems.

- **self-extracting file** — A compressed or archive file that includes an executable component, like an application program, that enables the file to separate into individual files and uncompress the files automatically. A self-extracting file does not require an external program to expand the file into its individual components.

- **serial port** — A computer input/output port used for modem, printer, and other connections. A serial port transmits data one bit after another in serial fashion, as compared to a parallel port, which transmits data 8 bits or more at a time.

- **slave** — In an IDE drive chain, the secondary storage device. See *master*.

- **Small Computer System Interface (SCSI)** — A computer input/output bus standard and the hardware that uses this standard. There are many types of SCSI in use today, providing data transfer rates from 10 Mbps to 40 Mbps.

- **StuffIt** — A Macintosh archive and compression utility.

- **SuperDisk (LS-120)** — An increasingly popular high capacity floppy disk design. SuperDisk / LS-120 drives can store as much as 120 MB of data on a single disk, but these drives also can read conventional 3½" floppy disks.

- **SyQuest** — The manufacturer of one of the earliest removable hard disk devices popular in Macintosh and PC systems. SyQuest drives use hard disk technology. Early drives stored only 40 MB, but later designs can hold upwards of 200 MB.

- **tar** — A UNIX file archive utility.

- **terminator resistor packs (TRPs)** — Sets of resistors used on a hard drive or other storage device. These resistors reduce the possibility of data echoes on the interface bus as information travels between the computer's controller and the storage device.

- **thermal-wax transfer** — A printer technology that creates high quality color printed output by melting colored wax elements and transferring them to the printed page.

- **Universal Serial Bus (USB)** — A relatively high-speed I/O port found on most modern computers. It is used to interface digital sound cards, disk drives, and other external computer hardware.

- **wheel mouse** — A new mouse design, popularized by Microsoft's IntelliMouse, that includes a top-mounted wheel in addition to the standard mouse buttons. The wheel is programmable for a variety of operating system and application functions. A switch integral to the wheel provides additional opportunity for programmable, custom functions.

- **WINZIP** — An archive and compression utility for Windows 95 and 98.

- **Zip disk** — A removable high capacity floppy disk design from the Iomega company. Zip disks store a nominal 100 MB of data.

REVIEW QUESTIONS

1. Printed (hard copy) output is frequently much easier to read accurately than the same information on a computer screen. True or False?

2. The two basic early printer technologies were line printers and _____ printers. Of the two, _____ printer technology is the most common today.

3. The main printer port on Windows computer systems is frequently designated

   a. Character Port

   b. LPT1

   c. Printer Port 1

   d. Main Printer Port

4. A printer that produces characters by slamming a group of wires from a rectangular grid onto a ribbon and then to paper is called a(n) _____ design.

5. Describe how an impact dot matrix printer with a low-resolution print head design can produce high quality output. Why does high quality output slow down the printer considerably?

6. Describe how ink-jet designs differ from impact designs.

7. High quality impact printers typically provide better output for color photographic and graphics needs than an ink-jet printer. True or False?

8. One type of popular computer printer could be described as a computerized copier. What printer technology is this? Is this analogy appropriate? Why or why not?

9. The Imagesetter printer is most often used for

   a. low-resolution proofs.

   b. high-resolution final output for publishing applications.

   c. computer animation.

   d. None of the above.

10. Most early computer printers used a(n) _____ port, although today this port is more commonly used as a two-way modem port or as an input port for a mouse.

11. A Centronics port can best be described as

   a. a serial port sometimes used to connect a printer to a computer.

   b. a high speed digital port frequently used for digital cameras.

   c. a parallel port that has become the standard printer interface for IBM-compatible PCs.

   d. an older printer interface that is rarely used today.

12. The traditional Centronics interface uses a 36-pin connector. A more common type of connector for this interface is _____.

13. Two or three users can access a single printer by using a switch box that changes which computer is attached to the printer. When multiple users need access to the same printer, however, a better solution is a printer that includes

  a. a network interface and support software.

  b. multiple parallel interfaces.

  c. multiple serial interfaces.

  d. more than two or three users can't use the same printer.

14. The basic display resolution in most desktop computers is 640 × 480 pixels. However most current machines can be set to maximum resolutions of

  a. 12,000 × 15,000

  b. 800 × 600

  c. 1,280 × 1,024

  d. 12,800 × 10,240

15. Although computer screens can display 640 × 480 pixels or more, the actual bit depth—the number of pixels per inch—is only _____ dots.

16. A bus that is common to PC, Macintosh, and UNIX computers and that is most often used as the interface for modern display adapters is

  a. PSI

  b. PCI

  c. IDE

  d. None of the above

17. Describe why it is important to leave a new expansion card inside its shipping container until you are ready to install it into the computer. What additional precautions should you take in handling adapter cards during the installation process?

18. Even if your hardware is brand new, the driver software shipped with it may not be the latest and greatest. What is a good source of the most recent software drivers for a manufacturer's hardware?

19. What do the software utilities PKZIP, StuffIt, and *tar* have in common? For which operating system is each designed?

20. Most operating systems include driver software for popular hardware including printers and display adapters. Should you always use these drivers to ensure maximum compatibility with the operating system? Why or why not?

21. Describe the basic differences between the digital pad or tablet and a standard mouse. Under what circumstances would you most commonly use each of these input devices?

22. Most operating systems support specialty input devices such as digital pads and scanners without requiring special drivers. True or False?

23. Which of the following devices include output capabilities as well as input capabilities (select all that apply)

    a. Scanner

    b. Mouse

    c. Keyboard

    d. Digital sound interface

    e. Digital video interface

    f. Digital tablet or pad

24. Some of the newer computer mice include a top-mounted wheel. What purpose does this wheel serve?

25. The most common hardware interface for a digital scanner is

    a. USB

    b. IDE

    c. RS-232

    d. SCSI

26. For what applications might you expect to use a joystick for data input (choose all that apply)

    a. Playing games

    b. Manipulating graphics objects

    c. Text documents

    d. Database applications

27. A controller is a piece of hardware that

    a. controls how fast the CPU functions to manipulate application requests.

    b. controls the operation of the computer monitor.

    c. provides for a data interface path and hardware control for a floppy or hard drive.

    d. None of the above.

28. Hard disks are very different from floppy disks in the way they read and write data. The hard disk read/write heads don't _____.

29. The most popular hard disk interface for most desktop computers today is

    a. SCSI—small computer system interface

    b. IDE—integrated drive electronics

    c. HSDI—high speed disk interface

    d. EDIE—extended drive interface electronics

30. Of these interface standards, _____ is the fastest and most commonly used in specialty applications such as graphics design or sound and movie editing.

6

31. RAID is a technology for

    a. eliminating programming bugs during application development.

    b. using multiple hard drives in various configurations to provide data security through redundancy and error checking.

    c. storing data in a Redundant Access Integrated Drive arrangement.

    d. communicating configuration information between the computer and a remote user interface.

32. Describe the major design differences between DVD and CD-ROM that enable the much larger storage capacities of DVD.

HANDS-ON PROJECTS

PROJECT 6-1

If you have experience only in the Windows or Mac OS environment, then installing drivers and configuring your system from the DOS prompt may seem a little strange. However, the process isn't difficult. Most DOS applications will automatically modify your CONFIG.SYS and AUTOEXEC.BAT files as necessary to install drivers or other support programs they need. And, it is quite easy for you to modify these configuration files yourself.

To view the contents of the CONFIG.SYS and AUTOEXEC.BAT files, and to modify them:

1. At the DOS prompt, type **cd** and press **Enter** to ensure that the root directory is the current one.

2. Type **copy config.sys config.tmp** and press **Enter** to make a backup copy of your computer's CONFIG.SYS file.

3. Type **copy AUTOEXEC.BAT autoexec.tmp** and press **Enter** to make a backup copy of your computer's AUTOEXEC.BAT file.

> If an AUTOEXEC.TMP or CONFIG.TMP file already exists, you may see a DOS message asking if you want to replace these files. This just means that another application has previously made a temporary backup of these files. It probably is OK to save the current file over them. If you don't want to overwrite an existing .tmp file, choose **no** to the question, and choose another name for your backup, such as config.bak.

4. Type **edit config.sys** and press **Enter** to launch the intrinsic DOS editor and load the CONFIG.SYS file into the editor window.

If you see an error message, such as invalid file or program name, check what you typed to be sure you didn't misspell one of the file names. If these are OK, you probably don't have a path statement that properly points to the location of your DOS external commands. Type **path** at the command prompt and press **Enter** to view the current path. It should include \DOS in the path line. If not, you can add this statement to your AUTOEXEC.BAT file later in this exercise. Continue to load the DOS editor by typing **\dos\edit** to provide a full path to the location of this utility.

5. Use the cursor keys to scroll through this file and view the contents. Do you see one or more *device=* commands? These statements load device drivers that help configure DOS or that enable proper operation of peripheral devices. Do not edit this file since most of the commands here are critical to proper operation of your computer.

6. Press **Alt+F** to display the File menu and choose **Open**. You will see a list of text files in the root directory.

7. Type **AUTOEXEC.BAT** on the command line, or use the cursor movement keys to select AUTOEXEC.BAT from the displayed list. Press **Enter**.

8. Use the arrow keys to scroll through this file. See if you recognize any of the programs or commands, based on the applications you are running on this machine. Do you see a path statement (see Note, above)? If you had trouble loading the DOS editor in the first step of this project:

   a. Move the cursor to the beginning of a line in the file and press **Enter**.

   b. Type **path \DOS**. Don't press Enter, since you don't want to leave a blank line in the file.

   c. Press **Alt+F** to display the **File** menu and choose **Save**.

9. Add a utility command to the file. Move the cursor to the beginning of a line and press **Enter** to open up a blank line.

10. Type **loadhigh doskey**. Do not press Enter.

11. Press **Alt+F** to display the File menu and choose **Save**.

12. Press **Alt+F** and choose **Exit**.

13. Reboot your machine for the change to take effect.

The DOSKEY utility adds some useful functionality to your DOS command line. For one thing it stores commands in a buffer so you can use the up and down arrow keys to step through previously used commands. To learn more about the DOSKEY utility, type **help doskey** or **doskey /?** at the DOS command prompt.

PROJECT 6-2

To find out what printers are installed in your Windows 3.1 system:

1. Locate the Main application window on your desktop. Remember, there may be a number of open application windows on your screen or you may see a virtually blank screen with one or more small, gray boxes. In the former situation, simply click anywhere inside the **Main** window to select it; in the latter situation, double-click **Program Manager** to open the application windows and then select **Main**.

2. Double-click the **Control Panel** icon to open the Control Panel.

3. Double-click the **Printers** icon to open the Printers window.

4. Note the available printer icons, which should be named according to the printer software you have installed on your system.

5. Close the Printers dialog box.

PROJECT 6-3

To find out what printers are installed in your Windows 95/98 system:

1. Move the mouse pointer to the bottom of the screen to display the taskbar, if it is not already displayed.

2. Click **Start**.

3. Point to **Settings**.

4. Click **Printers** to display the Printers window.

5. Now you can determine some of the settings for an individual printer by right clicking one of the printer icons.

6. Choose **Properties** from the shortcut menu. You will see different properties displays for different printers. You probably will see a tabbed dialog. Click on various tabs to view such information as paper trays available, quality setting, and so on.

7. Close the Properties dialog box by clicking **Cancel**, then close the Printers window.

PROJECT 6-4

To find out what printers are installed in Mac OS 8:

1. Open the Apple menu (click the **Apple** icon at the upper left of your desktop).

2. Open the **Chooser**, which you should find near the top of the Apple menu.

3. If you have printers installed you will see a separate icon for each one on the left side of the Chooser dialog box.

4. Click one of the icons to select it, and you will see information specific to that printer on the right side of the display.

5. Click the **Setup** button to display properties and options settings for this printer.

6. Click **Cancel** to close Setup, then close the Chooser to return to the Apple desktop.

PROJECT 6-5

The UNIX operating environment can be very different from any of the Windows implementations or Mac OS, or it can be fairly similar, depending on whether you are running the X-Window shell.

6

To find out what printers are installed in a UNIX system, using the command line prompt:

1. Type **lp –p** from a command prompt. You will see a list of all the printers that are available for use on the system.

2. The names of the printers are the names you use with the print command. You can also set the environment variable PRINTER to one of these names to make the printer in question the default printer.

PROJECT 6-6

To find out what printers are installed in Linux, using the X Window shell:

1. Type **printtool** from the X Window command prompt and press **Enter**. The list of printers will appear in the printtool window.

2. Click the **Close** box to close printtool.

PROJECT 6-7

To find out what printers are installed in Solaris, using the X Window shell:

1. Type **admintool** from the command prompt.

2. Select the **Browse** menu, then **Printers**. A list of the available printers appears.

3. Click the **Close** box to close admintool.

PROJECT 6-8

To add a printer using the printtool utility in Linux (note that you must have root privileges to do so):

1. Log in and start the X Window interface by typing **startx** at the command prompt.

2. Type **printtool** and press **Enter**. The printtool window will show you all the print queues on your system.

3. To add a printer, click the **Add** button at the bottom of the window. A window will appear asking what kind of queue you wish to add.

4. If you want to print to a printer connected to your local computer, select **Local**. To print to a printer connected to another UNIX machine, select **Remote Unix (lpd) Queue**.

5. Click **OK**. The Info window opens, showing Auto-Detection information. Click **OK**.

6. The Edit Printer Entry window will appear. In this window, enter all the names by which this printer is known on your system, separated by pipe (|) symbols. The default printer on a Linux system should include *lp* as at least one of its names. (Please note that as with almost all commands or text in UNIX, printer names are case sensitive.) Oftentimes, an abbreviated name that represents the printer type is used. For example, to make an Apple LaserWriter 2 the default printer as well as naming the printer *lw2*, you would enter *lp|lw2*.

7. Specify the spool directory. This directory is usually created automatically when you add the printer, and is where the temporary print files will be kept. In Linux, this will typically be a subdirectory of /var/spool/lpd. If it is necessary to create the directory, open a terminal and type **mkdir /var/spool/lpd/dirname** where *dirname* is the name of the directory you wish to create. Make certain that two printers never share the same spool directory!

8. Now enter the file size limit in KB. This will limit how large spool files in this queue may be. If you would like to allow any size file, set this to 0.

9. For local printers, the next task will be to specify the printer device. A printer connected to the parallel port would use the device */dev/lp1*. For network printers, you need to provide the name of the machine with the printer connected to it in the Remote Host field. This can either be an IP address or a host name. In addition, you have to provide the print queue name on the remote host.

Use the same queue name for the same printer on all machines; it makes keeping track of who prints to what printer a lot easier!

10. The last thing to do is to select a printer driver; you do this by pressing the **Select** button. The Configure Filter window appears. From the printer type list, pick the correct printer. You can configure the details for this printer in the color depth, paper size, and resolution boxes. Click **OK** to close the Configure Filter window. Click **OK** to complete printer installation.

11. You should now restart the print queue by opening the **lpd** menu in printtool, and choosing **Restart lpd**.

12. Pick a test from the Tests menu to see that the printer works as expected.

13. For a machine that is serving as a print server, you may have to perform one more step to allow remote queues to print to it. The file */etc/hosts.lpd* must be edited, and the machines that you want to be able to use your print server must be added to this file.

14. Click the **Close** box to close printtool.

PROJECT 6-9

Installing a printer under Solaris is similar to installing a printer in Linux. You use the *admintool* utility. The admintool will let you edit many things, including printers. You should have root privileges to do this.

To use the *admintool* utility in Solaris to install a printer:

1. Type **admintool** in a command prompt window.

2. To indicate that you wish to add a printer, select the **Browse** menu, then **Printers**.

3. To add a printer, select **Edit**, **Add** from the menu.

   a. If you want to print to a print queue on another machine, select **Access to printer**. You will see the Access to Printer window, where you have to fill in the printer name, which is the name of the queue on the machine you wish to print to, the print server, which is the host name or IP address of the print server, and a description. To make this the default printer, click in the **default** box. Click **OK** to add the printer.

   b. To add a local printer, after selecting Edit, Add in step 3, choose **Local printer**. Enter the printer name, which is the queue name. Also enter the description, which is purely for your reference.

4. You will see that there is a very limited list of Printer types: either PostScript or ASCII. This list is much smaller than the one in Linux. In the File Contents box, specify whether files sent to this printer will be PostScript or ASCII files. (If you have a PostScript printer and want to print ASCII text as well as PostScript files, you will have to set up two entries for the same printer with two different queue names.)

5. Next, specify whether this is the default printer.

6. Finally, you can select a list of users that may use this printer; by default this list will be set to All, making it possible for all users on the system to use this printer.

7. Click the **Close** box to close admintool.

PROJECT 6-10

One interesting facet of the operating system–hardware interface is the way various devices communicate with the operating system. How detailed this communication is depends to some extent on the operating system, but mainly is a factor of the hardware and custom software driver designs.

To experiment with the messaging that occurs between your operating system and your printer:

1. Make sure your printer hardware is connected to your computer and that the printer is turned on.

2. Load a software application that can print to the connected printer. It doesn't matter much which application: word processor, spreadsheet, presentation package, etc.

3. Remove all paper from the printer and send a document to the printer. Note the error message you receive. Replace the paper. Does the printer begin printing without user interaction on the computer?

4. Send a large print job to the printer and quickly unplug the printer cable before the print buffer can be transferred to the printer. Does your application happily print to nothing, or does it recognize that no printer is physically attached to the system?

5. Open a DOS window if you are working in Windows. Use the COPY command to copy a text file to the printer. Does the DOS window communicate properly to the printer?

6. Open an application that will support a large graphics image such as a photograph. Send a photograph to the printer. Does it have enough memory to process the print job? If not, what error message do you see when the printer runs out of memory?

PROJECT 6-11

Many of us never view or change the configuration settings for our computer's mouse. However, whether you are using a standard mouse or an extended version, such as a wheel mouse, configuration software is readily available to you.

To view or change your basic mouse settings:

1. Click **Start** on the taskbar.

2. Point to **Settings**.

3. Choose **Control Panel**.

4. Double-click the **Mouse** icon to open the Mouse dialog box.

5. View or change available mouse settings as desired.

6. Cancel the Mouse dialog box and close all open windows.

PROJECT 6-12

To view basic keyboard configuration settings:

1. Click **Start** on the taskbar.

2. Point to **Settings**.

3. Choose **Control Panel**.

4. Double-click the **Keyboard** icon to open the Keyboard dialog box.

5. View or change available keyboard settings as desired.

6. Cancel the Keyboard dialog box and close all open windows.

PROJECT 6-13

Does your computer include any specialty input hardware? You can physically view the back of your machine to find special devices, or you can check the drivers installed on your system to get a line on what's in there.

To review installed devices:

1. Click **Start** on the taskbar.

2. Point to **Settings**.

3. Choose **Control Panel**.

4. Double-click the **System** icon to open the System dialog box.

5. Click the **Device Manager** tab to display installed devices (see Figure 6-20).

System Properties

General | Device Manager | Hardware Profiles | Performance |

○ View devices by type   ● View devices by connection

- Plug and Play BIOS
  - Communications Port
  - Communications Port (COM2)
    - Global Village Communication NewsCatcher
  - EISA direct memory access controller
  - Motherboard resources
  - Numeric data processor
  - PCI bus
    - S3 Inc. ViRGE PCI
    - Intel 82371SB PCI Bus Master IDE Controller
    - Intel 82371SB PCI to ISA bridge
    - Intel 82437VX Pentium(r) Processor to PCI bridge
  - Printer Port (LPT1)
  - Programmable interrupt controller
  - PS/2 Compatible Mouse Port
  - Standard 101/102-Key or Microsoft Natural Keyboard

Properties | Refresh | Remove | Print...

Figure 6-20 Windows 98 Device Manager

6. If necessary, click the plus sign to display additional information about any entry.

7. Select an entry and click **Properties** to display detailed information about any entry in this list.

8. Cancel the Device Manager dialog box and close all open windows.

PROJECT 6-14

Mouse hardware is fairly standard, even between very inexpensive models and high-end devices. For the most part the mouse just works. However, it does require periodic cleaning.

To view basic mouse hardware design and to clean its mechanical parts:

1. Turn the mouse over.

2. Notice the plastic cover over the mouse ball. In most cases it is marked "open" and "close."

3. Apply pressure on the cover in the direction of the "open" label. The cover should slide a fraction of an inch to enable you to remove it.

4. Set the cover aside.

5. Place your hand over the bottom of the mouse and turn the mouse over. The mouse ball will fall into your hand. Set the ball aside.

6. Notice the internal components. You should see two horizontal rollers. In cheaper mice these are plastic. More expensive mice use stainless steel rollers. These connect to

potentiometers that send mouse movement information to your operating system. A third roller is a tensioning device that helps keep the ball in place and rolling smoothly.

7. Is there any lint, hair, or other residue on any of these rollers? If so, that could explain why you have had difficulty positioning the mouse pointer accurately.

8. Use a soft rag or tissue and a little rubbing alcohol to clean the rollers.

9. Clean the ball by rubbing it with a soft cloth (rubbing the ball on your clothing works well as long as you don't use a sweater or other garment that might produce lint).

10. Turn the mouse over and drop the ball into the hole.

11. Snap the cover in place and reposition the mouse on its pad or your desktop.

6

PROJECT 6-15

You can tell a lot about your system from the System Properties dialog box, as shown in Hands-on Project 6-13. There also are specialty utilities to let you view and configure other devices, such as multimedia.

98

To view and configure multimedia devices on your computer:

1. Click **Start** on the taskbar.

2. Point to **Settings**.

3. Click the **Control Panel**.

4. Double-click the **Multimedia** icon to open the Multimedia Properties dialog box.

5. Click any of the tabs to view audio, video and other settings.

6. To inspect available drivers and settings, click the **Devices** tab (see Figure 6-21).

7. Click **Cancel** or **OK** to close the dialog box. Close the Control Panel window.

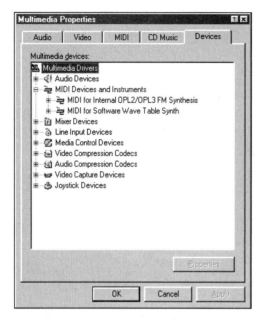

Figure 6-21   Windows 98 Multimedia Properties dialog box

PROJECT 6-16

Windows 98 includes some really useful system-level utilities that can help you find out more about your hard drive.

To use the Windows 98 System Information utility to study your hard drive configuration:

1. Click **Start**, point to **Programs**, point to **Accessories**, and point to **System Tools**.

2. Choose **System Information**. The Microsoft System Information dialog box opens, as shown in Figure 6-22.

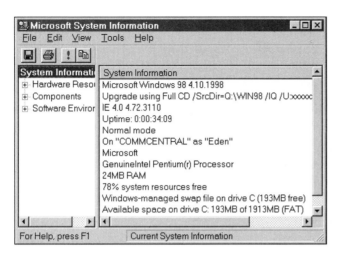

Figure 6-22   Microsoft System Information dialog box

3. Note the size of your hard drive and the amount of space used at the bottom of the first screen of System Information.

4. Use **File**, **Exit** from the menu to close this dialog box and return to your desktop.

PROJECT 6-17

You can find out information on the system configuration of your Macintosh with the Apple System Profiler, available from the Apple menu.

To view some of your Apple system configuration settings:

1. Pull down the Apple menu by clicking the **Apple icon** at the far left of your menu bar. This list of menu items won't change much from application to application. These are intrinsic applications and utilities that are part of your operating system and, while running other applications won't change this menu too much, it can change drastically from version to version of the operating system.

2. Choose **About this Computer** to display the dialog box shown in Figure 6-23. This shows basic information about your computer, including the version of the operating system and memory usage.

3. Close the About this Computer dialog box.

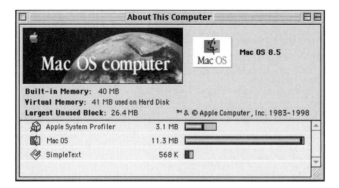

Figure 6-23   Mac About This Computer dialog box

4. Again, click the **Apple** menu and choose **Apple System Profiler** to produce the display shown in Figure 6-24. This is a tabbed display that provides more detail. Click on various tabs to browse the information about your system.

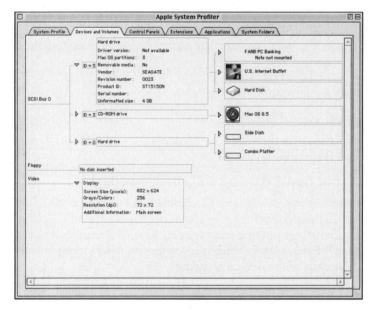

Figure 6-24   The Apple System Profiler

5. With the System Profiler still open, pull down the **File** menu and choose **New Report** to display the New Report dialog box shown in Figure 6-25.

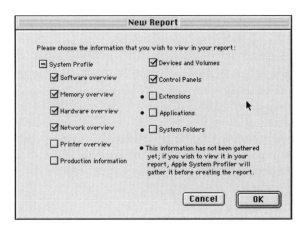

Figure 6-25   Creating a system report on the Mac

6. Put check marks by the information you want to see. Use the example in Figure 6-25, or try your own selections.

7. Click **OK** to produce a report similar to the one in Figure 6-26. Of course what you see will be different from this example, but you will see similar results.

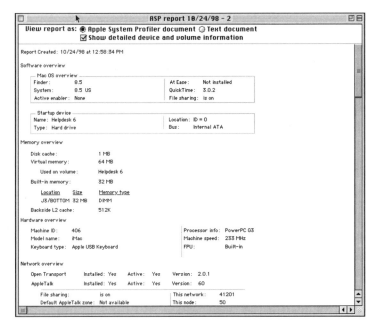

Figure 6-26   Sample Apple System Profiler report

8. Close and save the report as **Proj6-17**, then close the Apple System Profiler.

CASE PROJECTS

1. As MIS manager for a small business network, you have been asked to research possible expansion of your network printer hardware. You are currently supporting 10-15 users with a single, high-speed laser printer capable of 16 pages per minute. This printer has worked well for general business printing, but your firm is broadening its in-house technical capability to include advertising layout and Web page development. The public relations department additionally wants to begin publishing a newsletter for your corporate clients, which will require some color printing capabilities.

   From the information covered in this chapter, answer the following questions about your pending network printing upgrade:

   a. Assuming you will leave the existing laser printer in place, what additional shared printer might you install to expand general purpose business printing capabilities?

   b. Given that quality color printing is important—more important than speed for this application—what color printing solution might you suggest?

   c. The accounting department needs a dedicated printer shared among three users, to print private information such as financial reports and payroll checks. What type of printer might you suggest here?

   d. That sounds like three additional printers at least. Can you estimate a budget for this network expansion?

2. Your company's computer collection consists of a Macintosh for the graphics department, five PCs for management and accounting, and a UNIX-based Web and mail server to handle your email and Internet presence needs.

   All machines are equipped with standard input devices at this time. Based on the material covered in this chapter, answer the following questions:

   a. What additional input device or devices might you suggest for the Macintosh?

   b. Are there any advantages to changing or adding to the input devices already available on the PC platforms?

   c. Would you consider installing a digital pad on the UNIX server machine? Why or why not?

3. If you wanted to add digital photography capabilities to one of the machines in your company, which one would you recommend? Why?

MODEMS AND OTHER COMMUNICATIONS DEVICES

Long gone are the days when most computer users sat at isolated computers. Communications from your computer to another user's computer—one on one—and from your computer to many other computers on a wide area network such as the Internet are an important part of computer use today. We communicate among computers to share data and to conduct research. If your computer is part of a local area network you may communicate directly over the network connection. If you have a stand-alone computer, you probably communicate with other computers and networks using a modem attached directly to your computer.

This chapter discusses basic modem technology and architecture, modem applications, and operating system considerations in installing, configuring and using modems.

AFTER READING THIS CHAPTER AND COMPLETING THE EXERCISES YOU WILL BE ABLE TO:

- Understand analog modem architecture
- Relate the classic Hayes AT modem command set to computer communications applications
- Understand the basics of digital modem architecture
- Describe the basics of telephone line data communications
- Understand basic modem communications in different operating systems

ANALOG MODEM ARCHITECTURE

Computers handle information in a digital format. Everything the computer understands is stored as a series of ones and zeros, represented as the presence of voltage (a digital 1) or the absence of voltage (a digital 0). Information is sent over a telephone line in analog format, rising and falling sounds produced when you speak into the telephone handset. The computer doesn't recognize the telephone system's analog data and the telephone system—at its most commonly used level—can't use the computer's digital data format. A modem is a piece of hardware and associated software that connects these two incompatible systems in a way that lets them communicate with each other.

MODEM HARDWARE BASICS

A modem consists of three basic electronic hardware or software components: the data pump, the controller, and the UART. The name **modem** comes from a description of what the modem does. A modem is a *MODulator-DEModulator*. It modulates digital signals from the computer into analog signals that can be sent over the phone line, and demodulates incoming analog signals back into digital signals the computer can understand. The component that performs basic modulation/demodulation is sometimes called a **data pump**. Basic modem concepts are shown in Figure 7-1.

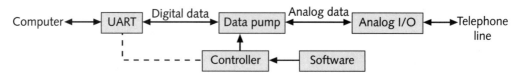

Figure 7-1 Basic modem concepts

The **controller** provides the modem's identity. This is where protocols for modulation (V.34, V.90, etc.), error correction (MNP-4, V.42) and compression (MNP-4, V.42bis) are stored. The controller also interprets AT. The AT command set communicates configuration and operational instructions to the modem. AT stands for Attention and tells the modem to interpret the next characters as a command instead of as data. More detailed information on communicating with modems with the AT commands is provided later in this chapter.

These protocols define some of the basic operational parameters of your modem and determine how compatible it is with other modems with which you communicate. The latest standard—**V.90**—defines a 56,000 bits per second (56 Kbps) communications protocol. It is by far the most popular choice for high-speed data communications requirements such as browsing the World Wide Web. (For more information on modem speed and testing your modem's performance, see Hands-on Project 7-2 at the end of this chapter.) Modem protocols are not covered in detail in this chapter. However, you should understand the basics of modem protocols and how their development has paralleled the development of modem technology. Historically, modem protocols have been a determining factor in modem speed and compatibility. As this book is written, this Web page provides a number of useful links to modem technology and protocol information:

http://www2.computerworld.com/home/online9697.nsf/All/980126modemlinks

Table 7-1 contains a reference list of modem standards and protocols that you may see as you read about modems here and elsewhere. Today's standard is V.90 and generally incorporates most of the earlier technologies and protocols listed in the table.

Table 7-1   Modem Standards and Protocols

Standard	Description
V.21	300 bps duplex
V.22	1,200 bps duplex
V.22bis	2,400 bps duplex
V.32	9,600 bps duplex
V.32bis	14,400 bps duplex. Adds improved training and fallback.
V.FAST	28,800 bps duplex (early standard)
V.34	28,800 bps duplex (replaces V.FAST)
V.34 (new)	33,600 bps duplex. Second V.34 standard.
V.42	Error correcting protocol with sync-to-async conversion
V.42bis	Data compression added to V.42 error correction. MNP-5.
X2	56,000 bps. U.S. Robotics standard.
K56Flex	56,000 bps. Motorola, Rockwell, Ascend and others.
V.90	56,000 bps. ITU international 56K standard.
MNP Levels 1-4	Microcom Networking Protocol. Asynchronous error correction.
MNP Level 5	Adds data compression to levels 1-4

Computer modems can be classified in a number of ways. One distinction is whether the modem is located inside the computer (an internal modem) or outside the computer (an external modem). Internal modems usually are built on expansion cards that plug into the computer's expansion bus, most commonly the PCI bus. They may also be part of the computer's main circuit board. External modems are circuit boards that are placed inside a stand-alone case with its own power supply. External modems usually plug into the computer via a serial port or, with newer modems, the USB port. An external USB modem is an excellent choice for a number of reasons. For one thing, the USB port is a high-speed port that can supply power to peripheral devices, obviating the need for external power supplies or power "bricks." USB devices are self-configuring. When you plug in a USB modem, the operating system recognizes the presence of the new device and automatically launches a configuration utility. In general, external modems are preferable to internal modems because they include status lights that tell you when the modem is connected, what state it is in, and whether data is being transferred. In addition, an external modem is a universal device that you can use with DOS, Windows, Mac OS, or UNIX (though a USB device may be less portable. Only the latest versions of Windows and Mac OS support USB devices at this time).

The **UART** (pronounced "you art") is an electronic chip, the Universal Asynchronous Receiver-Transmitter. The UART converts data from the computer into data that can be sent to serial ports. The UART reads in one byte of data at the computer's bus speed, adds a start bit at the beginning, a stop bit at the end, generates an interrupt, and feeds the bits to the serial port at a slow speed that won't overwhelm the peripheral (a modem in this case, but the same system applies to other serial devices). The 8250 UART was the standard for many years, but faster modems demand faster UARTs, and the 16550 UART is now standard for most uses. External modems use whatever UART is attached to the serial port, part of your computer hardware. Internal modems use their own UART, bypassing the computer's serial I/O port. (In Figure 7-1, you can see this internal UART concept. An external modem would have serial port hardware and use the computer's internal UART.)

Computers communicate with external serial devices with two basic protocols: synchronous and asynchronous. These terms refer to the method used to keep the data streams on the local and remote devices aligned so proper data transfer can occur. Asynchronous communication is the most common method for today's desktop computers. Sent and received data is synchronized by using fairly accurate clocks (timers) at both ends of the connection. The transmitting device sends a start bit, which is captured by the receiving device. The next eight bits are assumed to be data, and the final two bits are stop bits. The start and stop bits help the receiving device interpret data and stay in synch. Synchronous communication, on the other hand, sends information in blocks (frames) of data that include embedded clock signals. Alternately, the clock data can be sent over a separate, dedicated clock line that is part of the connection. Synchronous data transfer usually is more efficient, but it requires more processing at both ends of the link. For a discussion of synchronous and asynchronous communications, see *http://www.sangoma.com/sync&a.htm*.

SOFTWARE-BASED MODEMS

All modems need the functions of the data pump, controller, and UART. However, some modems do not implement these functions in hardware. Software-based modems (often referred to as **Winmodems**, after the trademarked name of 3Com/U.S. Robotics popular models) replace one or more of these components with software.

The 3Com (formerly U.S. Robotics) Winmodem is a controllerless modem that retains a hardware data pump (a **digital signal processor (DSP)**, in the case of the 3Com Winmodem), but implements the controller functions in software. So-called **host signal processor (HSP)** modems dispense with the controller and data pump hardware entirely. Instead of using their own signal processors, HSP modems use the host's central processing unit (such as the Pentium or PowerPC) along with special software, to handle the same jobs.

There's a third kind of modem unique to the Apple Centris and Quadra AV (Audio Visual) models. Apple's Geoport Telecom Adapter for these computers uses the AV computer's onboard DSP, rather than the computer's CPU, to perform modem functions. This DSP is also used for speech recognition, so you can conduct speech recognition and modem operations with these computers at the same time. The Geoport Telecom Adapter for the PowerPC models was a conventional HSP modem.

One disadvantage of implementing modem functions with software rather than hardware is that such software takes up memory and processor cycles, although these cycles have become increasingly cheap. The biggest disadvantage of software-based modems is their dependence on particular operating systems. A 3Com Winmodem won't work on a Mac or even on a PC running Linux or OS/2, and a Geoport Telecom Adapter won't work on a PC operating system. In addition, many communications software packages simply aren't compatible with the Winmodem design because they expect to find a serial port and modem hardware at traditional locations. Many software modem designs use non-standard address locations. Newer communications software can find such address locations, but older software won't always work properly with software-based modems because it can't find the hardware.

In contrast, any external Hayes-compatible modem (hardware-based) can be used on virtually any computer made in the past 20 years. All that is required is a serial port on the computer compatible with the modem's serial port, and communications software capable of sending compatible commands through the computer's serial port to the modem and of receiving feedback and data from the modem.

The advantages of using a software modem are cost savings and upgradeability. By eliminating physical parts, the unit cost falls dramatically. In a completely software-based modem, drastic upgrades are possible by rewriting the software. Many multimedia features—such as voicemail or speakerphone—also are easier to implement in a software-based modem design.

HAYES AT COMMAND SET

In the 1970s, modems were sold for specific purposes, such as connecting a particular remote dumb terminal to a specific host computer, and commanded high prices. Dennis Hayes devised a way to create a general-purpose modem that could be configured using a command language he invented, the **Hayes**, or **AT**, **command language**. When a modem is said to be Hayes compatible, it simply means that the modem supports all or part of the Hayes AT command set. Most chipset vendors support the standard Hayes command set, and supplement the command set with additional commands.

Dennis Hayes' commands begin with the letters AT, which stands for *AT*tention. The command interpreter ignores spaces and dashes (which people are accustomed to using to separate area codes, exchanges, and extensions). In this chapter the commands are shown in uppercase, but the commands are not case sensitive. Table 7-2 on the next page summarizes some of the more important AT commands. Although many modem manufacturers extend the basic AT command set for their own use, most modern modems respond to the basic commands in the traditional ways. This command set is used extensively to set up and control modems so that they are compatible with a variety of host hardware.

Table 7-2   AT Command Set Summary

AT Command	Description
DT and DP	Dial the phone number that follows. DT is for touchtone phones. DP is for pulse dial phones. A complete touchtone dialing sequence would be: ATDT 555-5555
, (comma)	Causes a delay before executing the next command. Often used to make sure the phone switch has recovered before dialing, as when dialing a 9 to get an outside line: ATDT 9,555-5555
W	Wait for dialtone before dialing: ATDT 9W555-5555
+++	Escape from online mode into command mode. In command mode, AT commands can be sent to the modem.
H	Hangup. A typical hangup sequence is +++ ATH.
O	Go from command mode back to online mode. This is the only occurrence of the letter "o" in the Hayes AT command set. All other occurrences of 0-like shapes are zeroes.
S0=n	Answer incoming calls after n rings. Setting n equal to zero tells the modem to not answer incoming calls.
Mn	Turn modem speaker off (n=0) or on (n=1).
Ln	Set speaker volume for values of n equal to 0 (lowest volume), 1 or 2 (medium volume) or 3 (highest volume).
&Fn	Set modem to factory template.
Z	Reset modem to defaults.

DIGITAL "MODEMS"

The name **digital modem** is a misnomer of sorts, since there is no actual modulation or demodulation (of analog signals), but the usage persists. A digital modem performs the same basic function as an analog modem: it moves data out of a computer, across a telephone line, and into another computer at a remote location. The major difference is that the data is digital from start to finish. Digital modems are digital devices that use digital transmission media. Digital modems can be network devices (connected directly to the network) or serial devices (connected to the serial port). When connecting to TCP/IP networks, they connect via PPP (Point-to-Point Protocol, a popular communications protocol when communicating with mainframe computers and over the Internet).

Integrated Services Digital Network (ISDN) uses a digital telephone line for high-speed computer communications, video conferencing, Internet connections, and so on. This technology has been around for nearly 20 years, but only with the rise in interest in the Internet and video conferencing has it gained much market penetration. ISDN uses standard copper telephone line pairs with digital equipment on either end of the connection to encode and transmit the information (an ISDN router and **terminal adapter (TA)**, a type of digital modem).

ISDN routers and TAs typically include analog telephone jacks so you can plug in a conventional telephone or modem for use over the digital line. With most ISDN hardware, you connect to a single telephone line copper pair (the same kind of wire that brings telephone service into your home or office—two wires twisted together), but you get two separate channels for computer data and two analog telephone lines. You can use one analog line and one data line simultaneously, or two digital lines, or two analog lines.

It is hard to predict the future role of ISDN. For one thing, newer technologies could replace ISDN (see the sections on Cable Modems and DSL later in this chapter). For another, ISDN can be prohibitively expensive for the average user. Costs in the U.S. as this book is written range from around $30 per month to $90 per month, with additional charges of $0.05 to $0.15 per minute of use.

ISDN TERMINAL ADAPTERS, ROUTERS, AND BRIDGES   **7**

You can think of an ISDN terminal adapter as an ISDN modem. It's a serial device, complete with UART. It accepts AT commands, and appears in the Windows Modems control panel and Mac OS Modem control panel in the same way as a modem. These devices use the PPP stacks built into the operating system, just as a modem does.

Routers and **bridges** are network devices (almost always Ethernet). Bridges simply connect or bridge one part of a network to another, sometimes remote, part of the network. Routers can route network packets to different networks, and can route multiple protocols. Figure 7-2 shows one possible connection of an ISDN router within a local area network. Schemes such as this are used to allow multiple users on a LAN access to the Internet or to remote corporate sites.

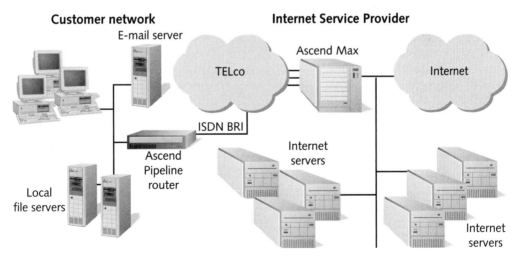

Figure 7-2   Typical ISDN bridge and LAN connection

Notice the two Ascend icons in this drawing. The "Pipeline" is an ISDN router used to connect a computer network to an ISDN line. The Ascend Max is a digital modem bank that answers remote calls from ISDN or analog telephone line users. The Max and similar hardware serves as the initial contact point for calling computers and modems, then passes the data across a network to the attached host or server computer. The ISDN BRI designation simply refers to the telephone company's ISDN line connection.

Routers and bridges use their own built-in PPP stacks to make a connection, and are programmed with the number they are to call, and the username and password of the login account.

Routers can be used to get a picture of how data passes through the Internet, and to find bottlenecks between your computer and an Internet site. A *traceroute* utility can determine the number of routers between your computer and the site, allowing you to "trace the route" that your data takes on its way to its destination. Traceroute sends a packet of data to the remote site. As each router receives the packet and passes it on to the next router, it sends back traceroute data. Graphical traceroute utilities are available as freeware or shareware, or you can use the commands built into UNIX (*traceroute*) and DOS (troute). Figure 7-3 shows a typical *traceroute* output.

```
traceroute www.linux.org

traceroute to www.linux.org (198.182.196.55), 30 hops max, 40 byte packets

 1  209.235.87.33 (209.235.87.33)  0.951 ms  0.909 ms  0.945 ms

 2  209.196.32.13 (209.196.32.13)  1.433 ms  0.774 ms  0.717 ms

 3  209.196.32.25 (209.196.32.25)  0.943 ms  0.736 ms  0.672 ms

 4  32.ATM0-0-0.GW3.ATL1.ALTER.NET (157.130.67.197)  12.400 ms  12.355 ms  8.949 ms

 5  106.ATM3-0.XR1.ATL1.ALTER.NET (146.188.232.114)  7.949 ms  6.244 ms  7.604 ms

 6  295.ATM2-0.TR1.ATL1.ALTER.NET (146.188.232.90)  10.538 ms  9.004 ms  6.233 ms

 7  109.ATM6-0.TR1.DCA1.ALTER.NET (146.188.136.14)  17.761 ms  17.955 ms  17.897 ms

 8  199.ATM6-0.XR1.TCO1.ALTER.NET (146.188.161.161)  27.107 ms  28.385 ms *

 9  193.ATM9-0-0.GW2.TCO1.ALTER.NET (146.188.160.57)  17.867 ms  20.803 ms  23.098 ms

10  uu-peer.pos-4-oc12-core.ai.net (205.134.160.2)  34.974 ms  30.970 ms  29.225 ms

11  border-ai.invlogic.com (205.134.175.254)  88.728 ms  33.566 ms  36.078 ms

12 router.invlogic.com (198.182.196.1)  94.452 ms  86.347 ms 126.998 ms

13 www.linux.org (198.182.196.55)  113.948 ms  135.998 ms  90.676 ms
```

Figure 7-3   Typical *traceroute* routine

Notice that the data went through the local network (209), then to alternet, to ainet, then finally to linux.org. Congestion on any one of those routers, or on any of the links between those routers, could cause slow Internet performance.

CABLE MODEMS

Another type of digital modem that is beginning to gain popularity is the **cable modem**. These devices connect to your television cable and use one or more channels to transfer data at very high speeds. The initial cable modem designs were hybrid devices that required an analog telephone line for transmitting data to the host; the digital cable channel was used only to download data from the remote host (the Internet gateway) to your PC. Later designs are two-way digital and don't require the extra analog telephone connection.

Cable modems aren't yet widely used, but as the technology improves and as local cable companies deploy the infrastructure required to support digital data delivery over cable, look for this technology to grow rapidly.

DSL MODEMS

Still another type of digital data service is **DSL**. DSL stands for Digital Subscriber Line, and it comes in a couple of varieties: asynchronous (ADSL) and synchronous (SDSL). Like ISDN, DSL uses standard telephone line wire pairs to bring high-speed data into your home or office. Digital modems at each end of the connection manage the task of data transfer. DSL is being deployed on an experimental basis by several telephone companies around the country, but there still is a lot of work to complete before the technology is widely distributed.

DSL modems can be relatively expensive. Getting this technology dispersed widely requires the local telephone company to spend millions of dollars in new hardware and in some cases new wiring. Nevertheless, many industry watchers believe that DSL is the data communication technology of the near future and, that it may someday replace ISDN as the digital connection of choice.

DATA COMMUNICATIONS OVER PHONE LINES

When two modems communicate, they must have a way to halt and resume the flow of data. Otherwise, data buffers would fill and then overflow, resulting in lost data. **Flow control** can be accomplished by software or hardware.

SOFTWARE FLOW CONTROL

A popular software flow control method from the early days of modems is called **Xon-Xoff**. Xon-Xoff uses the Ctrl+S character (ASCII 19) to stop the flow of data (Xoff), and Ctrl+Q (ASCII 17) to resume (Xon). When the receiving computer needs time to process the data in the buffers, perform disk I/O, and so on, it can send an Xoff request to the remote modem to stop the flow of data. Once it has processed the data in its buffer, it can send an Xon to begin receiving data again. This receive, stop, resume process continues repeatedly throughout the data transfer or communications session.

In the days before online services had graphical user interfaces, you could manu-ally type Ctrl+Q and Ctrl+S from the keyboard to issue the Xon-Xoff control sig-nals to suspend and resume the flow of onscreen text. This was a common tech-nique for users of dumb terminals connected to central computers as well. Some software in those days wasn't sophisticated enough to manage the dumb termi-nal screens automatically. And, communications software running on early PCs or Macs simply emulated a dumb terminal to access text-based host computers.

One problem with Xon-Xoff flow control is that the data being transferred may contain Ctrl+S or Ctrl+Q characters, which can interrupt the data transfer. Another problem is that Xon-Xoff is a form of signaling that uses the bandwidth of the data stream to pass data about the condition of the data stream. This is inefficient, as it reduces the amount of user data that can move over the phone line.

HARDWARE FLOW CONTROL

With the advent of faster modems, the industry moved to hardware flow control. Hardware flow control halts and resumes the movement of data by changing the voltage on specific pins in the serial interface. Controlling data flow with hardware eliminates the problems of the modem confusing data with control signals. If you are given a choice in configuring your modem for data communications, always use hardware flow control instead of Xon-Xoff. It is more reliable and permits faster modem performance.

See *http://www.myhome.org/pg/modem.htm* for an informative discussion of flow control and of modem technology in general.

ERROR CORRECTION

Sometimes errors are introduced into the data stream by the telephone lines or other equip-ment. Modems must check for these errors and re-send bad blocks of data to ensure that the receiving modem (and, thence the attached computer) get the information exactly as it was transmitted.

Modems transfer bits (ones or zeroes) over the phone line. Three possible errors can occur: a bit can be lost, an extraneous bit can be introduced, or a bit can be flipped (changed from zero to one or from one to zero). The most basic form of error correction involves the start bit and stop bit. Each eight-bit byte is framed by a **start bit** at the beginning and a **stop bit** at the end (see Figure 7-4).

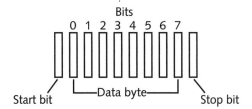

Figure 7-4   Data byte framing with start and stop bits

The start and stop bits always have the same value. If a bit is added or lost, the start and stop bits won't be in the right place. The receiving modem will notice this and request that the sending modem re-send that block of data. The modem's UART adds start and stop bits to outgoing data, and strips them from incoming data.

There are always eight bits between the start and stop bit, even when communicating with systems that only require seven bits. That makes it possible to use the eighth bit for another form of error checking: **parity checking**.

Parity can be either even or odd (or none, if parity checking is turned off). Say the seven bits are 0100101. Adding up the 1s yields 3. If parity were set to even, then an extra parity bit with a 1 value must be added to this byte: 01001011. The resulting byte + parity combination has an even number of 1s. A data byte that already had an even number of 1s would get a parity bit of 0 to maintain the even parity check. The receiving computer checks the number of 1s in each byte to make sure they sum to an even value (2, 4, 6, 8, etc.). If they are odd, the computer would know that a bit had been flipped, or some other error had occurred.

DATA COMPRESSION

In addition to error correction, modems today generally also compress the data they send. The concept behind data compression is fairly simple. Consider a screen displayed on your computer, for example. There may be several icons, an application dialog box, and a solid blue background. A data compression routine can study this picture and see that there's a lot of repetitive blue in the picture. So, in essence the program says, "Here's a blue spot at the start of this picture, how many times does it repeat itself?" The "compressed" representation of the screen would show a blue dot and a number that represents the number of times the blue dot is repeated. This would take a lot less room than physically representing each blue dot.

Other file types are compressed using this same—very simplified—theory. Text obviously contains repetitive data, as does program code. Virtually any computer file can be compressed to reduce the overall size of the file that must be transmitted. If you are familiar with compression utilities such as PKZIP or WINZIP for the PC, or StuffIt for the Mac, then you have seen the result of data compression. Compression can reduce the size of a TIF (Tagged Image Format) file, for example, by more than 90 percent.

Modem data compression uses a similar technique to reduce the total number of data bytes that must be transferred over the connection, but it does it "on the fly," while you work, so you don't have to manually compress the data before you send it. Data compression is one way modem manufacturers are able to achieve some of the high-speed data transfers expected today.

MODEMS AND THE OPERATING SYSTEM

The previous discussions provided an overview of basic modem technology with respect to the hardware components. Just as important is the software component of modem communications.

All operating systems include a communications component. In fact, data communications is one of the most basic of operating system duties. Data moves along the internal computer bus from the CPU to memory and to peripheral devices that may be connected to the internal bus or to external ports. Part of this data communications software intrinsic to the operating system was discussed in the coverage of printers and other output, input, and storage devices in Chapter 6. Components of the operating system manage the flow of data through the serial and parallel ports, working with the features of vendor-specific drivers.

In the case of modem communications, the intrinsic serial communication protocols are used to manage data flow through the serial port, and communications programs—external to the operating system—handle the specifics of communicating with a remote host. In addition, facilities supplied with the operating system (but actually external applications) dial a remote computer and establish a communication link using PPP or another protocol. For example, Microsoft Dialup Networking is supplied with Windows 95/98, and a PPP protocol and dialer is part of Mac OS. (Step-by-step instructions for setting up dial-up networking in Windows 95/98, Windows NT, Mac OS, and UNIX are given in the Hands-on Projects at the end of this chapter.)

The Mac OS uses two major TCP/IP stacks to configure your computer for Internet or other TCP/IP remote host access: the MacTCP Control Panel and the TCP/IP Control Panel. Older connection software and older Mac operating systems probably use MacTCP; newer versions of Mac OS use Open Transport or the TCP/IP Control Panel. Newer versions of Mac OS also have a built-in PPP Control Panel and Modems Control Panel. This is sometimes referred to as "PPP for Open Transport" because it requires Open Transport. Apple began including this software beginning with Mac OS 7.6, and it is available as a separate download for System 7.5.3 and 7.5.5.

On systems that have Mac OS version 7.5.3 or 7.5.5, users can switch between MacTCP and TCP/IP using Network Software Selector. Network Software Selector is easy to use. Double-click it, select either Classic Networking or Open Transport Networking, and restart the computer. Network Software Selector, if present, is located in Hard Drive:\Apple Extras\. If it is not present, you may need to re-install the 7.5.3 or 7.5.5 update.

In UNIX, as well as in some configurations of Windows, a modem has two purposes. It can either be a dial-in device, or it can be a dial-out device. When a modem is used as a dial-in device, it is treated similarly to a terminal connected to the computer using a serial connection. Any such terminal is still referred to as a teletype, from the old paper-based terminals that were used many years ago. As such, the device port used for a modem is referred to as a TTY port, an abbreviation for teletype. To support dial-in connectivity on one of these TTYs, UNIX uses a **daemon** (an internal, automatically running program) called *getty*. There are numerous versions of *getty*; some simply answer a call and let a user use the TTY as if they were on a terminal. More advanced versions are capable of using fax modems, detecting when a fax is being received on the modem line, and automatically invoking fax software. Today, fewer people are using dial-in modems connected to serial ports on UNIX machines. Instead, terminal servers are becoming more popular.

 Please be aware that *getty* is very picky when it comes to what the modem will report, both in the form of control lines used and messages sent to the computer. In general, a modem should be used in factory settings with UNIX, with DCD signaling enabled, DTR set to drop the phone line, DSR and DTS set to normal.

Set the modem to Auto Answer mode for use with *getty*. This means the modem will automatically answer the phone when there is an incoming call and make the connection to the other modem.

External communications programs can include simple terminal emulators (Microsoft Terminal), World Wide Web browsers (Microsoft Internet Explorer, Netscape), e-mail programs (Outlook Express, Eudora), audio and video communications applications (Microsoft NetMeeting), or anything that uses a modem link to exchange data with a remote computer or remote computer network. UNIX supports a large variety of software packages that can use the modem to dial out. The earliest packages were for message exchange using the Unix to Unix Copy Protocol, or UUCP. These packages are found on almost all UNIX versions, including the very simple terminal program *tip* (Telephone Interface Program).

In addition, many UNIX platforms, such as Solaris and Linux, include programs to make network connections using protocols such as PPP. These programs are used to make the actual connection to a remote host, then to send IP or other network traffic over that link. The Async PPP software provided with Linux and Solaris is discussed briefly in the Hands-on section of this chapter.

Finally, there are now some advanced terminal emulation programs available as third-party add-ons to most UNIX operating systems. These programs look and feel a lot like the terminal programs used in the DOS or Windows world. If you get your modem set up to work with *tip* or one of the PPP products, your modem will also work with any of these third-party programs.

Most standard *gettys* want to see no progress information from the modem. To achieve this, use the following initialization string on most modems:

    AT&F&C1&D2E0V0Q1S0=2&W

This string has the following components and meanings:

    AT—Modem command prefix
    &F—Reset the modem to factory settings
    &C1—Turns on RTS/CTS control
    &D2—Sets DCD control to follow carrier
    E0—Lets the modem not echo any commands sent to it back to the computer

V0—Instructs the modem to send numeric, as opposed to verbal error and progress messages

Q1—Tells the modem to not return any error or progress messages

S0=2—Tells the modem to answer the phone after two rings

&W—Writes these settings to the modem's NVRam (non-volatile RAM that stores configuration information), so the new settings will be used the next time the modem is power cycled.

Dial out can be done with the same modem, but in general a different device name is used. This is done because UNIX does not normally operate with a modem that does not have the Data Carrier Detect (DCD) line raised. The initialization string for most dial-out applications is very similar to that for dial-in applications. The only change for most software is to use Q0 instead of a Q1 setting, and for some software to use the V1 setting instead of V0. Some modems may differ, so consult your modem manual.

Once you install the modem hardware, you need to configure your operating system dialer to communicate with your modem, to dial a number, and to log onto a remote host. This process is detailed in the step-by-step exercises in the Hands-on section at the end of this chapter.

CHAPTER SUMMARY

This chapter is a good starting point for your understanding of modern computer communications. Analog modems have a three-part architecture, consisting of a data pump, controller, and UART (Universal Asynchronous Receiver-Transmitter). These components may be implemented completely in hardware, or partially in software.

The Hayes (AT) modem command set is used to control modem settings, and is compatible with a wide variety of host hardware.

Digital modems are not actually modems at all, since they are entirely digital and do not perform the modulation/demodulation required for analog devices. They are called modems because they perform the same basic functions as analog modems, allowing communications between computers. Digital modems work with digital telephone or cable systems such as ISDN (Integrated Services Digital Network). Digital modems that work with ISDN are called terminal adapters (TAs), and interface with ISDN routers and bridges. Other types of digital modems are cable modems, which connect to a television cable to transfer data at high speeds, and Digital Subscriber Line (DSL) modems.

Data communication over telephone lines involves software flow control, hardware flow control, error correction, and data compression.

All the operating systems covered in this book include a communications component and method for setting up dial-up networking. To set up a modem and dial-up networking, you must provide the operating system with information about your modem, networking protocol(s) and addresses, and a dial-up access telephone number.

KEY TERMS

- **AT commands** — A modem control command set designed by the Hayes company. This standard modem command set begins each command with AT (for Attention) and allows communications software or users to control many modem functions directly.

- **bridges** — Hardware devices that bridge two or more network segments so that computers on different physical networks can communicate with each other.

- **cable modem** — A digital modem device designed for use with the cable TV system, providing high-speed data transfer. It may include an analog modem component that is used with a conventional telephone line connection for information sent from the user to the ISP.

- **controller** — A hardware or software component of a modem that defines an individual modem personality. The controller interprets AT commands, handles communications protocols, and so on.

- **daemon** — An internal, automatically running program, usually in UNIX, that serves a particular function such as routing email to recipients or supporting dial-up networking connectivity.

- **data pump** — The hardware or software portion of a modem that is responsible for converting digital data into analog signals for transmission over a telephone line, and for converting analog signals into digital data for transmission to the computer.

- **digital modem** — A modem-like device that transfers data via digital lines instead of analog lines.

- **Digital Signal Processor (DSP)** — A software data pump used in such software-driven modems as the 3Com Winmodem.

- **DSL** — Digital Subscriber Line. An emerging digital technology supported by some telephone companies to provide data connections at T1 speeds (1.544 Mbps). Two varieties of DSL exist, synchronous (SDSL) and asynchronous (ADSL).

- **flow control** — A hardware or software feature in modems that lets a receiving modem communicate to the sending modem that it needs more time to process previously-sent data. When the current data has been processed successfully, the receiving modem notifies the sending modem that it is OK to resume data transmission.

- **Hayes command** — See AT command.

- **Host Signal Processor (HSP)** — A software approach to handling data pump duties in software-based modems such as the 3Com WinModem.

- **Integrated Services Digital Network (ISDN)** — A digital telephone line used for high-speed digital computer communications, video conferencing, Internet connections, and so on.

- **modem** — MOdulator-DEModulator. A hardware device that permits a computer to exchange digital data with another computer via an analog telephone line or dedicated connection.

7

- **parity checking** — A data communications process that ensures data integrity through a system of data bit comparisons between the sending and receiving computer.

- **routers** — Network hardware that can intelligently route network packets to different networks, and can route multiple protocols.

- **start bit** — In data communication, an extra bit inserted by the sending modem at the beginning of a data byte to help ensure that the received data is correct.

- **stop bit** — In data communication, an extra bit inserted by the sending modem at the end of a data byte to help ensure that the received data is correct.

- **terminal adapter (TA)** — A digital modem that permits computer-to-computer data transfer over a digital line, such as ISDN.

- **Universal Asynchronous Receiver-Transmitter (UART)** — An electronic chip that handles data flow through a serial port or modem.

- **V.90** — A modem communication protocol that defines the standards for 56 kbps communications.

- **Winmodems** — A software-driven modem from 3Com Corporation that uses minimal hardware and the computer's CPU with software to conduct data communications.

- **Xon-Xoff** — A software flow control protocol that permits a receiving modem to notify the sending modem when its data buffers are full and it needs more time to process previously received data.

REVIEW QUESTIONS

1. The three basic modem components are _____, _____, and _____.

2. These components are usually implemented in hardware—but not always. Describe the alternatives to all-hardware modem components.

3. There are distinct advantages—and some serious disadvantages—to non-hardware modems described in the previous question. List two main advantages and two main disadvantages of this design.

4. The term "modem" stands for

   a. Modulator-demodulator

   b. Modern Electronic Manipulator

   c. Model Emulator

   d. none of the above

5. International modem standards define how modems communicate with each other and at what speed. The latest standard for 56 Kbps modems is

   a. V.34bis

   b. V.90

   c. V.42

   d. V.190

6. A UART is the electronic device that manages serial input/output data transfers for modems and other serial objects. UART stands for

   a. Universal Asynchronous Receiver-Transmitter

   b. Universal Area Remote Transmitter

   c. United Access Reverse Transfer

   d. Universal Accessible Reverse Transfer

7. 3COM Corporation, among others, manufactures a modem that is a different design from conventional modems. How is their WinModem design different?

8. Flow control helps ensure accurate data transfer between modems. There are two general types of flow control in common use. They are _____ and _____.

9. Xon-Xoff flow control is which one of the types referenced in the previous question? What are the disadvantages to this type of flow control?

10. A byte of data transferred via modem is typically 10-bits in length. True or False?

11. Error correction ensures reliable data transfer from modem to modem, but it can seriously degrade data transfer speed. Describe why this is so.

12. Adding an extra bit to each data byte for error correction is called _____ checking.

13. The error checking in the previous question can be of two types. They are _____ and _____.

14. When this type of error correction is turned off, it is said to be set to none, or no _____.

15. The Hayes manufacturing company initiated in the early 1970s a command set used to configure and control modems. This command language is frequently referred to as the _____ _____ command set.

16. Conventional modems are used on analog telephone lines or direct connections. New digital lines permit faster, more reliable connections. One popular digital line is ISDN. Another is _____.

17. ISDN stands for Integrated Services Digital Network. True or False?

18. Routers and bridges are used with digital lines, frequently to provide network or Internet access to multiple computers. Briefly describe the basic differences between a router and a bridge.

19. Software-based modems use electronic circuits called Digital Signal Processors or DSPs to emulate what major modem hardware component?

20. The most versatile and universal modem is an external, serial modem. True or False?

HANDS-ON PROJECTS

PROJECT 7-1

Using a modem can be as simple as heating your coffee in a microwave, or as complex as rebuilding your computer from scratch. A lot depends on how interested you are in learning about the technology and how reliable your hardware/software/phone line combination is.

To expand on the topics introduced in this chapter, point your browser to the following locations and try to relate the information in this chapter to the expanded data you find there:

1. Columbia University - Modem Protocols Explained:
   http://www.cc.columbia.edu/acis/networks/protocols.html

2. John Navas 28800-56K Modem FAQ: *http://www.aimnet.com/~jnavas/modem/faq.html*

3. Les Jones' 56K Modem page: *www.56k.com*

PROJECT 7-2

You can't always depend on achieving a data transfer rate equivalent to the speed of your modem. A 56 Kbps modem may only connect at 48 Kbps or less, for example, and even if you connect at a full 56K you may not achieve an actual data throughput of 56K.

To test the performance of your modem:

1. Log onto an online service or remote computer with an FTP client.

2. Locate a *compressed* file of known size on the remote computer.

3. Start downloading the file.

4. Use a stopwatch or watch and time precisely how long it takes to download the file.

5. Conduct the following calculations, using your actual data, to calculate the actual transfer rate in bits per second:

Say that your 56K modem downloaded a 100 kilobyte compressed file in 20 seconds. A simplistic calculation would be:

100 kilobytes × 1024 bytes/kilobyte × 8 bits/byte = 819,200 bits
819,200 bits/20 seconds = 40,960 bits per second

This calculation assumes that the modem was transferring 8 bits per byte. But what about start bits and stop bits? That would make the number 10 bits per byte, which makes the modem performance 51,200 bits per second. However, a 56K modem is probably using V.42 hardware error correction, which strips out the start and stop bits, but adds other overhead. For quick calculations call it 9 bits per byte, or about 46,080 bits per second.

Take note that the file was compressed. Otherwise you would have to take into account the compressibility of the file and the efficiency of the modem's hardware compression!

PROJECT 7-3

Testing modem performance with only a single type of file and a file of only one length won't give you a reliable test of modem performance over the phone lines and with the hosts you use frequently. In this exercise you conduct data transfer (upload and download) experiments using different file types, such as .ZIP, .GIF, .JPG, and .TXT. .ZIP files are efficiently compressed. .GIF and .JPG files are somewhat compressed, and .TXT files are not compressed at all.

When conducting data transfer tests, use sufficiently large files to ensure reproducible results. That minimizes the effect of latency and TCP/IP slow start. Files of about 200 KB in length are sufficient for analog modem testing.

To further test your individual modem performance by downloading various types of files:

1. Use any available FTP program for the transfer—MS FTP that is part of Windows, WS_FTP (a shareware utility), Fetch for the Macintosh, or FTP in UNIX.

2. Using the FTP program, log on to a remote site (an Internet site, public FTP site, or dial-in remote access server). If you have an Internet service provider you can probably upload files to a directory on their host, or use files already available in a public FTP site.

3. Identify the file or files you want to transfer (try to select a .GIF file, a .ZIP or other compressed file, a .JPG file, and a .TXT file.) Download all files from the same location, and time the data transfer as described in Project 7-2. How much do the different file types affect modem efficiency?

PROJECT 7-4

When downloading a precompressed file (such as a .ZIP file), a 33.6 modem that connects at full speed has a maximum data rate of a little over 3 KB per second. If your downloads are much slower than that, you can determine the bottleneck as follows.

To test Internet performance problems to determine whether any bottlenecks are on the Internet or somewhere closer (the computer, modem, or the local network):

1. Download a .ZIP file from the Internet, and note the data transfer rate and the total time for the transfer.

2. Then download a .ZIP file from a local FTP or Web server. (If you're dialed into usit.net, for example, a download from www.usit.net or ftp.usit.net would be a local download.) Note the data transfer rate and total time for the transfer. If the Internet data transfer rate is significantly higher and the time significantly less, then the bottleneck may be local. If local rates/times are better, the slowdown may be on the Internet.

PROJECT 7-5

Dial-up networking is the Microsoft answer to modem communications in Windows 95/98. Although the Windows NT component operates slightly differently, the user interface and installation process is virtually the same. You'll need dial-up networking to enable modem communications to the Internet or another remote host if you're using Windows 95/98.

The figures in the following project are from Windows 95. Windows 98 screens are nearly identical.

To install and configure Windows Dial-up Networking:

1. Verify that Dial-Up Networking is installed.

   a. Choose **Start**, **Programs**, point to **Accessories**, and look for the **Dial-Up Networking** icon or entry.

If you don't see these items in your Start menu, double-click the My Computer icon, then verify that the Dial-Up Networking icon is present.

   b. If Dial-Up Networking is present, skip ahead to Step 2. If it is not present, continue with Steps c through j to install it.

    c. Click **Start**, **Settings**, **Control Panel**, and double-click the **Add/Remove Programs** icon.

    d. Click the **Windows Setup** tab.

    e. Click **Communications**.

    f. Click **Details** and make sure Dial-Up Networking is selected. (The other components are not necessary for this project.)

    g. Click **OK**.

    h. Click the **Have Disk** button.

    i. Insert your Windows 95 or 98 CD and click the **Browse** button. Select the CD. Windows 95 or 98 will install the Dial-Up Networking components.

    j. Restart your computer and continue with the next step.

2. Check your network settings.

    a. Click **Start**, **Settings**, **Control Panel** (if necessary), then double-click the **Network** icon.

    b. On the Configuration tab, the Primary Network Logon should be set to Windows Logon. If you are on a Novell network, Netware Login is appropriate. Client for Microsoft Network may cause problems and should not be selected as the Primary Network Logon.

    c. Check in the network components area for the following two components, which are necessary to use Dial-Up Networking: Dial-Up Adapter, and TCP/IP, or TCP/IP→Dial-Up Adapter. If you are missing one or both of these components, you will need to install them using the instructions in Steps 3 and 4. Otherwise, skip to Step 5.

3. Install the Dial-Up Adapter.

    a. Click the **Add** button.

    b. Double-click **Adapter**.

    c. Select **Microsoft**.

    d. Choose **Dial-Up Adapter** and click **OK**.

4. Install TCP/IP.

    a. Click **Start**, **Settings**, **Control Panel**. Open the **Network** icon.

    b. Click the **Add** button.

    c. Double-click **Protocol**.

    d. Select **Microsoft**.

    e. Choose **TCP/IP** and click **OK**.

    f. Click **TCP/IP** (or **TCP/IP →Dial-Up Adapter**) and click the **Properties** button. (In Windows 98 you may see a message box warning that changing settings could cause problems. Click **OK** to close this dialog box.)

    g. Click the **IP Address** tab. For most servers it should be set to "Obtain an IP address automatically."

7

h. Click the **WINS Configuration** tab. For most Internet services this is set to "Disable WINS resolution." If you are running on a local area network, check with your LAN administrator for the proper setting here.

i. Click the **Gateways** tab. Type **0.0.0.0** in the small box and click **Add**. If your Internet service provider or LAN administrator specifies a different setting here, use that instead.

j. Click the **DNS Configuration** tab.

k. Verify that **Enable DNS** is selected.

l. In the host text box, enter your username in all lowercase letters with no spaces.

m. The domain should be the domain to which you are connecting. If the connection is for an ISP, this is probably the ISP's domain, such as onemain.com. This should be entered in all lowercase characters with no spaces.

n. Under DNS Server Search Order, the Primary and secondary DNS should be an IP address such as 199.1.48.2. You'll need to check with your ISP or LAN administrator for the correct settings in these fields.

o. Under Domain Name Suffix Search Order, the domain should be your ISP's domain or whatever domain is specified by your ISP or LAN administrator. Enter this data in all lowercase with no spaces. Figure 7-5 shows the DNS Configuration tab of the TCP/IP Properties dialog box.

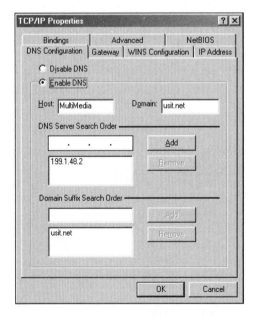

Figure 7-5   DNS Configuration tab of the TCP/IP Properties dialog box

p. Click **OK** to accept the configuration you have entered.

q. Click the **Dial-Up Adapter** and click the **Properties** button.

r. Click the **Bindings** tab. Only TCP/IP should be checked. Uncheck all other bindings.

s. Click **OK**.

t. Click **OK** again to close the Network control panel.

u. You are prompted to restart Windows for changes to take effect. Restart Windows before attempting to log in.

5. Create a new connection icon.

a. Choose **Start**, **Programs**, **Accessories** (Windows 95), or **Start**, **Programs**, **Accessories**, **Communications** (Windows 98), then **Dial-Up Networking**. If you don't see these items in your Start menu, double-click the My Computer icon, then double-click the Dial-Up Networking icon. If you have not previously installed dial-up networking, you will see a Connection Wizard that will step you through the process described here. If this happens, skip to Step 5c.

b. Double-click **Make New Connection**.

c. Type a title for the connection. Name the connection the same as your Internet service provider, or use another name that will help you identify it later. "U.S. Internet" is used in our examples.

d. Your modem should be listed in the "Select a modem" area (Win 95) or "select a device" area (Win 98). If it isn't, see the following Note.

If your modem is not listed in the Select a modem area, now is a good time to set up your modem to work with Windows 95. Go to Start, Settings, Control Panel and use the Add New Hardware Wizard. Click the Configure button. In the General tab, select your modem speed. For 14.4 modems, use 19200. For 28.8 modems, use 38400 or 57600. DO NOT select "Only connect at this speed." You can ignore the settings in the Connection tab. Click the Options tab. Make sure "Bring up terminal window after dialing" is unchecked. Click OK.

e. Click the **Next** button. Enter the dial-up access phone number you want to use and click **Next**. Click the **Finish** button. The icon for your new connection appears in the Dial-up Networking dialog box.

6. Set the properties of your dial-up connection.

a. Click the new icon you just created for the dial-up connection once, to select it.

b. Right-click and choose **Properties** from the menu. You should now see a dialog box named after your icon.

c. Click the **Server Type** tab.

d. Under Type of Dial-up Server, choose **PPP: Windows 95, Windows NT 3.5, Internet (Win 95)** or **PPP: Internet, Windows NT Server, Windows 98 (Win 98)**.

e. Verify that the advanced options are all OFF. Make sure Log on to network, Enable software compression, and Require encrypted password are not checked.

    f. Verify that TCP/IP is the only allowed network protocol. Make sure that **TCP/IP** is checked. NetBEUI and IPX/SPX Compatible should not be checked, as Figure 7-6 shows.

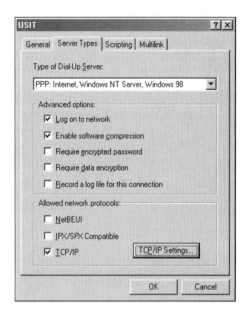

Figure 7-6   Windows 98 Server Types dialog box

    g. Click the **TCP/IP Settings** button.

    h. In the TCP/IP Settings dialog box, verify that **Server assigned IP address** is selected, and **Specify name server addresses** is selected. Primary DNS and Secondary DNS should be set to the name server addresses specified by your ISP or network administrator. **Use IP header compression** should be checked, as should **Use default gateway on remote network**. Figure 7-7 shows the completed TCP/IP Settings dialog box, with Primary and Secondary DNS addresses for U.S. Internet.

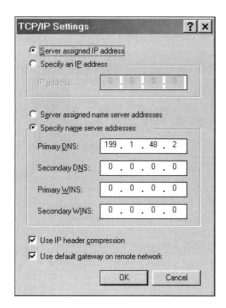

Figure 7-7   TCP/IP Settings dialog box

   i. Click **OK**. Click **OK** again to close the Properties dialog box.

   j. Set Dial-Up Networking to redial. From the **Connection** menu of the Dial-Up Networking window, choose **Settings**. Then put a checkmark in the **Redial** box and click **OK**.

7. Use these settings to connect to an ISP or other remote host.

   a. Double-click your dial-up connection icon.

   b. Enter your username and password in the provided boxes. Please note: your username and password are case sensitive. Uppercase and lowercase are not the same.

   c. Click the **Connect** button; your modem should dial and connect. Windows 95/98 should now tell you it is connected, and a timer will begin counting your time online. You can now launch your Internet software, such as a browser or e-mail software.

PROJECT 7-6

Configuring dial-up networking for Windows NT is almost identical to Windows 95/98, though the dialog boxes you use are slightly different.

To set up Windows NT for Dial-up Networking:

   1. Double-click the **My Computer** icon on your desktop, then double-click **Dial-Up Networking**.

If you have not previously installed dial-up networking, you will see a dialog box to begin the installation. You will need the Windows NT CD-ROM for these steps. Choose **Yes** when you are asked if you want RAS setup to invoke the modem installer.

2. If you see a dialog box saying that the phone book is empty, click **OK**.

3. Launching RAS (Remote Access Service) for the first time will start the Phonebook Entry Wizard. If you have run RAS before, simply click the **New** button to start the Phonebook Entry Wizard.

4. Enter a name for this connection. You should name the connection the same as your Internet service provider, or use another name that will help you understand what it is later.

5. Click the **Next** button.

6. The Server dialog box tells your system what to expect from the server it is connecting to. Put a check mark next to all of the following three options (see Figure 7-8).

   ▪ I am calling the Internet

   ▪ Send my plain text password if that's the only way to connect

   ▪ The non-Windows NT server I am calling expects me to type login information after connecting, or to know TCP/IP addresses before dialing

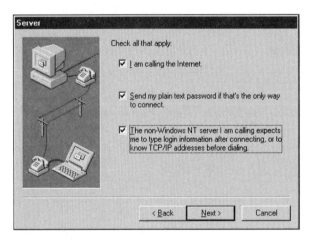

Figure 7-8   Windows NT Server dialog box

7. Click **Next**.

8. Supply a phone number for your dialup connection. Do not select Use Telephony dialing properties. Click **Next**.

9. Set the serial line protocol to **PPP** and click **Next**.

10. Under Login Script, select **Use a terminal window** and click **Next**.

11. If your ISP uses dynamic IP addressing, leave the IP address at 0.0.0.0. Otherwise, enter the IP address you were given for your workstation. Figure 7-9 shows the IP Address dialog box.

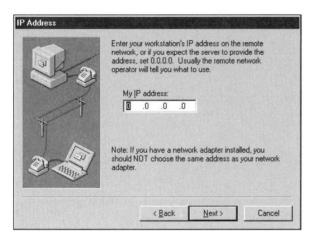

Figure 7-9   Windows NT IP Address dialog box

12. Click **Next**.

13. Set the Name Server Addresses. The DNS Server is the IP address you have been supplied for this server (the example uses the IP address of the U.S. Internet DNS server). WINS server will be left at 0.0.0.0 in most cases, as shown in Figure 7-10.

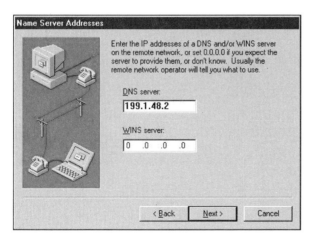

Figure 7-10   Windows NT Name Server Addresses dialog box

14. Click **Next**.

15. Click **Finish**.

16. At the main RAS connect screen, you need to supply a secondary DNS. In the Dial-Up Networking dialog box, click the **More** button, then select **Edit entry and modem properties,** as shown in Figure 7-11. The Edit Phonebook Entry dialog box appears, as shown in Figure 7-12.

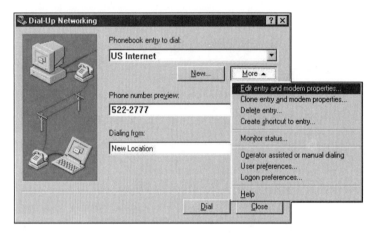

Figure 7-11   Windows NT Dial-Up Networking dialog box

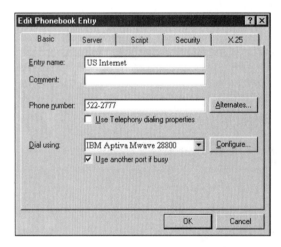

Figure 7-12   Edit Phonebook Entry dialog box

17. Click the Server tab, shown in Figure 7-13. The settings on this tab should be:

- Dial-up server type: **PPP: Windows NT, Windows 95 Plus, Internet**

- Network protocols: **TCP/IP** only

- **Enable software compression**: checked

- **Enable PPP LCP extensions**: checked

If any of these items is not checked, as in Figure 7-13, click the empty box to select the item.

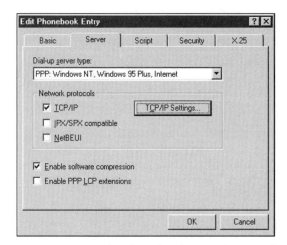

Figure 7-13   Edit Phonebook Entry Server tab

18. Click the **TCP/IP Settings** button to display the dialog box shown in Figure 7-14 on the next page. These settings are typical, but you'll need the actual figures from your ISP or other host:

- Server assigned IP address (unless you have been assigned a static IP address)

- Specify name server addresses

- Primary DNS: **199.1.48.2** (for U.S. Internet)

- Secondary DNS: **199.1.54.4** (for U.S. Internet)

- Primary WINS: **0.0.0.0** (not used)

- Secondary WINS: **0.0.0.0** (not used)

- **Use IP header compression**: checked

- **Use default gateway on remote network**: checked

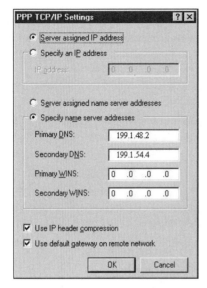

Figure 7-14   PPP TCP/IP Settings dialog box

19. Click **OK** to close all dialog boxes.

20. Click **OK** to close the main RAS connect screen.

PROJECT 7-7

To view or change your TCP/IP settings on the Mac:

    1. Choose **Apple Menu**, **Control Panels** and open the **TCP/IP** Control Panel, shown in Figure 7-15.

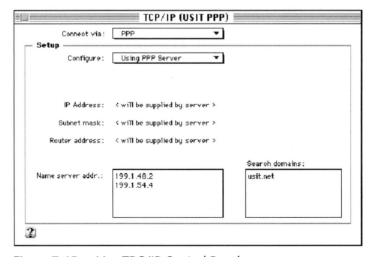

Figure 7-15   Mac TPC/IP Control Panel

2. There are several modes used in TCP/IP that affect the appearance of the Control Panel. The screenshot in Figure 7-15 shows the Basic mode. To change the user mode, select **User Mode** from the **Edit** menu (see Figure 7-16) to display the User Mode dialog box shown in Figure 7-17.

Figure 7-16   Use the Edit menu to change the user mode

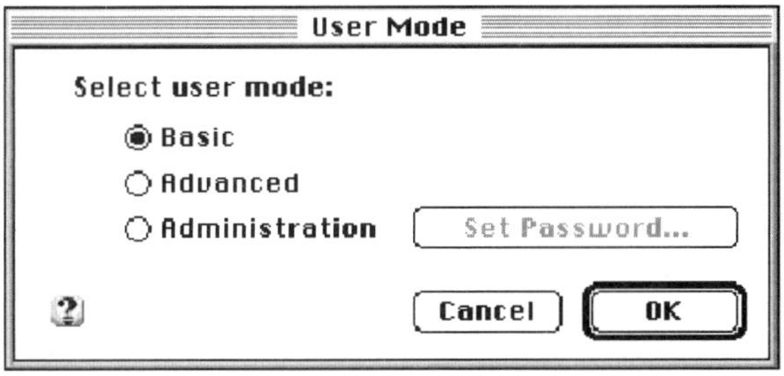

7

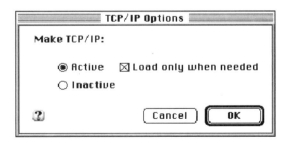

Figure 7-17   User Mode dialog box

3. Select the **Advanced** user mode and click **OK**. The TCP/IP dialog box will now show an Options button.

4. If the Mac tries to dial in every time it's restarted, you probably have "Load Only When Needed" unchecked in the Options dialog box. Click **Options** on the TCP/IP dialog box to display the TCP/IP Options dialog box shown in Figure 7-18. Put a check mark next to **Load only when needed**, and the problem will go away.

Figure 7-18   TCP/IP Options dialog box

5. The Connect via settings on the TCP/IP dialog box can be one of four things (though you may not see all options in all versions of Mac OS):

- Use "MacPPP" with FreePPP 1.05 or MacPPP 2.5

- Use "FreePPP" for use with FreePPP 2.5 and later

- Use "PPP" with Apple's PPP (part of 7.6 and later)

- Use "Ethernet" for computers attached to a router

All other settings should be as shown for server-assigned IP addresses. For static addresses used with an Ethernet-based ISDN router, change Configure to "Manually" and enter the correct numbers for IP, Subnet, and Router.

PROJECT 7-8

Under Linux, the serial ports on the PC are automatically set up for modem use. All you have to do is connect a modem that has been configured. When done, you can dial in to the machine with any terminal emulator. When you do, you will see the login prompt and you will be in business. The *getty* provided with Linux will self-detect the modem speed and parameters.

In order to complete this exercise and effectively configure network interfaces, you must have root privileges.

To set up a dial-out interface on Linux for use with the PPP protocol:

1. Launch the Network Configuration tool: type **netcfg** at the command prompt.

2. To add a PPP interface, select the **Interface** button.

3. Click **Add**. An Interface type dialog box appears.

4. Choose **PPP**.

5. In the Create PPP Interface box, enter the phone number, username and password you want to use.

6. Select the **Use PAP Authentication** option.

7. Click the **Customize** button to select the communication port and settings you wish to use.

8. Click **Save**.

PROJECT 7-9

In order to complete this exercise and effectively configure network interfaces, you must have root privileges.

To set up and configure a modem under Solaris:

1. Launch the Service Access Facility manager (SAF), which is part of the admintool, an X Window-based tool. From the command line, enter **admintool**. The Admintool window appears.

2. From the **Browse** menu, select **Serial** ports. The list of serial ports is shown.

3. Select one of the ports, then select **Edit**, **Modify** from the menu to change the settings for that port. The Modify serial window appears.

4. Click the **Expert** button to reveal all options.

5. From the Template list, choose **Modem**.

6. Check **Service Enable**.

7. In the options section, select **Initialize Only**, **Bi-Directional** and **Software Carrier**.

8. For normal dial-in operation on this port, set the service setting to **/usr/bin/login**, and the streams modules setting to **idterm,ttcompat**.

9. Click **OK**, and you are ready to accept incoming calls on your modem.

The command string sent to a modem for it to work correctly under Solaris is AT&F&C1&D2E0V0Q0S0=2&W. Without this setting, the operating system will not work correctly with the modem! If no auto-answer is desired, the S0=2 portion may be left off.

CASE PROJECT

1. Your company's small computer network uses a networked modem server, allowing multiple machines on the network to access a single modem to connect to online services. Although the modem is a modern 56 Kbps device, you consistently notice data transfer rates of less than 30 Kbps.

   a. Describe a process for testing this modem to determine where the slowdown is occurring. Based on just the data given and the information in this chapter, where do you surmise the problem is? Can you prove it?

   b. This modem connection uses a single analog telephone line for data connections. What alternative hardware and connection options might you investigate to ensure that these networked computers will achieve higher data transfer rates?

CHAPTER EIGHT

NETWORK CONNECTIVITY

Networking is really an extension of the desire to immediately share all kinds of information: word processed documents, graphs and charts, pictures, maps, x-rays, electronic mail, and full motion video. Through networks, a physician in New York City can help in diagnosing a patient who is with another physician in Los Angeles. Through networks, an engineer can coordinate the design of a new supersonic airplane by electronically sharing design diagrams with other engineers working on that project in the same building. Students now use networks to obtain assignments from teachers and to submit their completed assignments. Other students take entire classes or programs of study by using the Internet.

AFTER READING THIS CHAPTER AND COMPLETING THE EXERCISES YOU WILL BE ABLE TO:

- Explain basic networking theory such as network topologies, packaging data to transport, and how devices connect to a network

- Describe network transport and communication protocols and determine which protocols are used in specific computer operating systems

- Explain how bridging and routing are used on networks

- Explain LANs and WANs

- Describe how network and workstation operating systems are used for remote networking

As you learned in the last chapter, modems provide one of the first and most basic ways to build a network. Today, there are many new and evolving options to connect computers. Strong interest in setting up computers to communicate has spurred the development of an array of network technologies. In this chapter, you learn basic networking theory and how computers communicate through network protocols. You also learn how information is forwarded from one network to another. You discover the difference between local and wide area networks and you learn how telecommuters remotely access their work from home. Most important, you learn about networking features that are included in operating systems. These features make it possible for even the most diverse combination of operating systems to be partners in shared network communications.

BASIC NETWORKING THEORY

A **network** is composed of communications media, such as communications cable, that is used to link computers, printers, disk storage, CD-ROM arrays, and network communications equipment. The basic principle of networking is similar to connecting telephones for communications. In a telecommunications system, telephones are located in homes and businesses. Each telephone can communicate with other telephones by linking to the local main cable or trunk line that is on nearby telephone poles or run underground. For example, in a single neighborhood, 50 homes may connect to one trunk line. That trunk line goes to a local telephone switch that connects to other trunk lines throughout a city or town. The main components of a telephone system are telephones, telephone communication equipment like switches, and cable that links telephones and switches.

Most of us understand the basics of telephone communications because we have used them all of our lives. The basics of networking can be understood in a similar way, because computer networks mimic the principles of telephone systems. To understand networking, think of the computer as similar to the telephone in that each computer is linked to the network by cable, which is similar to telephone cable. The equipment between computers is similar to a switch or central hub that connects one telephone to another (see Figure 8-1).

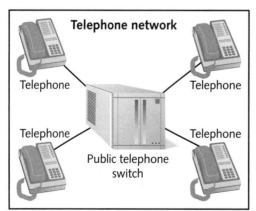
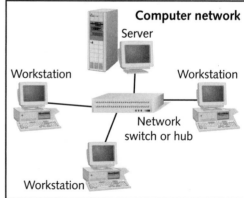

Figure 8-1   Telephone and computer networks compared

The hardware components of a computer network are computers, printers, communications cable, and internetworking devices, such as bridges, routers, and hubs (these devices are discussed later in this chapter). Computer networks also have software components consisting of client and server network operating systems. Windows 95 and Windows 98 are examples of client operating systems. A **client operating system** is one that enables a workstation to run applications and process information locally, and to communicate with other computers and devices over the network. A **workstation** is a computer that has a CPU and that can run applications locally or obtain applications and files from another computer on the network.

Sometimes the term *workstation* is confused with the term *terminal*. The difference is that a **terminal** has no CPU or local storage for running programs independently. The main use of a terminal is to access a mainframe or minicomputer and to run programs on that computer.

A **network operating system (NOS)** is one that enables the coordination of network activities and the sharing of resources—network communications, shared printing, shared access to files, and shared access to software, for example. Windows NT and Novell NetWare are examples of NOSs. A **server** is a computer running a NOS and which provides resources, such as shared files and programs, that are accessed by clients.

8

REASONS FOR A NETWORK

Networks were invented for three interrelated reasons: to share resources, to save money, and to increase productivity. Most important, networks allow organizations to save money by sharing resources. For example, consider an accounting office in which there are 35 people, each with his or her own computer. Each person in the office uses word processing software, spreadsheets, databases, and accounting software. Also, each needs to print documents and to regularly back up files. Purchasing individual software packages and then installing each one on every office computer can be expensive and time consuming. Also, purchasing a printer for each computer is expensive, especially when each person does not need to use a printer continuously; and purchasing 35 tape drives to back up important information on each computer in the office is another expense. Buying a printer for each computer user was a particularly common practice when PCs were introduced in the days before networks were common.

By installing a network, this office can save money by sharing resources (see Figure 8-2 on the next page). For example, a server with one or two printers and tape drives might be installed in a central location. One or two additional printers could be installed on the network in other locations and those printer operations coordinated through the server. Software installations are made easier, because a site license can be purchased so that an original copy of the software is placed on the server and each user installs the software to her or his workstation over the network. The advantage is that the software can be configured on the server so that it is installed in the same way on each workstation. Another advantage is that site licensing is often less expensive than purchasing individual software packages for each user.

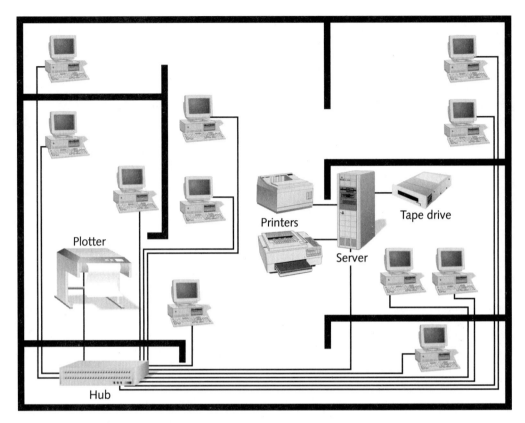

Figure 8-2   Sharing resources in an office

Productivity is another reason for having networks. Consider the same accounting office before the installation of a network. Each time an accountant needs to share a spreadsheet with another accountant, he or she makes a copy on a floppy disk and hand carries it to the other accountant. This is a process that we now call "sneakernet." Each act of sharing requires several time-consuming steps:

1. Finding and formatting the floppy disk

2. Copying the spreadsheet to the disk

3. Leaving your desk and walking to the other person's desk, which is perhaps on another floor or in another building

4. Taking time for conversation with the other person as you deliver the disk

5. Walking back to your desk and possibly having more conversations with other employees along the way

Without a network, sharing one spreadsheet with one other person might take 10 minutes to an hour. If you need to share the file with several people, the process takes even longer. In the past, organizations sometimes hired an individual whose job it was to carry disks with shared files and printouts to other people within the organization. With a network, your productivity is increased significantly without the need to hire an extra person. All you need to do is to take a minute or two to copy the spreadsheet to a shared location on your workstation or on a server. If you need to share a printout as well, you just send it to a network printer in a location near the person who needs it.

Electronic mail (e-mail) is another example of how networking can increase productivity. With e-mail, you can reach someone on the first try. You also can attach a file, such as a word processing document or spreadsheet, so that the recipient has it right away. If you need to contact several people, you can do so by sending one e-mail to a previously established address list or to multiple recipients. Many organizations schedule meetings through e-mail and they use it to send announcements automatically.

Electronic commerce is another network application that increases productivity. For example, computer companies such as Compaq and Dell can take thousands of orders a day through a Web site, as well as offer automated support or order information. The electronic capability to offer automated information saves time for customer service and support people, making them more productive.

Another growing area for networks is electronic conferencing. Advances in network technology coupled with advances in audio and video technologies enable organizations to hold conferences among sites in different parts of the country or around the world. For example, a company that has manufacturing plants in three different sites can use a network so that members of project teams at each site can confer without leaving town. Electronic conferencing can save thousands of dollars in travel and employee time.

THE DEVELOPMENT OF NETWORK OPERATING SYSTEMS

Novell NetWare was one of the first network operating systems, initially demonstrated in 1982 at the National Computer Conference as a groundbreaking PC networking system. Windows 3.1, released in 1992, was one of the first Windows-based operating systems with network capabilities, enabling it to connect to NetWare, Microsoft, and other networks. (In 1992, Microsoft added basic workgroup capabilities to an updated version of Windows 3.1.) In 1993, Windows 3.11, also called Windows for Workgroups (WFW), constituted another significant step up in Windows network connectivity because it added peer-to-peer networking, expanded workgroup capabilities, and provided more support to connect to servers. Peer-to-peer networking enables basic PCs or workstations to share resources, such as files with other computers. Workgroups (predefined groups of member computers) enable the ability to limit resource sharing on the basis of group membership. Windows 95 represents still another major step into networking because it expanded peer-to-peer networking and has the ability to connect to more kinds of networks. Although Windows 98 on the surface looks similar to Windows 95, it adds even more networking features such as the ability to connect to very high-speed networks.

Representing a different Windows operating system track, Windows NT 3.1 was released just a little later than Windows 3.1, but Windows NT 3.1 was intended for industrial-strength networking from the beginning. The server version of Windows NT 3.1 was called

Windows NT 3.1 Advanced Server and was targeted to compete with NetWare. In 1994, Microsoft renamed the two versions of Windows NT to Windows NT Workstation and Windows NT Server and considerably enhanced the network capabilities of the Server version. The dawning of the millennium has brought two new names for Windows NT: Windows 2000 Server and Windows 2000 Professional (Workstation). Besides the NetWare and Windows-based operating systems, there are several others designed for networking as follows:

- UNIX
- Banyan Vines
- Pathworks
- LAN Manager

Three of these operating systems have not been mentioned before in the text: Banyan Vines, Pathworks, and LAN Manager. All three are server operating systems that are currently in use on networks and that run on small to mid-sized computers. Banyan Vines is supported by Banyan Systems, and Pathworks is supported by Digital Equipment Corporation (now merged with Compaq). LAN Manager was an early server operating system developed by Microsoft prior to Windows NT Server and that is still in use on some networks. Along with NetWare and UNIX, all three operating systems were contenders for network server dominance at the beginning of the 1990s.

THE BASICS OF NETWORK TOPOLOGIES

Networks are designed in three basic patterns: bus, ring, and star. Each of these is called a network topology. A **topology** is the design of the network as if you were looking at it from above in a helicopter, or following the path information takes when it goes from one computer to another. (You can practice identifying network topologies in Hands-on Project 8-1.)

A network that uses a bus topology is designed like a climbing rope with knots tied along the way for a foothold. There is a beginning and end to the rope and junctures along the way for your feet. When you climb up the rope you go from end-to-end, passing through each juncture. Like the climbing rope, a bus topology has two ending points. Each ending point has a terminator to keep the electronic data signal from reflecting back along the path it just traveled. Also like the knots in the rope, the bus topology network communications cable has junctures at which computers are attached. A data-carrying signal is transmitted onto the cable from the source computer and it goes through all junctures on the bus. When the destination computer receives the signal, it picks it up from the cable and then codes it into data. Figure 8-3 shows a simple bus network.

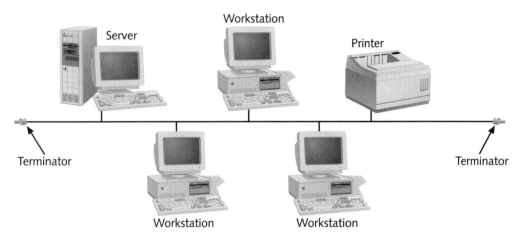

Figure 8-3   Bus topology

A ring topology is one in which the data-carrying signal goes from station to station around the ring, until it reaches the target destination. There is no beginning or ending point and so there are no terminators (see Figure 8-4).

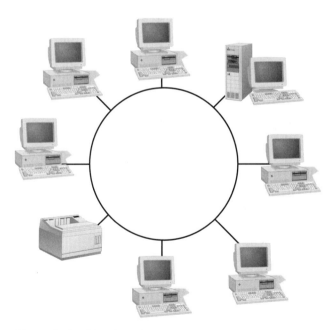

Figure 8-4   Ring topology

The star topology is one in which there is a hub in the middle with cable segments coming out of the hub in all directions, as Figure 8-5 on the next page shows. The hub sends the signal onto each segment, which has a computer at the end. Every segment is terminated inside the hub at one end and inside the computer at the other end (when it is used for Ethernet communications discussed later in this chapter). The star topology was derived from the topology most frequently used in telephone networks. It is the oldest communications topology and has evolved into the most popular network topology, because it has the most flexibility in terms of providing for future growth and in adding high-speed networking capability.

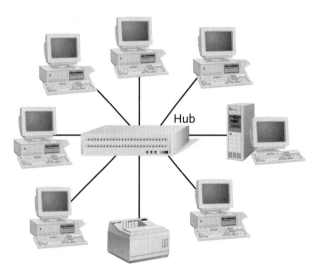

Figure 8-5   Star topology

Some hubs, called **passive hubs**, just pass the signal onto a segment without modifying the signal in any way. The disadvantage in using a passive hub is that the signal grows weaker each time it goes through the hub to the next segment. Networks that use passive hubs support fewer workstations, because the signal eventually becomes too weak for reception. Networks that use **active hubs** support more computers because the signal is amplified to its original strength each time it goes through the hub.

PACKETS, FRAMES, AND CELLS

Each computer or network device translates data into individual units and then places the units onto the network cable. For example, if you obtain a file from a server and transport it to your workstation, the file is broken into hundreds of small data units and transmitted a unit at a time from the server to your workstation. Each data unit is called a **packet** or a **frame**. These terms are sometimes used interchangeably, but they are not the same. Both consist of data and transmission control information contained in a header that is appended to the front of the data. The difference is that a packet contains routing information that can be read by specialized devices that are able to forward packets to specific networks. The actual data is placed after the header information and is followed by a footer or trailer that enables detection of a transmission error. Figure 8-6 shows a basic packet format. (Hands-on Projects 8-2 and 8-3 show how to view the computers connected to a network and the frame (packet) activity on a network.)

Figure 8-6   Basic packet format

Older networks transmit at speeds of 4 Mbps, 10 Mbps, and 16 Mbps. Newer networks transmit at 100 Mbps or consist of segments that transmit at 10 Mbps or 100 Mbps. Network **backbones**, which are segments that join main networks, typically run at 100 Mbps or higher. A backbone might join networks on individual floors in a building or link a LAN in one building to a network in another building.

Some networks require extra capacity for high-speed transmissions of over 100 Mbps, such as networks that have a high proportion of multimedia applications or on which large files (1 MB and more) are regularly transmitted. On these networks, data may be transported in cells. A **cell** is a data unit designed for high-speed communications; it has a control header and a fixed-length payload (see Figure 8-7). The **payload** is that portion of a frame, packet, or cell that contains the actual data, which might be a portion of an e-mail message or of a word processed file. One element of the cell header is path information that enables the cell to take the route through the network that is most appropriate to the type of data carried within the cell. For example, a large graphics file that holds a medical x-ray might take a different network path than a cell transmission containing streaming video for a movie clip.

Figure 8-7   Basic cell format

The exact format of a frame, packet, and cell is determined by the type of protocol used on a network. A **protocol** is a set of formatting guidelines for network communications, like a language, so that the information sent by one computer can be accurately decoded by another. Protocols also coordinate network communications so that data is transported in an orderly fashion, preventing chaos when two or more computers want to transmit at the same time. A network may use several different protocols, depending on the types of devices that are connected and on the NOS (protocols are discussed later in this chapter).

CONNECTING TO A NETWORK

Computers and internetworking devices connect to a network through a network interface card (NIC). A NIC is usually a card that goes into a computer's expansion slot or that is built into a network device or a computer. The NIC is equipped with a connector that enables it to attach to the network communications cable. Each NIC has a unique hexadecimal address, called a device address or physical address, that identifies it to the network. This address is used much like a postal address, because it enables a computer (the source) to create a frame or packet and send it to a specific destination computer (see Figure 8-8).

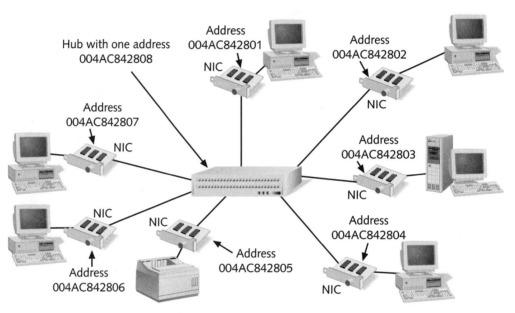

Figure 8-8   Devices on a network with unique physical addresses

A NIC is several devices built into one card. First, it is a transmitter and receiver (or transceiver) that can transmit a signal onto the cable and pick up a signal to decode. It also is a connection interface that matches the type of cable used on a network (twisted-pair or coaxial cable, for example). Finally, it contains computer circuits and chips that provide a home to software logic that translates data into packets and frames and then sends the translated data onto the cable as an electrical or optical signal. Some NICs also transform data into radio frequency communications, called packet radio, for wireless networks. The software logic consists of one or more programs called firmware, because it resides in a programmable chip on the card. Communication between the operating system and its NIC, like communication between the operating system and various input, output, and storage devices, is controlled by driver software written by the manufacturer of the device (in this case the NIC). Drivers are installed as part of the firmware on the NIC and into the operating system on the computer when the NIC is installed. (Try Hands-on Project 8-10 to build a network cable for connecting to a NIC.)

One important step related to installing a NIC is to make sure you have the most recent software drivers for that NIC and for the operating system that is running on its host computer, such as NetWare, Windows NT, UNIX, or Windows 98. Network communications are complex, and early versions of NIC drivers often contain errors that impede the NIC's performance. Most manufacturers offer the latest versions of drivers on their Internet Web sites.

NETWORKING PROTOCOLS

Network communications are made possible through protocols. Protocols are used for many types of network communications, including the following:

- Coordinating transport of packets and frames among network devices

- Encapsulating data and communication control information

- Providing communications to accomplish a specific function, such as enabling the destination computer to tell the source computer to slow its transmitting speed because it is too fast for the destination computer

- Enabling communications over a long distance network, such as the Internet

- Enabling remote users to dial into networks

Two of the most important types of protocols are those that coordinate transport and those that communicate and coordinate how data is encapsulated and addressed.

TRANSPORT PROTOCOLS

The commonly used transport protocols are Ethernet and token ring. Ethernet is in more installations than token ring, because there are more network equipment options for it and because modern Ethernet network designs are most easily expanded for high-speed networking. Token ring is used because it is reliable and because network problems were initially easier to troubleshoot in token ring networks than in the early Ethernet networks.

Improved design options and equipment now make the complexity of troubleshooting Ethernet problems on a par with troubleshooting token ring problems.

Both Ethernet and token ring are defined as part of the networking standards established by the Institute of Electrical and Electronics Engineers (IEEE) through its 802 standards committee. The 802 standards are followed by network administrators and manufacturers to ensure consistent network communications and the ability for one network to connect to another.

Ethernet

In **Ethernet** communications, only one station on the network transmits at a given moment. If two or more stations transmit at the same time, frames will collide. The transmission control method used by Ethernet is called Carrier Sense Multiple Access with Collision Detection (CSMA/CD). In CSMA/CD, the NICs of computers and devices check the network communications cable for a carrier signal that contains an encoded frame. If the device's NIC detects a carrier signal, and if the NIC decodes its own device address within the frame, it will forward that packet to its firmware for further decoding. If the frame does not contain its device address, then the NIC does not process the signal any further.

When the detected carrier signal is twice (or more) the strength of a normal carrier signal, this indicates at least two network stations have transmitted at the same time. In this situation, a collision has occurred and a transmitting station sends a "jam" signal to warn all other stations. After the jam signal is sent, every station waits a different amount of time before any attempts to transmit again. The amount of time that a particular station waits is determined by generating a random number for the wait period, on the assumption that each station will generate a different random number. If two stations generate the same random number and transmit simultaneously, then the collision recovery process starts again.

There are two varieties of Ethernet protocol communications: the IEEE 802.3 standard and Ethernet II. Both are nearly identical, but Ethernet II uses a slightly different frame format for modern network communications. In IEEE 802.3 and in Ethernet II, frames contain a header that has control information along with source and destination addressing. The data portion of both frame types contains from 576 to 12,208 bytes. Also, both frame formats contain a frame check sequence field as a trailer that is used to alert the receiving station when a transmission error has occurred, by showing that some portion of the received frame contents is not the same as when the frame was sent. If a transmission error is detected, the frame in error is retransmitted.

Networks that use Ethernet are designed in a bus topology, or in a star topology in which the internetworking devices simulate a logical bus. Ethernet bus-star networks are very common in modern network design because they are easier to troubleshoot and to expand for high-speed networking than simple bus networks.

Originally, the speed of Ethernet was 10 Mbps (megabits per second). Newer Ethernet standards now include 100 Mbps and 1 Gbps versions that are called Fast Ethernet and Gigabit Ethernet. Fast Ethernet is becoming commonplace and most NICs are currently designed to handle either 10 or 100 Mbps communications. Gigabit Ethernet is finding acceptance on busy network backbones in which even Fast Ethernet does not provide enough capacity.

All versions of Ethernet are compatible with popular network operating systems such as:

- UNIX
- NetWare
- Windows NT and Windows 2000
- Windows 3.1x

- Windows 95 and Windows 98

- Macintosh

- Banyan Vines

- Pathworks

Token Ring

In most versions of **token ring**, only one network station transmits at a time. The sequence of frame and packet transmissions is controlled by the use of a specialized frame, called a token. A token without data is transmitted around the network until it is captured by a station that wants to transmit. When the token is captured by a station, no other station can transmit until the station that has the token is finished (see Figure 8-9). The transmitting station packages data inside the token, so that part of the token is used as the frame header to indicate the beginning of a frame, and part is used as the frame trailer to indicate the last sequence of bytes in the frame.

8

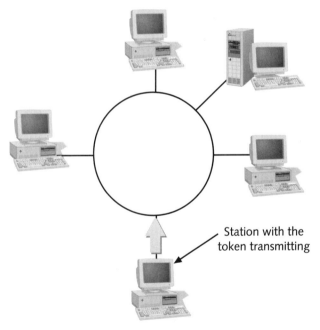

Station with the token transmitting

Figure 8-9   Station with the token in token ring

As the name suggests, token ring networks use the ring topology. Thus, the frame is transmitted from station to station around the ring, until it reaches the destination station. The destination station removes the frame from the network and decodes the frame's contents for local use. It also replicates the frame back onto the network to be forwarded around the ring to the sender, but changes two bits inside the frame indicating that the frame was successfully received and decoded at the destination.

On most token ring networks, the first station that is recognized as connected becomes the active monitor; all other stations are standby monitors. The active monitor is charged with assessing transmissions to make sure that a token frame exists, that the timing of packet transmissions is accurate, and that standby monitors are responding. Each standby monitor periodically transmits a message to show that it is present and available to take over for the active monitor, if it fails. If there is no token, the active monitor creates a new one and places it on the network. If the active monitor ceases to function or if there is no response from a standby monitor, the token ring network goes into a beaconing condition, which is started when a station sends a beacon frame to warn there is a problem. No tokens containing a data payload can be sent until the beaconing condition is solved, such as by assigning a new active monitor.

Older token ring networks transmit at 4 Mbps and newer networks transmit at 16 Mbps. IBM has recently developed 100 Mbps fast token ring technology that is compatible with existing 4 Mbps and 16 Mbps networks. Fast token ring is off to a slow start in the market and some manufacturers have discontinued production of internetworking devices that support it.

Token ring is compatible with the same mainstream network operating systems as used with Ethernet, including:

- UNIX
- NetWare
- Windows NT and Windows 2000
- .Windows 3.1x
- Windows 95 and Windows 98
- Macintosh
- Banyan Vines
- Pathworks

Implementing a Transport Protocol in an Operating System

A transport protocol is interfaced with an operating system through three elements: a network driver specification built into the operating system, a NIC, and a NIC driver. Network operating systems are built so that they offer special elements that programmers call "hooks" in the operating system kernel (program code) to enable the operating system to interface with a network. For example, Microsoft has designed the Network Device Interface Specification (NDIS) and Windows-based NDIS drivers for this purpose. Similarly, NetWare uses the Open Datalink Interface (ODI) and ODI drivers.

 One way to think of networking "hooks" in an operating system and how a NIC driver links into those hooks is by using the analogy of a lock and key. The combined hooks are like a lock and the NIC driver software is similar to a key that is specially cut to exactly match the unique configuration of the lock.

When you set up an operating system to work on an Ethernet or token ring network, the first step is to purchase an Ethernet or token ring NIC for the computer running the operating system. The NIC cable interface must also match the type of cable used on the network. After the NIC is installed in an open expansion slot in the computer, the next step is to boot the operating system and install the NIC driver software, which links the NIC into the network computing hooks in the kernel. For example, if you install an Ethernet NIC in a computer running Windows 98, then you must obtain an NDIS compatible driver for that NIC that is written for Windows 98 Ethernet communications.

After the NIC setup is complete and the computer is connected to the network, the operating system, NIC, and driver handle the work of converting data created at the computer to an Ethernet or token ring format for transport over the network. The same three elements also enable the computer to receive Ethernet or token ring packets or frames and convert them to data that the computer can interpret.

COMMUNICATIONS PROTOCOLS

The development of communications protocols (the protocols that carry data between two communicating stations and that are encapsulated in Ethernet or token ring transport protocols) has been interrelated to the network operating system in which they are used. For example, Novell NetWare grew out of experiments with network operating systems that began in the early 1980s and became the first true network operating system. The **Internet Packet Exchange (IPX)** protocol was developed to enable a NetWare file server to communicate with its client workstations. Also, in 1982, researchers implemented and combined two protocols for use on the Advanced Research Projects Agency network, ARPANET, which was the long distance network that set the foundation for the Internet. The ARPANET protocols that are now used worldwide over the Internet are **Transmission Control Protocol** (TCP) and **Internet Protocol** (IP). (Since these are usually used together, the combination is called **TCP/IP**.) Because many of the original ARPANET servers ran UNIX, this operating system was quickly adapted to employ TCP/IP. Two other important communication protocols are NetBIOS Extended User Interface (NetBEUI), a protocol developed for Microsoft networks, and AppleTalk, developed for Macintosh networks.

IPX

IPX is a protocol developed by Novell and modeled after the Xerox Network System (XNS) protocol. Xerox created XNS for Ethernet communications. Novell adopted XNS to use with NetWare and called the end product IPX. Although it was developed in the early 1980s, IPX is still widely used, because NetWare is one of the most commonly implemented network server operating systems. One reason IPX has survived is that it is tailored for NetWare environments and it can be routed, which means that it can transport packets to specific networks as designated in the packet addressing information.

IPX encapsulates data and transports it within a host transport protocol format, Ethernet or token ring for example. IPX is a connectionless protocol, which means that it does minimal checking to ensure that a packet reaches its destination, leaving this task for the Ethernet or token ring communications layer within the packet. When there is a need for more reliable data transport, such as for data out from a database, an application running via NetWare can use **Sequence Packet Exchange (SPX)**, a protocol that provides connection-oriented communications. The limitation of IPX/SPX is that it is a "chatty" protocol because servers and clients configured for IPX frequently broadcast their presence on the network, even when there are no requests to exchange actual data or information.

IPX works with other specialized service and NetWare protocols as follows:

- *Link Support Layer (LSL):* Enables one NIC to transmit and receive multiple protocols, such as IPX and TCP/IP

- *NetWare Core Protocol (NCP):* Used to access applications between a server and its client

- *NetWare Link Services Protocol (NLSP):* Enables routing information to be added to an IPX packet

- *Routing Information Protocol (RIP):* Enables a NetWare server to build tables of routing information about the location of particular network stations

- *Service Advertising Protocol (SAP):* Enables NetWare client computers to identify servers and the services offered by each server

IPX is the default communications protocol in all versions of NetWare up through version 5. The default protocol in NetWare 5 is TCP/IP, although it still supports IPX.

NetBEUI

NetBEUI was introduced in the early 1990s as the main protocol for LAN Manager, a network server operating system developed by Microsoft and IBM and the forerunner of Windows NT Server. NetBEUI became a widely implemented communications protocol as the use of Windows NT Server on small networks grew through the mid-1990s. This protocol continues to play an important role in all versions of Windows NT Server up through version 4. The role of NetBEUI in Windows 2000 Server (formerly Windows NT Server version 5) is diminished in favor of using the more versatile TCP/IP protocol.

NetBEUI was developed from the **Network Basic Input/Output System (NetBIOS)**, which is a technique to interface software with network services. NetBIOS also provides a naming service for computers on Microsoft networks. For example, if you view all of the computers on a Microsoft network that contains Windows NT servers and Windows 95 and Windows 98 workstations, you will notice that each has a unique name, such as a nickname of the user, an abbreviation of the user's title, or a name that is symbolic to the user, like Tophat or Sparrow. (You can view NetBIOS names in Hands-on Project 8-2.)

 NetBIOS should not be confused with a protocol. It acts as a software interface only, providing a way for an application to export data to a network service, such as linking data in a word processed document to a network mail service that attaches the document to an e-mail.

NetBEUI is designed to be used on networks of under 200 stations and is well suited for Microsoft networks. It is particularly compatible with applications that use NetBIOS and with computers that run Microsoft operating systems, such as Windows NT, Windows 3.1x, Windows 95, and Windows 98. Another advantage of NetBEUI is that later versions of this protocol can handle nearly limitless communication sessions (earlier versions were limited to 254). Thus the limit on the number of clients that can be connected to a Windows NT server using NetBEUI is dependent on the server hardware and network resources and not on the protocol. Other advantages of NetBEUI are:

- Low use of memory resources

- Quick transport of information on small networks

- Strong error detection and recovery

- Relatively easy configuration in the host operating system

An important limitation of NetBEUI is that it is not designed to carry routing information, which means it is not a good choice for medium and large sized networks. When it is used on these types of networks, it must be sent to every portion of the network, instead of being limited to only specific smaller networks within the larger network scheme. This characteristic creates unneeded traffic on a medium or large network that may already be bursting with high traffic. Figure 8-10 illustrates how NetBEUI is flooded to all networks within a large network setup when the goal is to reach only Station A.

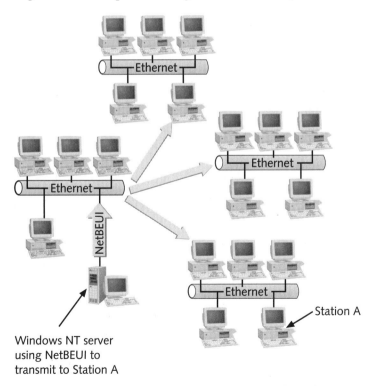

Windows NT server
using NetBEUI to
transmit to Station A

Figure 8-10 NetBEUI flooding all networks within a large network setup

TCP/IP

TCP/IP is one of the oldest protocols, initially developed for long distance networking on ARPANET and now used on most medium- to large-scale networks. One of the strongest influences on TCP/IP use has been the growth of the Internet. UNIX has always used TCP/IP as its main network communications protocol. NetWare version 5, Windows 2000 Server, and Windows 2000 Professional also have adopted TCP/IP as the protocol of choice. Besides these server operating systems, TCP/IP is used to network IBM mainframe computers that run the Multiple Virtual Storage (MVS) operating system and Digital Equipment Corporation (Compaq) computers that run the Virtual Memory System (VMS). TCP/IP is also compatible with the following operating systems:

- Windows 3.1 and 3.11
- Windows 95
- Windows 98
- Windows NT 3.0, 3.5, 3.51, and 4.0
- Macintosh
- Banyan Vines

TCP was developed for extremely reliable point-to-point communications between computers on the same network. This protocol establishes communication sessions among applications on two communicating computers, making sure there is a mutually agreeable "window" of transmission characteristics. Some of the communication functions performed by TCP are:

- Establishes the communication session between two computers
- Ensures that data transmissions are accurate
- Encapsulates, transmits, and receives the payload data
- Closes the communication session between two computers

The IP portion of TCP/IP is used to make sure that a frame or packet reaches the intended destination. IP performs the following complementary functions with TCP:

- Handles packet addressing
- Handles packet routing
- Fragments packets as needed for transport across different types of networks
- Provides simple packet error detection in conjunction with the more thorough error detection provided by TCP

IP addressing uses the dotted decimal notation that consists of four 8-bit binary numbers (octets) separated by periods. The format is as follows: 10000001.00000101.00001010.00000001, which converts to the decimal value, 129.5.10.1. Part of the address designates a unique identifier for a network, called the network identifier (NET_ID). For example, a school or a corporation will have its own NET_ID, which distinguishes its network from all others. Another part of the address is the host identifier (HOST_ID) that distinguishes a computer or network device from any other computer or device on a network. Some network administrators also designate a **subnet mask** within the IP address that enables them to uniquely identify smaller networks or subnetworks within their larger network setup.

For example, using a subnet mask enables the network administrator at a university to limit how much network traffic goes to certain networks on campus as a way to reduce congestion and to implement network security. In Figure 8-11, implementing a subnet mask enables a packet to be sent from one network on a campus to Station A on another network without flooding all networks with traffic. The exact allocation of the IP address into NET_ID, HOST_ID, and subnet masks depends on factors unique to each network such as its size, the number of computers connected to it, and the overall design of the network.

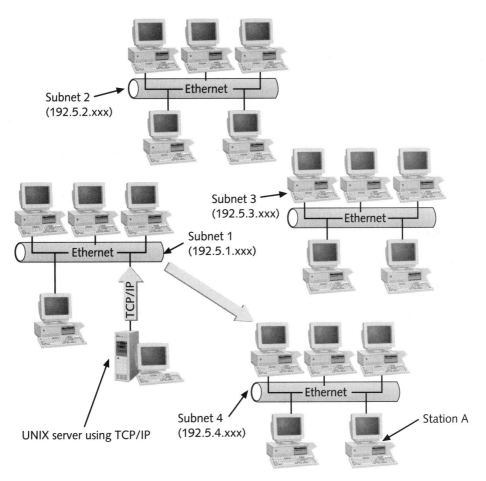

Figure 8-11   Using TCP/IP subnet masks

Consider a university's IP address of 129.72.22.124 in which the first half (first two octets) of the address is the NET_ID and the last octet is the HOST_ID. Also, the first three octets are used to specify the subnet. In this address, the 129.72 identifies the university (NET_ID), 129.72.22 identifies the subnet on which the station is located within the university, such as the network in the English building, and 124 is the HOST_ID of a particular computer on that subnet. In this designation, the subnet is useful in several ways. One is that data, such as e-mail intended for English faculty, can be directed to the English building subnet so that it does not saturate other parts of a busy university network. Another advantage is that the English department can set up its own private Web site containing salary, budget, and human resources information and limit access to only those having the subnet as part of their IP address.

 By Internet convention, an IP address in which the first octet translates to a decimal number between 128 and 191 signifies a medium to large network consisting of between 257 to 65,536 stations.

Computers and devices on a network that use IP addressing actually have two addresses: a physical address and an IP address. The use of two addresses provides better insurance that a packet will reach the right destination while expending the fewest network resources. For example, on a large network, a packet might be able to follow any of several paths to its destination, but some paths will be longer or will involve using more expensive resources, such as high-speed backbone links. IP addressing makes it possible to send a packet along the best or fastest route for the type of information it contains.

Today IP version 4 is in use on nearly all networks, but its 32-bit (4-octet) addressing capacity is a problem. The explosive growth of networks and the Internet has created an address shortage. IP version 6 (there is no version 5) or IP Next Generation is a new standard that is intended to solve the address shortage by using 128-bit addresses and providing for more specialized networking implementations, including the growth in voice, video, and multimedia applications. IP version 6 is primarily in use on experimental networks; it will be several years before IPv6 is broadly available.

TCP/IP works with a range of associated protocols that make this a powerful combination for networks of all sizes and types. Some of those protocols include the following:

- *Routing Information Protocol (RIP):* Enables network routing devices to build tables of routing information about the location of particular networks and network stations

- *Simple Mail Transfer Protocol (SMTP):* Used to transmit e-mail

- *File Transfer Protocol (FTP):* Used to send and receive files over a network

- *Telnet:* Used to enable a PC workstation to emulate a terminal for connections to mainframes and minicomputers over a network

- *Hypertext Transfer Protocol (HTTP):* Used for World Wide Web communications (for network browsers)

- *Point-to-Point Protocol (PPP):* Enables a computer to remotely access a network, through a dial-up modem connection, for example

- *Simple Network Management Protocol (SNMP):* Used to detect and track network activity, including network problems

- *Internet Control Message Protocol (ICMP):* Enables reporting of network errors

AppleTalk

AppleTalk is a network communications protocol used between Macintosh computers. It is designed primarily as a peer-to-peer protocol, rather than for combined peer-to-peer and client-to-server communications. As a peer-to-peer protocol, AppleTalk establishes equal communications between networked Macintosh computers without the need for a server (see Figure 8-12). Most mainstream network operating systems, such as Windows NT and NetWare, support AppleTalk as a means to communicate with Macintosh computers. For example, disk space can be specially configured on a Windows NT server for access by Macintosh computers. Network communications are then configured by installing AppleTalk in Windows NT.

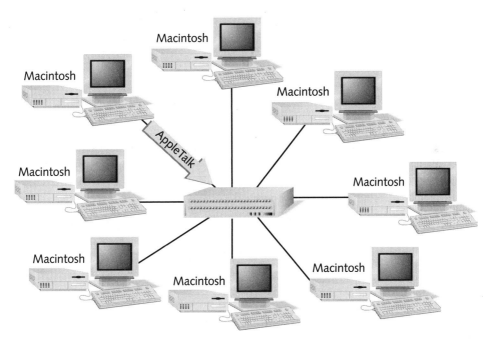

Figure 8-12   Peer-to-peer networking using AppleTalk and no server

AppleTalk performs three essential services: remote access to files over a network, network print services, and access to computers running MS-DOS or Windows operating systems. Examples of protocols designed for use with AppleTalk are as follows:

- *AppleTalk Address Resolution Protocol (AARP):* Converts computer names to IP addresses and vice versa for network and Internet communications

- *AppleTalk Data Stream Protocol (ADSP):* Ensures that streams of data are sent and received reliably

- *AppleTalk Session Protocol (ASP):* Used to ensure reliable network communications between two stations

- *Datagram Delivery Protocol (DDP):* Used for routing packets

- *Name-Binding Protocol (NBP):* Enables network services to be associated with specific computer names

- *Printer Access Protocol (PAP):* Used to communicate with network printers

- *Routing Table Maintenance Protocol (RTMP):* Enables routing table information to be built for routing packets

Early versions of AppleTalk have not been very compatible with large networks that use multiple combinations of protocols, such as TCP/IP, IPX/SPX, and NetBEUI over the same communication cable. AppleTalk Phase II is a newer version that is designed to work smoothly on large networks.

Implementing Communications Protocols in an Operating System

Most computer operating systems are designed to support one or more communications protocols. Those that support multiple communications protocols are able to do so through the same kernel interface hooks intended for transport protocols, such as NDIS for Windows-based operating systems and ODI for NetWare communications.

In general, there are two steps involved in setting up a communications protocol in an operating system. The first is to install the protocol software that is written for that operating system. For example, in Windows NT, you can install AppleTalk, IPX/SPX, NetBEUI, TCP/IP, or all four. The Windows-based software for each of these protocols is written to work in conjunction with NDIS so that these protocols can be carried over Ethernet or token ring networks. Step two is to bind the protocol with the NIC. Binding the protocol enables the NIC to format data for that protocol and to identify the most efficient methods for transporting it within Ethernet or token ring. When two or more protocols are used, binding also enables the NIC to set a priority for which protocol to process first. The protocol priority has a direct impact on how fast the computer and its NIC process network communications, and also affects network performance.

For example, consider a workstation that is configured for IPX/SPX, NetBEUI, and TCP/IP and on which TCP/IP represents 80% of the communications. If the binding priority is set so that TCP/IP packets are processed after IPX/SPX and NetBEUI, then that workstation will take longer to process network communications than if TCP/IP is given the first priority. The end result is that the network will have to wait longer on that workstation, delaying communications to other workstations.

The Mac OS provides one of the easiest methods for setting up communications protocols. In the Mac OS, you use a Control Panel to designate a port for network communications associated with the NIC. After designating the port, you simply turn on AppleTalk from the Chooser window (try Hands-on Project 8-5).

Most UNIX systems have TCP/IP networking support built in, and some of these automatically run a network configuration program when you first boot the computer with an installed NIC. NIC device drivers are loaded in the kernel. When the configuration program runs, you need to supply information about the network connection, such as the IP address. If TCP/IP networking is not automatically configured when you first boot, it can be configured later by using the *ifconfig* command when you log in as root. *Ifconfig* is a utility that is typically found in the /etc or /sbin directories and that enables you to assign an IP address, turn on the network interface, and assign a subnet mask (try Hands-on Project 8-6).

Communications protocols in NetWare, such as IPX and TCP/IP, can be set up in a window that is displayed when NetWare is installed. If TCP/IP is used, the setup process will need the IP address and subnet mask. Before version 5, NetWare uses IPX/SPX as that protocol of preference. In version 5, TCP/IP is the preferred protocol, but NetWare can be configured to interoperate with TCP/IP and IPX/SPX (there is no support for NetBEUI).

In Windows 3.1 and 3.11, communication protocols are set up through the Main program group by opening the Windows Setup icon and the Options menu. For Windows 3.1, the network protocol configuration is modified by clicking Change System Settings and selecting the new setup as in Figure 8-13. In Windows 3.11, the network protocol configuration is modified from the Options menu, by clicking Drivers and modifying the protocol setup. (Try Hands-on Project 8-7.)

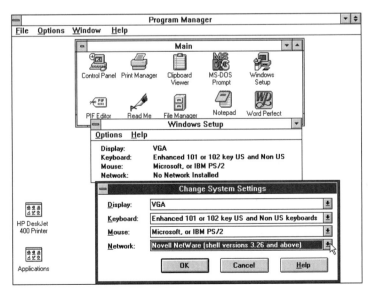

Figure 8-13   Installing IPX/SPX in Windows 3.1

Communications protocols are set up in Windows 95, Windows 98, and Windows NT 4.0 through the Network icon in the Control Panel. In Windows 95 and Windows 98, you open the Network icon in the Control Panel and click the Configuration tab. Next, click the Add button and then double-click Protocol in the Select Network Component Type dialog box. Windows NT 4.0 adds a slight variation in that you open the Network icon in the Control Panel, click the Protocols tab, and click Add to add a new protocol. (Try Hands-on Project 8-4 to practice installing a protocol in Windows 95, Windows 98, and Windows NT.)

Windows 2000 Server and Windows 2000 Professional use still a different method to set up a new protocol. In these versions of Windows, you open the Control Panel in the same way as in Windows 95, Windows 98, and Windows NT. Next, double-click the Network Connections folder. Use the Make New Connection wizard to add a new setup for a NIC. Or, if there is already a connection, right-click it and select Properties (see Figure 8-14). Click Add and then click Protocols to add a new protocol.

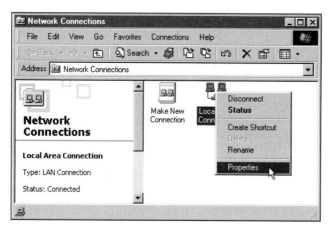

Figure 8-14   Installing a protocol in Windows 2000 Server

Integrating Different Operating Systems on the Same Network

The key to implementing multiple operating systems on one network is to select a transport protocol and communications protocols that are supported in all of the operating systems that must be connected. Ethernet is particularly well suited to a network that has different operating systems. It is supported by Mac OS, UNIX, Windows-based operating systems, server operating systems, and mainframe operating systems. Also, the TCP/IP communications protocol is supported by most operating systems.

Ethernet is also a strong choice for mixed networks because there are more equipment, NIC, and driver options for it than for token ring.

In situations where TCP/IP is not supported by all operating systems, then multiple protocols can be configured such as a combination of AppleTalk, TCP/IP, and IPX/SPX. For example, consider a network that has a combination of computers running Macintosh, Windows 95, Windows 98, Windows NT Server 4.0, and UNIX. This network might use AppleTalk and TCP/IP. AppleTalk might be used for communications between the Macintosh computers and enable them to access the Windows NT Server resources. TCP/IP might be used for communications between the Windows-based computers, the server, and the UNIX computers. Another example is a small network of 120 computers in which the workstations run Windows 3.11, Windows 95, and Windows 98 and that access Windows NT 4.0 and NetWare 3.12 servers. This network might use both NetBEUI and IPX/SPX to enable communications among all of the workstations and servers.

BRIDGING AND ROUTING

One or more networks can be linked by using internetworking devices such as bridges and routers. **Bridges** are used to link networks that are close together, such as on different floors in the same building or in different buildings. They also link remote networks, in two different cities for instance. Other uses for bridges are to extend networks, such as when more stations need to be added, but the primary network segment already contains the maximum length of cable or number of stations as permitted by network standards. Bridges are also used to segment a network into smaller networks as a way to control traffic and reduce bottlenecks at busy network intersections. Finally, bridges can be used to link networks that use different cable types, such as linking a network that uses twisted-pair cable to one that uses fiber-optic cable.

Bridges operate in what network administrators call promiscuous mode, which means that they examine the physical destination address of every frame that passes through them. Because they operate in promiscuous mode, bridge filters can be built that control which incoming frames are allowed to go out to which bridge ports. For example, if a bridge has four ports connected to networks A, B, C, and D, it can build a table of known destinations. A frame sent from network A that has a destination address which is on network D can be prevented from reaching networks B and C (see Figure 8-15). The network administrator can build "filters" that use the bridge table information to control which networks receive traffic from other networks. This characteristic enables bridges to manage network traffic as a way to circumvent bottlenecks. It also enables bridges to be used for network security, such as preventing all incoming Internet traffic from reaching a network that contains sensitive human resources or research data. A bridge used in this capacity is one example of a **firewall**, which is hardware or software that can control which frames and packets access or leave designated networks.

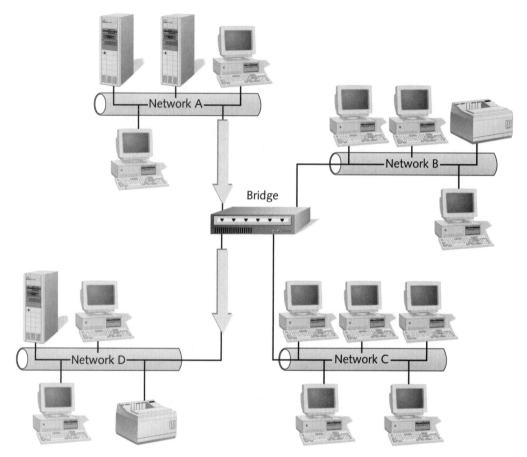

Figure 8-15   Using a bridge filter to direct Network A frames to Network D

Bridges are protocol-independent, a characteristic that permits them to forward all kinds of frame formats, for example TCP/IP, NetBEUI, or IPX/SPX. Bridges can also accept frames from any computer operating system that can send frames.

 Whenever two or more bridges are placed on a network, there is a potential that frames can be forwarded in an endless loop. Network administrators prevent looping by implementing a programmed system of checks called the spanning tree algorithm.

Bridges are not designed to route packets from one network to another, because they ignore routing information. This characteristic is used by network designers in two positive ways. One is that because bridges do not look at or process routing information, they are able to forward frames faster than devices that process routing information (although this advantage is quickly disappearing because new routing devices use specialized computer chips to enhance their speed). Another advantage is that bridges can forward frames constructed by protocols that do not contain routing information, such as NetBEUI.

Most network administrators today use internetworking devices called switches instead of bridges. **Switches** operate in promiscuous mode like bridges, but they provide additional logic that enables them to move network traffic more efficiently than the old-style bridges. Also, some switches are starting to use mainstream network operating systems, such as Windows NT, for managing the switch functions.

Like bridges, **routers** are used to join networks, either locally or remotely. Unlike bridges, routers are designed to look at routing information in packets before forwarding those packets to another network. Routers also are sensitive to different network protocols and the resulting differences in packet formats. These characteristics of routers enable them to direct and control network traffic more effectively than bridges. Routers also make excellent firewalls, because networks connected to a router can be divided into subnets as a way to control incoming and outgoing traffic to each subnet (see Figure 8-11). Because they truly route network traffic, routers are frequently used to prevent and cure network bottlenecks.

Routers that are equipped with multiple protocol interfaces can be used to translate traffic from one type of network to another, such as connecting a token ring network that uses TCP/IP, a token ring network that uses AppleTalk, and an Ethernet network that uses TCP/IP (see Figure 8-16). Like bridges, routers maintain tables, called routing tables, that store information about local networks and information obtained from routers connected to nearby and remote networks. Specialized routing protocols are used so that one router can transport part or all of its routing table information to another router. When a new computer is added to a network, its local router automatically polls the network and updates addressing and network location information about that computer. The updated information is later shared with other routers.

8

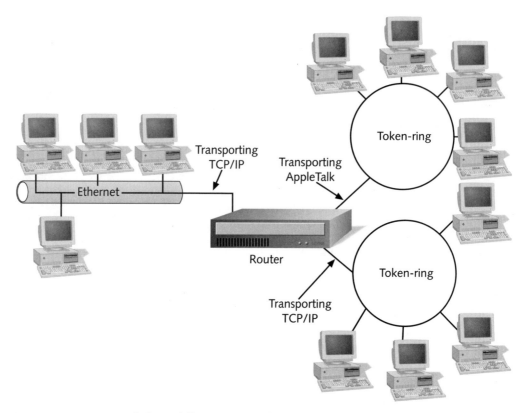

Figure 8-16   Router linking different types of networks and protocols

LOCAL AND WIDE AREA NETWORKS

Many networks are classified as local or wide area networks. A **local area network (LAN)** is one in which the service area is relatively small, such as a network in an office area or one spread throughout a floor in a building. On a college campus, the accounting department computers might be connected to a LAN in the top floor of a classroom building, and the English department computers might be on a different LAN within the main floor of the same building. Internetworking devices, a switch or a router for example, might be used to connect these LANs.

A **wide area network (WAN)** is one that offers networking services over a long distance, such as between cities, states, or countries. For example, consider a documentary film company in Chicago that has a LAN which connects through a telecommunications line to the LAN of a film distribution company in St. Louis. The LANs and the telecommunications link compose a WAN. Further, the telecommunications link alone is also a WAN because it links two LANs over several hundred miles. An example of a simple WAN is using a modem and telephone line at your computer to dial into your Internet service provider, such as AT&T.

Metropolitan area network (MAN) is another term that is used to describe networks that cover more geographic area than LANs, but less than WANs. A MAN might consist of networks joined throughout a city, such as joining LANs among eight hospitals in one city. Another example might be linking the suburban branch campuses of a community college to the main campus in the inner city. The term MAN is used less and less, often replaced by WAN.

Because of the complexity of networking, it can be difficult to determine where a LAN ends and a WAN begins. There are several interrelated elements that can be used to determine the intersection of a LAN with a WAN. One element is that the network topology may change between the two, such as a LAN that uses a ring topology and a WAN that uses a star. Another factor is a change in cable type. In the previous example, the LAN might use twisted-pair cable and the WAN might use fiber optics. Protocols may change between a LAN and a WAN, which is another indication of where one ends and the other starts. Ownership is another factor, because LANs often are private networks used by a restricted group and WANs often are public, such as telecommunications lines operated by a telephone company.

8

USING OPERATING SYSTEMS FOR DIAL-UP ACCESS

As you learned in Chapter 7, users on remote computers can access host computers and networks through dial-up networking and modem connections. For example, a specialized Novell server can be configured, with the appropriate software, to be a NetWare Access Server (NAS) on a LAN. A user who wants to access the LAN from home or while traveling simply dials up the NAS through software on his or her computer and a modem connection. Through the NAS, that user can gain access to files and software on one or more NetWare servers connected to the remote LAN.

Windows NT Server offers a similar option for dialing into a LAN through its remote access services (RAS) server. RAS is a set of network services that can be installed on any Windows NT server that is connected to one or more modems. Once the services are installed and started, a remote user can dial into one or more Windows NT servers and also access NetWare servers on the same network through a single RAS connection.

Besides setting up a remote access server, there must be a way to set up remote access capability on client workstations. Windows 95, Windows 98, and Windows NT all have a dial-up networking service that can be configured to access a remote network, as shown in the Hands-on Projects in Chapter 7. The dial-up service is set up by specifying the telephone number used to access the remote network, the communication protocol used (TCP/IP, IPX/SPX, or NetBEUI), and the remote communication protocol that is used. Most users configure dial-up networking to use the Point-to-Point Protocol (PPP), which can encapsulate packets already formatted in TCP/IP, IPX/SPX, and NetBEUI for transmission over a telecommunications line (try Hands-on Projects 8-8 and 8-9). A close relative, Point-to-Point Tunneling Protocol (PPTP) can also be configured for making a remote connection to a LAN over the Internet. Another protocol, Serial Line Internet Protocol (SLIP) is frequently used in UNIX for remote communications that transport TCP/IP.

CHAPTER SUMMARY

A network is a system of information resources and productivity tools that facilitates our human need to work, play, and learn. Networks were invented because they enable us to share information and information resources over short and long distances. Today, networking is a vital part of society that enables us to communicate by e-mail, order products rapidly, and accomplish work without leaving our homes or offices.

Networks are designed in standardized topologies (bus, star, and ring) and use standardized communication means, such as frames, packets, and protocols, with the end result that a network in Jackson, Wyoming can be connected to another in Denver, Colorado or in Montreal, Canada. Protocols are particularly important to networking because they act like a common language for communication. Some protocols are used to provide orderly transport of data between computers. Other protocols package data so that it can be decoded and checked for errors when it arrives at its destination. Protocols make communications reliable, they enable the delivery of e-mail, and they monitor networks for problems.

Modern computer operating systems can use a variety of network protocols for communication, such as TCP/IP, IPX/SPX, and NetBEUI. Even computers running very different operating systems, UNIX and Windows 98 for example, are able to communicate and exchange information over networks. Network operating systems such as Windows NT, NetWare, and UNIX offer a wide spectrum of services to client computers including file sharing, printer services, backing up files, access to software applications, and access to databases.

Tables 8-1, and 8-2 and 8-3 on the next page provide a summary of the transport, communications, and remote protocols introduced in this chapter and the operating systems that support those protocols.

Table 8-1   Summary of Transport Protocols

Transport Protocol	Communications Protocols Transported	Operating Systems that Support the Protocol
Ethernet	IPX/SPX, NetBEUI, TCP/IP, AppleTalk	Mac OS, NetWare, UNIX, Windows 3.1, 3.11, 95, 98, NT, 2000
Token ring	IPX/SPX, NetBEUI, TCP/IP, AppleTalk	Mac OS, NetWare, UNIX, Windows 3.1, 3.11, 95, 98, NT, 2000

Table 8-2   Summary of Communications Protocols

Communications Protocol	Operating Systems that Support the Protocol
AppleTalk (native to Mac OS)	Mac OS, NetWare, Windows NT, Windows 2000
IPX/SPX (native to early versions of NetWare)	NetWare, Windows 3.1, 3.11, 95, 98, NT, and 2000
NetBEUI (native to early versions of Windows-based systems)	Windows 3.1, 3.11, 95, 98, NT and 2000
TCP/IP (designed for Internet and general networking)	Mac OS, NetWare, UNIX, Windows 3.1, 3.11, 95, 98, NT, and 2000

Table 8-3   Summary of Remote Communications Protocols

Remote Communications Protocol	Communications Protocols Transported Over Remote Links	Operating Systems that Support the Protocol
SLIP	TCP/IP	NetWare, UNIX, Windows 95, 98, NT, and 2000
PPP	IPX/SPX, NetBEUI, and TCP/IP	Mac OS, UNIX, Windows 95, 98, NT, and 2000

8

Internetworking devices, bridges and routers for example, enable two or more networks to be connected. Bridges and routers can be employed for network security and to control network traffic patterns. Each of these devices is used to achieve different connectivity goals, based on their capabilities.

Networks are roughly categorized as LANs or WANs, depending on their areas of service. LANs are smaller networks that run throughout an office area or a floor in a building. WANs are long distance networks that can span states and continents to join LANs and individual users. One of the simplest WANs consists of deploying a server on a LAN that is able to communicate with users by modem and telephone line connections. Also called dial-up access, modem communications with a LAN are made possible through remote communications protocols, such as SLIP and PPP. PPP is most commonly used because it can transport a combination of protocols, such as TCP/IP and IPX/SPX.

In the next chapter, you learn how resources are shared through network operating systems. File sharing, printer sharing, Web services, and other functions are explored. You also learn about the different types of servers that provide these functions.

KEY TERMS

- **active hub** — A central network device that connects multiple communications cable segments; it amplifies the data carrying signal as it is transmitted to each segment.

- **AppleTalk** — Used for communications with Macintosh computers, this protocol is designed for peer-to-peer networking.

- **backbone** — A main connecting link or highway between networks, such as between floors in a building or between buildings. Main internetworking devices, such as routers and switches, are often connected via the network backbone.

- **bridge** — A network device that connects two or more networks into one or that is used to extend an existing network.

- **cell** — Format for a unit of data that is transported over a high-speed network, usually at speeds of 155 Mbps to over 1 Gbps. Cells are mainly used for network communications that employ Asynchronous Transfer Mode (ATM).

- **client operating system** — Operating system on a computer, such as a PC, that enables the computer to process information and to run applications locally, as well as to communicate with other computers on a network.

- **Ethernet** — A network transport protocol that uses CSMA/CD communications to coordinate frame and packet transmissions on a network.

- **firewall** — Hardware or software that can control which frames and packets access or leave designated networks, as a method to implement security.

- **frame** — A data unit sent over a network that contains source and destination (but not routing), control, and error detection information as well as data (related to the data-link layer of network communications between two stations).

- **Internet Protocol (IP)** — Used in combination with TCP, this protocol handles addressing and routing for transport of packets.

- **Internet Packet Exchange (IPX)** — Developed by Novell, this protocol is used on networks that connect servers running NetWare.

- **local area network (LAN)** — A series of interconnected computers, printing devices, and other computer equipment in a service area that is usually limited to a given office area, floor, or building.

- **NetBIOS Extended User Interface (NetBEUI)** — A protocol used on Microsoft networks that was developed from NetBIOS and that is designed for small networks.

- **network** — A system of computing devices, computing resources, information resources, and communications devices that are linked together by communications cable or radio waves.

- **Network Basic Input/Output System (NetBIOS)** — A technique to interface software with network services and to provide naming services for computers on a Microsoft network.

- **network operating system (NOS)** — Computer operating system software that enables coordination of network activities, such as network communications, shared printing, and sharing files. NetWare, UNIX, and Windows NT are examples of network operating systems.

- **packet** — A data unit sent over a network that contains source and destination, routing, control, and error detection information as well as data (related to the network layer of network data communications between two stations).

- **passive hub** — A central network device that connects multiple communications cable segments, but does not alter the data-carrying signal as it is transmitted from segment to segment.

- **payload** — That portion of a frame, packet, or cell that contains the actual data, which might be a portion of an e-mail message or of a word processed file.

- **protocol** — A set of formatting guidelines for network communications, like a language, so that the information sent by one computer can be accurately received and decoded by another.

- **router** — A device that joins networks and that can route packets to a specific network on the basis of a routing table it creates for this purpose.

- **Sequence Packet Exchange (SPX)** — A protocol used on Novell networks that provides reliable transmission of application software data.

- **server** — A computer running a network operating system and that enables client workstations to access shared resources, printers, files, software applications, or CD-ROM drives, for example.

- **subnet mask** — A designated portion of an IP address that is used to divide a network into smaller subnetworks as a way to manage traffic patterns, enable security, and relieve congestion.

- **switch** — A network device that connects LAN segments and that forwards frames to the appropriate segment or segments. A switch works in promiscuous mode similar to a bridge.

- **terminal** — A device that has a keyboard but no CPU or storage, and that is used to access and run programs on a mainframe or minicomputer.

- **token ring** — A network that uses a ring topology and token passing as a way to coordinate network transport.

- **topology** — The physical design of a network and the way in which a data-carrying signal travels from point to point along the network.

- **Transmission Control Protocol (TCP)** — A communications protocol that is used with IP; it facilitates reliable communications between two stations by establishing a window tailored to the characteristics of the connection.

8

- **wide area network (WAN)** — A system of networks that can extend across cities, states, and continents.

- **workstation** — A computer that has a CPU and that usually has storage to enable the user to run programs and access files locally.

REVIEW QUESTIONS

1. Which of the following computer operating systems are compatible with TCP/IP?

   a. NetWare 3

   b. Windows 95

   c. UNIX

   d. all of the above

   e. only a and b

   f. only b and c

2. Packet collisions are part of _____ networks, but not of _____ networks.

3. Which of the following resources can be shared through networks?

   a. files

   b. printers

   c. tape backup systems

   d. all of the above

   e. only a and b

   f. only a and c

4. The Internet Protocol (IP) handles _____ on networks.

5. Which of the following network topologies uses terminators?

   a. star

   b. bus

   c. ring

   d. all of the above

   e. only a and b

   f. only a and c

6. Which of the following protocols is not designed to enable routing?

   a. NetBEUI

   b. IPX

   c. TCP/IP

   d. None of the above can be routed.

   e. All of the above can be routed.

7. _____ is the protocol used by the Internet.

8. Which of the following operating systems cannot be used on an Ethernet network?

   a. Macintosh

   b. UNIX

   c. NetWare

   d. Windows 95

   e. None of the above can be used on Ethernet networks.

   f. All of the above can be used on Ethernet networks.

9. Dialing into a networked server at work from your home computer is a simple example of what type of network?

   a. Ethernet

   b. LAN

   c. WAN

   d. Token ring

10. A remote access services (RAS) server for remote dial-in access runs on which of the following operating systems?

    a. NetWare

    b. Windows NT

    c. IBM MVS

    d. DEC VMS

    e. all of the above

    f. only c and d because they are mainframe and minicomputer operating systems

11. A token ring network device that connects 16 workstations and that amplifies the data signal as the signal is sent from station to station is called a(n) _____.

12. You are setting up a UNIX server for communications on a network. Which of the following protocols are you most likely to implement in the UNIX operating system for communications?

    a. NetBEUI

    b. IPX

    c. TCP/IP

    d. SNMP

13. Which of the following protocols would you set up on your Windows 98 workstation to communicate with a UNIX server described in the previous question?

    a. NetBEUI

    b. IPX

    c. TCP/IP

    d. SNMP

8

14. You are configuring a Windows 95 portable computer that has an internal modem so that you can dial into Microsoft Windows NT servers that use TCP/IP, and NetWare servers that use IPX on your network. Which of the following protocols would you configure on your portable for communications through the modem?

   a. TCP/IP

   b. IPX

   c. PPP

   d. NetBEUI

   e. all of the above

   f. only a and b

   g. only a, b, and c

15. Fast Ethernet communications are at ———————— Mbps.

16. You are setting up a workstation running Windows NT so that it can access your network. To enable the computer to connect to the network cable, you need to install a hardware card in the computer called a(n) ———————— and then you need to install software into the operating system called a(n) ————————, which enables the hardware card to communicate with Windows NT.

17. Hypertext Transfer Protocol (HTTP) is used in association with which of the following protocols?

   a. TCP/IP

   b. XNS

   c. IPX

   d. NetBIOS

18. One problem with AppleTalk is that it cannot be used for network print services. True or False?

19. Which of the following topologies would you find on an Ethernet network?

   a. bus

   b. ring

   c. star

   d. all of the above

   e. only a and b

   f. only a and c

20. You want to link three LANs and each transports NetBEUI only. Which of the following would you use to connect them?

   a. A router

   b. A bridge

   c. A passive hub

   d. A terminal

21. When the active monitor on a token ring network stops working, this is called

_____.

22. A firewall must be a hardware device because network security cannot be reliably set up through software. True or False?

23. A network that has a combination of NetWare and Windows NT servers can be either Ethernet or token ring. True or False?

24. Token ring networks can operate at which of the following speeds?

    a. 10 Mbps

    b. 16 Mbps

    c. 100 Mbps

    d. all of the above

    e. only a and b

    f. only b and c

25. 144.79.22.122 is an example of a(n) _____ address.

HANDS-ON PROJECTS

PROJECT 8-1

In this hands-on activity, you examine a network to see if you can determine its topology.

To view a network topology:

1. Arrange to examine the network in a lab located in your school.

2. With the help of a lab assistant (or on your own), determine how each workstation is connected to the network. For example, are workstations connected directly to each other, to a wall outlet, or directly to a hub or switch?

3. If the workstations are connected to a wall outlet, ask if the connection eventually goes to a network device, such as a hub or switch.

4. Ask the lab assistant or your instructor if the network employs Ethernet or token ring communications.

5. Determine if you can see any visible terminators.

6. Using the information that you have gathered and what you have learned in this chapter, attempt to identify the network as a bus, ring, or star topology.

PROJECT 8-2

In this assignment, you examine the computers connected to your school's network. You will need a workstation running Windows 95 or Windows 98 that has access to your school's network.

To observe the computers on your network:

1. Double-click **Network Neighborhood** on the desktop.

2. Observe the number of computers on the network and their computer names.

3. Notice if there is any apparent naming scheme for computers or if users have a wide range of options in selecting their computer names.

4. Right-click one of the computers displayed and click **Properties**.

5. Look for the General tab in the dialog box and for Type, which shows the operating system run on the computer that you displayed (see Figure 8-17). Close the Properties dialog box.

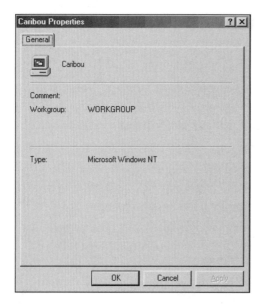

Figure 8-17   Viewing the connected computer's operating system

6. Repeat steps 4 and 5 to view other computers and their operating systems.

7. Back on the main Network Neighborhood screen, double-click **Entire Network**.

8. Notice if you see options, such as Microsoft Windows Network and NetWare or Compatible Network. If you do, first click one of the options to view its member

computers. If you are using Windows 95, close the window; or if you are using Windows 98, click the **Up** button. Then click the other option to view its contents.

9. Close the Network Neighborhood windows that you opened.

PROJECT 8-3

In this project you view the number of frames transported across a network. You will need access to a computer running Windows NT Server or Workstation 4.0 that has the Network Monitor Agent and SNMP service installed. You also need to ask your instructor for an account name and password to use in Windows NT Server or Workstation.

To view the frame activity:

1. Click **Start**, point to **Programs**, and point to **Administrative Tools (Common)**.
2. Click **Performance Monitor**. Maximize the window, if necessary.
3. Click the plus sign (**+**) on the button bar.
4. In the Add to Chart dialog box, make sure that the name of your computer is displayed in the Computer box, or open the list box to find and select your computer.
5. Open the Object list box and select **Network Segment**.
6. Select **Total frames received/second** in the Counter: list box.
7. Click **Add** and then close the Add to Chart dialog box.
8. View the graph for several minutes to see the frame activity.
9. Close Performance Monitor when you are finished.

PROJECT 8-4

In this project, you practice installing NetBEUI in Windows 95, Windows 98, or Windows NT Server or Workstation 4.0.

To install NetBEUI in Windows 95 or Windows 98:

1. Click **Start**, point to **Settings**, and click **Control Panel**.
2. Double-click the **Network** icon (applet).
3. Click the **Configuration** tab, then click the **Add** button.
4. Double-click the **Protocol** selection in the Select Network Component Type dialog box.

5. Click **Microsoft** in the Manufacturers text box and notice the protocols that can be installed under the Network Protocols text box (use the scroll bar if you are using Windows 98).

6. After you view the protocol selections, click **NetBEUI** in the Network Protocols: text box.

7. Click **OK**.

8. If the setup program asks for a path from which to install the protocol software, insert the Windows 95 or Windows 98 CD-ROM. Then click **Continue** or **OK** (depending on the dialog box that appears).

9. Close the Network dialog box and click **Yes** to reboot the computer (save any other work you have open first).

To install NetBEUI in Windows NT 4.0:

1. Log on to the Administrator account or to an account with Administrator privileges.

2. Click **Start**, point to **Settings**, and click **Control Panel**.

3. Double-click the **Network** icon.

4. Click the **Protocols** tab and click **Add**.

5. Click **NetBEUI Protocol** and click **OK**.

6. If the setup program asks for a path from which to install the protocol software, insert the Windows NT 4.0 CD-ROM and provide a path to the \i386 folder on the CD-ROM drive. Then click **Continue** or **OK** (depending on the dialog box that appears).

7. Close the Network dialog box and click **Yes** to reboot the computer (save any other work you have open first).

PROJECT 8-5

In this project, you set up the Mac OS for AppleTalk communications.

To set up AppleTalk in the Mac OS:

1. Make sure that the network cable is connected to the computer's NIC. If it is not, obtain a cable and connect it following directions from your instructor or lab assistant.

2. Open the **Apple** menu and **Control Panels**.

3. Select the **AppleTalk** Control Panel.

4. Select **Ethernet** as the port in the pop-up menu.

5. Close the AppleTalk Control Panel. (If the save changes warning box appears, click **Save**.)

6. Open **Chooser** in the AppleTalk menu.

7. Click **Active** in the lower-right corner of the dialog box. Click **OK** for the warning to make sure you are connected to the network.

8. Exit Chooser.

PROJECT 8-6

In this project, you turn on TCP/IP networking and assign an IP address in UNIX.

To set up and start TCP/IP communications in UNIX:

Do not execute this assignment if you are unable to obtain an IP address in advance, because you run the risk of creating an address that may conflict with others or of causing network problems. If you do not have an IP address in advance, try only Step 6 to view the current configuration information.

1. Make sure that a NIC is installed in the computer and ask your instructor for the NIC interface name, IP address, subnet mask, and broadcast address that you will use for this assignment.

2. Make sure that the network cable is connected to the computer's NIC. If it is not, obtain a cable and connect it following directions from your instructor or lab assistant.

3. Log in as root.

4. Switch to the /etc directory and determine if it contains ifconfig. If ifconfig is not in /etc, then switch to the /sbin directory.

5. Run *ifconfig interface_name ip_address netmask subnetmask_value broadcasts broadcast_address*, such as **ifconfig ln0 129.72.10.188 netmask 255.255.0.0 broadcasts 129.72.1.1** (if you are using the SCO version of UNIX, use the format *ifconfig interface_name netmask subnetmask_value ip_address* and omit the broadcast address). You will see configuration information after you run the *ifconfig* utility. Note that when you designate an IP address, *ifconfig* also starts the interface.

6. Check the configuration again by entering **ifconfig interface_name**.

7. Log off when you are finished.

PROJECT 8-7

In this project, you set up Windows 3.11 to use IPX/SPX communications with a NetWare version 3.26 server.

To set up IPX/SPX in Windows 3.11:

1. Double-click the **Main** program group in the Program Manager.

2. Double-click the **Windows Setup** icon.

3. Click the **Options** menu and click **Change Network Settings**.

4. Click the **Drivers** button, then click the **Add Protocol** button.

5. Click **IPX/SPX Compatible Transport**, then click **OK**.

6. Click **Close**, then **OK**.

7. Click **OK** again to change the SYSTEM.INI file.

8. Save any previously opened work, if necessary, then click **Restart Windows** to reboot.

PROJECT 8-8

In this project, you find out how to set up PPP for remote networking in Windows NT 4.0. You need access to Windows NT Server or Windows NT Workstation. Ask your instructor for an account and password into Windows NT.

1. Double-click **My Computer** on the desktop.

2. Double-click the **Dial-Up Networking** icon (applet).

3. In the Dial-Up Networking dialog box, click the **More** button.

4. Click the menu option to **Edit entry and modem properties**.

5. Click the **Server** tab in the Edit Phonebook Entry dialog box.

6. Notice the Dial-up server type box to see if **PPP: Windows NT**, **Windows 95**, **Internet** is the selected protocol.

7. Also on the Server tab, notice that you can specify which protocols will be carried via PPP.

8. Click **Cancel** on the Edit Phonebook Entry dialog box.

9. Click **Close** on the Dial-up Networking dialog box.

PROJECT 8-9

As an alternative to Project 8-8 or in addition to that project, check the remote protocol setup in Windows 95 or Windows 98.

To check the remote protocol setup:

1. **Double-click** My Computer.

2. Double-click the **Dial-Up Networking** icon (applet).

3. Right-click an existing dial-up networking icon.

4. Click **Properties**.

5. Click the **Server Type** button.

6. Notice which protocol is set up in the Type of Dial-Up Server list box.

7. Observe which network protocols are checked for transport over a remote connection.

8. Click **Cancel** on the Server Types dialog box.

9. Click **Cancel** on The Microsoft Network dialog box.

PROJECT 8-10

In this Hands-on Project, you attach a 4-pair unshielded twisted pair (UTP) cable to an RJ-45 connector. You will need the cable, a crimper, a connector, and a wire stripper. (These instructions and Figure 8-18 follow the EIA/TIA-568 standard for constructing UTP network cable.)

To attach UTP cable to an RJ-45 connector:

1. Lay out the wires on a flat surface in the arrangement shown in Figure 8-18.

2. Trim the wires with a pair of wire cutters, all to the same length.

3. Use a wire stripper intended for twisted-pair cable.

4. Follow the directions of the manufacturer of the stripper to strip the cable.

5. Insert the wires into the RJ-45 connector, ensuring that the connector is oriented the correct way, with the first pair of wires (blue and blue/white) to connectors 4 and 5 inside the RJ-45 connector, connecting the blue wire to connector 4 and the white/blue wire to connector 5 (see Figure 8-18).

6. Make sure the second pair of wires go to connectors 1 and 2, connecting the white wire to connector 1 and the orange wire to connector 2.

7. Make sure the third pair go to connectors 3 and 6, connecting the white/green wire to connector 3 and the green wire to connector 6.

8. Make sure the fourth pair go to connectors 7 and 8, connecting the white/brown wire to connector 7 and the brown wire to connector 8.

9. Make sure a portion of the cable jacket is inside the connector.

10. Insert the RJ-45 connector into the crimp tool and crimp the connector to the wires.

11. Test the installation by pulling the cable and connector in opposite directions to make sure your work does not come loose.

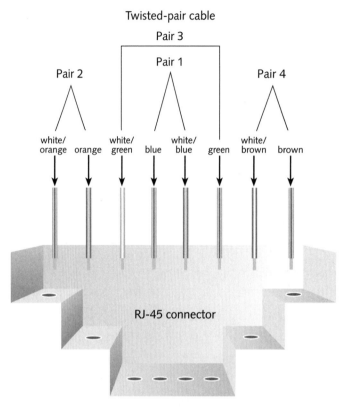

Figure 8-18   Attaching a connector to UTP cable

CASE PROJECT

1. You are the network administrator for a group of 18 groundwater hydrologists who work in two adjacent buildings. Their company works with new housing construction all over the United States to determine if there is enough local ground water to support a new housing development. Each hydrologist has her or his own computer workstation. Two use computers running UNIX, three use Macintosh computers, and the rest use computers running Windows 95. These hydrologists work with a variety of software, including word processing, research databases, spreadsheets, mapping software, and mathematical calculation software. The buildings in which the hydrologists work are not networked, but the company plans to network each building and connect both networks. The company also has decided to purchase a UNIX server and a NetWare server for all of the hydrologists to access. Both servers will be in a secure

computer room in one of the buildings. Also, the company plans to connect to an Internet service provider so that each hydrologist can easily access the Internet. Explain how you would handle the following immediate concerns:

a. What type of network, Ethernet or token ring, do you believe should be implemented? Why?

b. What topology do you think should be installed?

c. What equipment will have to be purchased in order for each hydrologist's computer to be connected to the network?

d. What protocols will you need to set up on each server and on all of the workstations? Why will you need these particular protocols?

e. Ten of the hydrologists travel frequently, and will need to remotely access the network from portable computers that are running Windows 95 or Windows 98. What will need to be set up on the network for them to dial into it? What will need to be set up on each portable?

f. What internetworking device would you use to connect the networks in each building? Do you anticipate a need for routing capability on this network?

g. As you are working to set up the network, two of the hydrologists are curious about the function of protocols. Briefly explain to them the function of network protocols.

8

RESOURCE SHARING OVER A NETWORK

The power of networks and of network-capable operating systems lies in their ability to share resources. The last chapter discussed resource sharing as the most fundamental rationale for having a network. This chapter brings the concept to life by showing you how resources are shared in several network server and client operating systems. Most modern operating systems have the capability to share files, programs, printers, CD-ROM drives, tape drives, modems, fax machines, and other resources.

A cartoon appeared several years ago in a popular computer magazine, showing two network experts attempting to connect an air conditioning unit to share its cooling capabilities over the network cable. The cartoon is a humorous illustration of the real trend toward sharing more types of resources over a network. In keeping with this trend, newer operating system releases offer more ways to accommodate resource sharing.

AFTER READING THIS CHAPTER AND COMPLETING THE EXERCISES YOU WILL BE ABLE TO:

- Explain the principles behind sharing disks and files on a network
- Explain how to set up accounts, groups, security, and disk and file sharing on network server operating systems
- Explain how to set up file and disk sharing on client operating systems
- Explain how to set up printer sharing on server and client operating systems
- Discuss how network and Internet servers are used for vast information sharing networks

In this chapter, you learn how to share resources through operating systems such as Mac OS, NetWare, UNIX, Windows 3.11, Windows 95, Windows 98, and Windows NT. You also learn about deploying user accounts, groups, and security to manage and protect shared resources, and how these capabilities enable network server operating systems to propagate information for businesses, schools, and government organizations.

SHARING DISKS AND FILES

Most modern and many older computer operating systems have the capability to share files, directories, and entire disks on a network. Sharing files was one of the first reasons for linking a workstation's operating system onto a network, and it remains one of the most important reasons for networking. In terms of network operating systems, NetWare was early on the scene at the start of the 1980s to enable file sharing through a server. This was possible through two methods: (1) by downloading a file from a file server to a workstation, and (2) by purchasing third-party software to create a special shared drive for other computers or workstations to access over a network. Downloading a file directly from a file server was one of the first methods for sharing files and was incorporated in the first version of NetWare.

 Although NetWare is not one of the operating systems covered in this book, because of its importance in the development of network OSs, and the common use of computers running DOS, Windows, UNIX, and Mac OS as clients to NetWare servers, it is given more extensive coverage in this chapter and in Chapter 10.

When network operating systems such as NetWare, UNIX, and Windows NT became available, it was difficult for many users of mainframe computers to grasp the idea that entire applications could be loaded as files onto a networked workstation, instead of running on the mainframe. For instance, a word processing package could be loaded onto the server and accessed by workstations. Each workstation would simply download the executable files, and perhaps a document file from a server, and run them in the local workstation's memory. Only one version of the word processing software was needed at the server, which could be downloaded multiple times by authorized workstations, eliminating the need to have the software loaded on each workstation. In this arrangement, each workstation housed a specialized setup file for the word processing software, but the executable files were always loaded from the server. Of course, it was still necessary, as it is today, to have the appropriate licenses as mandated by the software vendor.

 Although it was common to download applications software from a server and run it in memory on a workstation, it is less common today, because many applications are too large to download each time a workstation needs to run them.

Another complexity is that as software applications have grown in size, downloading them each time you want to run them on a workstation creates excessive network traffic. For example, early versions of word processors might have executable files in the range of a few thousand kilobytes, but today executable files and associated components can be in the range of 1 MB and more, because they contain many more functions. Consider a business where 100 employees arrive at work at 8 a.m. and all access the WordPerfect or Microsoft Word executable files from the server simultaneously. The resulting network traffic would be immense.

The concept of sharing resources quickly blossomed into other ways for accessing files, such as by making shared drives available on a network and the ability to make each shared drive look just like another local drive at the client. When a workstation accesses a shared drive, the process is called **mapping**. Mapping is a software process that enables a client workstation to attach to the shared drive of another workstation or server, and to assign it a drive letter. The network drive that is attached is called a mapped drive.

SHARING DISKS AND FILES THROUGH SERVER NETWORK OPERATING SYSTEMS

NetWare, UNIX, and Windows NT Server are three prime examples of server network operating systems that are able to share disks and files over a network. Each of these operating systems offers a way for client workstations to access a combination of disk, file, and other shared resources. Further, each operating system enables the network administrator to establish security through techniques such as assigning accounts, account passwords, groups, and access privileges. NetWare, UNIX, and Windows NT Server are described in the next sections in terms of their capabilities to share disk and file resources combined with the ability to secure those resources on a network.

NETWARE

When a Novell NetWare server is installed, one of the first projects is to design a file structure that makes it easy to establish drive mappings. For example, important commands available to users are contained in a directory called PUBLIC. The SYSTEM directory contains operating system files and utilities that the server administrator uses to manage the server. The LOGIN directory has files that users can access before they log into a server, such as the executable file (LOGIN.EXE) used to log in and other start up files needed by clients. Other information important to users is contained in home directories setup for each user. **Home directories** are areas on the server in which users store data. Users typically have control over whether to enable other users to access their data. Also, on NetWare servers there may be directories from which to install applications such as WordPerfect or Microsoft Word (or perhaps to run other applications that do not have much network overhead).

Consider, for example, a NetWare server set up for use by accountants. The main disk volume composing the root directory is the system volume, called the SYS volume. The server would have directories on the SYS volume that are available to users, such as PUBLIC, LOGIN, HOME, APPS, and DATA (see Figure 9-1 on the next page). The SYSTEM directory is also on the SYS volume, but full access is limited to the server administrator. If workstations access the server using a Windows-based client operating system, then the PUBLIC directory can have a subdirectory for utilities and programs related to a particular version of Windows, such as a subdirectory called WIN98 for Windows 98. The APPS directory might contain subdirectories for applications such as word processing, spreadsheets, and accounting software. The HOME directory would have one subdirectory for each user and the DATA directory would contain database files for the accounting system.

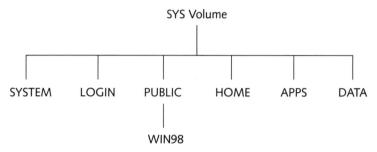

Figure 9-1 Sample NetWare directories available to users

Before users can access any shared directory, the network administrator performs several tasks to prepare the server before it is made available on the network. These tasks include the following:

- Set security on each directory, subdirectory, and on particular files
- Create an account and account password for each user who needs to access the server
- Set up groups as a way to provide shortcuts for managing security

After the server is prepared for network access, individual users log onto their accounts and map to particular drives. This can be done as a manual process by mapping each drive at the beginning of every login session, or it can be done by using a login script. Table 9-1 illustrates how drives might be mapped at the client workstation, which might be running DOS, Windows 3.1x, Windows 95/98, or Windows NT, for example.

Table 9-1   NetWare Network Drive Mappings

Mapped Drive Letter at the Workstation	Mapped Directory on the Server	Purpose of the Mapped Directory
F	SYS volume root	Access to the main volume and log-on utilities
H	SYS volume HOME directory, and user's subdirectory (SYS:HOME\userdirectory)	Storing the user's files
P	SYS volume applications directory (SYS:APPS)	Accessing program files to download to the client
Q	SYS volume data directory (SYS:DATA)	Access to data files or to a database
S1	SYS volume PUBLIC directory (SYS:PUBLIC)	Search access for NetWare utilities
S2	SYS volume, PUBLIC directory, and Windows 98 subdirectory (SYS:PUBLIC\WIN98)	Search access for clients using Windows 98

9

With an account and the appropriate security, a client can access directories and files within NetWare directories over the network. The directories that are mapped using a letter of the alphabet are available as shared drives for users to view and access files, and to copy files to their client workstations. The letters for these drives generally start after letters already allocated for local drives on the workstation, which include local drive A: for a floppy drive, local drive C: for a hard drive, and CD-ROM drive D: (depending on the number of hard drives installed).

In MS-DOS, Windows 3.1, Windows 3.11, Windows 95, and Windows 98, the last drive letter allocated for a local drive can be specified in the CONFIG.SYS boot file using the LASTDRIVE command. Typically a computer that is not attached to a network is set up with the command LASTDRIVE=E; if it is connected to a network LASTDRIVE=Z is used. Using this command occupies 40 KB of overhead in memory. When you do not use the command, these client operating systems default to using A: through E: for local drives, thus the first network drive is mapped as F:. When you install Windows 3.11 for use on a network, the setup process automatically changes the LASTDRIVE command to drive Z, if you authorize the change to the CONFIG.SYS file.

NetWare recognizes another type of network drive, called a **search drive**, which is given drive letters such as S1 for the first drive, S2 for the second drive, and so on. The difference between a mapped network drive and a mapped search drive is that NetWare can execute a file on a search drive, regardless of whether the file is in the main directory or in a subdirectory under the search drive. For example, if you want to execute a utility in a subdirectory under the S1 mapped directory for PUBLIC, you simply type the name of the program and NetWare searches all subdirectories under PUBLIC in order to execute it.

There are several ways to map a NetWare drive from a client workstation operating system. One way is to use the MAP command from the MS-DOS prompt or MS-DOS command window for Windows-based operating systems. The syntax of the MAP command is MAP drive: = volume:directory[\subdirectory] for regular network drives, and it is MAP S#: = volume:directory[\subdirectory] for search drives. For example, to map the PUBLIC directory as search drive S1, you would type MAP S1:=SYS:PUBLIC (try Hands-on Project 9-1). Another way to set up the same search drive (so that you map it each time you log onto your account) is to put the MAP command in a NetWare login script. A login script is a file of commands that is stored on the NetWare server and associated with an account or a group of accounts. The login script runs automatically each time a user logs onto her or his account. The network administrator can set up login scripts and can enable users to customize their own login scripts. Figure 9-2 is an example of a NetWare login script (the arrows in the figure point to the description of each command).

MAP DISPLAY OFF ⟶ Turns off the display of map commands as they are executed
CLS ⟶ Clears the screen
WRITE "Welcome to the First National Bank network server" ⟶ Displays a message
PAUSE ⟶ Requires that a key be pressed to continue
MAP F:=SYS: ⟶ Maps drive F: to the SYS: volume
MAP H:=SYS:USERS\HERRERA ⟶ Maps drive H: to the home directory location
MAP INS S1:=SYS:PUBLIC ⟶ Maps search drive S1 to the PUBLIC directory
MAP INS S2:=SYS:PUBLIC\WIN98 ⟶ Maps search drive S2 to the WIN98 subdirectory in PUBLIC
#CAPTURE Q=HPLASER ⟶ Directs printer files from a local printer port to a network printer

Figure 9-2 Sample NetWare login script

The MAP INS command is used to insert a search drive between two existing search drives. It is also used in login scripts to ensure that search drive mappings supercede those from another source.

Access to a NetWare shared drive is granted through creating an account for each user. A user account can be set up using several kinds of restrictions. The restrictions include:

- Requiring a password

- Setting a minimum password length

- Requiring that a password is changed within a specified interval of time

- Requiring that a new password is used each time the old one is changed

- Limiting the number of unsuccessful attempts to log on to an account

- Setting time restrictions that specify when users can log on

- Setting intruder detection capabilities

User accounts and restrictions are set up in NetWare by using the NetWare Administrator (see Figure 9-3). Also, multiple accounts can be set up by using the UIMPORT utility. UIM-PORT is run in conjunction with an ASCII text file that contains information about the accounts to be set up, such as the login name, the user's actual name, information about the location of a home directory, password restrictions, and other information pertinent to each account.

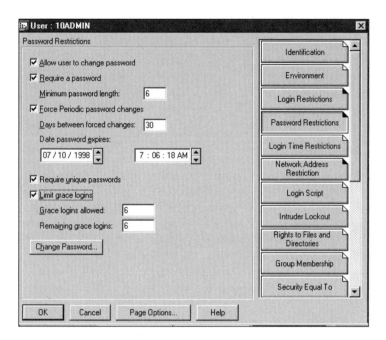

Figure 9-3   Password restrictions in NetWare Administrator

Many server operating systems, such as NetWare, automatically create a Guest account. Sometimes when an upgraded version of the operating system is just released, the Guest account is not automatically assigned a password and may even have broad permissions to the server resources. Make sure these types of accounts have a password (or are disabled) and that they are given appropriate permissions.

After accounts are set up, the network administrator can grant rights to access specific directories, subdirectories, and files. The rights control the ability to:

- Perform a directory listing
- Create a new directory, subdirectory, or file
- Read the contents of a directory, subdirectory, or file
- Write to the contents of a file
- Delete a directory, subdirectory, or file
- Change the security associated with a directory, subdirectory, or file
- Copy a directory, subdirectory, or file
- Rename a directory, subdirectory, or file

Rights are assigned by making a user or group a directory or file trustee. Rights also can be inherited on the basis of the rights already assigned to higher level directories; and they can be inherited based on container objects. A **container object** is an entity that is used to group together resources, such as an organizational unit, an organization, or a country as specified in the directory services of NetWare.

An effective way to manage the rights granted to accounts is by creating groups that need the same kinds of access. After a group is created, the network administrator assigns rights to the group and also assigns accounts to the group. Likewise, a group can be assigned to a specific login script containing mapped drives and other network parameters, such as network printer assignments, applicable to each group.

User accounts, groups, printers, directories, subdirectories, files, and other resources in NetWare are considered **objects**. Information about objects, such as rights that are associated with them, is stored in the **Novell Directory Services (NDS)**. NDS is a comprehensive database of shared resources and information known to the NetWare operating system. A portion of the NDS is used to store information about clients, which are one example of NDS **leaf objects** in an organization container and which are given various levels of authorization to access NetWare servers. The information that is stored in the NDS includes the client login name, full name of the client, home directory location, and password information.

UNIX

Access to directories and files on a UNIX server is also governed through user accounts, groups, and access permissions. Each user account in UNIX is associated with a unique **user identification number (UID)**. Also, users who have common access needs can be assigned to a group via a **group identification number (GID)** and then the permissions to access resources are assigned to the group, instead of to each user. When the user logs on to access resources, the password file is checked to permit logon authorization. The password file (\etc\passwd) contains the following kinds of information:

- The user name, which can be up to eight characters long

- An encrypted password or a reference to the **shadow file**, a file associated with the password file that makes it difficult for intruders to determine the passwords of others

- The UID which can be a number as large as 60,000

- A GID with which the user name is associated

- Information about the user, such as a description or the user's job

- The location of the user's home directory

- A command that is executed as the user logs on, such as which shell to use

The shadow file (\etc\shadow) is normally available only to the system administrator. It contains password restriction information that includes the following:

- The minimum and the maximum number of days between password changes

- Information on when the password was last changed

- Warning information about when a password will expire

- Amount of time that the account can be inactive before access is prohibited

A group file is associated with each group that is created. It contains the name of the group, an encrypted group password, the GID, and a list of group members. Every account must be assigned to at least one group and can be assigned to more. User accounts and groups can be created by editing the password, shadow, and group files, but a safer way to create them is by using UNIX commands created for this purpose. If you edit the files, you run the risk of an editing error that can create unanticipated problems. Also, it is important to make sure that each group has a unique GID, because when two or more groups use the same GID, there is a serious security risk. For example, an obvious risk is that the permissions given to one group also inappropriately apply to the other.

The *useradd* command enables you to create a new user. The parameters that can be added to *useradd* include the following:

- *-c* gives an account description

- *-d* specifies the user's home directory location

- *-e* specifies an account expiration date

- *-f* specifies the number of days the account can be inactive before access is prohibited

- *-g* specifies group membership

- *-m* establishes the home directory if it has not previously been set up

- *-s* designates the default shell associated with the account

- *-u* specifies the unique UID

The parameters associated with an account can be modified by using the *usermod* command. Also, account setup can be automated by writing a shell script that contains prompts for the desired information. Accounts are deleted through the *userdel* command, which enables you to specify the username and home directory that are to be deleted.

Groups are created using the *groupadd* command. There are typically two inputs associated with this command. The *–g* parameter is used to establish the GID, and the group string creates a group name that can be eight characters or less. For example to create the auditors group, you would enter *groupadd –g 2000 auditors*. Once a group is created, it is modified through the *groupmod* command. Groups are deleted through the *groupdel* command. (Try Hands-on Project 9-9.)

UNIX files are assigned any combination of three permissions: read, write, and execute. The permission to read a file enables the user to display its contents and is signified by the letter *r*. Write permission entails the ability to modify and save a file, as signified by a *w*. The execute permission, indicated by an *x*, enables a user or a group of users to run a program. When a directory is flagged with an *x*, that means a user or a group can access and list its contents. A directory can also be designated as read, write, or both, but these permissions have no meaning unless the directory is given the execute permission for a user or a group.

Executable programs can have a special set of permissions called Set User ID (SUID) and Set Group ID (SGID). When either of these is associated with an executable, the user or group member who runs it can do so with the same permissions as held by the owner. This can provide more access permissions than when the file is executed simply by the user.

Permissions are granted on the basis of three criteria: ownership, group membership, and other (or World). The owner of the file or directory typically has all permissions and can assign permissions. Group members are users who may have a complete set of permissions, one permission, or a combination of two, such as read and execute. The designation other (or World) consists of non-owners or non-group members who represent generic users. For example, the owner of a file would have read, write, and execute permissions. A particular group might have read and execute permissions, while all others (World) might only have read permissions or perhaps no permissions.

Permissions are set up by using the *chmod* command in UNIX. *Chmod* has two different formats, symbolic and octal. In the symbolic format, you specify three parameters: (1) who has the permission, (2) the actions to be taken on the permission, and (3) the permission. For example, consider the command, *chmod go-rwx* * that is used on all files (signified by the *) in a directory. The *g* signifies groups and *o* signifies others. The – means to remove permission, and *rwx* signifies the read, write, and execute permissions (all three would be removed). In this example, only the owner is left with read, write, and execute permissions on the files in this directory. (Try Hands-on Project 9-2 to practice setting permissions in UNIX.)

The octal permission format is more complex, because it assigns a number on the basis of the type of permission and on the basis of owner, group, and other. Execute permission is assigned 1, write is 2, and read is 4. These permission numbers are added together for a value between 0 and 7. For instance, a read and write permission is a 6 (4 + 2) while read and execute is a 5 (4 + 1). There are four numeric positions (*xxxx*) after the *chmod* command. The first position gives the permission number of the SUID/SGID, the second position gives the permission number of the owner, the third gives group permissions, and the last position gives the permission number of other. For example, the command *chmod 0755* * assigns no permissions to SUID/SGID (0); read, write, and execute permissions to owner (7); and read and execute permissions to both group and other (5 in both positions), for all files (*).

WINDOWS NT SERVER

Windows NT Server uses accounts, groups, and permissions; in this respect it is similar to UNIX and NetWare. The steps involved in sharing Windows NT Server resources over a network include setting up the following:

- Groups
- Account policies
- User accounts
- Permissions
- Shared disks and folders

With Windows NT Server, you use groups to manage resources and permissions to resources in a way that is similar to NetWare and UNIX. Windows NT Server adds the use of two kinds of groups: local and global. A **local group** is generally used to manage resources such as shared disks, folders, files, and printers. A **global group** typically consists of user accounts, and can be made a member of a local group that is in the same domain or in a different domain. A **domain** is a grouping of servers in a particular geographic area, business unit, department, or other functional area. The process of controlling shared resources in Windows NT involves creating the resource, such as a shared folder, and then creating a local group that has specific permissions to that shared resource. Finally, a global group is created and user accounts are added to that global group, which is then designated as a member of an appropriate local group.

On the surface, this technique of managing shared resources sounds complex, but it ultimately reduces management effort. For example, consider a corporation that has business units and networks in five different geographical areas. Each network is designated as a separate domain and has accounting and sales databases that are in shared folders. In this scenario, each domain would have a local group with permissions to the databases. The corporate headquarters domain would have a global group consisting of all members at each location who need access to the databases. Access could be controlled by making the headquarters global group a member of each local group (see Figure 9-4 on the next page). If three employees leave the organization, the network administrator simply removes their accounts from the headquarters domain and global group. This is a simpler process than removing each account from each domain and from a group in each domain, which would require several times the effort. Likewise, when three new people are hired, the network administrator creates an account for each person in the headquarters domain and makes each a member of the global group in that domain.

9

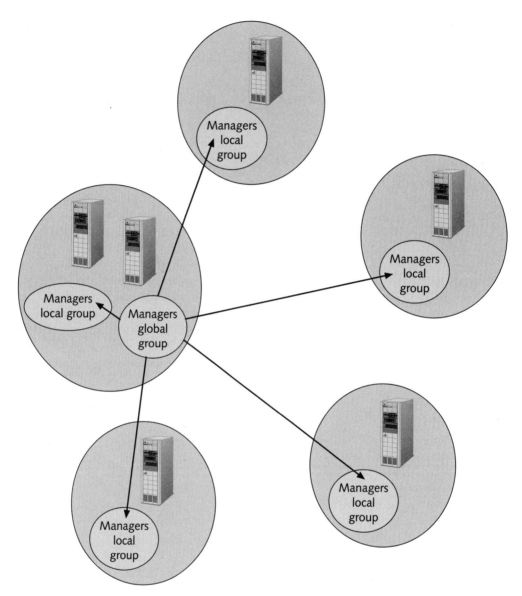

Figure 9-4   Managing shared resources using local and global groups

Directories are called folders in Windows 2000, Windows NT, Windows 95, and Windows 98. Windows 2000 Server adds a new type of group called a universal group, because this operating system is enhanced to provide new levels of resource groupings beyond domains.

Global and local groups are created by using the GUI tool, User Manager for Domains, in Windows NT Server. You access this tool in Windows NT Server 4.0 by clicking the Start button, Programs, Administrative Tools (Common), and User Manager for Domains. Next, click the User menu and select to create a new global or local group. Figure 9-5 illustrates the Windows NT dialog box that is used to create a new global group. (Try Hands-on Project 9-3 to view the global and local groups on a Windows NT Server.)

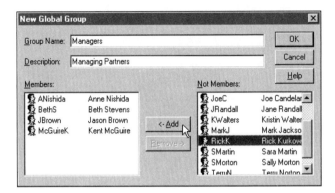

Figure 9-5   Creating a global group in Windows NT Server 4.0

  By now you understand that groups are a valuable tool for managing shared resources, but they can also introduce complexity in resource management when too many groups are used and when there is no documentation on them. As a rule, in NetWare, UNIX, and Windows NT, keep resource management simple by planning groups in advance and keeping their numbers to a minimum.

In Windows NT Server, access rights are controlled through setting rights policies in the User Manager for Domains and by associating them with local groups. For example, the right to access a particular server over the network can be controlled in this way, and also the right to directly log onto a server from its console.

User accounts are also created through the User Manager for Domains. Windows NT Server uses account policies and restrictions, as does NetWare, which accomplish many of the same ends (but use different utilities) as follows:

- Require a password
- Set a minimum password length
- Require that a password is changed within a specified interval
- Require that a new password is used each time the old one is changed
- Limit the number of unsuccessful attempts to log on to an account
- Set time restrictions that specify when users can log on
- Set intruder detection capabilities
- Specify from which workstations an account can be accessed
- Control remote access to a server, such as over a dial-up line

Figure 9-6 shows the Account Policy dialog box in Windows NT Server 4.0, which is one place in which account restrictions can be set. Another is through utilities provided at the time an account is created.

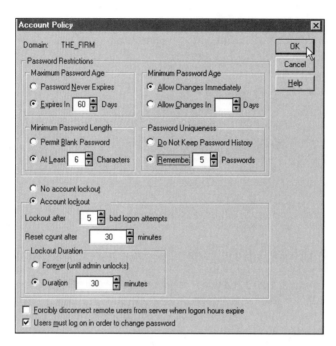

Figure 9-6 Windows NT Server 4.0 account policies

As is true for UNIX and NetWare, access privileges (permissions) are associated with Windows NT Server disks, folders, and files. The ease with which you assign permissions is closely related to how the folder structure is set up. For example, it is easiest to share access for the installation of application programs, by placing those programs in subfolders within a main folder intended for installing applications. The main folder might be called Apps and there might be subfolders such as MSOffice, Accounting, Drivers, CAD, WIN98, and so on.

Windows NT Server recognizes two main file systems, File Allocation Table (FAT) and the NT File System (NTFS). (See Chapter 3 for more information on file systems.) In virtually all cases, files that are shared to the network are set up in NTFS, because this file system has better security. FAT can offer security through DOS attributes, while NTFS can offer security by using a combination of DOS attributes and NTFS permissions (see Table 9-3 in the summary section of this chapter for a comparison of security offered by FAT, NTFS, and other file systems).

After groups, user accounts, and permissions are set up in Windows NT Server, disk volumes, folders, and files can be accessed through the network by creating shares. A **share** is an object, a disk or folder for example, that is given a name and made visible to network users, such as through Network Neighborhood in Windows 95, Windows 98, and Windows NT.

A disk or folder is shared through its properties. This is possible because Windows NT Server objects have associated properties that include sharing, setting permissions, and ownership. For example, to set up a shared folder, you locate that folder in My Computer or Windows NT Explorer and then right-click the folder. Next, click the Sharing option and the Sharing tab in the properties dialog box. Sharing a folder entails clicking the Shared As radio button and setting up the parameters for sharing, particularly the share permissions. Figure 9-7 illustrates the sharing properties for a folder called Public. Share permissions are another type of permissions in addition to regular file and folder permissions. Share permissions cannot exceed the regular permissions already established on a disk, folder, or file. For example, if a folder already has no access permissions for all users, then it does no good to set share permissions to read, because the no access permissions supersede the shared read permissions. (You can practice setting up a shared folder in Windows NT Server in Hands-on Project 9-4.)

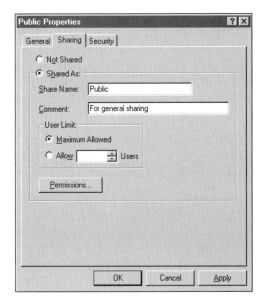

Figure 9-7   Setting up a shared folder in Windows NT 4.0

There are only four share permissions, as follows:

- *No access*: The specified groups and users have no access.
- *Read*: The specified groups and users can read and execute files.
- *Change*: The specified groups and users can read, add, modify, execute, and delete files.
- *Full Control*: The specified groups and users have full access to the files and folders, including the ability to take ownership or change permissions.

Sharing resources through Windows NT Workstation involves nearly the same processes as sharing resources through Windows NT Server. The important differences are that Windows NT Workstation supports only local groups (not global groups) and Windows NT Workstation is designed to support 10 or fewer simultaneously logged on users.

ACCESSING AND SHARING DISKS AND FILES THROUGH CLIENT (WORKSTATION) NETWORK OPERATING SYSTEMS

Many operating systems include the ability to act as clients, to map to disks and directories on servers. Some client operating systems can share files and folders, as well. In the sections that follow, you learn about the capabilities of major client operating systems including:

- Macintosh
- UNIX
- Windows 3.11
- Windows 95
- Windows 98

MACINTOSH

The Mac OS offers two ways to connect to shared resources on a network: the Chooser and the Network Browser. The Chooser is the original way to access shared network volumes, which can be an entire disk drive or a directory, depending on the way in which the resource is set up. The Network Browser is a utility that is new to Mac OS 8.5. For example, you might use either utility to mount a shared drive set up for AppleTalk on a NetWare or Windows NT Server. Another way to use these utilities is to connect to shared files and volumes on another Macintosh computer.

The Mac OS uses the terminology *mount* instead of *map* when accessing a shared disk volume over the network.

To use the Chooser, you select it from the Apple menu and then click the AppleShare icon in the Chooser window. If your network consists of more than one zone, select the zone that is home to the computer you want to access. Next, choose the computer that contains the shared volume or files and click OK (see Figure 9-8). A dialog box appears that enables you to mount the resource as a guest or as a registered user. Typically, you access the shared resource as a registered user, providing your name and password. If you access the resource as a guest, you do not enter your name and password, because guest access is intended for anonymous users who access resources available for anyone on the network. After you make your selection, click Connect. A list of resources, called volumes, appears in the next dialog box enabling you to click the one you want to access. You can select multiple volumes by pressing the Shift key and clicking those you wish to mount. There is also an option to check volumes that you wish to open at system startup time, which means that these volumes are automatically connected each time you start up the operating system. Once your selection is made, click OK to have it appear as an icon on the desktop.

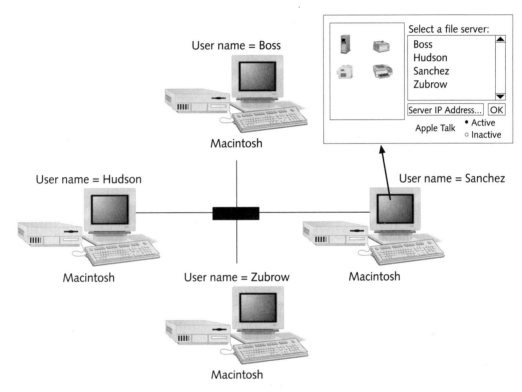

Figure 9-8 Using the Chooser

 If the Mac OS is set up to use TCP/IP, then you can use the Chooser to connect to a server by entering its IP address. Also, you can set up the operating system for PPP communications over a remote network (see Chapter 8).

The Mac Network Browser presents an interface that is similar to a Windows drop-down or scroll box, or like the Open dialog box that is new to Mac OS 8.5. The Open dialog box is a scroll box that lists items and presents a small identifying icon in front of each item. Hands-on Project 9-5 demonstrates how to use the Network Browser. Unmounting a volume entails dragging its icon to the trash, which does not delete the volume contents, but only disconnects access to the volume at the computer that mounted it.

Files are shared from a Macintosh workstation by first creating users and groups and then by defining which files to share. As in server operating systems, a Macintosh user is set up by assigning an account and a password for the account. Also, groups can be established that consist of accounts which have the same access. Users and groups are set up by opening the Apple menu, clicking Control Panels, and then Users & Groups. Computers running the Mac OS have two users already defined, which are Owner and Guest. After a user is created, it can be added to one or more groups.

The process of creating a new user involves these steps (which you can practice in Hands-on Project 9-6):

1. Provide the user's name.

2. Provide a password.

3. Enable the user to change her or his password (an optional check box).

4. Enable sharing and allow the user to link to programs on the computer.

Creating a group is an equally straightforward process in which you define the name of a group and then drag selected users into the group. Also, you can modify or delete users and groups from the Users & Groups control panel. As is true with network server operating systems, it is a good practice to keep the number of groups to a minimum for easier management.

After the users and groups are created, you are ready to share files. The first step in preparing to share files is to establish a network identity for the computer. You establish a network identity in the File Sharing control panel by providing your name as the owner, the password to associate with the owner name, and a computer name. The computer name is the one that other computers on the network use to identify yours. After the network identity is established, it is necessary to turn file sharing on, which is accomplished through the File Sharing control panel. Also, it is possible for users to "link" to your computer so that you can share programs with them. If your computer has programs that can be linked, you can choose to turn linking on as part of the file sharing process. File sharing and linking can be turned off through the File Sharing control panel at any time.

Privileges are set in order to enable users and groups to access the folders and files you wish to share. There are four kinds of privileges that can be set:

- *None*: No access to files

- *Read only*: Access to read the contents of files only

- *Write only*: Access to write files but not to open them

- *Read & write*: Access to open and write files

The access privileges can be assigned to any of four types of users: owner, users and groups, and everyone. The owner is the one who holds all access privileges and can set them. Users and groups consist of the user accounts and groups currently set up on the computer. Last, everyone consists of those who do not belong to any of the following: users already assigned privileges, groups already assigned privileges, or the owner.

UNIX

UNIX computers can access resources on other computers that support the **Network File System (NFS)**, which provides file transfer capabilities. Accessing shared resources on a Windows NT Server provides one example of how UNIX can participate as a network client with the ability to access shared resources. One way to support a UNIX client in Windows NT Server is to implement third-party disk sharing software that employs NFS, such as Intergraph DiskShare (recommended by Microsoft as compatible).

With the third party's software installed, you can copy the UNIX password file, located in \etc\passwd to a Windows NT Server at the folder location, Winnt\System32\Drivers\Etc. This step enables the Windows NT logon authentication to work along with the third-party software to match the authentication used at the UNIX workstation, so both employ the same username and password, for example. The authentication is performed by creating an account in Windows NT Server and linking the same rights and privileges assigned to the UNIX user account with those of the corresponding Windows NT Server account. Intergraph DiskShare, for instance, is installed in Windows NT Server and provides an NFS server and administrator utility that is used to link and administer the rights and permissions granted to the NT Server account. The NFS server utility is used to set up shares that are available to UNIX and to assign share permissions. With this in place, the UNIX client accesses the shared disk or folder through its *mount* command, which is the same command that is used to mount local and remote resources, including non-UNIX file systems such as FAT and NTFS. Typically UNIX share permissions include:

- *Root*: Includes all permissions and is similar to Full Control in Windows NT

- *Read-write*: Encompasses permissions to mount the shared disk or folder, read the contents of files and folders, and modify files and folders

- *Read-only*: Gives permission to mount the shared resource, but only to read the contents of files and folders

- *No access*: Prevents mounting the shared disk or folder

The NFS server acts as a two-way utility, because it also permits a Windows NT Server or NT Workstation to access a computer running UNIX. When Windows NT is a UNIX client, the UNIX computer authorizes the logon and enables the Windows NT computer to mount the UNIX shared resources as a mapped drive that appears in the Windows NT Explorer and in My Computer. The drive is mapped in Windows NT using the same utility as for mapping any other network drive.

WINDOWS 3.11

The ability to truly share disks and directories in Windows-based client operating systems is implemented first in Windows 3.11 (Windows for Workgroups (WFW); or the WFW special enhancement for Windows 3.1). Windows 3.11 offers the ability to configure sharing when you first install it. The Setup program contains a Network Setup Window that is used to configure the operating system for network access, such as setting up network drivers, the NIC, and protocols. The Network Setup Window also has a Sharing button that, when clicked, enables you to install the capability to give others access to your files and printers (Figure 9-9).

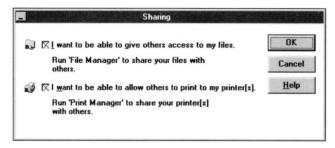

Figure 9-9 Setting up file and printer sharing during Windows 3.11 installation

With file sharing enabled, you can share a disk, directory, or file for others to access over the network. For example to share a folder, open File Manager, click the folder, click the Disk menu, and click Share As (or click the Share As icon on the button bar). In the Share Directory dialog box (Figure 9-10):

1. Provide the share name that others will see over the network.

2. Make sure the path is correct to the share or enter the path in the Path: box.

3. Enter a comment to describe the share.

4. Determine if you want to offer the share each time you boot the computer.

5. Specify the security to place on the share.

6. Specify a password, if desired, for the type of access (Read-Only, Full, or specify a different password for each).

7. Confirm the password, if provided in step 6.

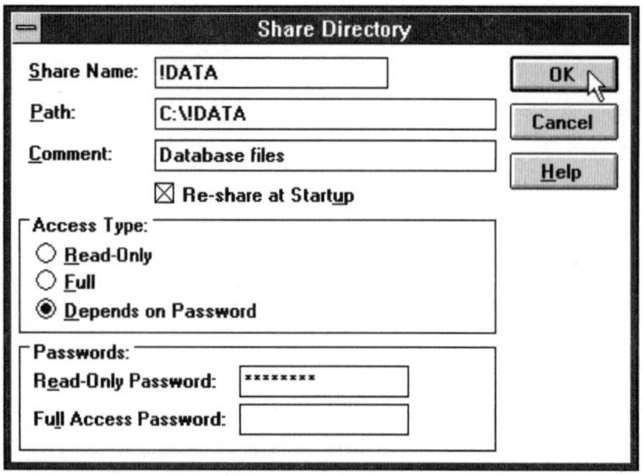

Figure 9-10 Sharing a directory in Windows 3.11

The Windows 3.11 security that is available for a shared disk or directory includes the following:

- *Read-Only*: Clients can read the contents of files and directories and copy them, but clients cannot modify files and directories.

- *Full*: Clients can read, copy, add, remove, and modify files and directories.

- *Depends on Password:* Clients must enter a password for the type of access, Read-Only or Full.

To discontinue sharing, open the File Manager, click the shared disk, directory, or file, click the Disk menu and click Stop Sharing (or click the Stop Sharing icon on the button bar).

Windows 3.11 can be configured through File Manager to access a disk, directory, or file that is shared by another computer on the network. To access a shared directory on another computer (practice these steps in Hands-on Project 9-10):

1. Open File Manager.

2. Click the Disk menu and click Connect Network Drive (or click the Connect Network Drive icon on the button bar).

3. In the Connect Network Drive dialog box, select the computer and shared directory in the Show Shared Directories on: and Shared Directories boxes.

4. Assign an unused drive letter.

5. Specify the path to the shared directory (if it is not already provided).

6. Specify whether to reconnect to the share each time you log on.

The Connect Network Drive dialog box in Windows 3.11 also contains an option to enable you to browse domains, workgroups, and computers connected to the network. If this option is checked (which is the most likely response), then Windows 3.11 may contend with Windows NT Server (and NT Workstation) computers as the Master Browser. This can cause computers running Windows 95, Windows 98, and Windows NT to experience problems in using Network Neighborhood, such as not seeing some or even all computers connected to the network. The solution is to modify the SYSTEM.INI file in Windows 3.11 to include the line: MaintainServerList=no. As a Windows NT Server administrator, you can identify the contending Windows 3.11 system by checking the server system log for Master Browser contention. Figure 9-11 shows an example of a log entry in which the Windows 3.11 computer named REV is contending with the server CARIBOU. (Practice changing the SYSTEM.INI file in Hands-on Project 9-10).

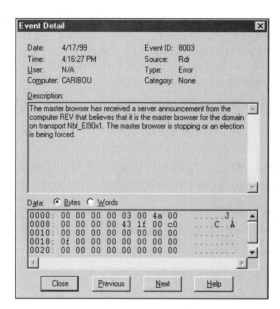

Figure 9-11   Windows NT system log showing Master Browser conflict with
Windows 3.11

A connection to a shared directory can be disconnected at any time by opening File
Manager, selecting the shared directory, and clicking the Disk menu and Disconnect
Network Drive—or click the Disconnect Network Drive icon on the button bar.

WINDOWS 95 AND WINDOWS 98

Windows 95 and Windows 98 have nearly the same capabilities to access shared disks and
folders. Both also can offer shared resources for other network workstations to access. These
operating systems enable access to resources through two access control techniques. One,
called **share–level access control**, creates a disk or directory share that is protected by share
permissions and on which the share owner can require a password for access. The second
technique, called **user–level access control**, requires the share owner to create an access list
of groups and users who are allowed to access the share. Both techniques are set up through
the Control Panel and Network icon. After you open the Network dialog box, click the
Access Control tab to select one of these methods (see Figure 9-12).

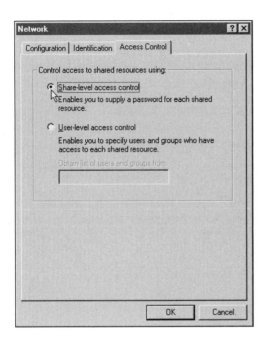

Figure 9-12   Windows 95 and Windows 98 access control

In share-level access, you create a share that is similar to a share created on a Windows NT Server. The difference is that several hundred simultaneous users (depending on the server resources, such as CPU and memory) can access a Windows NT Server share, whereas a share on a computer running Windows 95 or Windows 98 is designed to host 10 or less (also depending on the workstation resources). Further, Windows NT Server provides a more comprehensive set of regular permissions and of share permissions. There are three share-level access permissions in Windows 95 and Windows 98:

- *Read-Only*: Clients can read the contents of files and folders and copy them, but clients cannot modify files and folders.

- *Full*: Clients can read, copy, add, remove, and modify files and folders.

- *Depends On Password*: Clients are given access on the basis of a read-only password or a full-access password.

The Read-Only and Full permissions can be assigned with or without a password. The default is to use no password, which simply means that you leave the password box empty. The Depends On Password permission requires that you enter a password on the basis of whether the client is to have read-only or full access. There is no option to leave the password boxes empty.

User-level access enables you to specify access on the basis of user accounts and groups that are already defined through Windows NT Servers that authorize users to log onto a domain. A list of users and groups also can be obtained from Windows NT workstations. To obtain a list of valid users and groups, you specify either the domain name or the name of a computer that has a defined set of users and groups. Users and groups are given three kinds of access:

- *Read-Only*: Clients can read the contents of files and folders and copy them, but clients cannot modify files and folders.

- *Full*: Clients can read, copy, add, remove, and modify files and folders.

- *Custom*: Clients are given access using any combination of the permissions listed in Table 9-2.

(Try Hands-on Project 9-7 to practice setting up a shared folder in Windows 95/98.)

Table 9-2   Windows 95 and Windows 98 Custom Share Permissions for User-Level Access

Permission	Description
Read-only	Read the contents of files and folders and copy, but not modify files and folders
Full	Read, copy, add, remove, and modify files and folders
Read (R)	Read the contents of files and copy them
Write (W)	Modify the contents of files
Create (C)	Create new files and folders
Delete (D)	Delete files
Change file attributes (T)	Change share permissions on files, such as adding or removing read, write, and delete to the customized access granted to a list of users and groups
List files (F)	View a listing of files in a folder
Change access control (A)	Change the type of access to files and folders, such as to read-only or full

Before setting up share-level access or user-level access, it is necessary to install file and printer sharing services. These services can be installed for Microsoft networks, for older NetWare networks, and for newer NetWare networks that use NDS. File and printer sharing services are installed from the Control Panel and Network icon. Click the Add button, double-click Service, and double-click File and printer sharing for Microsoft Networks, to install the services for a network running Microsoft operating systems. After you install the services, return to the Configuration tab and the Network dialog box, and check the options to enable others to have access to files and printers.

With file and printer sharing services installed and the access level selected, you are ready to create a shared disk, folder, or file (or printer). For example, to share a folder, right-click the folder in My Computer or in Explorer, click the Sharing option on the menu and click the Shared As radio button. The parameters that you complete will depend on which access level has been designated previously.

To map a drive that is shared by another computer, Windows 95 and Windows 98 use the Network Neighborhood utility on the desktop. You map a drive by double-clicking Network Neighborhood to view the computers on the network. Network Neighborhood displays a list of computers by name. To access the resources offered by a particular computer, double-click that computer to view the shared resources, which can be folders and printers. Next, map a folder by right-clicking it and selecting Map Network Drive on the menu (see Figure 9-13). In the Map Network Drive dialog box (see Figure 9-14) you specify a drive letter to which it is mapped and you can check a box to make sure the drive is mapped each time you start the operating system. After the drive is mapped, it appears in My Computer and in Explorer.

Figure 9-13   Selection menu

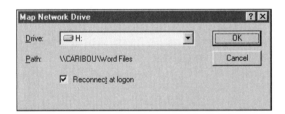

Figure 9-14   Mapping a drive

To disconnect a mapped drive, you right-click the drive in My Computer or Explorer, and click Disconnect on the menu.

 Shared drives in Windows NT Server and Windows NT Workstation are mapped using the same utilities as in Windows 95 and Windows 98—Network Neighborhood and the Map Network Drive dialog box. Also, mapped drives appear in My Computer and Explorer.

SHARING PRINTING DEVICES

Mac OS, NetWare, UNIX, Windows 95, Windows 98, and Windows NT all have the ability to share printers as well as disks, directories, and files. The sections that follow describe how printers are shared through these operating systems. (For more information on setting up printers in various operating systems, see Chapter 6.)

MACINTOSH

The Mac OS can make a local printer connected to it available to other computers running the Mac OS on a network. Also, the Mac OS can attach to a shared printer offered by another workstation on the network. You use the Chooser utility to set up a printer to share and to attach to a shared printer through the network.

To share a printer, first install the printer and set it up in the Mac OS. Once a printer is installed, it appears in the Chooser window. Select the printer and the Chooser window, and click Setup. In the Sharing Setup dialog box, click the check box next to Share this Printer and enter a name for the shared printer. There are also optional parameters that enable you to set a password required by others to access the shared printer and a check box to enable the Mac OS to keep a log of its use.

Accessing a shared printer requires that you first install a printer driver for the printer, such as a driver for a LaserWriter 8 or a StyleWriter 1200. After the printer driver is installed, click it in the Chooser window, and select the appropriate zone, if applicable. A list of shared printers appears, enabling you to select the one to use over the network.

NETWARE

Shared printing in NetWare is accomplished by using two different approaches. Both approaches are relatively complex and are only summarized in this chapter. The first approach is to employ queue-based printing, which is used for MS-DOS or Windows applications. The second is Novell Distributed Print Services (NDPS), which is used for Windows applications and for printers that have options tailored to NDPS.

In queue-based printing, the network administrator performs several functions to set up a shared printer. The first is to install the printer and its driver in NetWare. The next step is to create a print queue for the printer. For versions of NetWare that use NDS, the next step is to set up an NDS printer object, which defines the printer to NDS. After the printer object is defined, a print server object is also defined which links a printer to one or more print queues. The last step is to load the print server on the NetWare server so that the printer and its queue are shared through the NetWare server's operating system. After the printer is shared, clients access it by using the NetWare capture command, which captures the output from the client's designated printer port, such as LPT1, to the network printer associated with the queue.

NDPS is a new print service capability added in NetWare 5.0. It is designed to work with printers that have NetWare's printer agent software built in. These printers are simply attached to the network as a printing agent and the NDPS on the NetWare server handles the details of directing client print requests to the correct printer. Because most printers currently do not come with printer agent software, NetWare provides a printer gateway that acts as printer agent and that runs on the NetWare server. When printers are attached that do not have the agent software built in, NetWare provides the NDPS Manager utility to manage their connectivity for client access.

UNIX

UNIX printing in a networked environment is essentially the process of logging on to the UNIX server and printing to one of its printers. Typically, when a UNIX server is accessed through network connectivity, it is set up to use the BSD or the SVR4 spooling systems as described in Chapter 6. As a review, BSD uses three components for printing: the *lpr* print program, the *ldp* daemon, and the file, \etc\printcap to specify printer properties. The file \etc\printcap is a text file that can be modified via a text editor. In SVR4, the spooling system consists of the *lp* print program and the *lpsched* daemon. SVR4 printer properties are stored in the file, \etc\printcap, which is modified by using the *lpadmin* utility.

If your version of UNIX can use either BSD or SVR4 spooling, note that administrators often consider BSD spooling to be more adaptable for network clients.

WINDOWS 3.11

Printers are shared in Windows 3.11 by opening the Print Manager in the Main program group. A printer must first be installed before it can be shared. After you install the printer, select the printer in the Print Manager, click the Printer menu, and click Share Printer As (or use the Share Printer icon on the button bar). In the Share Printer dialog box, make sure the printer is entered in the Printer: box, enter the name for the share, and enter a comment to describe it. For security, you have the option to require that users enter a password to enable them to use your shared printer. To discontinue printer sharing, select the printer in the Print Manager, click the Printer menu, click Stop Sharing Printer, and click OK to confirm the action.

To connect to a shared printer on another network computer, open the Printer menu, click Connect Network Printer, and select the printer in the Connect Network Printer dialog box. You will also need to specify a local printer port from which to capture the print file. Disconnecting from a printer is accomplished by highlighting the network printer in the Print Manager, opening the Printer menu, and clicking Disconnect Network Printer.

WINDOWS 95, WINDOWS 98, AND WINDOWS NT

Windows 95, Windows 98, and Windows NT use the Add Printer Wizard to set up a printer locally (see Chapter 6). Once a printer is set up, it appears in the Printers folder. In all three operating systems, you share a printer by first opening the Printers folder, such as from the Start button and Settings option. Select the printer you want to share and right-click it to access the menu options shown in Figure 9-15 on the next page. Click Sharing and then click the Shared As: radio button. Enter a name for the shared printer and a comment to describe it. In Windows 95 and Windows 98, if share-level access is used, then you also have the option to require a password to access the printer (see Figure 9-16 on the next page). Also, if user-level access is used, then you can specify a list of users and groups who have access to the printer.

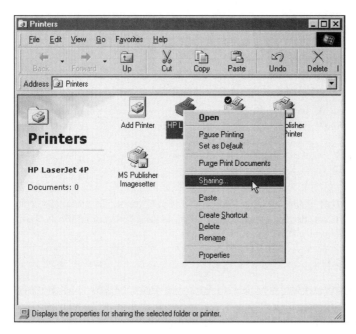

Figure 9-15   Sharing a printer in Windows 98

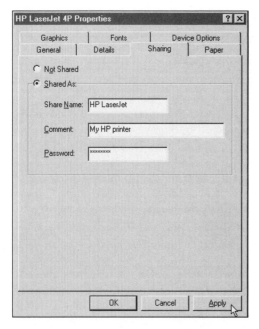

Figure 9-16   Setting up shared printer parameters in Windows 98

To share a printer, file and printer sharing services must first be installed in Windows 95 and Windows 98. In Windows NT, the server, spooler, and workstation services should be running (you can check these through the Control Panel and Services icon).

Sharing a printer in Windows NT 4.0 entails setting up two printer property tabs, Sharing and Security. To set up sharing, open the Printers folder, right-click the printer, and click Sharing. On the Sharing tab, click the radio button to share the printer and then provide a name for the shared printer. Because computers using different Windows operating systems may access the printer, you also have the option to install drivers for operating systems other than Windows NT, such as for Windows 95. The Security tab is used to set up share permissions for the printer, auditing of printer activity, and printer ownership. Use the Security tab and Permissions button (see Figure 9-17) to specify users and groups who have access and which permissions are granted. The Windows NT share permissions are as follows:

- *No Access*: Cannot access the shared printer

- *Print*: Can send print jobs and manage your own jobs

- *Manage Documents*: Can send print jobs and manage yours or those sent by any other user

- *Full Control*: Have complete control, including the ability to change share permissions, turn off sharing, and delete the share

Figure 9-17   Windows NT shared printer security

The Windows NT Add Printer Wizard enables you to designate a printer as shared at the same time that you install it. It also enables you to set up and manage shared printers at other Windows-based workstations on the network. Because the wizard does not include setting share permissions, make sure that you set these after the wizard completes the printer installation.

Mapping to a shared printer is an easy process in Windows 95, 98, and NT (try Hands-on Project 9-8). To map a printer, open Network Neighborhood and double-click the computer that offers the shared printer. In the list of shared resources, right-click the printer and click Install from the menu (see Figure 9-18).

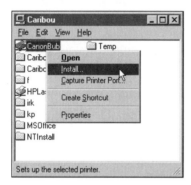

Figure 9-18   Installing a shared printer in Windows 95

NETWORK AND INTERNET RESOURCE SERVERS

NetWare, UNIX, and Windows NT Server can be set up as resource servers to provide network and Internet resources. All of these operating systems can act as servers for many kinds of functions. One of the most common is to handle e-mail. There is a wide range of programs that can turn a NetWare, UNIX, or Windows NT Server system into an e-mail server. By 1997, there were over 16 million Internet hosts, many of them NetWare, UNIX, or Windows NT servers processing and sending e-mail. The close relative of e-mail is e-commerce, which consists of thousands of servers connected to the Internet conducting business, such as taking and fulfilling product orders. It is estimated that by the year 2002, e-commerce servers will have processed over $300 billion in business transactions.

Another area in which these operating systems participate as resource servers is in videoconferencing and multimedia. Many companies are implementing videoconferencing capabilities on servers and workstations as a way to save money by reducing their travel expenses. For example, meetings that once required people to fly to a location from different parts of the country are now conducted through networks and server operating systems. Multimedia servers are also growing in use for business applications, education, government, and entertainment purposes. In a short time, computer owners will access a variety of rental movies through multimedia servers connected to the Internet. Currently, you can go to virtually any news organization's site and play news clips from a multimedia server. Many of these servers run NetWare, UNIX, and Windows NT Server. Another growing use for multimedia is to provide classes that you can access from a home computer over the Internet.

Client/server applications are also a reality and are made possible by networks and servers. A typical **client/server application** consists of three components: a workstation running a Windows-based operating system, a server from which to run applications, and one or more database servers. These applications are made possible because database software runs well on NetWare, UNIX, and Windows NT Server. For instance, Oracle and Sybase are two database systems that can run on these operating systems. Informix is another database system designed for UNIX, and SQL Server is a database system designed for Windows NT Server. All four of these database systems are used frequently in client/server applications.

Web servers are another fast-growing implementation of NetWare, UNIX, and Windows NT servers. Web servers provide a huge range of services that include the ability to quickly access information and to download it through FTP. This means that a large portion of Web servers also act as FTP servers. Already, many software companies enable you to provide a credit card number through a Web server and then download software. Before long, most software that you purchase will be downloaded from an Internet server instead of purchased in a box at a store.

9

Companies, schools, and government organizations are quickly implementing intranet servers that enable information to be obtained through private networks. For example, some companies enable employees to change personnel information by accessing an intranet server and completing a form in a Web-based environment. You may already have services at a bank that enable you to access your account information from a home computer by dialing into an intranet server available over the Internet. Or, your school may post grade and degree completion information on a server that you access through your campus network or through the Internet.

The uses for network servers are growing at an unimaginable rate. As networks are able to transport higher volumes of traffic at faster speeds, the implementation of servers grows reciprocally. Complementing the growth in the use of servers is equivalent growth in the capabilities of their operating systems and in the number of server programs written for them. For example, only a few years ago most database systems were written for mainframe computers. NetWare and Windows NT servers, in particular, were not considered robust enough to handle large databases. Today, major database systems run on both and databases often grow to be multigigabyte-sized files.

CHAPTER SUMMARY

Resource sharing is why networks exist and are thriving. At first, networks were particularly designed to share files. One of the first methods of doing this was by using protocols such as FTP to upload and download individual files. Network file servers quickly followed with the ability to share disks, directories, and files. Before long, they were also sharing other services such as printing and program services. Today, these functions on servers are commonplace and compose the vital network infrastructure of information and services.

One way to distinguish network-capable operating systems is by classifying them as server or client operating systems, although in some cases the distinctions are slight. NetWare, UNIX, and Windows NT Server are three extremely popular server network operating systems. Each of these enables you to create user accounts to access shared resources and to create groups to help manage user accounts, resources, and security. Security is becoming a critical capability as more servers are implemented on networks and more resources are shared. Some server network operating systems offer extensive security, such as Windows NT Server 4.0, which is certified by the federal government as having top secret or C2 level security capability.

Mac OS, UNIX, Windows 3.11, Windows 95, Windows 98, and Windows NT Workstation are examples of client network operating systems. All of these operating systems can share disks, directories, and files for other computers to access through a network. Each of these also can map to the shared resources made available on a network. Most of these operating systems enable you to control who accesses their shared resources. Table 9-3 presents a security summary by comparing FAT attributes (DOS and Windows-based systems configured for FAT), NetWare attributes and trustee rights, Windows NT (NTFS) attributes and permissions, and UNIX permissions.

Table 9-3   Attributes and File Permissions Compared

DOS Attributes (FAT)	NetWare Attributes and Trustee Rights	UNIX Permissions	Windows NT Attributes and Permissions (NTFS)	Description
N/A	N/A	Absence of X permission	No access —permission	No access
N/A	Read (R)	Read (R)	Handled through special NTFS permission (R)	Can read the contents of a file or directory
Read only (R)	Read only (Ro)	N/A	Handled through special NTFS permission (R)	Prevents directory or file from being changed or deleted
Archive (A)	Archive (A)	N/A	Archive (A)— file attribute	Directory or file is new or changed and needs to be backed up
N/A	Immediate Compress (Ic)	N/A	Compress (C)— file attribute	Compresses files to save disk space
N/A	Cannot Compress (Cc) and Do not Compress (Dc)	N/A	N/A	In NetWare Cc is automatically placed on files that should not be compressed and Dc is placed on files by the administrator

Table 9-3   Attributes and File Permissions Compared (continued)

DOS Attributes (FAT)	NetWare Attributes and Trustee Rights	UNIX Permissions	Windows NT Attributes and Permissions (NTFS)	Description
System (S)	System (Sy)	N/A	System (S)— file attribute	File is used by the operating system and should not be viewed with ordinary list commands— used by NetWare directories but not NT directories
Hidden (H)	Hidden (H)	N/A	Hidden (H)— file attribute (also can create a hidden share)	Directory or file cannot be viewed with ordinary list commands
N/A	Read Write (RW)	Read Write (RW)	Handled through special NTFS permissions (RW)	Directory or file can be viewed, changed, or deleted
N/A	Read and Execute (RX)	Read and Execute (RX)	List or Read (RX)— NTFS permissions List prevents access to folder contents, but can execute them	Can read and execute files, but not modify them
N/A	Write and Execute (WX)	Write and Execute (WX)	Add (WX)	Can modify files and execute them
N/A	N/A	N/A	Add & Read (RWX)	Can read files, add new files, execute programs, but cannot modify the file contents
N/A	Read, Write, and Execute (RWX)	Read, Write, and Execute (RWX)	Change (RWXD)	Can read, add, delete, modify, and execute files and directories
N/A	Copy Inhibit (Ci)	N/A	Handled through special NTFS permissions	Cannot copy a file

9

Table 9-3   Attributes and File Permissions Compared (continued)

DOS Attributes (FAT)	NetWare Attributes and Trustee Rights	UNIX Permissions	Windows NT Attributes and Permissions (NTFS)	Description
N/A	Delete Inhibit (Di)	N/A	Handled through special NTFS permissions	Cannot delete a directory or file
N/A	Execute only (X)	Execute (X)	Handled through special NTFS permissions (X)	Can only execute a file (run the program)
N/A	Indexed (I)	N/A	Handled by the NT operating system	Flags large files for fast access
N/A	Purge (P)	N/A	Handled by the Recycle Bin	Purge deleted directories and files so they cannot be salvaged
N/A	Rename inhibit (Ri)	N/A	Handled through special NTFS permissions	Cannot rename a directory or file
N/A	Read audit (RA)	N/A	N/A	Can be assigned, but has no function in NetWare 3.1 and later systems
N/A	Sharable (Sh)	Execute (X)	Handled by creating a network share	Files can be accessed by more than one user at a time
N/A	Transactional (T)	N/A	Handled by NTFS through directory and file recovery options	For recovery of data files after a system interruption, such as a power failure
N/A	Write (W)	Write (W)	Handled by creating a special NTFS permission (W)	Can modify the contents of a file or folder
N/A	Write audit (Wa)	N/A	N/A	Can be assigned, but has no function in NetWare 3.1 and later systems

Table 9-3 Attributes and File Permissions Compared (continued)

DOS Attributes (FAT)	NetWare Attributes and Trustee Rights	UNIX Permissions	Windows NT Attributes and Permissions (NTFS)	Description
N/A	N/A	N/A	Full Control	Can read, add, delete, execute, and modify files and directories, plus change permissions and take ownership
N/A	Normal (N)	N/A	N/A	Removes all attributes

Network server operating systems will be particularly interesting to watch as they provide more and more shared network and Internet resources. Already, network server operating systems handle functions such as e-mail, e-commerce, network conferencing, multimedia distribution, database access, and education through the Internet.

In the next chapter, you learn about techniques for managing and maintaining computer operating systems, such as performing backups, managing accounts, and maintaining hard disk drives. You also learn about techniques for installing and managing application software.

9

KEY TERMS

- **client/server application** — A software application that divides processing between a client operating system and one or more server operating systems (often a database and an application server). Dividing processing tasks is intended to achieve the best performance.

- **container object** — An entity that is used to group together resources, such as an organizational unit, an organization, or a country as specified in the directory services of NetWare.

- **domain** — A grouping of resources into a functional unit for management. The resources can be servers, workstations, shared disks and directories, and shared printers.

- **global group** — In Windows NT Server, a group that is used to manage user accounts, such as for security access.

- **group identification number (GID)** — A unique number that is assigned to a UNIX group that distinguishes that group from all other groups on the same system.

- **home directory** — A user work area in which the user stores data on a server and typically has control over whether to enable other server users to access his or her data.

- **leaf object** — An object, such as an account, that is stored in an organization or organizational unit container in the NetWare NDS.

- **local group** — In Windows NT Server, a group that is used to manage shared resources, such as disks, folders, and printers.

- **mapping** — The process of attaching to a shared resource, such as a shared drive, and using it as though it is a local resource. For example, when a workstation operating system maps to the drive of another workstation, it can assign a drive letter to that drive and access it as though it is a local drive instead of a remote one.

- **Network File System (NFS)** — Enables file transfer and other shared services which involve computers running UNIX.

- **Novell Directory Services (NDS)** — A comprehensive database of shared resources and information known to the NetWare operating system.

- **object** — An entity, such as a user account, group, directory, or printer, that is known to a network operating system's database and that the operating system manages in terms of sharing or controlling access to that object.

- **search drive** — A mapped NetWare drive that enables the operating system to search a specified directory and its subdirectories for an executable (program) file.

- **shadow file** — With access limited to the root user, a file in UNIX that contains critical information about user accounts, including the encrypted password for each account.

- **share** — An object, such as a folder, in Windows 3.11, Windows 95, Windows 98, and Windows NT, that is made visible to other network users for access over a network.

- **share-level access control** — Access to a shared folder in Windows 95 and Windows 98 by creating a disk or folder share that is protected by share permissions and on which the share owner can require a password for access.

- **user identification number (UID)** — A unique number that is assigned to a UNIX user account as a way to distinguish that account from all others on the same system.

- **user-level access control** — Access to a shared folder in Windows 95 and Windows 98 in which the share owner creates a list of groups and users who are allowed to access the share.

REVIEW QUESTIONS

1. Which of the following enables you to access a shared volume in Mac OS 8.5?

   a. Chooser

   b. Network Neighborhood

   c. My Computer

   d. all of the above

   e. only a and b

   f. only b and c

2. The _____ spooling system is the one most recommended on a net-worked UNIX computer.

3. Which of the following is an access method that can be used in Windows 95?

   a. user-level

   b. share-level

   c. privilege level

   d. all of the above

   e. only a and b

   f. only a and c

4. Which operating system uses a permission called Full Control?

   a. Windows 3.11

   b. NetWare

   c. Windows NT

   d. None of the above permit Full Control, except to the workstation administrator.

5. Which operating system enables you to set up a search drive?

   a. Mac OS 8.5

   b. NetWare

   c. Windows NT

   d. UNIX

6. The utility that is used to set up accounts in Windows NT Server 4.0 is called

   a. Server Manager

   b. Network Browser

   c. User Manager for Domains

   d. Account Manager

7. The *x* permission on a UNIX directory enables you to

   a. write to a file in the directory.

   b. read the contents of a file in that directory.

   c. list the directory contents.

   d. keep date stamps on files in the directory.

8. Each account created in UNIX has a unique _____.

9. Shared printing in Windows 98 is set up as a(n) _____ of a printer object.

10. Which of the following is a security measure that you can associate with a NetWare account?

   a. intruder detection

   b. requiring a minimum password length

9

   c. requiring the user to periodically change his or her password

   d. all of the above

   e. only a and b

   f. only b and c

11. Which of the following is a security measure that you can associate with a Windows NT Server account?

    a. intruder detection

    b. requiring a minimum password length

    c. requiring the user to periodically change his or her password

    d. all of the above

    e. only a and b

    f. only b and c

12. The share permissions used to share a folder in Windows NT Server are _____, _____, _____, and _____.

13. Which of the following file systems recognized by Windows NT Server has the greatest security capabilities?

    a. NTFS

    b. NFS

    c. FAT

    d. OSPF

14. One problem with the Mac OS is that it does not support using groups to help manage shared resources. True or False?

15. Which of the following methods is used by the UNIX *chmod* utility for setting up permissions?

    a. symbolic

    b. binary

    c. octal

    d. all of the above

    e. only a and b

    f. only a and c

16. The _____ utility in NetWare enables you to quickly set up multiple accounts.

17. In Windows NT Server, it is not possible to set up a shared printer by using the Add Printer Wizard. True or False?

18. Which type of Windows NT Server group is typically used for managing resources?

   a. resource

   b. global

   c. share

   d. local

19. In the Mac OS 8.5, it is possible to access another network computer by using its IP address. True or False?

20. Which of the following are privileges supported by the Mac OS 8.5 operating system?

   a. read only

   b. write only

   c. none

   d. all of the above

   e. only a and b

21. Set User ID is an example of a special set of _____ in the _____ operating system.

22. Windows NT Workstation is designed to effectively handle up to _____ simultaneous users.

23. Which of the following resources can be shared in Windows 95?

   a. disks

   b. directories

   c. printers

   d. all of the above

   e. only a and b

   f. only b and c

24. Which of the following operating systems enable(s) you to associate a password with a shared resource?

   a. Windows 3.11

   b. Windows 95

   c. Mac OS

   d. all of the above

   e. only a and b

   f. only b and c

9

25. You see a drive mapping to S4. What operating system is offering this as a shared resource?

   a. Windows 98

   b. Windows NT

   c. UNIX

   d. NetWare

   e. all of the above

   f. only a and b

   g. only b and d

HANDS-ON PROJECTS

PROJECT 9-1

In this hands-on activity, you practice mapping a search drive to a NetWare server and then delete the drive. You will need network access from Windows 3.11, Windows 95, Windows 98, or Windows NT and an account on a NetWare server.

To map and then delete a search drive:

1. Log on to the NetWare server.

2. Open an MS-DOS command window and type **MAP** at the prompt and then press **Enter** to view the current drive mappings. If the MAP command does not work, access the PUBLIC directory by typing **CD SYS:PUBLIC**, press **Enter**, type **MAP** at the network prompt, and then press **Enter**.

3. Determine the last search drive in use from the list of mapped drives, which is the S# drive that has the highest number.

4. Using the next S# number (use S1 if no search drives are defined), map a search drive to the PUBLIC directory or to another directory specified by your instructor. Type **MAP S1:=SYS:PUBLIC** and press **Enter**.

5. Type **MAP** again to see if your search drive is in the list of mapped drives.

6. Finally, type **MAP DEL S1:** (or S and the number of the drive you used in step 4) and press **Enter** to delete the drive mapping.

7. Type **exit** at the command prompt to close the DOS window.

Project 9-2

In this assignment, you give read permissions to all user accounts on a UNIX server. You will need access to a UNIX computer, a user account, and a practice directory containing files.

To set the permissions:

1. Log on to the UNIX computer and switch to your practice directory.
2. At the command prompt, type **chmod a=r ***.
3. View the change by listing permissions via the command **ls −1**.
4. Log off when you are finished.

Project 9-3

In this project, you view the global and local groups on a Windows NT Server. You will need access to a computer running Windows NT Server and access to an account that has administrator privileges (ask your instructor how to access the account).

9

To view the global and local groups:

1. Click **Start**, highlight **Programs**, and highlight **Administrative Tools (Common)**.
2. Click **User Manager for Domains**. Maximize the screen, if necessary.
3. View the groups listed in the bottom half of the screen, under the Groups column.
4. Notice which groups have the word Domain in front, such as Domain Admins and Domain Guests, and notice their descriptions. These are global groups.
5. Notice the groups that do not start with the word Domain. These groups are local.
6. Double-click a global group to view its members. Next, close that dialog box and double-click a local group to view its members. Close that dialog box when you are finished viewing the members.
7. Create a word processed document containing a table that has two columns, one in which to record the groups and one in which to record the descriptions of the groups.
8. Close the User Manager for Domains when you are finished.

PROJECT 9-4

In this project, you practice setting up a shared folder in Windows NT Server 4.0. You also set up share permissions by deleting the Everyone group from access and then by giving full access only to the Backup Operators local group. As in the previous Hands-on project, you will need access to a computer running Windows NT Server (formatted for NTFS) and access to an account assigned administrator privileges.

To set up the shared folder:

1. Open **My Computer** on the desktop and double-click drive C: (or another appropriate drive).

2. Select an existing folder to share, such as the **Temp** folder and right-click it.

3. Click **Sharing** on the menu.

4. Click the **Shared As** radio button. Enter a name for the shared folder in the Share Name box, such as **TestShare**.

5. Enter **Share test** in the Comment box.

6. Click the **Maximum Allowed** radio button, so that there are no restrictions to the number of users who access the share simultaneously.

7. Click the **Permissions** button to open the Access Through Share Permissions dialog box.

8. Select the **Everyone** group from the Name list, and click **Remove**.

9. Click **Add**.

10. Select **Backup Operators** in the Names list box, and click **Add**.

11. Select **Full Control** in the Type of Access list box.

12. Click **OK**, and then click **OK** again. Server Operators now have Full Control access to that folder.

 Your instructor may ask that you remove the share when you are finished. If so, repeat Steps 2 and 3. On the Sharing tab, click the Not Shared radio button, then click Apply and OK.

PROJECT 9-5

In this project, you try out the Network Browser, new (at this writing) in Mac OS 8.5. Besides a Macintosh that runs this operating system, you will need shared resources set up on other network computers.

To use the Network Browser:

1. Open the Apple menu and click the **Network Browser**.

2. Double-click the appropriate zone containing the computer with the shared volume.

3. Double-click the computer containing the shared volume.

4. Enter your name and password (or a name and password provided by your instructor) in the text boxes. Click **OK**.

5. Double-click the volume you want to access.

6. Make sure that the icon for the volume is now on the desktop and that you can open it.

7. Close the Network Browser.

9

PROJECT 9-6

This project enables you to practice creating a new user in the Mac OS.

To create a new user:

1. Open the Apple menu.

2. Select **Control Panels** and click **Users & Groups**.

3. Click **New User**.

4. Enter the new user's name and password in the **New User** dialog box.

5. Check **Allow user to change password**.

6. Select **Sharing** in the Show box, to view the sharing options.

7. Check the box to **Allow users to connect to this computer**.

8. Check **Allow users to link to programs on this computer**.

9. Close the dialog box and look for the user that you created in the Users & Groups Control Panel dialog box.

10. Close the Users & Groups Control Panel dialog box when you are finished.

PROJECT 9-7

In this project, you create a shared folder in Windows 95 or Windows 98 that employs user-level access. You need a computer running Windows 95 or Windows 98 that is set up for user-level access and on which file and printer sharing services are installed. The computer should also be set up in advance as a member of an NT domain or workgroup.

To create the shared folder:

1. Open **My Computer** or **Explorer**.
2. Right-click a folder to share, such as **Temp**.
3. Click the **Sharing** option on the menu and then the **Sharing** tab, if necessary.
4. Click the **Shared As** radio button and enter a name for the share, such as **Test** or **Temp** in the Share Name box. Also, document your share by entering a comment, such as **Temporary share**, in the Comment box.
5. Click **Add**.
6. In the Add Users dialog box, select a user, such as **Administrator**, and click the **Full Access** button. Notice that Administrator moves into the box at the right of the Full Access button.
7. Select another user on the list, such as **Guest**, and click the **Read Only** button. Also, notice that Guest moves into the box at the right of the Read Only button.
8. Click **OK**.
9. Click **Apply** and **OK**.

PROJECT 9-8

In this project, you install a network printer in Windows 98.

To install the shared printer:

1. Open **Network Neighborhood**.
2. Double-click the computer that has the shared printer (if you are not sure which computer to click, ask your instructor).
3. Find a printer in the list of resources and right-click it. Shared printers are identified by a printer icon.
4. Click **Install**, which starts the Add Printer Wizard.

5. Click **No** to indicate you will not be using DOS-based programs and click **Next**.

6. Enter a name for the printer and click **No** so that it is not installed as the default printer for your workstation and click **Next**.

7. Click **Yes** to print a test page and click **Finish**.

8. Check to make sure that the test page printed.

PROJECT 9-9

In this project, you create a new group, change the group's name, and finally delete that group. Before starting, ask your instructor for a GID to use. For the group name, use the first and last initials of your name appended to test, such as mptest.

UNIX

To create, modify, and delete a group:

1. Log on to the UNIX computer as root.

2. At the command prompt, enter a *groupadd –g GID* (provided by instructor) *groupname* (your first and last initials + test), such as **groupadd –g 200 mptest**.

3. In some versions of UNIX, you will see a return code of zero that indicates you successfully added the group. (If a return code is displayed that is other than 0, make sure that you have correctly typed the command, used a unique GID and group name, and that you have proper access to create groups; or ask your instructor for help.)

4. Change the group name by using your first and middle initial appended to test using the command, *groupmod –g GID –n newname oldname*, such as **groupmod –g 200 –n mjtest mptest**.

5. Again you should see a zero return code to indicate that you have successfully changed the group name.

6. Delete the group by entering the *groupdel* command and the group name, such as **groupdel mptest**. (Look for a zero return code.)

7. Log off when you are finished.

9

PROJECT 9-10

In this project, you use Windows 3.11 to connect to a shared network drive and enable network browsing. After enabling network browsing, you change the SYSTEM.INI file to ensure that Windows 3.11 does not compete on the network as a Master Browser. Before starting, make sure that there is at least one other network computer that is set up to share a directory, such as a computer running Windows 95, Windows 98, or Windows NT.

To connect to a network drive:

1. Open **File Manager**.

2. Click the **Disk** menu and click **Connect Network Drive**.

3. In the Connect Network Drive dialog box, select the computer and shared directory in the Show Shared Directories on and Shared Directories boxes.

4. Assign an unused drive letter, such as **D:** (the dialog box will suggest the next available drive letter).

5. Specify the path to the shared directory (if it is not already provided).

6. Check the **Reconnect at Startup** box.

7. Check the **Always Browse** box.

8. Click **OK**.

To edit the SYSTEM.INI file:

1. Make sure that .INI files are associated with the Notepad text editor. Click the **File** menu and **Associate**, then enter **ini** in the Files with Extension box and make sure it is associated with **Text File (notepad.exe)**.

2. Access the Windows directory and double-click **SYSTEM.INI**.

3. Scroll down to the [Network] section in the file and look for the variable, MaintainServerList.

4. Make sure the variable equals **no**.

5. If the variable is not in the SYSTEM.INI file, enter it under the [Network] section as **MaintainServerList=no** (see Figure 9-19).

6. Close Notepad and then close File Manager.

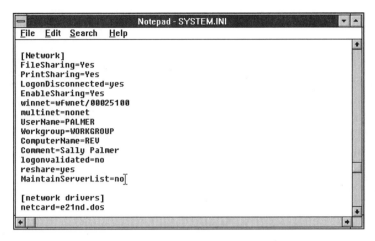

```
┌──────────────────────────────────────────────────┐
│ ▬              Notepad - SYSTEM.INI           ▼ ▲ │
│ File  Edit  Search  Help                          │
├──────────────────────────────────────────────────┤
│ [Network]                                       ▲ │
│ FileSharing=Yes                                   │
│ PrintSharing=Yes                                  │
│ LogonDisconnected=yes                             │
│ EnableSharing=Yes                                 │
│ winnet=wfwnet/00025100                            │
│ multinet=nonet                                    │
│ UserName=PALMER                                   │
│ Workgroup=WORKGROUP                               │
│ ComputerName=REV                                  │
│ Comment=Sally Palmer                              │
│ logonvalidated=no                                 │
│ reshare=yes                                       │
│ MaintainServerList=no                             │
│                                                   │
│ [network drivers]                                 │
│ netcard=e21nd.dos                               ▼ │
│ ◄                                               ► │
└──────────────────────────────────────────────────┘
```

Figure 9-19   Modifying the SYSTEM.INI file in Windows 3.11

CASE PROJECT

1. Your state's university has a large Engineering College consisting of 52 faculty members who use computers that run Windows NT Workstation 4.0, UNIX, and Mac OS 8.5. The department also maintains four labs. One of those consists of computers running Mac OS 8.5, while the other three labs have computers that run a combination of Windows 95 and Windows NT. Further, the dean's office maintains a NetWare server and a Windows NT server. You are employed by the department as the main support person for all of these computer operating systems.

   a. Ten faculty members use Mac OS 8.5 and have their students use the Macintosh lab. They want to enable students to submit assignments over the network from the lab. Also, they want to make new assignments available for students to pick up at any time of day through the network. Are these goals possible? If so, how can the Macintosh computers be set up to accomplish these goals?

   b. The dean wants to set up the NetWare server so that the five department heads in the Engineering College can access her spreadsheets reflecting the college's budget and several department management programs that have been written and installed by graduate student employees. You have been charged with explaining to the department heads how the NetWare server will be set up to share the spreadsheets and management programs. What explanation would you give in a presentation? Also, the dean asks you to show each department head how to access the shared information from their computers that run Windows 98. Develop a set of instructions for the deans and explain how you would use the instructions to supplement a live demonstration.

c. The electrical engineering department head has two kinds of folders that he wants to share over the network. One folder contains professor evaluations that he wants to enable his faculty members to access and review, but so that each faculty member can only view her or his evaluation. A second folder consists of text files that are assigned readings for his class of 19 students. How would you advise him to set up these shared folders? Keep in mind that the faculty members use Windows NT, Windows 95, and Windows 98. His students use a lab that has a combination of Windows operating systems.

d. The dean's office associate wants you to make two expensive color laser printers in the front office available to any department member. One is attached to his Macintosh computer and the other is attached to the Windows NT server. Can you make the printers available department-wide? If so, how?

e. The dean has purchased an Oracle database of technical information for all members of the Engineering College to access. What department computer would you use as home for this database? Why?

f. Eight faculty members have UNIX workstations. How can you set up the Windows NT server to be accessed by these workstations? Can they use their existing accounts and passwords for access? How?

g. A faculty member who uses Windows 98 wants to set up a shared folder so that others can only read the contents and access it via a password. How would you set up the computer to accomplish this?

STANDARD OPERATING AND MAINTENANCE PROCEDURES

Computer operating systems are similar to cars in that they need regular maintenance to achieve the best performance. A new car, like a new computer, delivers fast response and every component usually functions perfectly. To keep the car at its best, you need to perform regular maintenance such as changing the oil and performing tuneups. If you neglect maintenance, the car's performance suffers and the wear shows quickly. Maintenance is as important for computers as it is for cars, because it does not take long for an operating system, software, and hardware to degrade in performance. Computer operating system maintenance consists of deleting unnecessary files, tuning memory, regularly backing up files, defragmenting disks, and repairing damaged files. Maintenance is particularly important for computer systems that are connected to a network, because a poorly responding computer has an impact on network operations.

AFTER READING THIS CHAPTER AND COMPLETING THE EXERCISES YOU WILL BE ABLE TO:

- Explain file system maintenance techniques for different operating systems

- Perform regular file system maintenance by finding and deleting unused files and directories

- Perform disk maintenance that includes defragmenting, relocating files and folders, running disk and file repair utilities, and selecting RAID options

- Set up and perform disk, directory, and file backups

- Explain how to install software for best performance

- Tune operating systems for optimal performance

In this chapter, you learn a variety of techniques for maintaining and tuning workstations and servers. One of the most important steps in making disk and file maintenance easy is to start with a well designed directory structure, which makes finding unused files and folders a straightforward process. Two other important tasks are to perform regular backups and to run disk maintenance utilities. How and where software is installed is also vital to how a computer performs. Finally, there are tuning options, such as adjusting virtual memory, that can immediately enhance performance.

FILE SYSTEM MAINTENANCE

Successful file system maintenance is closely linked to the file structure on a computer. On both workstation and server operating systems, a well-planned file structure makes it easy to locate files, update files, share folders and files, back up and archive files, and delete unwanted files. In addition, on server operating systems, well-designed file structures favorably impact network performance and security.

Some basic rules for creating a file structure include:

- Keep the number of directories in the root directory to a manageable number.
- Keep operating system files in the default directories recommended by the vendor.
- Keep different versions of software in their own directories.
- Keep data files in directories on the basis of the function of those data files.
- Design home directories to match the functions of users in an organization.

It does not take long for the number of directories in the root directory (often called the "root") to proliferate. For example, many software vendors attempt to install their software into the root by default. If you have very many software applications, this kind of file structure quickly becomes confusing and hard to manage. It makes more sense to create one or two directories within the root that are intended for software applications, and then to create subdirectories within each main applications directory to contain particular applications. In the last chapter, you learned that software applications can be placed in a directory called Applications or Apps. Another technique is to create a general applications directory and separate directories for main software vendors. If you use Microsoft applications, consider using the Microsoft default directory, which is Program Files, or if you use Corel applications such as the WordPerfect Suite, use their default Corel directory. An example of a file structure in which you might use three directories for applications in the root of the main volume, Applications, Corel, and Program Files, is illustrated in Figure 10-1. The figure also shows two other directories usually found in the root, for Windows system files and utility programs.

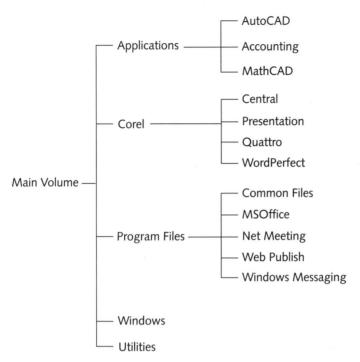

Figure 10-1 Example applications directories and subdirectories

 Some users and system administrators prefer to limit the number of entries in the root directory to only the number that can be displayed in one or two screens when you are at the command level in an operating system, or in a utility such as Windows Explorer. On a typical system, this might translate into a maximum of 10 to 15 directories per hard disk volume.

Well-organized directories and subdirectories enable you to have a relatively small number of main directories in the root. Figure 10-2 on the next page, illustrates a typical root directory structure in UNIX. The directories in this example have the following functions:

- \bin houses system files
- \dev is for device files
- \etc holds configuration files
- \home is for user home directories
- \mnt is for mounting removable drives such as CD-ROM drives
- \sbin contains system files
- \tmp holds temporary files
- \usr is for programs
- \var holds files that change frequently

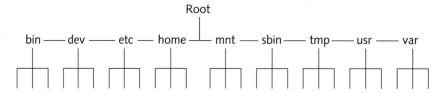

Figure 10-2   Typical UNIX root directory structure

Operating system directories are typically placed in the root directory, and have appropriate subdirectories under a main directory. For example, Windows 98 operating system files are contained in the Windows folder (see Figure 10-3), which has subdirectories such as System. Macintosh system files are likewise kept in a System folder. Table 10-1 illustrates typical locations for system files.

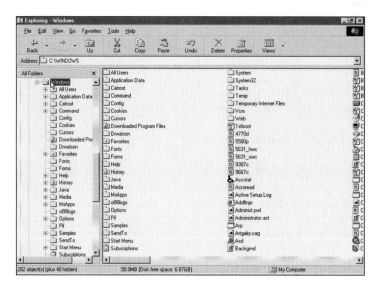

Figure 10-3   Windows 98 operating system files in the Windows folder

Table 10-1   Operating System Directories

Operating System	System Directory or Directories from the Root
Mac OS	System
NetWare	System
UNIX	bin, etc, and sbin
Windows 3.x	Windows
Windows 95	Windows
Windows 98	Windows
Windows NT	Winnt
Windows 2000 Server and Professional	Winnt

There are several advantages to installing and leaving operating system files in the directories created by the operating system, instead of trying to hide these files or use other directory locations (see the caution that follows). One reason is that it is easier for others to help with computer problems as they arise. For example, in organizations that have user support departments, it is easier for a user support professional to assist in solving problems with drivers and network access when system files are easy to find. Another reason for leaving system files in the default directories is that many software installations expect operating system files to be in the default locations, and work best when it is easy for them to find specific subdirectories and key files related to the operating system.

 When you install server operating systems there may be a temptation to hide or rename default system directories as a way to protect them from intruders. However, most intruders are not going to be deterred by this attempt at hiding files. A better approach is to understand and implement the security available in the operating system.

In Windows NT, software that is installed is also tracked in the Registry, which contains configuration information as well as information about individual components of a software installation. Thus, it is easier for the operating system to assist when it is necessary to uninstall or upgrade software, because it is able to quickly identify and find the components that are to be deleted or upgraded. In Windows 3.x, Windows 95, Windows 98, and Windows NT these vital files are kept in the operating system's folder and subfolders. For example, in Windows 3.1x, Windows 95, and Windows 98, these files are located in the \Windows and \Windows\System folders. In Windows NT, they are found in the \Winnt and \Winnt\System32 folders. Table 10-2 lists examples of typical Windows-based application software components. Applications software and operating system enhancements are easier to install when these components are in known locations.

10

Table 10-2 Examples of Windows-Based Application Software Components

File Type	File Extension	File Type	File Extension
Application	.exe	Help context	.cnt
Backup	.bak	Initialization	.ini
Bitmap image	.bmp	Installation	.inf
Control Panel extension	.cpl	MS-DOS application	.com
Configuration	.cfg	OLE common control	.ocx
Data	.dat	Precompiled setup information	.pnf
Device driver	.drv	Text	.txt
Dynamic link library	.dll	TrueType font	.ttf
Help	.hlp	Visual Basic application	.vbx

Sometimes, particularly on network servers, it is necessary to keep several versions of a software application available for different kinds of uses. For example, an organization may have some users who still use earlier versions of WordPerfect or Microsoft Word. In a department or organization in which software applications are developed, it may be necessary to keep different versions of compilers or development tools available. This is because some users may have operating systems that only support 16-bit applications, whereas other users may have operating systems that support 32-bit applications. In these situations, one way to easily handle having more than one version of the same software is to put different versions in different subdirectories under a main application directory. For example, in Windows NT Server, you can support different versions of Microsoft Word by having a Program Files directory, and subdirectories called Word2, Word95, Word97, and Word2000. In this case, you would have one of these versions installed to run locally and the other versions would be available to clients to support network installations (with appropriate licensing considerations).

Some directory structures include special locations for data files. For example, if the computer contains files for word processing, spreadsheets, and databases, then those files might be stored as subdirectories under a root directory called Data. On a file server the files might be stored on the basis of directories set up for departments. In a company that has a business department and a research department, the main directories might be Business and Research, with subdirectories under each for shared word processing, spreadsheet, and database files.

Home directories on a server often reflect the organizational structure. In a college, the home directory might be called Home within the root directory. Under the Home directory there might be subdirectories for each department in the college: Business, Registrar, Anthropology, Biology, Chemistry, English, Music, Psychology, and so on. Finally, under each department subdirectory there would be subdirectories for that department's faculty and staff members.

FINDING AND DELETING FILES

A solid file structure on the computer makes it easier to find and delete unneeded files on a regular schedule. It does not take long on any computer system for such files to accumulate and to occupy a large amount of disk space. One example is the temporary files that are created when you install new software and when you run many types of applications. Most installations create a temporary directory and a set of temporary files that are stored in the temporary directory. Some software applications do not completely delete temporary files when the application installation is finished. These files may be stored in a temporary directory in the root or in the operating system directory. Also, some software applications create temporary files that are not deleted when the application is improperly terminated. For example, many word processing programs create temporary files that are used for backup purposes or to save the most immediate changes. These files may not be completely deleted when the application is closed or when the application is shut down improperly, such as because of a power failure. It is a good practice to implement a regular schedule for finding and deleting these unneeded files, using the methods available in different operating systems, detailed in the following sections.

Deleting files is vital as a means to make the best use of disk storage resources and it can help extend the life of hard disks. One rule of thumb is that hard disk drives should be kept under 80% full. Those that grow over 80% full are subject to excessive wear and are more likely to have problems or fail. This provides added incentive to make sure that files are regularly deleted as a means to help keep disk utilization under 80%.

MAC OS

One particularly important reason for deleting files in the Mac OS is to make sure that you do not run out of disk space. Regularly deleting files enables you to make sure there is enough disk space on hand for all needs. The Mac OS provides an easy way to assess available disk space by simply checking the header information when you open the Macintosh HD window or a window to display the contents of any folder. The header provides information about the number of items and the available disk space in MB.

The Mac OS has a Find utility on the File menu that can be used to find files which are no longer needed. To use the Find utility, you simply click the folder and in the dialog box enter the string you want to use to find an unneeded file, such as a Web related graphics file called *netnews.gif*. Once an unneeded file is found, drag it into the trash. The Mac OS is forgiving because the deleted item can be brought back from the trash by opening the trash and moving the item back to the desktop.

10

 Use the Sherlock utility as described in Chapter 3 for complex search criteria including name, kind of file, creation date, modification date, size, version, and folder attribute. Sherlock also has the ability to index information for faster access.

 Files are not truly deleted until they are purged by emptying the trash. The trash should be emptied on a regular schedule so that disk space occupied by deleted files is returned for use by other files. (Try Hands-on Project 10-1 to practice emptying the trash.)

NETWARE

There are several ways to manage files and folders in NetWare. NetWare Administrator is one tool that is available to view and manage directories and files. Another option for Windows-based NetWare clients is to use Network Neighborhood to view folder and file information, including information about properties.

A third utility that can be very effective is called NDIR and is run from a NetWare DOS window. NDIR includes a number of commands that enable you to find files on the basis of specific criteria, such as by date or by owner. NDIR can also provide important information about directory space that is in use. The commands include the following:

- /AC BEF to view files that have not been accessed since the date specified
- /DATE to view information based on the date

- /DO to view all information on directories

- /OW to view files by owner

- /REV SORT SI to sort files listing the largest first

- /SPA to view how directory space is used

- /SORT SI to sort files on the basis of size

- /SORT OW to sort files on the basis of ownership

- /VOL to view the information by volume

You can delete directories and files by using NetWare Administrator or by using the delete (DEL) command in a DOS window. As is true for the Mac OS, NetWare files can be salvaged until they are purged. To salvage files from Network Neighborhood, right-click the folder containing the files to be salvaged, and then click Salvage Files. Another option to salvage files is to use the Salvage command in the DOS window. Because file space is not returned until deleted files are purged, it is wise to establish a schedule for regularly purging them. For example, the deleted files in a directory called Data can be listed and purged by right-clicking the directory and clicking Purge Files. Next, click Purge all and click Yes. Another way to purge files is to open the DOS window, switch to the Data directory and enter the PURGE command at the DOS prompt, such as PURGE *.* to purge all files or PURGE *.doc to purge word processed files only.

 When you create a home directory for a user, make sure you restrict the size of the directory by using NetWare Administrator. This technique makes sure that there is a limit to the amount of disk space that is available to a single user. In fact, there have been instances in which users have produced so many undeleted temporary files that they have occupied all available disk space on a server. When this happens, no space is left to perform even the simplest functions until the administrator deletes these files.

UNIX

You can view UNIX files by using the *ls* command along with one or more options for listing particular file qualities. Some of the options associated with this command are as follows:

- *-a* lists all files

- *-d* presents file information on the basis of the specified argument

- *-F* identifies the directory contents on the basis of directory, executable files, and symbolic links (since UNIX is case sensitive, this option should be capitalized while the others are not)

- *-i* displays the inode number for each file

- *-l* presents a detailed information listing including permissions and file size

- *-n* displays UIDs and GIDs of those who have access to files

- *-r* sorts files in reverse alphabetic order

- *-s* displays the size of files

- *-t* displays files on the basis of the date when they were last modified

- *-u* displays files on the basis of the time when they were last modified

Files and folders are deleted in UNIX by using the remove (*rm*) command. Two options can be added to the command: *-i* and *-r*. The *-i* or interactive option results in a query about if you really want to delete the file or directory; and the *-r* or recursive command is used to delete the entire directory contents, including all subdirectories and files within a directory.

A file can be found by using the *find* command. This command enables files to be found on the basis of the filename, a wildcard character (*) associated with part of the name, the size of the file, and the last time it was accessed or modified. For example, to find and print a list of all temporary files that have been modified in the last 30 days, you would enter *find -name temp* -mtime -30 -print*. (Try Hands-on Project 10-2 to practice finding and deleting temporary files in UNIX.)

The options used with *find* are as follows:

- *-atime* for last accessed time

- *-ctime* for last changed time

- *-mtime* for last modification time

- *-name* for the filename, including the use of wildcard searches

- *-print* to print the results of the find

- *-size* for file size (in blocks or in bytes; with bytes specified by a "c" after the size value)

UNIX provides commands to help you assess the allocation of disk space. One command is *df*, which enables you to view information on the basis of the file system. It provides statistics on the total number of blocks, the number used, the number available, and the percent of capacity used. While *df* provides gross file system statistics, the *du* command is used to display statistics for a given directory and its subdirectories, or for a subdirectory alone. (Try Hands-on Project 10-9.)

On a UNIX computer that acts as a server, the administrator has the option to set up disk quotas. For example, a disk quota can be established in blocks for each user as a way to make sure that users do not occupy all of the disk space (see Figure 10-4 on the next page). A quota is set by using the *edquota* command that opens the quota file so that it can be edited. The quota file must first be created by the administrator, or in some versions of UNIX, it is created automatically when you first use *edquota*.

10

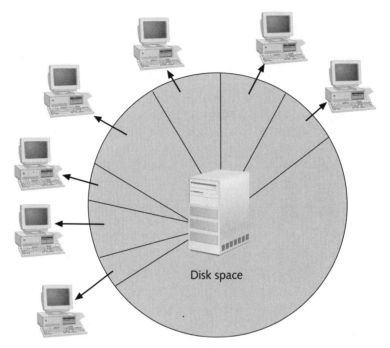

Figure 10-4   UNIX disk quotas for server users

 It is easier to start off by establishing an agreed-upon disk quota for each user rather than to start with no quotas and then to attempt to impose them later. Disk quotas are a good reminder to server users that they must periodically delete temporary and unused files. Providing training at the time accounts are created or when a new server is installed is one way to help users to learn to monitor their disk usage before they receive a notification that their disk quota is exceeded.

DOS, WINDOWS 3.1, AND WINDOWS 3.11

There are many Windows-based programs that create temporary files. These files are created as work files or backup files for programs such as word processors, spreadsheets, databases, queries, and backups. Although most application software is designed to clean up temporary files when those files are no longer needed, the files often are not deleted because the user may exit the program prematurely, the program may hang due to memory problems, or it may not successfully locate all of the temporary files it created. Users of all current Windows operating systems should schedule regular maintenance to find and delete temporary files. This process is important because these files can be quite large, up to several megabytes in size. The files are often located in the following places:

- A temporary directory in the root, such as C:\Temp

- A temporary directory in the Windows directory, such as C:\Windows\Temp

- A DOS directory in the root, for Windows 3.1, 3.11, and Windows 95

- A data directory in which word processing, spreadsheet, or database files are stored

- The applications directory that contains the executable file which created the temporary file

- Any temporary directory specified by an environment variable in the AUTOEXEC.BAT file, such as by the command SET TEMP=C:\Windows\Temp

 Sometimes a temporary file that is created as a backup for a word processing application or another type of Windows application can create problems if it is not deleted. One such problem is that the existence of the temporary file can cause corruption in the original file when the original file is next opened. A corrupted file often is indicated by a warning dialog box when you open the file.

Temporary files in DOS and Windows-based systems frequently are indicated by a tilde (~) at the beginning of the file, such as ~WRA1731.wbk, or by a .tmp extension at the end of the file, ~WRL3229.tmp or ~DF725.tmp, for example.

Use the DIR command in DOS to locate temporary files to delete. Before you start, make sure that there are no programs running, if you shell out to DOS (start a DOS session) from a DOS application such as WordPerfect or if you access the DOS command window from any of the Windows-based operating systems. To search for the temporary files in a specific directory, use the CD command to switch to that directory, such as *CD \WP51*, and enter *DIR ~*.** or *DIR *.tmp*. This will give you a listing of all files preceded by a tilde, or with the .tmp extension, respectively.

An easy way to quickly search the entire disk volume is to go to the root directory and use the /s switch to search all directories and subdirectories. Add the /p switch to cause the listing to pause a screen at a time so that you can view the results without scrolling faster than the eye can follow. For example, to search for all files that have a .tmp extension in the root of hard drive C, enter the following commands:

```
CD C:\
DIR *.tmp /s/p
```

Use the DOS DEL command to delete the files, but keep in mind that DEL does not support the /s (include all subdirectories) option so you must switch to each directory in which the temporary files reside in order to delete them. For example, to delete .tmp files from the TEMP directory, enter the following:

```
CD C:\TEMP
DEL *.tmp
```

In Windows 3.1 and Windows 3.11, you can use the File Manager utility to locate temporary files. Before you start, make sure that all applications are closed, because active applications may have opened temporary files that you do not want to delete. To perform a search for temporary files, open File Manager and click the File menu and then the Search option on the menu. Enter *.tmp in the Search For: text box, and enter C:\ in the Start From: text box. Also, check the box to Search All Subdirectories and click OK (see Figure 10-5 on the next page).

10

The Search Results dialog box shows a list of all the files found (Figure 10-6). Use the scroll bar to review the list and determine the files to delete, which in most cases will be all of the files listed. In the Search dialog box, hold down the Ctrl key and click each file you wish to delete, or click the first file on the list, hold down the Shift key, scroll to the last file, and click it. To delete the selected files press the Delete key or click the File menu and click Delete, and then click OK to delete the selected file or files.

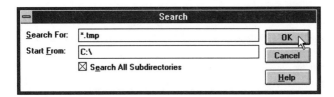

Figure 10-5   Windows 3.1x File Manager search dialog box

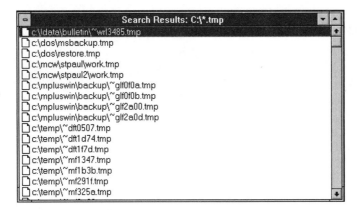

Figure 10-6   Windows 3.1x search results

WINDOWS 95, WINDOWS 98, AND WINDOWS NT

Temporary files are equally a problem in Windows 95, Windows 98, and Windows NT. As in Windows 3.1 and Windows 3.11, the temporary files often begin with a tilde (~) as a first character or have a .tmp extension and typically are found in the same locations. One exception is that in Windows NT the operating system is located in the \Winnt folder, which means that temporary files are found in this folder and in the \Winnt\System32 and \Winnt\Temp folders.

Web browsers also write an impressive number of temporary Internet files that are not deleted until you delete them using a Windows utility or a utility that comes with the Web browser. In Windows 3.1, Windows 3.11, Windows 95, and Windows 98, these files are typically found in a temporary Internet file folder in the \Windows folder. For example, in Windows 95 and Windows 98 that folder is called \Windows\Temporary Internet Files. In Windows NT, the temporary Internet files are found in one of two places, \Winnt\Temporary Internet Files and \Winnt\Profiles*account*\Temporary Internet Files (where *account* is the name of a particular account set up for Internet access). These files often have extensions such as .html, .htm, .jpg, and .gif. In most cases, the files can be deleted regularly except for **cookies** that contain specialized information for accessing particular Web sites. Cookies are text files that have the preface Cookie:, for example a cookie in Windows NT used for the Administrator account would have a filename such as Cookie:administrator@lycos.com. When you use a Windows-based utility or a browser utility to delete files, the utility provides a warning dialog box for each cookie that is encountered, and you can choose whether or not to delete a cookie by selecting Yes or No.

Before you search for temporary files, make sure that you close all active applications so that there are no open temporary files. Next, to search for temporary files, open Explorer from the Start button and Programs menu. Click the Tools menu, move to Find, and click Files or Folders. In the Find: All Files dialog box, enter *.tmp in the Named: text box, enter C:\ in the Look in: box, check the box to include subfolders, and click Find Now (see Figure 10-7). Select the files you wish to delete in the Find Files Named window (see Figure 10-8 on the next page; or press Ctrl + A to select all files), press the Delete key, and click Yes to delete the files. Windows 95, Windows 98, and Windows NT show a warning box in case any files are still open, such as temporary files in current use by the operating system.

10

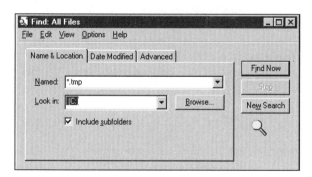

Figure 10-7   Windows NT 4.0 Find dialog box

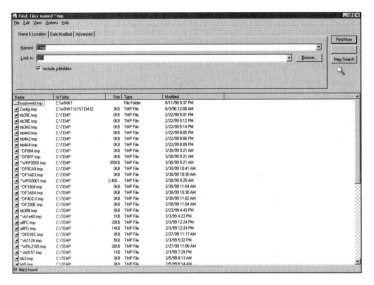

Figure 10-8   Temporary files found in Windows NT 4.0

Windows 95, Windows 98, and Windows NT retain deleted files in the Recycle Bin by default. You have the option to turn off retention of deleted files or to periodically empty the Recycle Bin. To empty the Recycle Bin, double-click its icon on the desktop, in Explorer, or in My Computer. Use the scroll bar to view the files before you delete them and then select to delete all the files or only certain files. To delete selected files, highlight those files, click the File menu, and click Delete; and to delete all files, click the File menu and click Empty Recycle Bin (try Hands-on Project 10-3).

By default, the Recycle Bin can grow to occupy 10% of the available hard disk storage. Computers that are configured for two or more volumes can have a Recycle Bin on each volume. You can resize the maximum allocation for the Recycle Bin by right-clicking its desktop icon, selecting Properties, clicking the Global tab, and moving the slider bar to the desired maximum size.

MAINTAINING LARGE AND SMALL SYSTEM DISKS

In addition to finding and deleting unneeded files, there are other disk maintenance techniques that are valuable in terms of maintaining the integrity of files and ensuring disk performance. These include the following:

- Defragmenting disks

- Moving files to spread the load between multiple disks

- Using disk utilities to repair damaged files

- Deploying RAID techniques that extend the life of disks and provide disk redundancy

DEFRAGMENTING DISKS

Hard disks in any operating system are subject to becoming fragmented over time. **Fragmentation** means that unused space develops between files and other information written on a disk. When an operating system is first installed, disk files are positioned contiguously on a disk, which means there is little or no unused space between files. Figure 10-9 is a simple conceptual illustration of a hard disk that has no fragmentation. The shaded areas represent files that are arranged in contiguous fashion and the white areas are unused disk space.

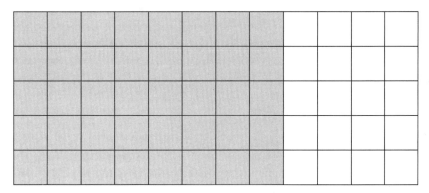

Figure 10-9 Files located contiguously on a disk

10

As the operating system deletes files, creates new files, and modifies files, the unused space between them grows and becomes scattered throughout the disk (see Figure 10-10). The greater the fragmentation, the more space that is wasted. Equally important, the disk read-write head begins to work harder to find individual files and data in files. When the disk read-write head has to move over more disk area to find information, two problems result. One problem is that disk performance suffers because it takes the read-write head longer to find information it is seeking to read and it takes longer to find an appropriately sized unused location on which to write information. The second problem is that the read-write head works harder when there is more disk fragmentation.

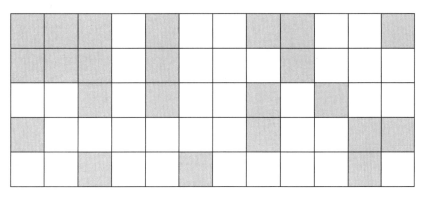

Figure 10-10 A fragmented disk

In mainframes and minicomputers that have large hard disks, fragmentation is sometimes obvious because the constant activity of the read–write head causes the disk drive cabinet to literally move across the floor. In small disk drives, the problem is apparent through excessive noise and hard disk activity.

Defragmentation is the process of removing the empty pockets between files and other information on a hard disk drive. There are two ways to do this. The oldest method is to take a complete backup of a disk's contents and then perform a full restore. Some administrators also run a **surface analysis** of a disk before performing the full restore, as a means of finding damaged disk sectors and tracks. Some surface analysis tools are destructive to data and attempt to reformat the damaged area to determine if it can be recovered. Others are not destructive to data, because they relocate information from a damaged disk area to an undamaged location and then mark the damaged area as off limits, so that no files can be written there.

As a precaution, back up a hard disk before running a disk surface analysis and before defragmenting it. Also, consult the documentation to make sure you know if a disk analysis tool is destructive to data before you run it. For example, sometimes disk analysis tools provided on the system troubleshooting disk provided by computer manufacturers perform a format along with the surface analysis of hard drives. Also, some disk troubleshooting tools that accompany hardware RAID are destructive to data because they initialize and format individual or all disks within the RAID.

A second option that is usually easier than backing up and restoring a hard disk is to run a disk defragmentation tool. Many operating systems come with a built-in tool to defragment disks. In some cases, it is necessary to purchase the tool from a third–party vendor, which is true for Windows NT 4.0 owners. Modern defragmentation tools can be run in the background as you continue to use the operating system. Many also provide a quick analysis of the hard disk and advise whether or not it is necessary to defragment it. For example, if disk fragmentation is 20% or less, the disk does not need to be defragmented immediately. Server operating systems often experience more rapid fragmentation than workstation operating systems. Server administrators develop a regular schedule to defragment the hard disks. Some administrators defragment once a week to once a month, during times when no one is on the server other than the administrator. In some situations where a server is under constant and heavy use, such as one used for a client/server application, it can be necessary to defragment disks every few days.

As introduced in Chapter 3, DOS, Windows 3.1, Windows 3.11, Windows 95, and Windows 98 are examples of operating systems that have built-in defragmentation utilities. The defragmentation utility in DOS 6.x, Windows 3.1, and 3.11 is a DOS utility called DEFRAG.EXE, that is run from the DOS prompt and is located with other DOS system files in the \BIN or \DOS directory in the root. You start the utility by setting a path to the DOS directory (if one is not already set) and typing *defrag* at the DOS prompt. The first screen presents options to defragment any of the floppy or hard disk drives attached to the computer. Select the drive to defragment, and click OK. The utility analyzes the drive to determine the percent of fragmentation. If you want to defragment the drive, select

Optimize to start the process and select OK when it is finished. The utility gives you an option to defragment another drive or exit.

In Windows 95 and Windows 98, defragmentation is accomplished through a Windows utility that you access from the Start button, Programs menu, and Accessories menu. On the Accessories menu select System Tools and Disk Defragmenter. Choose the drive to defragment in the Select Drive dialog box and click OK. The Disk Defragmentation dialog box reports the amount of fragmentation on the disk and recommends whether or not to proceed on the basis of the amount of fragmentation. Click Start to defragment the disk and click Show Details to view a complete cluster by cluster display of the defragmentation process. Figure 10-11 shows the Windows 98 Disk Defragmenter at work.

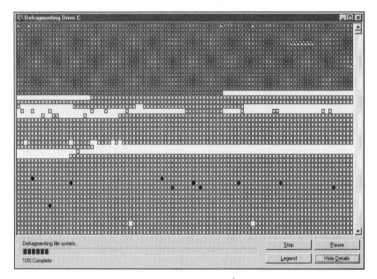

Figure 10-11   Disk Defragmenter in Windows 98

Tip

If a disk contains an error, the Disk Defragmenter detects the error and requires that it is repaired prior to defragmenting that disk. Errors can be repaired by using the ScanDisk or Chkdsk utilities discussed later in this chapter.

Windows NT 4.0 does not come with a defragmenting tool, but third-party software companies offer them. Executive Software, for example, has developed a Windows NT version of Diskeeper that can defragment disk drives, including the page file (or files) on disk volumes (paging is discussed later in this chapter). SYMANTEC's Norton Utilities for Windows NT also includes the SpeedDisk defragmenting tool. Defragmenting a Windows NT server can be an effective way to enhance performance, depending on how the server is used. For example, a Windows NT server that has frequent write and update activity may need to be defragmented every month, such as one that provides flat file database services to multiple users. Also, active Internet and intranet servers may need regular page file defragmentation.

Some versions of UNIX come with defragmenting tools, such as *defragfs*. The tools are limited in that they defragment and return to use existing empty space, but they may not rearrange files. Compunix, DEC (Compaq), Eagle Software, and other companies offer full-feature UNIX disk defragmentation tools.

 As for any system, an alternative to defragmenting disks on UNIX systems is to perform a full backup and restore.

The Mac OS is designed to minimize disk fragmentation, but third-party tools are available for systems that experience high use. For example, SYMANTEC's Norton Utilities for Macintosh includes a Mac OS version of SpeedDisk for defragmenting. One problem that is more likely to need attention in the Mac OS is memory fragmentation, in which pockets of empty unused space develop in memory. An indication of memory fragmentation is when you receive a message that there is not enough memory. There are four ways to handle memory fragmentation. The first and simplest is to implement virtual memory as described later in this chapter. Two other approaches are to close all open applications or to shut down and restart the computer. The fourth technique is to open your least used applications first and the most used applications last; and close the applications in the reverse order of that in which they were opened.

Moving Disk Files to Spread the Load

Another technique that can help extend the life of disk drives is to spread files evenly across disks when there is more than one disk. This technique is used mainly on computers that have multiple user access, such as servers, and on which there is frequent disk activity. Before files are moved, the server administrator examines disk and file activity to determine how to spread files across the disk drives to achieve even loading in terms of activity. Also, files have to be moved on the basis of their function so that files that contain related information are on the same drive. Disk activity is monitored in Windows NT, for example, by using the Performance Monitor tool and monitoring the LogicalDisk and PhysicalDisk objects. At the same time, resources that are in use are monitored by clicking the Server icon in the Control Panel.

 The DISKPERF utility must be started in Windows NT in order for Performance Monitor to gather statistics on disk use.

Using Disk Utilities to Repair Damaged Files

Some operating systems have utilities that enable you to repair damaged files and file links. Four examples of these utilities are:

- Disk First Aid in the Mac OS
- *fsck* and *p_fsck* in UNIX

- Chkdsk in DOS, Windows 3.1, Windows 3.11, Windows 95, Windows 98, and Windows NT

- ScanDisk in DOS, Windows 3.1, Windows 3.11, Windows 95, and Windows 98

Disk First Aid is a Mac OS utility that verifies files, folders, and mounted disks. Before you verify a disk, it is necessary to turn file sharing off. You start Disk First Aid by opening the Disk First Aid icon. Click the disk that you want to verify, or hold the Shift key and click several disks, and click the Verify button. Another option is to click the Repair button, if you know that a disk needs to be repaired.

The *fsck* utility in UNIX is used to check one or more file systems. For example, it looks for orphaned files that have no names, bad directory pointers, inode problems, directories that do not exist, bad links, bad blocks, blocks that are duplicated, pathname problems, and makes other file system checks. If it discovers there is a problem with one or more files, it gives you the opportunity to fix or to disregard the problem. Unless you have a reason not to (such as for a database file for which you want to try a database repair tool first), the best approach is to fix any problem it finds. To use *fsck*, enter the command along with a file list which is provided in one of two formats. One format is to specify the device name of the file system, such as \dev\devicename (try Hands-on Project 10-5). Another format is to specify the mount point of a particular file system so that the utility can determine it from the file \etc\fstab which contains a list of file systems. If you do not specify a file system to check, *fsck* assumes that it should check all file systems, or you can instruct it to check all file systems by including the -*A* option. Also, some versions of UNIX have a -*y* option that causes *fsck* to make its own decision about whether to fix a problem it finds and a -*n* command to have *fsck* check the file system, report problems, but not fix them.

Besides *fsck* there is the *p_fsck* utility in UNIX. This utility checks two or more file systems simultaneously, instead of checking only one at a time as is done by *fsck*. The drawback in using *p_fsck* is that it should not be applied to the root file system.

In most UNIX systems, *fsck* is started automatically each time the operating system is booted. If *fsck* cannot run when you boot these systems, that means the root system is very likely corrupted. To fix this problem you will need to use the rescue disk or emergency boot disks for your version of UNIX to boot to a minimal system and restore the root system.

The Chkdsk disk utility runs in DOS (or at the command prompt in Windows NT) and is used by Windows 3.1, Windows 3.11, Windows 95, Windows 98, and Windows NT. The Windows NT version of the utility is more powerful than the ones used in other versions of Microsoft Windows, because it incorporates some of the features of ScanDisk (Windows NT does not have a ScanDisk utility). In the other versions of Microsoft Windows, ScanDisk is usually recommended because it has a GUI-like interface and contains more interactive utilities for checking the integrity of a disk. In Windows 98, Chkdsk does not check for errors, but only provides information about the volume serial number, disk space allocation, and lower memory allocation (under 640 KB). Also, switches for Chkdsk that are available in other versions of Microsoft Windows are not implemented in Windows 98 (try Hands-on

Project 10-6 to run Chkdsk in Windows 98). Figure 10-12 shows Chkdsk results on a system that has MS-DOS 6 and on which there are over 244 MB of bytes in bad sectors, which have been marked previously as bad through a surface scan.

```
C:\>chkdsk
     1 lost allocation units found in 1 chains.
         32,768 bytes disk space would be freed

1,622,343,680 bytes total disk space
    36,896,768 bytes in 14 hidden files
     5,439,488 bytes in 166 directories
   361,398,272 bytes in 5,807 user files
   244,744,192 bytes in bad sectors
   973,832,192 bytes available on disk

        32,768 bytes in each allocation unit
        49,510 total allocation units on disk
        29,719 available allocation units on disk

       647,168 total bytes memory
       557,872 bytes free

Instead of using CHKDSK, try using SCANDISK.  SCANDISK can reliably detect
and fix a much wider range of disk problems.  For more information,
type HELP SCANDISK from the command prompt.

C:\>
```

Figure 10-12   Chkdsk in DOS

For the versions of Windows other than Windows 98, Chkdsk can find and fix the following:

- Damage to the root directory or to another directory

- Problems with the directory structure that causes Chkdsk to be unable to process the full tree

- Disk space that is not allocated

- Files that share the same allocation units

- A file pointer to an allocation unit that does not exist

- Files that are assigned more allocation units than they need

- Directories that have no entries

- Damaged directories that cannot be repaired

- A full root directory (the limit is 512 files)

- Disk sectors that cannot be read

- Damaged subdirectory entries, such as damaged pointers to parent directories

- File Allocation Table entry problems or a damaged File Allocation Table

- Allocation units that contain partial information but that have no links to files

- Bad file attributes

 Chkdsk only checks the first 640 KB of RAM and only for the purpose of determining how much of that is free for use by programs.

There are two options or switches that can be used with Chkdsk: /f and /v. The /f switch instructs Chkdsk to repair errors without a yes or no interactive query. The /v switch causes Chkdsk to display all files as it checks them. The advantage to this is that you can see a particular file that is damaged, but the disadvantage is that you may have to watch it display hundreds of files. You can also instruct Chkdsk to check a specific drive, directory, or file by using the drive letter or path after the Chkdsk command. For example, *Chkdsk D: /f* will check drive D and automatically fix errors.

 Use the /f option with care: when Chkdsk finds and fixes file errors it may need to eliminate data that it cannot associate with a file; it will fix errors automatically and you may lose data.

If you do not specify the /f option, Chkdsk will report errors in terms of a query such as: "*xx* lost allocation units found in *yy* chains. Convert lost chains to files (Y/N)?" If you automatically fix errors or reply with yes to fix errors, Chkdsk writes the lost data to one or more files in the root directory that have a .chk extension as in Figure 10-13. Use an editor to examine the contents of the .chk files (some of the information will consist of values you cannot read or interpret) in case there is information you want to retain. Once you have extracted the useful information or determined that the information in the files is not needed, make sure that you delete the files to recover the space they occupy.

10

```
IMAGE     BAK       137,728 05-19-96  10:23p
TREEINFO  IDX           871 10-10-96   1:28p
FILE0001  CHK        32,768 11-10-98  10:14p
FILE0002  CHK        98,304 11-10-98  10:14p
FILE0003  CHK        32,768 11-10-98  10:14p
FILE0004  CHK        32,768 11-10-98  10:14p
FILE0005  CHK        65,536 11-10-98  10:14p
FILE0006  CHK        98,304 11-10-98  10:14p
FILE0007  CHK        65,536 11-10-98  10:14p
FILE0008  CHK        65,536 11-10-98  10:14p
FILE0009  CHK        98,304 11-10-98  10:14p
FILE0010  CHK        32,768 11-10-98  10:14p
FILE0011  CHK        32,768 11-10-98  10:14p
FILE0012  CHK        32,768 11-10-98  10:14p
COLLWIN   <DIR>             03-04-99   3:45p
SCANDISK  LOG           520 03-31-99  11:10a
DOSBAK    <DIR>             04-05-99  11:22a
DOSMJP    <DIR>             04-16-99   3:45p
WIN31     <DIR>             04-16-99   3:48p
CONFIG    SYS           305 04-17-99  12:08p
AUTOEXEC  BAT           178 04-16-99   5:39p
        51 file(s)       1,031,178 bytes
                       973,766,656 bytes free

C:\>
```

Figure 10-13   Examples of .chk files

Two additional switches are available in the Windows NT Chkdsk version: /r and /l:size. The /r switch instructs Chkdsk to look for bad sectors and attempt to relocate information that it is able to read. The /l:size switch is used to change the size of the log file in NTFS. Another difference between Windows NT and other versions of Microsoft Windows is that Chkdsk is run automatically when the operating system boots and determines that there may be disk or file corruption.

ScanDisk is a disk verification utility that is available in DOS, Windows 3.1, Windows 3.11, Windows 95, and Windows 98. ScanDisk is a DOS-based utility in Windows 3.1 and Windows 3.11 and should be run from DOS with Windows shut down. It can also be run in the MS-DOS Prompt window, but ScanDisk cannot be used to fix errors when Windows 3.1 or Windows 3.11 are running.

To run ScanDisk from DOS, enter SCANDISK at the DOS prompt. ScanDisk initially checks the media descriptor, file allocation tables, directory structure, and file system on a hard drive and creates a log of the results. It also provides an optional surface scan that looks for areas of physical damage and attempts to rewrite data in damaged areas to areas that are not damaged (see Figure 10-14). The surface scan, therefore, is not destructive to data and takes about half an hour to examine a 1 GB drive.

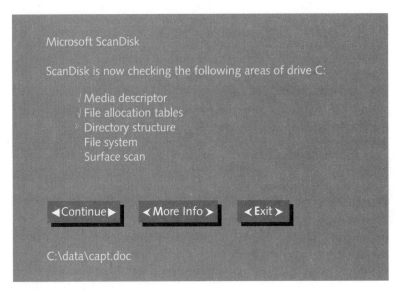

Figure 10-14   Windows 3.11 ScanDisk

In Windows 95 and Windows 98, ScanDisk is a Windows-based application that is run from the Start button, Programs menu, Accessories menu, and System Tools. The Windows-based version has more options than the DOS-based version, which can be set after ScanDisk is started. Another advantage of the Windows-based version is that it can be set up to start automatically each time you boot Windows 95 or Windows 98. The Windows-based version has two initial options, to perform a standard test or a thorough test. The standard test verifies files and folders, whereas the thorough test is a complete disk surface analysis that is not destructive to data. When you use the thorough option you can specify whether to scan the system and data areas, only the system area, or only the data area. You can also specify whether or not to perform write testing and whether or not to repair bad sectors in hidden and system files. This version of ScanDisk also has the following advanced options:

- Selections for how to display the summary information

- Selections for handling cross-linked files

- Selections about how to handle lost file fragments

- Selections about how to verify files

- Selections on whether or not to report DOS name length errors

(Try Hands-on Project 10-7 to practice using ScanDisk and to view its options.)

Deploying RAID Techniques

As you learned in Chapter 6, deploying a redundant array of inexpensive drives (RAID) is a technique that is used by server operating systems, such as UNIX, NetWare, and Windows NT, for three purposes: increased reliability (providing data recovery when a disk drive fails and extending the useful life of disks), increased storage capacity, and increased speed. This section focuses on how RAID is used to extend the life of a set of disks. RAID does this by using **disk striping**, a technique for spreading data over multiple disk volumes. For example, when a file is written to a striped disk set, portions of that file are spread across the set. Striping ensures that the load resulting from reading and writing to disks is spread evenly across the set of disks. This means that the disks experience equal wear, rather than placing extra load on one or two disks that are likely to wear out sooner.

There are six basic RAID levels:

- RAID level 0: Provides disk striping only and requires the use of two or more disks

- RAID level 1: Uses two disks that are mirror images of one another so that if one fails, the other one takes over, however it does not use disk striping to extend the life of disks

- RAID level 2: Provides disk striping and all disks contain information to help recover data in case one fails

- RAID level 3: The same as RAID level 2, but error recovery information is on one disk only

- RAID level 4: Provides disk striping as in RAID level 2 and adds checksum verification information that is stored on one disk in the array

- RAID level 5: The same as RAID level 4, except that checksum verification information is stored on all disks in the array and level 5 includes the ability to replace a failed drive and rebuild it without shutting down the drive array or server

There are two general ways to deploy RAID: hardware RAID and software RAID. Hardware RAID is controlled through a specialized RAID adapter that has its own RAID software on a chip and that usually provides extra redundancy, such as a battery backup for the RAID logic in the adapter. Software RAID is set up and managed by the server operating system and does not have as many redundancy features as hardware RAID.

 When given the choice, most server administrators use hardware RAID, because it enables them to bypass some restrictions that the operating system places on software RAID. For example, Windows NT Server does not permit boot and system files to reside on software RAID, but the restriction does not apply to hardware RAID. Also, most hardware and software RAID is deployed as RAID level 1, RAID level 5, or a combination of these in order to achieve the best performance combined with optimal data protection.

10

MAKING BACKUPS

In Chapter 5 you learned that it is vital to back up your operating system and data files before an operating system upgrade. It is also essential to back up these files as a regular mainte-nance practice. Disk drives fail, files can be lost or corrupted, and database files can get out of synchronization on any workstation or server. The best line of defense is to develop a strong backup plan. Most computer operating systems have built-in backup software or backup software can be purchased as a separate software add-on. Typically, backups are writ-ten to tape, but other backup options include backing up to floppy disks or CD-ROMs.

In general, there are several types of backup techniques. One type of backup is called a **binary backup** because it backs up the disk contents in binary format to create an exact image of the disk contents. The advantage of this backup is that it is simple to perform and includes everything on the disk. The disadvantages are that in many versions you cannot restore indi-vidual files or directories, and when you perform a restore the target disk drive must be the same size or larger than the disk drive from which the backup was made.

Another backup technique is called a **full file-by-file backup** in which all of the disk con-tents are backed up, but as individual directories and files. This type of backup is commonly used on workstations because it enables you to restore a single directory or a given set of files without having to restore the entire disk contents. Full file-by-file backups also are performed on servers, depending on the backup scheme that is in place. Some backup schemes call for a full file-by-file backup to be performed at the end of each workday, as long as the total amount of information on the disks is not too large. If the disks hold a large amount of infor-mation, then it is common to perform a full file-by-file backup once a week and to perform partial backups on the other days in the week. There are typically two kinds of partial back-ups, differential and incremental. A **differential backup** backs up all files that have an archive attribute (file attribute that indicates that the file needs to be backed up), but does not remove the archive attribute. An **incremental backup** backs up all files that have the archive attribute, and removes the attribute from each file after it is backed up. The difference between using differential or incremental backups between full backups, is in the number of tapes required for these backups and the number of days that have to be restored when a complete restore is necessary. For example, assume that a business needs to restore all files because it has had a catastrophic disk failure during the day on Thursday. Also, assume that the business per-forms a full file-by-file backup each Saturday evening and differential backups Monday through Friday evenings. To recover after the disk drives have been replaced, they will first restore the full file-by-file backup from the previous Saturday and then restore the differen-tial backup from Wednesday night. If the same business had been performing incremental backups, they would restore the full file-by-file backup from Saturday and then restore the incremental backups from Monday, Tuesday, and Wednesday.

UNIX

Two main utilities in UNIX for backing up files are *volcopy* and *dump*. *Volcopy* is a binary backup that creates a mirror image of a disk onto the backup medium, such as a tape or a Zip drive. *Volcopy* requires that you provide specifics about the length and density of the information to be backed up. *Volcopy* can write to one or multiple tapes, calling for additional tapes if the information does not fit on the first one. The utility also can back up to multiple tape drives. *Volcopy* is sometimes used with the *labelit* utility that can put a label on file systems or unmounted volumes to provide unique identification for each one that is copied in the backup.

The *dump* utility is used for full or partial file-by-file backups. (These backups are often called "dumps.") The *dump* utility backs up all files, files that have changed by date, or files that have changed after the previous backup. Files can be backed up using a dump level that correlates a dump to a given point in time. For example, a Monday dump might be assigned level 1, Tuesday's dump level 2, and so on. Up to nine dump levels can be assigned. A dump is restored via one of three commands depending on the flavor of UNIX: *restore*, *ufsrestore*, and *restor*.

 A third backup utility, called *tar*, is sometimes used in addition to *volcopy* and *dump*. *Tar* is designed for archiving tapes and includes file information as well as the archived files, such as security information and dates when files have been modified. (You used *tar* in a Hands-on Project in Chapter 5 to back up configuration files before upgrading UNIX.) Also, there are several third-party utilities that employ *tar*-based backups and restores that have many added features. Two examples of these utilities are CTAR from UniTrends Software and BRU 2000 from Enhanced Software Technologies. A comprehensive backup and restore solution for networked systems is available in Cheyenne's ARCserve/Open.

NETWARE

NetWare uses its Storage Management System (SMS) for creating backups. Typically, three NetWare Loadable Modules (NLMs) are loaded at the server console by using the LOAD command. They include the target server software (TSA410), the target NDS agent (TSANDS; to back up the NDS database), and backup device drivers (SBACKUP).

After these NLMs are loaded, you highlight the Backup From or Restore To option on the SBACKUP menu at the console and select the server to back up. Next, access the Backup menu and provide a name and location for the backup log file. Specify the directories and files to back up using the Backup Selected Target selection and provide a name for the backups. Use the Start backup now option to run the backups.

WINDOWS NT

Windows NT Server and Windows NT Workstation have a Backup utility that allows different combinations of full and partial backups along with the ability to restore backed up information. The options in the Backup utility are as follows:

- Normal backup (full file-by-file backup)
- Incremental backup
- Differential backup
- Daily backup for files that have changed on the same day as the backup
- Copy backup that is performed only on specified files

10

Prior to backup, the backup media and the driver that integrates the backup media with the operating system must be installed. For example, if you back up to tape it is necessary to have the tape adapter installed, the tape device driver installed, and the tape drives detected by the operating system. With these installed, you are ready to start a backup by starting the utility from the Start button, Programs menu, Administrative Tools (Common) menu, and Backup selection. When you start the Backup utility, it will automatically detect the tape system. To back up a particular disk volume, click its check box (see Figure 10-15); or check all volumes to backup the entire server. Click the Backup button to specify the backup parameters, which include whether to back up the Registry, a description of the backup, and the type of backup, such as normal or incremental.

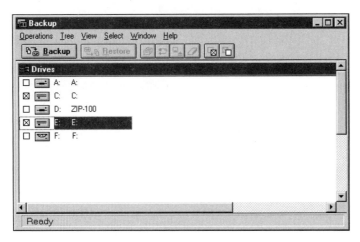

Figure 10-15   Windows NT 4.0 backup

 The Windows NT Backup utility is only compatible with Windows NT and not other versions of Windows.

WINDOWS 95 AND WINDOWS 98

Windows 95 and Windows 98 have a Backup utility that you access from the Start button, Programs menu, Accessories menu, and System Tools menu. Backups are created as jobs that are given titles. The Backup utility displays all drives recognized by Windows 95 or Windows 98, including mapped drives. You can back up an entire drive, a directory, a file, or any combination of these by placing a check in the box in front of the entity (see Figure 10-16). Also, there are options to back up all files (full file-by-file) or only files that are new or have changed since the last backup (incremental). After you check what you want to back up, provide a job name, specify parameters for the backup, and start the backup. The parameters include the ability to compress files on the backup medium and to perform a read verification after each file is backed up.

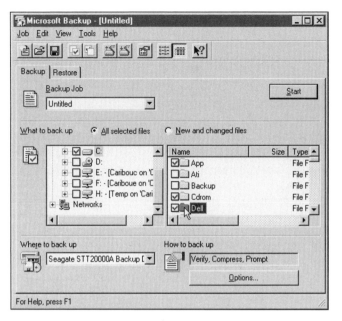

Figure 10-16   Windows 98 backup

A read verification is advantageous because it provides initial assurance that a file can be read from the backup medium; it is disadvantageous in that it makes the backup take twice the time.

The Windows 95 and Windows 98 backups are only compatible with these versions of the operating system.

DOS, WINDOWS 3.1, AND WINDOWS 3.11

DOS, Windows 3.1, and Windows 3.11 all use the same DOS-based backup utility, called BACKUP, and backed up files are restored via the RESTORE command. The BACKUP utility copies the specified files to floppy disks, creating two files per disk: BACKUP.xxx and CONTROL.xxx—where xxx is the number of the disk in the set. The BACKUP.xxx file contains the saved file contents and the CONTROL.xxx file has information about which files are contained in the BACKUP.xxx file. The BACKUP command can back up an entire disk, specified directories, or specified files through the use of switches which include the following:

- /a — Adds files to a backup disk that already contains backup files

- /d — Backs up files that are new or changed, on or after the specified date

- /f — Formats the disk prior to backing up files

- /l — Causes a log file to be created with the name that you enter after the /l command, such as /l:backlog

- /m — Backs up files that have the archive bit only

- /s — Backs up subdirectories and their contents

- /t — Backs up the files created or changed on or after the specified time

The syntax of the BACKUP command is:

```
BACKUP [drivespec] [path and filespec] switch
```

Thus, to back up only new or changed files in the data directory on drive C you would enter:

```
BACKUP C:\data /m.
```

The BACKUP utility in Windows 3.1 and Windows 3.11 is not compatible with Windows 95, Windows 98, or Windows NT.

In DOS version 5 and beyond, the BACKUP utility has the ability to back up to tape. Any time you back up to tape with any system, test the backup process from start to finish to make sure it is working properly and saving all of the files you want to save. Some problems with backups include the omission of critical files, such as the Windows-based Registry, and a tape subsystem error in which the backup prematurely quits after the first tape when there are two or more tapes of information. Make sure the operating system or third-party backup software is working properly by trying a restore on a test computer, or use the backup software tape catalog to view the directories and files on the tape.

OPTIMIZING SOFTWARE INSTALLATION

One aspect of software installation has already been discussed in this chapter, which is to plan and set up a well-organized directory structure. The directory structure influences the ease of the installation, provides the ability to keep different versions in separate places, and enables you to smoothly uninstall software. The following is a checklist of additional guidelines for software installation:

- Make sure that the software is compatible with your operating system.

- Check the CPU, RAM, disk storage, audio, and other requirements to make sure your computer is a match for the software.

- Find out if there are different installation options, such as one with or without tutoring applications to help you to learn the software.

- For Microsoft operating systems, determine if the software is DOS-based or Windows-based and if any special drivers are required. Keep in mind that Windows NT may not run some DOS-based software, games, and 16-bit Windows-based software.

- Check to determine if there are programs that attempt to directly manage hardware and peripherals, because these may not be allowed to function in Windows NT since these functions must go through the system kernel.

- Use any utilities provided by the operating system for installing software. For example, Windows 95, Windows 98, and Windows NT use an Add/Remove Programs utility in the Control Panel.

- Look in the documentation or ask your vendor for software that is written to take advantage of the Registry for Windows 95, Windows 98, and Windows NT applications.

- Check the vendor's "bug" list for the software to make sure there are no bugs that impact the way you will be using it. Bug lists are often posted on the vendor's Internet site in the software support area.

- Make sure that the software is well documented and supported by the vendor and that the vendor can provide the required drivers, if applicable.

- Determine in advance how to back up important files associated with the software and find out the locations and purposes of all hidden files.

- Determine if running the program requires adjustments to page or swap files used by the operating system.

- Find out what temporary files are created by the program and where they are created.

- For Windows-based software, always install the latest versions of Window's components, including .DLL, .OCX, .INI, .INF, and .DRV files. (These are generally available directly from the software vendor or on the vendor's Web site.)

- Do not mix .INF and driver files between different versions of Windows, because some other software on the computer may no longer work.

- Always keep service patches up to date for all software. **Service packs** are issued by the vendor to fix software problems, address compatibility issues, and to add enhancements.

Installing software on a network server requires some additional considerations, which include:

- Make sure there are enough licenses to match the number of users or that you have metering software that limits simultaneous use to the number of valid licenses.

- Determine if the software is network compatible by testing it before releasing it to users.

- Determine the network load created by software, such as by client/server, database, and multimedia applications.

- Consider purchasing management software, such as Microsoft System Management Server, that can automatically update system-wide software when there is a new release. This ensures that all users are on the same version of word processing or database software, for example.

- Determine if the software will be loaded from the server each time it is used or if it will be installed permanently at workstations from the server.

- Determine if the server or if client workstations must be tuned for the software in a particular way, such as by modifying page files or Registry entries.

- For operating systems that support two or more file systems, make sure that the software is compatible with the file system that is in use by the operating system.

TUNING THE OPERATING SYSTEM

After an operating system is installed, you may notice that its performance is not what you expected or that performance seems to decrease with time. Just as a car needs periodic tuning, so do workstation and server operating systems. One critical reason for tuning operating systems is that slow workstations and servers have a cumulative impact on a network. Sometimes poor network performance is not the result of network problems or too little bandwidth, but instead the result of a preponderance of workstations and servers that cannot keep up with the network. This is an often overlooked area that can result in huge dollar savings for an organization. It is much less expensive to tune servers and workstations (often at no cost) compared to investing in faster and very expensive network devices such as routers and switches. There are many ways to tune operating systems to achieve better performance, including tuning virtual memory, installing operating system updates and patches, and tuning for optimal network communications.

TUNING VIRTUAL MEMORY

Some operating systems supplement RAM by employing virtual memory techniques. **Virtual memory** is disk storage that is used when there is not enough RAM for a particular operation or for all processes that are currently in use. The computer's CPU, in conjunction with the operating system, can swap to disk processes and data that temporarily have a low priority or that are not in immediate use. When the operating system and CPU need to access the information on disk, they swap something else to disk and read the information they need back into RAM, using a process called paging. The information that is swapped back and forth from RAM to disk and from disk to RAM is stored in a specially allocated disk area called the **paging** or **swap file** (or swap file system in UNIX).

Some operating systems that use virtual memory and paging enable you to tune the paging file by adjusting its size. Tuning the paging file can result in better operating system performance. For example, you can adjust the virtual memory allocation, disk cache, and RAM disk settings in the Mac OS by opening the Apple menu, Control Panels, and the Memory option. To adjust the allocation, click the radio button to turn on virtual memory and make sure that it is set to equal the amount of RAM in the computer plus 1 MB or more (try Hands-on Project 10-8).

In UNIX, you can use the *vmstat* utility along with the *-s* option to monitor paging. Another tool that you can use to track disk activity is *iostat*. Paging in UNIX is accomplished by creating a swap file system by using the make file system command appropriate to the flavor of UNIX (see Chapter 3), such as the *nsfs* or *mkfs* commands in Solaris and Linux. The swap file system is mounted like any other file system. If the swap file system is often over 80% full, increase its size. Also, if there frequently is a high rate of swapping, consider spreading the swap space over multiple disks that are on different controllers.

Virtual memory in Windows NT is adjusted to set an initial starting size and a maximum size to which it can grow. Generally, the rule for sizing the page file is to set the initial size to equal the amount of RAM (in megabytes) plus 12 MB. The maximum page file size should allow for adequate growth in order to handle the most active times. You can monitor RAM and page file activity through the Task Manager's Performance tab and through the Performance Monitor. To adjust the page file size, open the Control Panel, double-click the System icon, and then click the Performance tab. The page file size is specified in the Initial Size (MB): and Maximum Size (MB): boxes. Also, you have the option to create a page file on each physical hard disk. As a general rule, it is a good idea to create multiple page files (one for each disk) with the following exceptions:

- Avoid creating a page file on the disk that contains the system files (if possible).

- Do not create a page file on a RAID set of disks when using software RAID levels 0 or 5 (not a problem in hardware RAID).

- Do not create a page file on the backup volume in a mirrored set.

These restrictions are another reason to use hardware RAID instead of software RAID.

10

Windows 3.1, Windows 3.11, Windows 95, and Windows 98 all make use of paging. To adjust paging in Windows 3.1 and Windows 3.11, open the Control Panel in the Main program group and double-click 386 Enhanced (you must have this option installed to use virtual memory). Click the Virtual Memory button, click Change, and enter your adjustment in the New Size box. In Windows 3.1 and Windows 3.11, the best indication that you need to increase the page file size is when the system frequently hangs or you often see messages that you are out of memory.

In Windows 95 and Windows 98, you can adjust the page file size by opening the Control Panel, double-clicking the System icon, and clicking the Performance tab. Click the Virtual Memory button and click "Let me specify my own virtual memory settings" to enter the minimum and maximum sizes for the page file.

Unless it is specifically required by a software application or you frequently see messages that you are out of memory, it is recommended that you let Windows 95 and Windows 98 automatically adjust the page file size.

INSTALLING OPERATING SYSTEM UPDATES AND PATCHES

One of the most important ways to keep your operating system tuned is by installing operating system updates and patches that are issued by the vendor. Often problems with an operating system are not fully discovered until it has been released and used by thousands or even millions of users. Once enough problems are discovered and reported, the vendors create updates or patches. For example, Microsoft issues service packs for operating systems and software that contain a wide range of updates and patches. If problems are discovered in between service packs, you can obtain individual program fixes. System updates and patches can be downloaded from the vendor's Web site or ordered on the appropriate medium, such as on CD-ROM.

 Often when you call a vendor to get help for an operating system problem, their representative will ask what service releases, upgrades, or patches you have installed and may request that you install them as the first step in problem resolution.

(For a more complete discussion of preparing for and executing an operating system upgrade, see Chapter 5.)

TUNING FOR NETWORK COMMUNICATIONS

Any computer that is connected to a network should be checked periodically to make sure that the connectivity is optimized. An obvious, but often ignored step is to periodically inspect the cable and connector into the computer for damage. A crushed or severely bent cable or one in which wires are exposed at the connector should be replaced immediately. Also, make sure that the NIC connector is in good condition. When the NIC is purchased, it should be high-quality and designed for use in the fastest expansion slot in the computer, such as a PCI slot in an Intel-based computer.

Just as operating systems need periodic patches, so do NIC drivers. Periodically check the NIC vendor's Web site for updated drivers that you can download and use immediately. Another problem with NICs is that they occasionally experience problems that cause them to saturate the network with repeated packet broadcasts. Network administrators can regularly monitor the network and individual nodes to make sure none are creating excessive traffic.

Sometimes an operating system is configured for protocols that are not in use on a network. An easy way to tune the operating system is to periodically check which protocols are configured and to eliminate those which are no longer used. On many networks, only TCP/IP is in use, but workstations and servers are still configured for IPX, NetBEUI, or both.

A workstation running Windows NT enables you to specify the order in which the workstation handles protocols on a multi-protocol network. One very effective way to tune the response time of the workstation and to improve the network response is to set the protocol order so that the most frequently used protocol is handled first. For example, consider a network that uses peer-to-peer communications and server communications that involve TCP/IP, NetBEUI, and IPX, plus printer communications that use IPX. In this example, most of the peer-to-peer and server communications involve TCP/IP, then NetBEUI, and last IPX. The workstation owner in this situation should set the order of Network Providers in Windows NT as TCP/IP, NetBEUI, and IPX. Also, he or she should set the order of Printer Providers so that IPX is first. You can tune the access order in Windows NT 4.0 by opening the Control Panel, double-clicking the Network icon, clicking the Services tab, and then Network access order (see Figure 10-17).

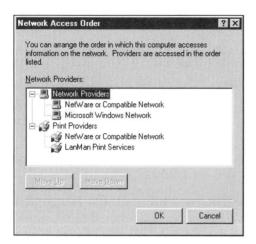

Figure 10-17   Windows NT Network Access Order

CHAPTER SUMMARY

Maintaining an operating system is as important as setting it up. There are many procedures you can follow on a regular schedule to ensure that your operating system is at its best. Although there is not room in this chapter to cover all of the possibilities, it does provide a foundation on which to build. One important technique for maintaining an operating system is to regularly find and delete unused files. Disk space is often at a premium and there is no reason to leave unused files on a system, particularly because they are easy to delete. Designing a well-organized file structure is a vital part of this maintenance technique.

Other ways to maintain disks include defragmenting disks, moving files to relatively unused disks, finding and repairing disk problems, and setting up RAID. Many operating systems have built-in utilities that can determine if disks are fragmented and defragment them. Regularly defragmenting disks is an inexpensive way to extend disk life and improve performance. Disk scan and repair tools are another inexpensive way to work on disk problems to prevent them from growing more serious. Equalizing the disk load by periodically moving files is another way to extend the life of disks. Also, RAID techniques are frequently used to add longer disk life as well as to protect data when a disk fails.

There are many considerations when installing software. Two of the most important are to make sure that the software is compatible with the computer hardware and operating system. Another is to use the software installation tools and features built into the operating system.

Finally, all operating systems should be tuned periodically. Adjusting paging is one way to tune for better performance. Another way is to make sure that you keep current with operating system patches and updates. Networked systems should be tuned so that only the necessary protocols are in use, NIC drivers are current, and the network cable is in good condition.

KEY TERMS

- **binary backup** — A technique that backs up the entire contents of one or more disk drives in a binary or image format.

- **cookie** — A text-based file used by Web sites to obtain customized information about a user such as the user's name, the user's password to access the site, and information about how to customize Web page displays.

- **defragmentation** — The process of removing empty pockets between files and other information on a hard disk drive.

- **differential backup** — Backs up all files that have an archive attribute, but does not remove that attribute after files are backed up.

- **disk striping** — A disk storage technique that divides portions of each file over all volumes in a set as a way to minimize wear on individual disks.

- **full file-by-file backup** — A technique that backs up the entire contents of one or more disk drives on the basis of directories, subdirectories, and files so that it is possible to restore a combination of any of these.

- **fragmentation** — Developing more and more empty pockets of space between files on the disk because of frequent writing, deleting, and modifying files and file contents.

- **incremental backup** — A technique that backs up all files that have an archive attribute, and then removes the attribute after each file is backed up.

- **paging file** — Also called the page or swap file, an allocated portion of disk storage reserved for use to supplement RAM when the available RAM is exceeded.

- **service pack** — Software "fixes" that are issued by the vendor to fix software problems, address compatibility issues, and add enhancements.

- **surface analysis** — A disk diagnostic technique that locates damaged disk areas and marks them as bad. Some surface analysis tools are destructive to data, because they also format a disk. Others can be run without altering data, except to move data from a damaged location to one that is not.

- **swap file** — Also called the page or paging file, an allocated portion of disk storage reserved for use to supplement RAM when the available RAM is exceeded.

- **virtual memory** — Disk storage that is used when there is not enough RAM for a particular operation or for all processes that are currently in use.

REVIEW QUESTIONS

1. In disk striping

   a. a disk array is specially coated to reduce wear.

   b. portions of files are spread over several disks in a set.

   c. redundancy is not needed because mirrored data is stored on a chip in the disk adapter.

d. all of the above

e. only a an b

f. only b and c

2. Which of the following utilities might you use in NetWare to find files that you want to delete?

    a. Windows-based client utilities, such as Network Neighborhood

    b. NetWare Administrator

    c. NDIR

    d. all of the above

    e. only a and b

    f. only a and c

3. Which of the following enables you to adjust virtual memory?

    a. Mac OS

    b. Windows 3.1

    c. Windows NT

    d. all of the above

    e. only a and b

    f. only a and c

10

4. A normal backup in Windows NT is

    a. a full file-by-file backup.

    b. a binary backup.

    c. a backup only of files that have changed or been created on the day of the backup.

    d. a backup only of files that do not have an archive bit.

5. Performing a complete backup and then fully restoring a disk is one way to eliminate heavy fragmentation. True or False?

6. The _____ file contains information stored via virtual memory.

7. If you are not sure of which protocols are used on a network, the best approach is to configure as many as possible at your workstation. True or False?

8. What might you find in the \bin directory in UNIX?

    a. temporary files

    b. user files

    c. system files

    d. home directories

9. NLMs are used in the _____ operating system for backups.

10. _____ and _____ are examples of partial backups.

11. Which operating system uses the dump utility for backups?

    a. NetWare

    b. Windows NT Server

    c. Mac OS

    d. UNIX

12. Which of the following utilities would help you acquire information about paging in Windows NT Server?

    a. Task Manager

    b. ScanDisk

    c. PageScan

    d. all of the above

    e. only a and b

    f. only a and c

13. The utility in Windows 3.1 that is used to address fragmentation is called

    _____.

14. Only UNIX has no built-in tools to fix file and directory problems. True or False?

15. It is best to keep directories for individual users, individual applications, and nearly every function in the root as a way to optimize performance. True or False?

16. The UNIX *ls* command can be used to display files in which of the following ways?

    a. by date

    b. by time

    c. alphabetically

    d. all of the above

    e. only a and b

    f. only a and c

17. Disk quotas can be set up in UNIX to control how much disk space is available to specific users. True or False?

18. Another name for disk mirroring in terms of RAID is _____.

19. The _____ command in UNIX enables you to create an image backup.

20. Chkdsk can repair file and directory problems in which of the following?

    a. Windows 3.11

    b. Windows 95

    c. Windows 98

    d. all of the above

    e. only a and b

    f. only b and c

21. How many backup options are available in Windows NT?

    a. five

    b. four

    c. two

    d. one

22. One operating system that enables you to optimize the network protocol order is _____.

23. You look at the contents of a backup medium and see two files, CONTROL.010 and BACKUP.010. Which of the following operating systems generated that backup?

    a. UNIX

    b. Mac OS

    c. Windows 3.11

    d. Windows 95 or Windows 98

24. A Windows 98 utility that can perform a surface analysis and fix file allocation errors is called _____.

25. In most directory structures, the directory that contains the operating system is

    a. in the root.

    b. hidden in a remote subdirectory for security.

    c. in server operating systems, located as a subdirectory under the \usr directory, a technique used to enhance performance.

    d. placed as a subdirectory in the main directory for all software applications.

10

HANDS-ON PROJECTS

PROJECT 10-1

In this hands-on activity, you empty the trash in the Mac OS.

To empty the trash:

    1. Double-click the **Trash** icon to view its contents.

    2. Make sure that there are no files you want to salvage from the trash.

    3. Open the **Special** menu on the menu bar.

    4. Click **Empty Trash**.

    5. The warning dialog box provides a summary of the contents that will be deleted and the disk space occupied by the contents. Click **OK** to finish emptying the trash.

PROJECT 10-2

In this assignment, you search for and delete all temporary files in the temp directory on a UNIX computer. (*Note*: Use the \temp directory created by your instructor for this assignment, or use the \tmp directory if it is specified by your instructor.)

To find and delete the files:

1. Change to the temporary directory. Enter **cd \temp** or **cd \user\temp**, for example.
2. Type **ls –l temp.***.
3. Type **rm temp.***.
4. Type **ls –l temp.*** again to make sure the files are deleted.
5. Log off when you are finished.

PROJECT 10-3

In this project, you find and delete temporary files in Windows 95, Windows 98, or Windows NT. Then you purge the files from the Recycle Bin.

To find, delete, and purge the temporary files:

1. Close all active windows and programs.
2. Click **Start**, point to **Programs**, and click **Windows Explorer** (or in NT, click Windows NT Explorer).
3. Click the **Tools** menu, move to **Find**, and click **Files or Folders**.
4. Enter ***.tmp** in the Named box and enter **C:** in the Look in list box (or click the list arrow and select (C:) from the list).
5. Check **Include subfolders** if necessary, and click **Find Now**.
6. Press **Ctrl+A** and press **Del**. Click **Yes** to confirm the deletion.
7. Close the Find dialog box.
8. Scroll to the bottom of the left window pane in Explorer and double-click **Recycle Bin**.
9. Scroll through the right window pane in Explorer to view the Recycle Bin contents.
10. Click the **File** menu, click **Empty Recycle Bin**, and click **Yes**.
11. Close Explorer.

PROJECT 10-4

In this project, you practice using Disk Defragmenter in Windows 95 or Windows 98.

To start the Disk Defragmenter:

1. Click **Start**, highlight **Programs, Accessories, System Tools**, and click **Disk Defragmenter**.

2. Select drive **C:** in the Select Drive dialog box and click **OK**.

3. Click **Start**, if necessary, in the Disk Defragmenter dialog box.

4. Click **Show Details** to see the complete step-by-step sequence of the defragmentation process.

5. Click the **Legend** button to see an interpretation of the color coded activities.

6. Click **Yes** to exit the Disk Defragmenter when the process is complete.

PROJECT 10-5

10

In this project, you perform a file system check in UNIX. Before starting, obtain a device name to use for the file system check.

To check the file system:

1. Log on as root.

2. Enter the command, **fsck /dev/***devicename*.

3. Notice that there are five phases of *fsck* operations: check blocks and sizes, check pathnames, check connectivity, check reference counts, and check free list.

4. Select **Yes** to correct any problems that the utility finds as it works.

5. Notice the statistics that show the number of files, the number of blocks, and the amount of free space.

6. If you see a message to reboot the system, use the **halt –n** command and reboot.

PROJECT 10-6

In this project, you run Chkdsk in Windows 3.1, Windows 3.11, or Windows 95. Next, you run it in Windows 98 and then in Windows NT 4.0 for comparison.

To run Chkdsk in Windows 3.1, Windows 3.11, or Windows 95:

1. If you run the utility in Windows 3.1 or Windows 3.11, double-click the **MS-DOS Prompt** icon in the Main program group window. If you run the utility in Windows 95, click **Start**, highlight **Programs**, and click **MS-DOS Prompt**.

2. At the DOS prompt, type **chkdsk** and press **Enter**.

3. Notice the information about the disk volume that is presented on the screen.

4. Type **exit** and press **Enter** to go back to Windows 3.1 or Windows 3.11; or close the MS-DOS Prompt window if you are in Windows 95.

To run Chkdsk in Windows 98:

1. Click **Start**, highlight **Programs**, and click **MS-DOS⋅ Prompt**.

2. At the DOS prompt, type **chkdsk** and press **Enter**.

3. Notice the information that appears on the screen. At the beginning, you should see a comment that says chkdsk has not checked the drive for errors and that you must use scandisk to detect and fix errors.

4. Close the MS-DOS Prompt window.

To run Chkdsk in Windows NT:

1. Click **Start**, highlight **Programs**, and click **Command Prompt**.

2. Type **chkdsk** at the command prompt and press **Enter**.

3. Notice the information on the screen and any errors that are fixed. You can run chkdsk on a FAT or NTFS volume.

4. Close the Command Prompt window when you are finished.

PROJECT 10-7

In this project, you run ScanDisk in Windows 95 or Windows 98.

To run ScanDisk:

1. Click **Start**, highlight **Programs**, **Accessories**, and **System Tools**, and click **ScanDisk**.

2. Select or click drive **(C:)**.

3. Click **Standard** as the type of test.

4. Check **Automatically fix errors**.

5. Click the **Advanced** button.

6. Check all three boxes under Check files for, which includes **Invalid file names**, **Invalid dates and times**, and **Duplicate names** (if you get a message asking if you are sure you want to check for duplicate names, click Yes). Click **OK**.

7. Click **Start** and notice the action bar as the utility checks files and folders.

8. Notice the ScanDisk Results dialog box and click **Close**.

9. Click **Close** to exit ScanDisk.

PROJECT 10-8

In this project, you tune memory settings in the Mac OS.

To tune the memory settings:

1. Open the Apple menu.

2. Point to **Control Panels** and click **Memory**.

3. For Disk Cache, click the **Custom setting** radio button and set the disk cache using the following formula: **(32 KB) * (Amount of RAM in megabytes)**. If you see a message which warns that you may decrease performance by changing this setting, click **Custom** to continue.

4. For Virtual Memory, click the **On** radio button and set the amount according to the formula: **(1 MB) + (Amount of RAM in megabytes)**.

5. Close the Memory Control Panel.

PROJECT 10-9

In this project, you use the *df* and *du* commands to examine disk space use.

To examine disk space use:

1. Log on as root.

2. Enter **df -a** to view information on all mounted file systems.

3. Enter df *directory*, such as **df /var** to view information about the file system in which that directory resides.

4. Switch to a directory of your choice and enter **du** to view how large each directory is within the main directory.

5. To view the total size of a directory and the directories under it, enter **du -s** *directoryname*.

CASE PROJECT

1. The National Center for Weather Research (NCWR) is funded by 22 state universities and by eight foundations to study all areas relating to weather patterns, forecasting, cloud seeding, and other weather phenomena. In NCWR's building there is a network consisting of 295 workstations, UNIX computers, supercomputers, Windows NT and NetWare servers. The workstations run UNIX, Windows 3.11, Windows 95, Windows 98, Windows NT, and Mac OS. The network protocols are TCP/IP,

10

AppleTalk, NetBEUI, and IPX/SPX. You are one of ten computer professionals who provide support to users on this network.

a. Over 50 users who run Windows 3.11, Windows 95, and Windows 98 are certain they need to purchase additional disks because they are nearly out of space. What options can you show them before their department heads order new disks?

b. The executive director of NCWR is experiencing slow network response at her Windows NT workstation, but the network administrator can find no apparent network problems after monitoring the network with a protocol analyzer. What alternatives might you examine to solve this problem?

c. Your boss has hired a new computer professional who formerly worked as a database support specialist in the business office, but who is relatively inexperienced in operating systems. The boss has assigned you to train your new colleague. One area that you are covering now is how to find and repair disk and file problems. Explain the tools available for the following operating systems:

- UNIX

- Mac OS

- Windows 95

- Windows 98

- Windows 3.11

d. As you are discussing the progress of the new employee, your boss mentions that he has an important word processing file that opens with a message that it is corrupted. Is there anything he might do to keep this from happening again in Windows 95?

e. The chief financial officer of NCWR keeps a huge number of reports, spreadsheets, and other critical financial information on his computer, which runs Windows 98. As you walk by the CFO's office, you notice that the disk drive on his computer sounds like it might have some mechanical problems. The CFO does not have a tape drive and has not backed up his computer in over a year. However, you have a tape drive on your computer that runs Windows 98 and there is a tape drive on one of the Windows NT servers in the machine room. Can you back up his computer on either of these computers? How?

f. The director of publications uses the Mac OS and has been working on so many projects for the past six months that she has had no time to perform maintenance tasks. She wants to spend some time tomorrow morning on these tasks. What maintenance tasks do you recommend?

g. Your new associate has not yet learned how to adjust the page file size in Windows 95 and in Windows NT. Explain how this is done.

GLOSSARY

8086 An early 16-bit personal computer CPU. It was released soon after the 8088 and was used in machines at the same time 8088 machines were popular. The 8086 CPU was never as popular as the 8088.

8088 The first popular personal computer CPU. The 8088 ran at 4.7 MHz, used a 20-bit address bus and an 8-bit data bus.

80x86 A general designation for a popular line of Intel PC CPUs that started with the 80286 and continued through the 80486. There were several subdesignations within this chip line.

A

active hub A central network device that connects multiple communications cable segments and that amplifies the data carrying signal as it is transmitted to each segment.

active partition The logical portion of a hard disk drive that is currently being used to store data. In a PC system, usually the partition that contains the bootable operating system.

ActiveX An internal programming standard that allows various software that runs under the Windows 95 and later operating systems to communicate with the operating system and with other programs.

address bus An internal communications pathway inside a computer that specifies the source and target address for memory reads and writes. The address bus is measured by the number of bits of information it can carry. The wider the address bus (the more bits it moves at a time) the more memory available to the computer that uses it.

alias In the Macintosh file system, a feature that presents an icon that represents an executable file. Equivalent to the UNIX link and the Windows shortcut.

allocation blocks In the Macintosh file system, a division of hard disk data. Equivalent to the Windows disk cluster. Each Macintosh volume is divided into 2^{16} (65,535) individual units.

Apple Desktop Bus (ADB) A serial bus common on the Apple Macintosh computer. ADB is used to connect the Macintosh keyboard, mouse, and other external I/O devices.

AppleTalk Used for communications with Macintosh computers, this protocol is designed for peer-to-peer networking.

AT commands A modem control command set designed by the Hayes company. This standard modem command set begins each command with AT (for Attention) and allows communications software or users to control many modem functions directly.

ATTRIB A DOS command that is used to review or change file attributes.

AUTOEXEC.BAT A system file that is part of DOS and other operating systems. This file contains lines of text that are used as commands to configure the system hardware and software as the operating system loads.

B

backbone A main connecting link or highway between networks, such as between floors in a building or between buildings. Main internetworking devices, such as routers and switches are often connected via the network backbone.

bad clusters On a hard disk drive, areas of the surface that cannot be used to store data safely. Bad clusters usually are identified by the FORMAT command or one of the hard drive utilities such as CHKDSK or SCANDISK.

base memory The memory areas that are directly addressable by computer programs. In early PCs this was the first 640 KB of memory.

BASIC Beginner's All-purpose Symbolic Instruction Code. An English-like computer programming language originally designed as a teaching tool, but which evolved into a useful and relatively powerful development language.

batch processing A computing style frequently employed by large systems. A request for a series of processes is submitted to the computer and information is displayed or printed when the batch is complete. Batches might include processing all of the checks submitted to a bank for a day, or all of the purchases in a wholesale inventory system, for example.

Berkeley Systems Distribution (BSD) A variant of the UNIX operating system upon which a large proportion of today's UNIX software is based.

Bernoulli A semi-rigid hard drive based on the Bernoulli principle. These high-capacity, removable cartridge drives provide reasonably high-speed, high-density add-on storage for desktop and laptop computers in data-intensive applications such as graphics.

beta software During software development, software that has successfully passed the alpha test stage. Beta testing may involve dozens, hundreds, or even thousands of people and may be conducted in multiple stages: beta 1, beta 2, beta 3, and so on.

binary backup A technique that backs up the entire contents of one or more disk drives in a binary or image format.

BinHex In the Macintosh file system, a seven-bit file format used to transmit data across network links.

BIOS Basic Input/Output System. Low-level computer program code that conducts basic hardware and software communications inside the computer. A computer BIOS basically resides between computer hardware and the higher level operating system, such as DOS or Windows.

block allocation A hard disk configuration scheme where the disk is divided into logical blocks, which in turn are mapped to sectors, heads, and tracks. Whenever the operating system needs to allocate some disk space, it allocates it based on a block address.

block devices In the UNIX file system, devices that are divided or configured into logical blocks. See also *raw devices*.

boot block In a Mac-formatted disk, the first of two important system sections on the disk. The boot blocks identify the filing system being used, the names of important system files, and other important information. (See also *volume information block*).

bridge Hardware device that bridges two or more network segments so that computers on different physical networks can communicate with each other.

C

cable modem A digital modem device designed for use with the cable TV system. Cable modems can provide very high speed data transfer, and may include an analog modem component that is used with a conventional telephone line connection to carry information sent from the user to the ISP.

cache controller Internal computer hardware that manages the data going into and loaded from the machine's cache memory.

cache memory Special computer memory that temporarily stores data used by the CPU. Cache memory is physically close to the CPU and is faster than standard system memory, enabling faster retrieval and processing time.

catalog b-tree In the Macintosh file system, a list of all files on a given volume. Similar to a directory in the Windows file system.

CD-ROM Compact Disk Read Only Memory. A hardware device used to play and in some cases to record computer data, music, and other multimedia information in a write once, read many format.

cell Format for a unit of data that is transported over a high-speed network, usually at speeds of 155 Mbps to over 1 Gbps. Cells are mainly used for network communications that employ Asynchronous Transfer Mode (ATM).

Centronics interface An industry standard printer interface popularized by printer manufacturer Centronics. The interface definition includes 36 wires that connect the printer with the computer I/O port, though all of these pins aren't always used, particularly in modern desktop machines.

CHKDSK A DOS external command and Windows utility that analyzes a specified disk drive to determine drive configuration and to locate and repair, where possible, bad disk locations.

clean machine A computer from which all unnecessary software and hardware have been removed. A clean machine is useful during software upgrade testing since a minimum number of other software and hardware elements are in place, making it easier to track down problems with new software.

client In a networking environment, a computer that handles certain user-side software operations. For example, a network client may run software that captures user data input and presents output to the user from a network server (See *server*).

client operating system Operating system on a computer, such as a PC, that enables the computer to process information and to run applications locally, as well as to communicate with other computers on a network.

client/server application A software application that divides processing between a client operating system and one or more server operating systems (often a database and an application server). Dividing processing tasks is intended to achieve the best performance.

client/server systems A computer hardware and software design wherein different portions of an application execute on different computers or on different components of a single computer. Typically client software supports user I/O and the server software conducts database searches, manages printer output, and the like.

clustering A special computer networking configuration in which multiple computers are connected in such a way that they can share processing tasks, frequently working on portions of the same software job at the same time. In a Windows NT cluster, for example, the NT operating systems on the various machines share all of the connected resources as if they were one large computer.

code Instructions written in a computer programming language.

Complex Instruction Set Computer (CISC) A computer CPU architecture in which processor components are reconfigured to conduct different operations as required. Such computer designs require a larger number of instructions and more complex instructions than other designs.

CONFIG.SYS A text-based configuration file in DOS (similar to AUTOEXEC.BAT). The commands in CONFIG.SYS are executed early in the bootup process and normally are used to configure memory, to load special drivers, and so on.

container object An entity that is used to group together resources, such as an organizational unit, an organization, or a country as specified in the directory services of NetWare.

Control Panel In Windows operating systems, an application window that contains utilities for system configuration, such as the modem settings, mouse, printers and so on.

controller A hardware or software component of a modem that defines an individual modem personality. The controller interprets AT commands, handles communications protocols, and so on.

cookie A text-based file used by Web sites to obtain customized information about a user such as the user's name, the user's password to access the site, and information about how to customize Web page displays.

cooperative multitasking A computer hardware and software design wherein the operating system hands off control to an application temporarily and waits for the application to return control to the operating system.

CPU central processing unit. In today's computer typically a single chip (the microprocessor) with support devices that conducts the majority of the computer's calculations.

creator codes Hidden file characteristics in the Macintosh File System that indicate the program (software application) that created the file.

Cyclic Redundancy Check (CRC) An error correction protocol that determines the validity of data written to and read from a floppy or hard disk.

D

daemon An internal, automatically running program, usually in UNIX, that serves a particular function such as routing e-mail to recipients or supporting dial-up networking connectivity.

data bus An internal communications pathway that allows computer components such as the CPU, display adapter, and main memory to share information. Early personal computers used an 8-bit data bus. More modern machines use 32- or 64-bit data buses.

data fork That portion of a file in the Macintosh file system that stores the variable data associated with the file. Data fork information might include word processing data, spreadsheet information, and so on.

data pump The hardware or software portion of a modem that is responsible for converting digital data into analog signals for transmission over a telephone line, and for converting analog signals into digital data for transmission to the computer.

DB-25 A 25-pin D-shaped connector commonly used on desktop computers, terminals, modems, and other devices.

defragmentation The process of removing empty pockets between files and other information on a hard disk drive.

device driver Computer software designed to provide the operating system and applications software access to specific computer hardware.

dial-up networking (DUN) A facility built into Windows 95, Windows 98, and Windows NT to permit operation of a hardware modem to dial a telephone number for the purpose of logging into a remote computer system via standard telephone lines.

differential backup Backs up all files that have an archive attribute, but does not remove that attribute after files are backed up.

digital modem A modem-like device that transfers data via digital lines instead of analog lines.

digital pad (tablet) An alternative input device frequently used by graphics artists and others who need accurate control over drawing and other data input.

Digital Signal Processor (DSP) A software data pump used in such software-driven modems as the 3Com Winmodem.

digital versatile disc (DVD) A high-capacity CD-ROM-like hardware device used for high quality audio, motion video and computer data storage.

DIN8M An 8-pin connector common on Macintosh computers for printer connections.

directory A special file on a disk drive that is used to store information about other data stored on the disk. A directory typically records a file name, a physical starting and ending point on the disk, file type, and file size.

Disk First Aid A Macintosh utility program that analyzes a Macintosh hard drive and files. It is useful in overall maintenance of a Mac hard drive.

disk geometry Critical information about a hard drive's hardware configuration. This information is often stored in an area of nonvolatile memory in the computer.

Disk Operating System (DOS) Computer software that manages the interface between the user and computer components, and among various components inside the computer. A disk operating system manages the low-level computer instructions for operation of and communication with such devices as storage hardware, a keyboard, a display adapter, and so on.

disk striping A disk storage technique that divides portions of each file over all volumes in a set as a way to minimize wear on individual disks.

domain A group of computers or resources that share a common security database. The resources can be servers, workstations, shared disks and directories, and shared printers.

dot matrix printer A character printer that produces characters by arranging a matrix of dots. Dot matrix printers can be impact, ink jet or other technologies.

Drive Setup A Macintosh file system utility that helps configure Macintosh hard drives.

DSL Digital Subscriber Line. An emerging digital technology supported by some telephone companies to provide data connections at T1 speeds (1.544 Mbps). There are two varieties of DSL, synchronous DSL (SDSL) and asynchronous DSL (ADSL).

DUN Server In Windows 95, Windows 98, and Windows NT, a software utility that permits a desktop machine to answer incoming calls, log on a user, and, with other software, permit the user access to the computer's resources.

dye sublimation A printer technology that produces high quality, color output by creating "sublimated" color mists that penetrate paper to form characters or graphic output.

E

e-mail Electronic mail. A method of sharing written communications and other computer data over a networked connection.

EMM386.SYS Extended Memory Manager. In personal computers running certain versions of DOS, an intrinsic utility that helps manage software access to memory above the 1 MB address.

Ethernet A network transport protocol that uses CSMA/CD communications to coordinate frame and packet transmissions on a network.

extended IDE (EIDE) A more modern, faster version of IDE.

extension In DOS, that part of a file name that typically identifies the type of file associated with the name. File extensions traditionally are three characters long and include standard notations such as .SYS, .EXE, .BAT, and so on.

external clock speed The speed at which the processor communicates with the memory and the other devices in the computer; usually one-fourth to one-half the internal clock speed.

external commands Operating system commands that are stored in separate program files on disk. When these commands are required, they must be loaded from disk storage into memory before they are executed.

F

FDISK A DOS and Windows command (utility) that is used to partition a hard disk drive or to change or review existing partitions.

file allocation table (FAT) A file management system that defines the way data is stored on a disk drive. The FAT stores information about file size and physical location on the disk.

file attributes File characteristics stored with the file name in the disk directory that specify certain storage and operational parameters associated with the file. Attributes are noted by the value of specific data bits associated with the file name. File attributes include hidden, read only, archive, and so on.

File Manager In Windows 3.1 and Windows for Workgroups, a software utility that provides a graphical interface to the computer's files, including programs and data files.

file system A design for storing and managing files on a disk drive. File systems are associated with operating systems such as UNIX, DOS, and Windows.

file system checker (*fsck*) In UNIX, a program utility that checks the integrity of the file system.

File Transfer Protocol (FTP) In some networking environments, a software utility that facilitates the copying of computer files across the network connection from one computer to another.

firewall Hardware or software that can control which frames and packets access or leave designated networks, as a method to implement security.

flow control A hardware or software feature in modems that lets a receiving modem communicate to the sending modem that it needs more time to process previously-sent data. When the current data has been processed successfully, the receiving modem notifies the sending modem that it is OK to resume data transmission.

FORMAT A program utility in DOS, UNIX and other operating systems that is used to prepare a disk drive for data storage. The FORMAT utility usually removes any existing data, checks the disk for bad storage locations and can optionally install some operating system files.

fragmentation Developing more and more empty pockets of space between files on the disk because of frequent writing, deleting, and modifying files and file contents.

frame A data unit sent over a network that contains source and destination, (but not routing), control, and error detection information as well as data (related to the data-link layer of network communications between two stations).

full file-by-file backup A technique that backs up the entire contents of one or more disk drives on the basis of directories, subdirectories, and files so that it is possible to restore a combination of any of these.

G

G3 An Apple computer design that uses a relatively new RISC CPU, so named as a third-generation PowerPC processor.

global group In Windows NT Server, a group that is used to manage user accounts, such as for security access.

group identification number (GID) A unique number that is assigned to a UNIX group that distinguishes that group from all other groups on the same system.

H

hard link In Windows NT, a file management technique that permits multiple directory entries to point to the same physical file.

Hardware Compatibility List (HCL) A list of hardware compatible with the version of the operating system being installed. Adherence to the HCL

will ensure a more successful operating system install. HCLs can often be found on the OS vendor's Web site.

Hayes command See *AT command*.

Hierarchical Filing System (HFS) An early Apple Macintosh file system file storage method that uses hierarchical directory structure. Developed in 1986 to improve file support for large storage devices.

home directory A user work area in which the user stores data on a server and typically has control over whether to enable other server users to access his or her data.

Host Signal Processor (HSP) A software approach to handling data pump duties in software-based modems such as the 3Com WinModem.

I

I/O Input/output.

IFSHLP.SYS In Windows for Workgroups, one of the final files to load during the bootup process and which helps facilitate the network component of Windows 3.1x.

Imagesetter A high end printer frequently used for publishing; it is capable of producing film output.

incremental backup A technique that backs up all files that have an archive attribute, and then removes the attribute after each file is backed up.

information node (inode) In the UNIX, a system for storing key information about files. Inode information includes the inode number, the owner of the file, the file group, the file size, the file creation date, plus the date the file was last modified and last read, the number of links to this inode, and information regarding the location of the blocks in the file system in which the file is stored.

ink jet printer A character printer that forms characters by spraying droplets of ink from a nozzle print head onto the paper.

instruction set In a computer CPU, the group of commands (instructions) the processor recognizes. These instructions are used to conduct the operations required of the CPU by the operating system and application software.

Integrated Drive Electronics (IDE) A storage protocol popular in today's desktop computer systems. IDE is significant because it simplifies the hardware required inside the computer, placing more of the disk intelligence at the hard drive itself.

Integrated Services Digital Network (ISDN) A digital telephone line used for high-speed digital computer communications, video conferencing, Internet connections, and so on.

internal clock speed The speed at which the CPU executes internal commands, measured in megahertz (millions of clock ticks per second). Internal clock speeds can be as low as 1 MHz and as high as 500 MHz.

internal commands Operating system commands that load with the main operating system kernel or command module.

Internet A global network used by individuals and businesses to connect standalone workstations and networks for the exchange of electronic mail, shared research information, commercial advertising, and other purposes.

Internet Packet Exchange (IPX) Developed by Novell, this protocol is used on networks that connect servers running NetWare.

Internet Protocol (IP) Used in combination with TCP, this protocol handles addressing and routing for transport of packets.

IPX/SPX protocol In various Windows versions, a networking protocol that is compatible with Novell networking. A Microsoft client running this protocol as part of its networking configuration can communicate with Novell clients as well as Microsoft clients.

J

Jaz An Iomega company removable hard disk design capable of storing 1 GB or 2 GB of data, depending on the model.

K

Kernel In a computer operating system, the lowest level and most basic instructions.

L

Large Block Allocation (LBA) In DOS, a technique to allow the creation of files larger than 512 MB. With LBA, DOS is told that the sector size of the hard disk is greater than 512 bytes per sector, which results in the ability to have much larger file systems.

laser printers A high quality page printer design popular in office and other professional applications.

LCD Liquid crystal display, the display technology in some laptops and other electronic equipment.

leaf object An object, such as an account, that is stored in an organization or organizational unit container in Novell NetWare.

LED Light emitting diode. An electronic device frequently used to display information in electronic devices such as watches, clocks, and stereos.

Level 1 (L1) cache Cache memory that is part of the CPU hardware. See *cache memory*.

Level 2 (L2) cache Cache memory that, in most computer CPU designs, is located on hardware separate, but situated close by, the CPU.

line printer A printer design that prints a full line of character output at a time. Used for high speed output requirements.

Linux A version of UNIX developed for Intel processors, available as freeware. Red Hat Linux is used for most UNIX examples in this book.

local area network (LAN) A series of interconnected computers, printing devices, and other computer equipment in a service area that is usually limited to a given office area, floor, or building.

local group In Windows NT Server, a group that is used to manage shared resources, such as disks, folders, and printers.

LPT1 The primary printer port designation on many desktop computers. Also designated Line Printer 1.

M

Macintosh Filing System (MFS) The original Macintosh filing system, introduced in 1984. MFS was limited to keeping track of 128 documents, applications, or folders.

mapping The process of attaching to a shared resource, such as a shared drive, and using it as though it is a local resource. For example, when a workstation operating system maps to the drive of another workstation, it can assign a drive letter to that drive and access it as though it is a local drive instead of a remote one.

master In an IDE drive chain, the main, or first drive. Most IDE interfaces can support two drives. One is the master (Drive 0) and the second drive is the slave. See *slave*.

Master Boot Record (MBR) An area of a hard disk that stores partition information about that disk. MBRs are not found on disks that do not support multiple partitions.

Master File Table (MFT) In Windows NT, a file management system similar to the FAT and directories used in DOS and Windows. This table is located at the beginning of the partition. The boot sector is located ahead of the MFT just as it is in the FAT system.

medium file names In the Macintosh file system, the 31-character file name length that Macintosh OS has supported from the beginning.

microprocessor A solid state electronic device that controls the major computer functions and operations. See also *CPU*.

Microsoft CD Extension (MCDEX) In Microsoft Windows, a software driver that enables CD-ROM hardware support.

Microsoft Foundation Classes (MFC) A series of core routines used by almost all applications on a Windows 95 machine.

micro-switch A small electronic switch used in a computer mouse, gamepad, or joystick to connect and disconnect electronic circuits. These openings and closings can be monitored by driver software to enable certain software features or functions.

Mkdir An operating system utility (UNIX and DOS) program that is used to create a new directory.

modem MOdulator-DEModulator. A hardware device that permits a computer to exchange digital data with another computer via an analog telephone line or dedicated connection.

MS-DOS A disk operating system designed by Microsoft Corporation. See *DOS*.

Multimedia Extension (MMX) A CPU design that permits the processor to manage certain multimedia operations—graphics, for example—faster and more directly. MMX technology improves computer performance when running software that requires multimedia operations.

multiprocessor machines A computer that uses more than one CPU.

multi-user A computer hardware and software system that is designed to service multiple users who access the computer's hardware and software applications simultaneously.

multi-user environment A computer environment that supports multi-user access to a computer's hardware and software facilities.

N

NetBEUI A protocol used on Microsoft networks that was developed from NetBIOS and that is designed for small networks. NetBEUI is the default networking protocol in Microsoft Windows environments.

Netware Loadable Modules (NLMs) In a Novell NetWare network, special files that store software that provides various network services.

network A system of computing devices, computing resources, information resources, and communications devices that are linked together by communications cable or radio waves.

Network Basic Input/Output System (NetBIOS) A technique to interface software with network services and to provide naming services for computers on a Microsoft network.

network bindings Part of the NT Server system used to coordinate software communications among the NIC, the network protocols, and network services.

Network control panel In Windows 95, Windows 98, and Windows NT, a graphical user interface to network configuration settings.

Network File System (NFS) In UNIX and other operating systems, a system-level facility that supports loading and saving files to remote disk drives across the network.

network operating system (NOS) Computer operating system software that enables coordination of network activities, such as network communications, shared printing, and sharing files. NetWare, UNIX, and Windows NT are examples of network operating systems.

networking A process for physically connecting two or more computers to permit them to share hard disk storage, printers, scanners, software, and other resources.

New Technology File System (NTFS) The 32-bit file storage system that is the native system in Windows NT. (Windows NT also supports the DOS FAT system.)

newfs A program utility in UNIX used to create a new file system.

Novell Directory Services (NDS) A comprehensive database of shared resources and information known to the NetWare operating system.

O

object An entity, such as a user account, group, directory, or printer, that is known to a network operating system's database and that the operating system manages in terms of sharing or controlling access to that object.

operating system (OS) Computer software code that interfaces with user application software and the computer's BIOS to allow the applications to interact with the computer hardware.

P

packet A data unit sent over a network that contains source and destination, routing, control, and error detection information as well as data (related to the network layer of network data communications between two stations).

paging file Also called the page or swap file, an allocated portion of disk storage reserved for use to supplement RAM when the available RAM is exceeded.

parallel port A computer input/output port used primarily for printer connections. A parallel port transmits data 8 bits or more at a time, using at least 8 parallel wires. A parallel port potentially can transmit data faster than a serial port.

parity checking A data communications process that ensures data integrity through a system of data bit comparisons between the sending and receiving computer.

partitioning A hard disk management technique that permits the installation of multiple file systems on a single disk or the configuration of multiple logical hard drives that use the same file system on a single physical hard drive.

passive hub A central network device that connects multiple communications cable segments, but does not alter the data-carrying signal as it is transmitted from segment to segment.

path In a computer directory structure, a command that specifies the complete location to a specific file or directory. Computer files are stored in files, which in turn reside in directories (folders). Directories can be stored within other directories. To access a specific file you must also specify the series of directories that must be traversed to reach the desired file.

payload That portion of a frame, packet, or cell that contains the actual data, which might be a portion of an e-mail message or of a word processed file.

PC DOS An operating system very similar to MS-DOS, customized and marketed by IBM.

PCMCIA Personal Computer Memory Card International Association. Standard for expansion cards used in laptops and desktop machines. Now usually shortened to PC Card.

peer-to-peer networking A computer networking configuration in which the various connected computers are essentially equal.

Pentium An Intel Corporation CPU (essentially an 80586), and often the computer system that uses this chip. Variations on the Pentium chip include the Pentium Pro, Pentium MMX, Pentium II, Pentium III, and others. Chip technology changes too quickly to provide a current comprehensive list.

per-seat licensing A software licensing scheme that prices software according to the number of individual users who install and use the software.

per-server licensing A software licensing scheme that prices software according to a server configuration that permits multiple users to access the software from a central server.

pipelining A CPU design that permits the processor to operate on one instruction at the same time it is fetching one or more following instructions from the operating system or application.

pixel Short for picture element. The small dots that make up a computer screen display.

PKZIP A utility program that archives files and compresses them so they require less disk storage and can be transmitted over a network faster.

plotter Computer hardware that produces high-quality printed output, often in color, by moving ink pens over the surface of paper. Plotters are often used with computer-aided design (CAD) and other graphics applications.

Plug and Play (PNP) In Windows 95 and Windows 98, software utilities that operate with compatible hardware to facilitate automatic hardware configuration. Windows can recognize PNP hardware when it is installed and in many cases can configure the hardware and install required software without significant user intervention.

Portable Operating System Interface (POSIX) A UNIX standard designed to ensure portability of applications among various versions of UNIX.

potentiometer A hardware device used to vary the amount of resistance in an electronic circuit. In computer I/O hardware this variable resistance can be used to monitor mouse movement, joy stick positioning, and so on.

power management A hardware facility in modern computers that permits certain hardware to shut down automatically after a specified period

of inactivity. Proper use of power management facilities reduces hardware wear and tear as well as energy usage.

PowerPC A RISC CPU designed jointly by Motorola, Apple, and IBM. PowerPC chips are used primarily in Apple computer designs.

preemptive multitasking A computer hardware and software design for multitasking of applications in which the operating system retains control of the computer at all times. See *cooperative multitasking* for comparison.

print queue (print spooler) A section of computer memory and hard disk storage set aside to hold information sent by an application to a printer attached to the local computer or to another computer or print server on a network. Operating system or printer drivers and control software manage the information sent to the queue, responding to printer start/stop commands.

Program Manager In Windows 3.1x, a software utility that provides a graphical user interface into certain components of the operating system. Program Manager displays directories and files and lets the user launch applications without resorting to DOS commands.

protocol A set of formatting guidelines for network communications, like a language, so that the information sent by one computer can be accurately received and decoded by another.

R

raw devices In the UNIX file system, devices that have not been divided into logical blocks.

real mode A limited, 16-bit operating mode in PCs running early versions of Windows.

Reduced Instruction Set Computer (RISC) A computer CPU design that dedicates processor hardware components to certain functions. This design reduces the number and the complexity of required instructions and, in many cases, results in faster performance than CISC CPUs.

Redundant Array of Inexpensive Drives (RAID) A relatively inexpensive, redundant storage design that uses multiple disks and logic to reduce the chance of information being lost in the event of hardware failure. RAID uses various designs, termed Level 0 through Level 5.

Registry A Windows database that stores information about a computer's hardware and software configuration.

Remote Access Service (RAS) A computer operating system subsystem that manages user access to a computer from a remote location, including security issues.

removable disks A class of relatively high capacity storage devices that use removable cartridges. These devices are used for data backup, for long-term offline storage, and for data portability among multiple computer systems.

resource fork In the Macintosh file system, that portion of a file that contains fixed information such as a program's icons, menu resources, and splash screens.

RESTORE A software utility available as part of many operating systems that permits the copying of backed up data from the backup medium to the computer hard drive.

ROM Read only memory. Special memory that contains information that is not erased when the voltage is removed from the memory hardware. ROM is used to store computer instructions that must be available at all times, such as the BIOS code.

root In a computer directory system, the highest level or main directory; in UNIX, root also refers to a user with supervisor privileges.

router A device that joins networks and that can route packets to a specific network on the basis of a routing table it creates for this purpose. Routers can also support multiple protocols.

S

ScanDisk A DOS and Windows utility that is used to locate bad disk drive storage locations and to mark and repair these areas.

search drive A mapped NetWare drive that enables the operating system to search a specified directory and its subdirectories for an executable (program) file.

self-extracting file A compressed or archive file that includes an executable component, like an application program, that enables the file to separate into individual files and uncompress the files automatically. A self-extracting file does not require an external program to expand the file into its individual components.

Sequence Packet Exchange (SPX) A protocol used (along with IPX) on Novell networks that provides reliable transmission of application software data.

sequential processing A computer processing style where each operation is submitted, acted upon, and the results displayed before the next process is started. Compare to *batch processing*.

server A computer running a network operating system and that enables client workstations to access shared resources, printers, files, software applications, CD-ROM drives, for example.

service pack Software "fixes" that are issued by the vendor to fix software problems, address compatibility issues, and add enhancements.

shadow file With access limited to the root user, a file in UNIX that contains critical information about user accounts, including the encrypted password for each account.

share An object, such as a folder, in Windows 3.11, Windows 95, Windows 98, and Windows NT, that is made visible to other network users for access over network.

share-level access control Access to a shared folder in Windows 95 and Windows 98 by creating a disk or folder share that is protected by share permissions and on which the share owner can require a password for access.

shell The operating system user interface. In MS-DOS, UNIX and some other systems, the shell interface is text-based, and command oriented.

Sherlock In the Macintosh file system Version 8.5, a file search utility that can find file names or text within files.

Simple Mail Transfer Protocol (SMTP) In a networked computer environment, a software utility that manages the transfer of electronic messages among various users.

SimpleText   A Macintosh utility program for text editing.

single-processor machines   Computers capable of supporting only a single CPU.

single-tasking   A computer hardware and software design that can manage only a single task at a time.

slave   In an IDE drive chain, the secondary storage device. See *master.*

Small Computer System Interface (SCSI)   A computer input/output bus standard and the hardware that uses this standard. There are many types of SCSI in use today, providing data transfer rates from 10 Mbps to 40 Mbps.

Solaris   A Sun Microsystems operating system based on UNIX.

start bit   In data communication, an extra bit inserted by the sending modem at the beginning of a data byte to help ensure that the received data is correct.

startup disk   A bootable floppy disk that includes the basic Windows 95 operating system, key disk utilities and drivers (such as for the CD-ROM drive). This disk can be used to start the system in the event that the hard drive or its operating system are damaged.

status bits   Bits used as part of a directory entry to identify the type of file name contained in each entry. The status bits in use are Volume, Directory, System, Hidden, Read-Only, and Archive.

stop bit   In data communication, an extra bit inserted by the sending modem at the end of a data byte to help ensure that the received data is correct.

StuffIt   A Macintosh archive and compression utility.

subnet mask   A designated portion of an IP address that is used to divide a network into smaller sub-networks as a way to manage traffic patterns, enable security, and relieve congestion.

superblock   In the UNIX file system, a special data block that contains information about the layout of blocks, sectors and cylinder groups on the file sys-

tem. This information is the key to finding anything on the file system, and it should never change.

SuperDisk (LS-120)   An increasingly popular high capacity floppy disk design. SuperDisk / LS-120 drives can store as much as 120 MB of data on a single disk, but these drives also can read conventional 3½-inch floppy disks.

surface analysis   A disk diagnostic technique that locates damaged disk areas and marks them as bad. Some surface analysis tools are destructive to data, because they also format a disk. Others can be run without altering data, except to move data from a damaged location to one that is not.

swap file   A hard disk file that is used by the operating system to swap out portions of running programs when RAM memory resources become low.

switch   (1) A network device that connects LAN segments and that forwards frames to the appropriate segment or segments. A switch works in promiscuous mode similar to a bridge. (2) An operating system command option that changes the way certain commands function. Command options, or switches, are usually entered as one or more letters separated from the main command by a forward slash (/).

symbolic link   A special file in the UNIX file system that permits a directory link to a file that is on a different partition. This is a special file, which has a flag set in the inode to identify it as a symbolic link. The contents of the file is a path that, when followed, leads to another file.

symmetric multiprocessing (SMP)   A computer design that supports multiple, internal CPUs that can be configured to work simultaneously on the same set of instructions.

SyQuest   The manufacturer of one of the earliest removable hard disk devices popular in Macintosh and PC systems. SyQuest drives use hard disk technology. Early drives stored only 40 MB, but later designs can hold upwards of 200 MB.

System scheduler   A Windows utility program that can be configured to execute other programs at a specified time or at the completion of other system events.

T

tar   A UNIX file archive utility.

task supervisor   A process in the operating system that will keep track of the applications that are running on the machine and the resources they use.

task-switching   A single-tasking computer hardware and software design that permits the user or application software to switch among multiple single-tasking operations.

TCP/IP   Transfer Control Protocol/Network Protocol, the networking protocol used by UNIX computers and on the Internet.

terminal   A device that has a keyboard but no CPU or storage, and that is used to access and run programs on a mainframe or minicomputer.

terminal adapter (TA)   A digital modem that permits computer-to-computer data transfer over a digital line, such as ISDN.

terminator resistor packs (TRPs)   Sets of resistors used on a hard drive or other storage device. These resistors reduce the possibility of data echoes on the interface bus as information travels between the computer's controller and the storage device.

thermal-wax transfer   A printer technology that creates high quality color printed output by melting colored wax elements and transferring them to the printed page.

time sharing systems   A central computer system, such as a mainframe, that is used by multiple users and applications simultaneously.

token ring   A network that uses a ring topology and token passing as a way to coordinate network transport.

topology   The physical design of a network and the way in which a data-carrying signal travels from point to point along the network.

Transmission Control Protocol (TCP)   A communications protocol that is used with IP and that facilitates reliable communications between two stations by establishing a window tailored to the characteristics of the connection.

type   In the Macintosh file system, embedded file information that denotes what applications were used to create the files. Mac OS type codes are used in much the same way as Windows file extensions that identify file types with .TXT, .DOC and other extensions.

U

Unicode   A 16 bit character code that allows for the definition of up to 65,536 characters.

uninstall disks   A set of operating system diskettes that contain information from a previous version of the operating system. These disks are used to restore the original operating system in the event the user wishes to remove an upgraded system.

Universal Asynchronous Receiver-Transmitter (UART)   A hardware device that handles data flow through a serial port or modem.

Universal Serial Bus (USB)   A relatively high-speed I/O port found on most newer computers. It is used to interface digital sound cards, disk drives, and other external computer hardware. It supports up to 127 discreet devices with data transfer speeds up to 12 Mbps.

UNIX   A popular networked, multitasking, multiuser operating system.

user identification number (UID)   A unique number that is assigned to a UNIX user account as a way to distinguish that account from all others on the same system.

user-level access control   Access to a shared folder in Windows 95 and Windows 98 in which the share owner creates a list of groups and users who are allowed to access the share.

V

V.90   A modem communication protocol that defines the standards for 56 kbps communications.

virtual memory   Disk storage that is used when there is not enough RAM for a particular operation or for all processes that are currently in use.

volume information block   In a Mac-formatted disk, the second of two system sectors. The volume information block points to other important areas of information, such as the location of the system files and the catalog and extents trees.

volume label A series of characters that identifies a disk drive or the file system it is using.

W

Web browsers Software to facilitate individual computer access to graphical data presented over the Internet on the World Wide Web, or over a local area network in a compatible format.

Web server In a networked environment, a computer that runs special software to host graphical data in a World Wide Web format. Data on a Web server is accessed with a computer running a Web browser.

wheel mouse A new mouse design, popularized by Microsoft's IntelliMouse, that includes a top-mounted wheel in addition to the standard mouse buttons. The wheel is programmable for a variety of operating system and application functions. A switch integral to the wheel provides additional opportunity for programmable, custom functions.

wide area network (WAN) A system of networks that can extend across cities, states, and continents.

WIN In Microsoft Windows, the command that launches the Windows operating system. Win is an executable program.

Windows Explorer A graphical software utility that provides access to a computer's files and applications in the Windows operating system variants.

Windows for Workgroups A networked version of the Windows 3.1 operating system. Also known as Windows 3.11.

Winmodems A software-driven modem from 3Com Corporation that uses minimal hardware and the computer's CPU with software to conduct data communications.

WINZIP An archiving and compression utility for Windows 95/98.

workstation A computer that has a CPU and that usually has storage to enable the user to run programs and access files locally.

X

X Window A windowed user interface for UNIX and other operating systems.

Xon-Xoff A software flow control protocol that permits a receiving modem to notify the sending modem when its data buffers are full and it needs more time to process previously received data.

Z

Zip disk A removable high capacity floppy disk design from the Iomega company. Zip disks store a nominal 100 MB of data.

INDEX